BEVERLEY MINSTER:

An illustrated history

1   The western towers and
the south side of the nave
from the south east.

BEVERLEY MINSTER:

An illustrated history

Edited by Rosemary Horrox

The Friends of Beverley Minster 2000

PUBLISHED BY THE FRIENDS OF BEVERLEY MINSTER
THE MINSTER, BEVERLEY

ISBN 0-9538517-1-0

British Library Cataloguing-in Publication Data
A catalogue record for this book is available from the British Library

Designed by Angela Ashton
Printed by University Printing Services, University Press, Cambridge.

Contents

Editor's Acknowledgements

My first thanks must be to the Friends of Beverley Minster, who invited me to edit this volume and thus allowed me to revisit four very happy years spent in Beverley. My second thanks are to the contributors, for their unfailing tolerance and good humour. More specifically, I am extremely grateful to Paul Barnwell, who not only stepped in at short notice to provide the best part of the Introduction but was a tower of strength when it came to tracking down pictures and references. Nicholas Dawton threw himself enthusiastically into providing photographs and drafted in his cousin, Anthony Dawton, to help. I am more grateful to them both than I can well say. David and Susan Neave cheerfully and uncomplainingly answered my cries for help with picture research and other matters. Melanie Legg, then cartographer in the Geography Department of Anglia Polytechnic University, prepared the map on which Fig. 4 is based. The formal picture acknowledgements which follow do not really do justice to the courtesy and efficiency which greeted my requests for illustrations. Everyone I approached was not only helpful but friendly, which made my task much easier than it might otherwise have been.

Picture credits:
28 His Grace the Archbishop of York and the Borthwick Institute of Historical Research, York; 55, 56 © The Bodleian Library, University of Oxford; 40, fig.1 by permission of the Syndics of Cambridge University Library; 15 The College of Arms, London; pl.1 © Anthony Crawshaw; 12, 16, 21a, 22, 23, 25, 30, 44, 45, 48 a & b, 49, 51, 52, 54, 60, 61, 62, 63, 64, 65, 69, 78, 81, 84, 85, pls 6, 12 © Anthony Dawton; 46, 47, 50, 57, 58, 59, 86, pls 14, 15, 16 © Nicholas Dawton; 53 © Anthony & Nicholas Dawton; 27 © East Riding Museums Service; 31, 33, 35, 36, 41, 42, 91, 92, 94 © East Riding of Yorkshire Council Library and Information Services; 34 R. Elvidge; 1, 2, 3 a & b, 4, 5, 10, 11, 13, 14, 20, 26, 27, 37, 66, 83, pls 4, 5, 10, 11 © English Heritage; pl. 3 © The Hunt Museum, Custom House, Limerick, Ireland; 38, pl.13 Ivan Hall; pl.13 photograph by Dr J. Hall; 7, 8, 9, 93 Humber Archaeology Partnership; 18, 68, 72a, 73, 75, 77 Malcolm Jones; 17 © David O'Connor; pl. 2 Michael & Lesley Smith; 39, 43 © The Society of Antiquaries of London; 87, 88, 89, 90, Alan Spedding; 82 Ian Sumner; pls 7, 9 David Thornton; 32 S. Todd; 19 The Master and Fellows of University College, Oxford; 29, 79, 80 © University of Hull photographic service; 6, 21b, 67, 70, 71, 74, 76 © University of Manchester, schools' photographic collection; pl. 8 © Frank Woodman.

front cover: the west towers © Frank Woodman
back cover: detail from the Percy tomb, a boss attributed to the Evangelist Master © Nicholas Dawton

Abbreviations

BIHR	Borthwick Institute of Historical Research, York
BL	British Library
DNB	*The Dictionary of National Biography*, eds L. Stephen and S. Lee, 22 vols (1908-9)
EETS	Early English Text Society
ERAO	East Riding Archive Office
EYLHS	East Yorkshire Local History Society
HUL	Archives in the Brynmor Jones Library, University of Hull
L. & P. Hen. VIII	*Letters and Papers, Foreign and Domestic, of the reign of Henry VIII*, eds J.S. Brewer, J. Gairdner and R.H. Brodie, 22 vols in 35 (HMSO, 1862-1932)
Leach, *Memorials*	A.F. Leach, ed., *Memorials of Beverley Minster: the chapter act book of the church of S. John of Beverley AD 1286-1347*, 2 vols, Surtees Society 98 & 108 (1898-1903)
MED	Middle English Dictionary (Ann Arbor, Michigan, 1956-)
OED	Oxford English Dictionary
Poulson, *Beverlac*	G. Poulson, *Beverlac; or the antiquities and history of the town of Beverley* (1829)
PRO	Public Record Office
TERAS	*Transactions of the East Riding Antiquarian Society*
VCH	*The Victoria History of the Counties of England*
VCH Beverley	K.J. Allison, ed., *The Victoria County History of York, East Riding. VI: The borough and liberties of Beverley* (Oxford, 1989)
YAJ	*Yorkshire Archaeological Journal*
YASRS	Yorkshire Archaeological Society record series

In the notes the place of publication is London unless otherwise stated.
Quotations have been rendered in modern English throughout.

Foreword by the Archbishop of York

To say that Beverley Minster is steeped in history is more than somewhat of an understatement. Located on what has been identified as a trade route going back thousands of years, the site has been home to a place of worship for the better part of thirteen hundred years. The church that we see today is essentially the same as that whose rebuilding was completed some six hundred years ago.

To be old is not always to be beautiful but Beverley Minster can justly claim to be both. Acknowledged as being amongst the finest Gothic churches in Europe, it also drew high praise from the great John Wesley: it was, he said, 'such a parish church as has scarce its fellow in England'.

Rising almost abruptly from a flat countryside, this 'mother-church' of the East Riding broods hugely but benevolently over the town of Beverley and the whole surrounding area. Down the centuries, it has excited admiration and affection in equal measure, while luminaries of the genius and stature of Nicholas Hawksmoor and Gilbert Scott are numbered among those who have devoted themselves to its care and preservation. That same sense of devoted dedication lives on today and finds its focus in the work of the Friends of Beverley Minster.

The Friends bring together those 'whose love of the Minster inspires them to have a share in preserving it in all its beauty for future generations', and over these last sixty-four years their vision and commitment have contributed in rich abundance to the *bene esse* of the Minster's life and worship. As Patron, I am greatly privileged to be associated in some small way with that which they have achieved.

As their latest initiative, the Friends have commissioned this most splendid volume. Authoritative and fascinating, it represents a fine and fitting millennial tribute to a great and much-loved church which is itself both a living testament to the faith and witness of centuries past and a beacon of hope for the future.

+ David Ebor:

2   The interior of the nave
from the west end.

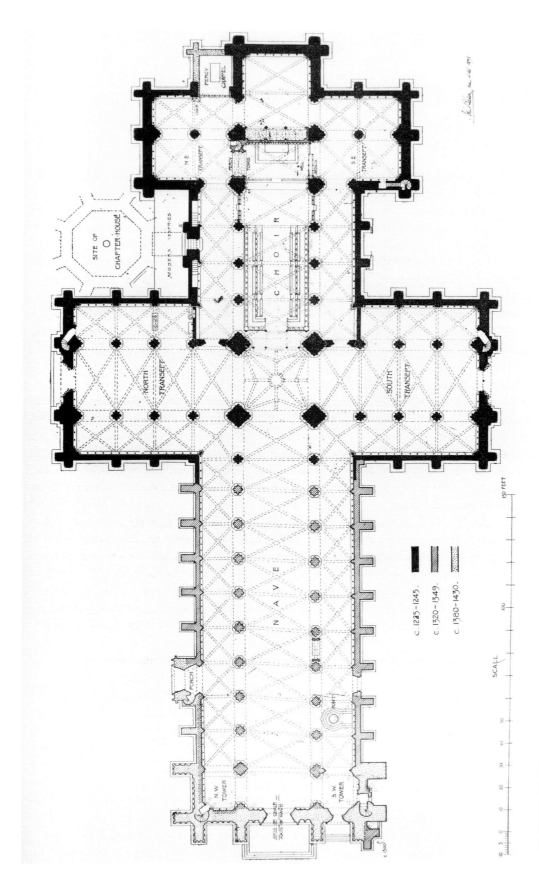

GROUND PLAN: MEASURED AND
DRAWN BY JOHN BILSON.

PAUL BARNWELL & ROSEMARY HORROX

Introduction

Beverley Minster is one of the great parish churches of England. Indeed, it is sometimes difficult to remember that is only a parish church. Instinctive comparisons are with cathedrals, even if, in absolute terms, it is smaller than most of them. In fact, it has never been the seat of a bishop, although the possibility has been mooted on occasion. George Gilbert Scott suggested as much in 1854, commenting that, 'It is quite perfect, being kept in more perfect repair than perhaps any church in England'.[1] There is a sense, however, in which Beverley's importance derived from a bishop: Bishop John of Hexham, later of York, who retired to his monastery 'in the wood of the men of Deira' in c. 714 and whose tomb, after his death in 721, became a focus of pilgrimage. Most recent historians have been willing to identify John's retreat with the modern Beverley, although Bede, our main source for John's life, does not say so. The saint's relics were certainly later housed in Beverley, and it was to John, in the person of his church, that Athelstan was later believed to have made the famous grant of liberties: 'As free make I thee, as heart can think or eye can see' [pl. 9].

The story is apocryphal. But it does testify to the influence wielded by Beverley Minster in the pre-Conquest period, even if that influence was in reality the result of a slow accretion of power rather than a single generous royal action. And St John himself remained a potent force in the Minster's fortunes. His tomb and shrine, and the miracles worked there, drew pilgrims from all over Britain, whose offerings must have helped to fund successive medieval building campaigns. John also secured royal favour for the Minster and for the town beside it. Local tradition later credited him with saving Beverley from the worst consequences of the 'harrying of the north' by William the Conqueror in 1069–70. Royal respect for the saint was further strengthened by the attribution of military powers to him and his banner. The first reference to the banner's use in battle was at the Battle of the Standard in 1138, when a Scottish force was defeated by local troops led by Archbishop Thurstan of York. The first three Edwards were all to borrow the banner, and the saint's reputation received a further boost in 1415 when Henry V won the battle of Agincourt on the feast of his translation (25 October) – although the great speech which Shakespeare put into Henry's mouth has meant that the battle is now popularly associated with the martyrs Sts Crispin and Crispinian, whose feast it also was. At the time, however, the Lancastrian kings were in no doubt where credit was due and the feast of St John's translation, hitherto of only local significance, became a national observance.[2]

Until the Reformation the Minster was a collegiate church, that is, a church served by a community of clergy rather than by a single parish priest. This is still reflected in the organisation of the choir, with its tiers of stalls for the clergy attending the services as congregation rather than officiants – a layout more characteristic of cathedrals or Oxbridge college chapels [66]. Indeed the existence of the stalls was, in Scott's eyes, a powerful argument for selecting the Minster as one of the projected new cathedrals: 'it might be entered upon and used as a cathedral without the necessity of any outlay whatever'.[3] In the later middle ages the clerical community of the Minster numbered around fifty, not including the chantry priests, most of whom lived in what was effectively the Minster precinct, although Beverley has never had a defined close. The most eminent, and the best endowed, of the Minster clergy were the canons and

fig. 1 Plan of the Minster drawn by John Bilson, *Architectural Review*, 3 (1898).

throughout the middle ages a prebend at Beverley was regarded as a significant rung on the ecclesiastical career ladder. This meant that many of the canons were absentees, leaving their pastoral duties to be performed by their vicars, while the *berefellarii* (a term unique to Beverley) took over their liturgical duties. But although the medieval canons may not have been very active locally, their national standing made them valuable patrons, with influence and wealth that could be put at the Minster's disposal. The great east window, now home to the Minster's surviving medieval glass [pl. 4], was the result of one such clerical benefaction in 1416.

The college of priests and the shrine of St John were swept away at the Reformation, and Beverley was left with a church considerably too large for the parish it served. Too large to be maintained by parish resources, and by the early 18th century parts of the fabric were on the point of collapse. Too large, also, as a liturgical space. In the middle ages the great church had been divided into many separate spaces. The heart of the church, accessible only to the clergy, was the choir, housing the high altar and, above and behind it, the shrine of St John. On feast days, pilgrims had access to the retrochoir, the space east of the high altar, which allowed them to approach the shrine, and to the Lady Chapel at the extreme east end of the church. Normally, however, the laity worshipped in the nave, itself invisibly broken up into smaller spaces focussed on the numerous altars and images housed there. The Reformation largely did away with these gradations of holiness, and made the interior of the Minster a single space, albeit one physically divided by the choir screen. Later centuries saw the focus of parochial worship shift back and forth between nave and chancel, usually for reasons of practical convenience.

It is not only, however, the scale of the Minster which gives it its grandeur and dignity. As virtually every commentator on the building has noted, in spite of a history which is essentially a succession of building and restoration campaigns, the Minster remains, to a surprising degree, an architectural unity. This may sometimes have been the result of a lack of money, but even well-endowed restoration campaigns were generally sympathetic to what was there already, with major changes being restricted to the fittings rather than the structure of the building. This, however, is true only of developments from the later middle ages onwards. The great building campaign which began in the 13th century, and is broadly responsible for the Minster as we see it today, must have marked a radical departure from the Romanesque building that preceded it, let alone the earliest church on the site.

Nothing now remains of the earliest Minster building, and no written records from the time cast light on its form or appearance. Whatever the truth of a refoundation by Athelstan in the 920s or 930s, the original building was almost certainly replaced, or at least substantially altered and enlarged, during the later Anglo-Saxon period, but the earliest references to the fabric relate to a time no earlier than the middle of the 11th century, shortly before the Norman Conquest. Although the documents concerned were composed much later, there is no reason to doubt their description of a major building campaign following the canonization of St John in 1037, when Aelfric was archbishop of York. The promotion of Beverley as a pilgrimage site would not only have required a larger building, but would also have generated the income necessary for constructing the requisite facilities. Although it must have been impressive compared with what went before, nothing of the eleventh-century Romanesque building remains. All that is known is that it had a tall stone tower (with bells), a new presbytery, and a substantial gilded ceiling; there is also a tantalizing reference to a crypt or undercroft (perhaps for St John's relics). Beyond that all is conjecture, and it is even a matter of debate whether the tower lay in the centre of the church (like the present one), or at its west end, though the latter is perhaps more likely.[4]

The extent to which building, or re-building, continued after the Norman Conquest is not known, although the presence of fragments of twelfth-century sculpture embedded in later

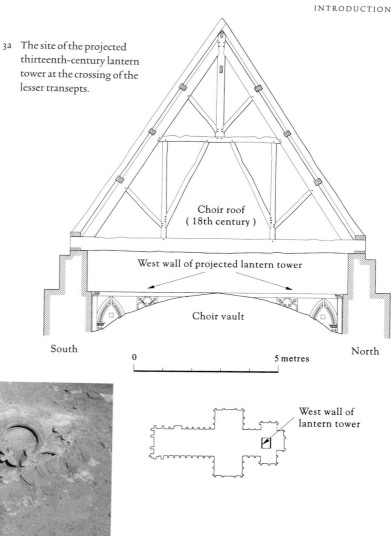

3a The site of the projected thirteenth-century lantern tower at the crossing of the lesser transepts.

3b The south-west corner of the unfinished eastern tower above the vaulting of the choir.

work in the choir roof and of re-used stones (of the 1120s or 1130s) carved with chevron designs in the back of the nave triforium,[5] suggests that work not only continued but was of a high quality. In 1188, however, the Minster sustained substantial damage from fire, following which an over-ambitious restoration scheme led, in c.1213, to the collapse of a tower (perhaps, but not certainly, that of the 11th century). Rather than continue with attempts at reconstruction, the decision was taken to build an entirely new Minster, starting with the eastern arm.

The new church was planned on the scale of a small cathedral, and forms part of a wider thirteenth-century trend of development at, and promotion of, cult sites. The design of the east end (c.1220-c.1260) was influenced by the leading buildings of its day, particularly those associated with other significant cults (Lincoln) and the great Cistercian monasteries of Yorkshire.[6] The plan of the east end incorporated two sets of transepts, as at Lincoln and Salisbury, and allowed for access to the tomb of St John, which was ultimately sited to the east of the choir and high altar.[7] As originally conceived, both crossings were to be surmounted by lantern towers of similar design. The eastern lantern was never completed, having been abandoned at an early stage and hidden from view by the insertion of a vault, perhaps on account of structural instability [3].[8] The story of the main crossing is less certain. Although a late sixteenth-century drawing (known from an engraving of 1656) shows a tower [27], it is not clear either whether its upper parts were of thirteenth-century date or represent a later addition or alteration, or whether they were built of stone or timber (which would have been less liable to cause subsidence). However that may be, the medieval tower hardly survives above vault level, having been demolished (probably in the 17th century) and replaced by the present eighteenth-century structure designed by Nicholas Hawksmoor, at a time when the thirteenth-century roofs were also completely replaced (see below).

The overall impression created by the east end of the Minster is one of uniformity and height, the former aided by the coherence of the system of proportions used in designing both the plan and elevations of the structure.[9] The sense of height is achieved by the narrowness of the building, relative shortness of the bays, emphasis on vertical lines, high springing point of the vaulting, and relatively compact 'band'-like triforium with tall clerestory above. Had the vaulting been punctuated by the two tall lanterns, through which light would have flooded down into the main crossing and onto the high altar, the sense of space would have been even greater. Awareness of both uniformity and height is increased by the relative restraint of the architectural embellishment (perhaps influenced by Cistercian ideals), which gives an uncluttered appearance, while the homogeneity of the design is highlighted by the intrusion of discordant piers at the eastern crossing which, instead of having the usual clustered shafts, are flat with heavily corbelled-out upper parts, perhaps to support four angle stairways to the unfinished lantern above. The other major feature of the decorative scheme is the restrained use of Purbeck marble to create contrasts between light and dark which were complemented by the original glazing scheme in which coloured glass was contrasted with plain grisaille.[10] During the 14th century the focus of new work switched to the nave, but a new reredos and the related Percy tomb were erected in the curvilinear style of the age.

Contemporary with the main eastern part of the Minster was the chapter house which lay between the two north transepts. The chapter house itself was demolished after the Reformation, but the entrance to it remains in the north choir aisle, in the form of an elaborate stone stairway, worked into the decorative scheme with great ingenuity [pl. 8]. Its existence demonstrates that the chapter house lay at first-floor level, above an undercroft. The fact that it was entered directly from the aisle, rather than from a vestibule (as at York or Southwell minsters) or a cloister (as at Salisbury or Wells cathedrals) is unusual, as is its first-floor position, and was presumably dictated by physical constraints on the site. Excavations at the end of the 19th century revealed that the building was octagonal in plan and about 9.5 m. (31 ft) across with, probably, a central pillar supporting the floor of the chapter house proper and perhaps extending upwards to carry a vault.[11]

For much of the 13th century the Romanesque nave seems to have remained in use, probably dwarfed by the new work rising towards the east, and with the intention that it would eventually be replaced. It was not until c.1309, some time after the east end had been completed, that work began, and even then progress was slow, the main part of the nave not being finished until the end of the century,[12] and the western bay and façade not being added until the 1390s or shortly afterwards. In comparison to the east end, the nave generally attracts little scholarly attention, largely because its overall conception was not at the leading edge of fourteenth-century design as the eastern end had been in the 13th, but represented an adaptation of the earlier scheme, both in form and embellishment. The most obvious departures from the earlier work are the absence of Purbeck marble, which had been used in modest quantities in the east end, changes in the window tracery, which is of its period (being Decorated rather than Early

4 View along the fourteenth-century nave roof from the east, between the collar beams.

English in form), and the form of the blind arcading on the inside of the aisle walls. The continuity of design increases the harmonious appearance of the interior of the church as a whole and, even allowing for the presence of nave altars, bright paint on the stone carvings, and devotional objects, must have concentrated attention on the east end which accommodated both the high altar and the shrine of St John.

One of the most distinctive features of the plan of the nave is its irregularity, the piers on the two sides of the building being misaligned. There is no consensus regarding the reasons for this: some (like Ivan Hall in this volume) see it as the result of deliberate aesthetic judgement; others (such as Nicholas Dawton, also in this volume) suggest it was the result of building round the Romanesque nave, the presence of which precluded clear sighting from one side of the nave to the other;[13] and yet others elaborate this to suggest that it stems from differences in the thirteenth-century buttresses from which initial measurements for the north and south walls were taken.[14] The vault, which follows the skewed plan, displays a mixture of conservatism and innovation: it is of a simple quadripartite form, but represents an unusual example of the use of brick, rather than stone, for the infill. Above the vault of the nave itself (as opposed to the nave aisles) the fourteenth-century roof survives [4]: it is the only medieval roof to remain, and, like so much of the rest of the nave, is conservative, if not old-fashioned, in form.[15]

The nave took about eighty years to complete, and it was not until the very end of the 14th century that the west front with its great twin towers was erected [37]. In contrast to the body of the nave, the design reflects its own age, incorporating many features characteristic of the Perpendicular style. The whole system of proportions is different from what lies behind, the great west window with its reticulated tracery projecting up beyond the vault of the main part of the nave, so that the new west bay has a higher vault, which is built of timber rather than continuing with brick or reverting to stone. With the completion of the west front, the fabric of the Minster almost reached its mature medieval form, the only significant alterations thereafter being the addition of the north porch [14], erected early in the 15th century, the replacement of the east window by a great Perpendicular 'wall' of glass painted by John Thornton of

York, the construction of the Percy chapel at the end of the north choir aisle later in the 15th century, and the refurnishing of the choir with new stalls and their sixty-eight misericords in c.1520.[16]

Apart from the demolition of the chapter house and charnel, and possibly a south porch, the structure of the Minster was not greatly affected by the Reformation. By contrast, the interior furnishing and appearance of the building must have been profoundly altered by the dismemberment of the shrine, the dismantling of the subsidiary altars and general clearing-out of the furnishings, although this is not a process that can be traced in detail. In the ensuing century and a half, the history of the building is one of poverty, neglect and decay. It appears likely that during the 17th century the medieval tower at the main crossing was demolished, and by the early years of the 18th century the fabric generally was in a very poor state, with part of the north-west transept in imminent danger of collapse. The consequence was a major programme of restoration and reconstruction undertaken from shortly after 1716 until the 1730s under the auspices of Nicholas Hawksmoor, and conducted by William Thornton and his York-based firm of craftsmen. The story of the partial demolition of the north-west transept, the ingenious

5 The eighteenth-century treadwheel in the roof above the central crossing. The guard rail in the bottom left hand corner surrounds an opening stopped by a boss which can be lifted to allow building materials to be winched into the roof space.

levering of its north wall back into place [39], and the subsequent restoration of that part of the building (including the construction of timber vaulting) is well known,[17] and it is generally recognized that the present central tower (originally capped with an ogival dome) results from the same programme of works, which also saw a major re-ordering of the interior of the building (discussed in chapter 7). What has until recently been much less well appreciated is that the structural restoration went considerably further, involving replacement of all the roofs over the thirteenth-century east end of the Minster, as well as those of the nave aisles, and an inventive attempt to prevent the gable wall of the south-west transept moving outwards and repeating the near disaster on the north side of the building.[18] It was to facilitate this enormous undertaking that the famous treadwheel was erected in the new tower [5], to lift the vast quantities of building materials up to the roof.[19] Although much of this structural work is not apparent to the casual visitor, its scale is immense: without it, the future of the building as a whole would have been at risk, and the 18th century deserves recognition as the third great phase in the history of the present Minster.

For all the care and skill lavished upon the building in the Hawksmoor/Thornton period, however, the story of the fabric does not end there. The dome Hawksmoor placed on the central tower was never regarded as aesthetically successful – except, it seems, by the Yorkshire antiquary Thomas Gent, who wrote enthusiastically of the Minster's beauty on a summer's day 'with its beautiful Dome, and a Ball, gilt with Gold, glittering by the refulgent Beams of the Sun'.[20] Poulson's judgement, that it 'had a most deformed and wretched effect', was more typical of later opinion, and the dome was removed in the 1820s, at the same time as the interior was again substantially re-ordered (under the influence of Thomas Rickman).[21] Half a century later, in a campaign beginning in 1866 and ending in 1880, further re-ordering and refitting of the interior was conducted by Sir George Gilbert Scott, who also undertook some structural restoration, notably in stabilizing the medieval roof by strengthening it with a system of iron tie rods. The last major addition to the building as such,[22] however, was almost exactly a century ago when, between 1897 and 1908, Robert Smith carved the figures which now adorn the niches on the west front.

As this implies, the Minster is a constantly evolving organism. As well as major alterations triggered by dramatic events, such as the collapse of the crossing tower in 1213 or the destruction of the chapter house and charnel at the Reformation, there is a more subtle flux, the result of much unspectacular and routine repair and replacement. Items wear out or get broken. Glass is particularly vulnerable. The Minster almost certainly had a full programme of medieval glass, of which only fragments now remain, enough to reveal that it included windows telling the stories of St Martin, St Nicholas and perhaps St Leonard [17].[23] Some, perhaps much, of the glass may have been destroyed at the Reformation, when its subject matter became theologically unacceptable. But some at least of what is now lost escaped the iconoclasts. The armorial glass in the chapel of the fourth earl of Northumberland survived long enough to be sketched by the antiquary William Dugdale in 1641, but only one armorial panel now survives [pl. 5].[24] More ephemeral still are the textiles associated with worship. Like any great medieval church, the Minster amassed such textiles in huge quantities. Wealthy parishioners contributed lavishly embroidered bed coverings to be turned into hangings, the clergy preferred to bequeath vestments. Robert Rolleston, for instance, gave a set of vestments of cloth of gold on silk to the chapel of St Katherine. Even such sumptuous and cherished fabrics did not last forever, and the more modest vestments of later centuries would have had an even shorter life.

Tastes also changed. Successive generations would have agreed with George Oliver when he castigated the 'want of judgment in our predecessors, which can only be attributed to the defective taste of the age in which they lived' and congratulated his contemporaries on their 'improved ideas and matured experience'.[25] Vestments provide a good example. They became a sensitive issue in the post-Reformation church, providing one of the clearest guides to the religious views of their wearers. The lavish vestments of the medieval church were abandoned everywhere, but it was a sign of the protestant temper of the Minster clergy that in 1566 John Atkinson had to be ordered to wear a surplice. Another dramatic change was from the highly coloured interior of the medieval Minster to the bare stone which has been the norm ever since. Until the 19th century such changes in taste were generally a matter of 'modernization'. The Victorians, by contrast, were more interested in turning the clock back, and restoring the church to their perception of the Gothic, removing the Georgian fittings and inserting coloured glass in the windows. But even the pursuit of 'authenticity' could be cavalier. It is now thought likely that the tomb chest which is shown standing under the canopy of the Percy tomb in Carter's drawing of 1791 was original [55], but it was assumed to be a later addition and ruthlessly removed in the 1820s.

This constant process of change means that many details of the Minster's development are still obscure – and this is true not only of the early medieval Minster but of something as recent as aspects of Hawksmoor's restorations in the 18th century. The position of St John's shrine relative to the high altar is likely to remain a matter for debate among historians, but we arguably have a clearer sense of the appearance of the medieval high altar than of its Georgian counterpart. Our only extant image of the great Georgian screen behind the high altar is a glimpse of it looming over the Percy tomb in John Carter's drawing [55]. More recently still, it is unclear whether the medieval choir screen survived into the 19th century behind a Georgian facing or was removed in the course of the eighteenth-century restoration. In offering a survey of the current state of research, the present volume thus also draws attention to what is *not* known about the Minster, and to continuing disagreements about the interpretation of the evidence.

If the Minster itself is a book, it is a book with some missing and illegible pages. Also very largely missing from the record are the people who created the church and its fittings. With the exception of the men who oversaw the restoration campaigns of the 18th century onwards, they are generally at best just names. Often, particularly in earlier centuries, they are not even that. Although carvings on the Percy tomb and reredos can be ascribed to individuals, those individuals remain anonymous and must, like the Clifford Master, be called after their work. Some masons did sign their work, although only rarely can masons' marks be identified with a known individual.[26] A few craftsmen may have left portraits of themselves or their colleagues, as in the jocular misericord image of two carvers thumbing their noses at two of their, perhaps senior, colleagues [6]. But for most their memorial is the Minster itself and through it they, like the vicar Thomas Mease (d. 1750) 'being dead, yet speak' [30].

6 Woodcarvers: misericord 29 [see Fig. 3 for its location].

NOTES

1 G. Gilbert Scott, *Additional Cathedrals. A Letter* (1854), p. 5.

2 J. Catto, ' Religious Change under Henry V', in G. Harriss, ed., *Henry V: the practice of kingship* (Oxford, 1985), p. 108.

3 Scott, *Additional Cathedrals*, p. 5.

4 The best discussion of the evidence for the early building is R. Morris and E. Cambridge, 'Beverley Minster before the early thirteenth century', in C. Wilson, ed., *Medieval Art and Architecture in the East Riding of Yorkshire* (British Archaeological Association Conference Transactions, 9, 1989), especially pp. 13-16.

5 J. Bilson, 'Norman work in the nave triforium of Beverley Minster', *The Antiquary*, 27 (1898), 18-23 is the definitive account.

6 The best general recent discussion is C. Wilson, *The Gothic Cathedral* (2nd ed., 1992), pp. 170-3. For a more detailed analysis, including discussion of other influences, see *idem*, 'The early thirteenth-century architecture of Beverley Minster: cathedral splendours and Cistercian austerities', in P.R. Coss and S.D. Lloyd, eds, *Thirteenth-century England*, iii (Woodbridge, 1991), pp. 181-95; L. Hoey, 'Beverley Minster in its thirteenth-century context', *Journal of the Society of Architectural Historians*, 43 (1984), especially 215-24.

7 The tomb was placed there perhaps in the 1320s: A. Hamilton Thompson, *The Cathedral Churches of England* (1925), p. 78.

8 The most recent investigation of the towers is described in P.S. Barnwell, '"The Church of Beverly is fully repaired": the roofs of Beverley Minster', *Transactions of the Ancient Monuments Society*, 44 (2000), 11-13, 20-1.

9 Wilson, *Gothic Cathedral*, pp. 172-3.

10 D. O'Connor, 'The medieval stained glass of Beverley Minster', in Wilson, ed., *Medieval Art and Architecture in the East Riding*, pp. 62-90.

11 J. Bilson, 'On the discovery of some remains of the Chapter-house of Beverley Minster', *Archaeologia*, 54 (1895), 426-32.

12 For the phases of construction see chapter 8 below.

13 e.g. Hamilton Thompson, *Cathedral Churches*, p. 78.

14 J. Bilson, 'Beverley Minster', *Architectural Review*, 3 (1898), 252.

15 Barnwell, '"Church of Beverly is fully repaired"', 15-18.

16 Bilson, 'Beverley Minster', 257.

17 The fullest account is that by I. Hall, 'The first Georgian restoration of Beverley Minster', *Georgian Group Journal*, 3 (1993), especially 17-19.

18 This work is described and discussed in Barnwell, '"Church of Beverly is fully repaired"', 18-21.

19 Ibid., 23.

20 T. Gent, *The Antient and Modern History of the Loyal Town of Rippon* (York, 1733), p. 88.

21 Poulson, *Beverlac*, p. 679.

22 Apart from the introduction of fire doors into the main tower, which may have been the response to a potentially serious fire in the roof in 1889: W.M. Stevenson and J. Bilson, *Two Beverley Churches, being papers read before the British Association at their visit to Beverley, September 11th 1890* (Hull, 1890), p. 19.

23 O'Connor, 'The medieval stained glass', pp. 63-6.

24 Ibid. p. 73 and plate XVIA.

25 G. Oliver, *The History and Antiquities of the Town and Minster of Beverley* (Beverley, 1829), p. 262.

26 M.R. Petch, 'William de Malton, Master Mason', *YAJ*, 53 (1981), 37-44.

D. H. EVANS

1 · The Archaeological Origins of Beverley Minster

Comparatively little archaeological investigation has taken place within the Minster itself, and what little there has been has mainly revealed evidence of post-medieval activity.[1] However, during the past twenty years a great deal of archaeological work has taken place in the surrounding area – including a large-scale excavation at Lurk Lane, immediately to the south of the Minster church [7] – and the evidence from these various excavations has shed a considerable amount of light on the environment and form of the buildings which preceded the present Minster.[2] This chapter presents a summary of the archaeological evidence for the pre-Conquest use and settlement of this site.

There are a number of topographical factors which made Beverley an ideal site for early settlement. Before the 18th century, much of the Hull valley and the Holderness plain were poorly drained areas of wetland, with large expanses of marsh, meres and small creeks. Much of the present town has been built over just such a landscape, and water clearly played a very significant part in shaping its development: the winding shape of many of the older streets stems from the fact that they were laid out alongside existing watercourses. Even the very name of the settlement betrays this watery past, being thought to derive from the lake (or stream) of the beavers.

Beverley's position on the edge of the Wolds offered a sheltered location on the only reasonably dry crossing-point in this stretch of the Hull valley. Thus, it controlled a natural route-way from the Wolds to the rich fishing and fowling grounds of the Holderness plain to the east. Evidence has been accumulating over the last twenty years to demonstrate Neolithic and Iron Age settlement on the eastern edges of the future town,[3] and part of a Roman farmstead, dating to the 2nd and 3rd centuries AD, has been located at the northern limits of the medieval settlement.[4] The probability is that this natural route across the Hull valley has been regularly used from at least the Mesolithic period (perhaps 8,000 BC) onwards.

The original landscape of this part of the Hull valley would have been dominated by large tracts of marshy peat-lands, interspersed with low islands of better drained gravels or boulder clay. In consequence, early settlement tended to be attracted to these slightly raised islands - and the Minster is no exception to this rule, being sited on a slight ridge of boulder clay. In prehistory, some of the area would have been wooded. Mature oak trees were growing around a spring on Park Grange Farm in nearby Long Lane at the beginning of the Neolithic period,[5] whilst elsewhere, carrs would have been surrounded by wetland species such as alder trees. Pollen cores taken from a number of sites on the south side of the town show that by the onset of the Iron Age (around 600 BC) the immediate environment comprised a mixed oak forest. During the next thousand years (probably during the later Iron Age or the Romano-British period), parts of this were gradually cleared to allow the cultivation of cereals: this part of the pollen record is marked by the appearance of new invasive species of trees (such as ash), along with grasses and cereals.

Excavations on the Lurk Lane site revealed the traces of parallel enclosure ditches and lines of stake-holes, which probably represent the remains of hedges, fences and ditches defining small agricultural enclosures. Unfortunately, the lack of any associated finds means that these

7   The Lurk Lane excavation in progress, with the south transept of the Minster in the background.

structures cannot be closely dated, and may belong anywhere between the later Iron Age and the early Anglo-Saxon period; however, they are demonstrably earlier than the Anglo-Saxon monastic phase which was to follow.

The foundation of that monastic community is traditionally associated with one of the leading figures of the early English church, the future St John of Beverley – who had been bishop of Hexham and of York before his retirement to the monastery at *Inderauuda* (or, in its latinized form, *in Silva Derorum*), where in 721 he died, and was buried in the *porticus* of St Peter, within his own monastic church. As no evidence has ever been found to suggest that any monastery had existed here before John's retirement, it is generally accepted that this religious house was founded by Bishop John.

Thus, the association of Bishop John with the monastery at *Inderauuda* is indisputable. However, the identification of that place with Beverley was more questionable, until the excavations at Lurk Lane in 1979–82 revealed the presence of a substantial middle Saxon site which appeared to extend beneath the Minster. This coincided with the publication of a major new study of a middle and late Saxon list of saints' resting places, which survives as a medieval copy of a document known in an abbreviated form as the *Secgan*. Detailed textual analysis showed that this list now consists of two separate sections, which were compiled at different dates. The part which includes the reference to St John's resting place at *Beferlic* appears to pre-date the Viking settlement in Northumbria, and was probably compiled in the mid 9th century.[6] There is no evidence that John's remains were ever moved (translated) to Beverley from any other site – and, where this is known to have happened to any of the other saints on this part of the list (such as St Cuthbert), this has been indicated by later amendments in one or other of the surviving manuscripts. This suggests that John's remains were already at Beverley in the mid 9th century, and there is every reason to suppose that *Beferlic* and *Inderauuda* were one and the same site.

Environmental samples from the Lurk Lane excavations show that by the beginning of the 8th century the area around the future Minster was still covered with woodland, in which oak trees were common (alongside water-loving species, such as alder and willow). This is at least consistent with the descriptive place-name *Inderauuda*: 'in the woods of the men of Deira'. The choice of this particular location is more likely to have been influenced by the grant of an available tract of dry ground, on the edge of marshland (a rich food resource), rather than by any preference for a secluded woodland environment. Certainly, the monastic foundation had an immediate and dramatic impact on this landscape: an initial phase of woodland clearance seems to have been followed by cultivation of some of the surrounding ground, to meet the needs of the burgeoning monastic community.

The excavation revealed the southern edge of a large monastic enclosure which appeared to underlie the present Minster, and which was surrounded by an enormous precinct ditch and rampart (a monastic *vallum*). A length of some 26m of this precinct ditch was exposed within the excavated area, on the south side of Minster Yard South/Keldgate, and varied between 2.5 and 3m wide, with a depth of some 0.8m. Adjoining its northern edge was an internal bank which had been constructed from the clay upcast of the ditch; this would presumably have been topped either with a timber palisade, or with a quickset hawthorn hedge. The combined width of the bank and ditch (in its best-preserved form – in Phase 4a, dating to the early 9th century) would have been c. 4.5m. If topped with a palisade, the actual bank or rampart could conceivably have been as high as 4–5m. Not only would this have served to demarcate the monastic enclosure, but it would also have represented quite an effective first line of defence against wild animals and unwanted visitors. However, the sheer size of the enclosure would have precluded any realistic hope of withstanding a determined or prolonged attack. In its early stages, the ditch certainly held water, and could well have been used for some functional purposes beyond mere demarcation - for example, retting flax or hemp, and trapping fish. This is suggested not only by environmental residues recovered from soil samples taken from the ditch, but also by the presence of small feeder channels, which led into it from the south (that is, from outside the monastic precinct), and wood-lined sluices which may have served to control the flow of water.

Very little can be said about the overall size of John's monastery, as only a relatively small portion of its southern perimeter has been defined. Complete, or even substantially complete, monastic plans for this period are restricted to a handful of sites in rural settings, mainly in the west of Britain and Ireland;[7] whereas John's monastery at *Inderauuda* is more likely to have been modelled on or influenced by contemporary monastic sites within the kingdom of Northumbria – such as Jarrow, Wearmouth (or Monkwearmouth), Hartlepool, Tynemouth, Whitby, or even Hexham (where he had previously been bishop). Few of these Northumbrian sites have been investigated sufficiently for their overall plans to be restored with any degree of confidence. Even at Hartlepool, where the early north-eastern perimeter has been established by excavation, and the maximum limits of its southern and eastern sides would seem to be determined by the headland and a cemetery, respectively, there is still considerable room for doubt about the overall size of the monastic enclosure.[8] At Beverley, a major determining factor on the final size of the monastery will have been the availability of well-drained land on which to site the precinct. Its medieval successor appears to have had an informal oval-shaped close measuring c.160m (east-west) x 190m (north-south), giving a total area of c. 3.04 ha. Its Saxon predecessor is unlikely to have exceeded this, and may well have been considerably smaller.

The internal layout of the precinct is almost a complete unknown, as none of its major buildings has yet been located. It is reasonable to assume that the actual church would have lain somewhere under the present site of the Minster – perhaps under its eastern end, or the crossing, if continuity in the position of the altar had persisted in the late Saxon and medieval churches which succeeded it. If this were indeed to be the case, then the most likely way in which this might be located would be with ground-sensing radar.

The ground plan of such a church is a matter for pure speculation. However, it is likely that it would have been influenced by other contemporary Northumbrian churches, such as those built by Benedict Biscop (628-89) at Wearmouth and Jarrow, or by the work of Wilfrid (c. 633-709) at Hexham, Ripon and York. Bishop John began his life as a monk at Whitby, and was subsequently bishop of both Hexham and York; hence, he would certainly have been very familiar with St Wilfrid's work, but may also have absorbed other architectural influences from the region. Bede closes his account of John's life by relating that he was buried in 721 in the *porticus* of St Peter in his own monastery of *Inderauuda*.

The use of the term *porticus* usually implies that the church had at least one lateral chamber - if not a pair: the term is used by both archaeologists and architectural historians to describe 'a subsidiary cell opening from the main body of a pre-Conquest church', or, more simply, 'a small side chamber or chapel characteristic of Saxon churches'. The function of such chambers is not very clear: many contained altars, whilst burials were often made within them - sometimes of important dignitaries. At St Peter and St Paul, Canterbury, not only was St Augustine (the founder of the English church) buried in a side *porticus*, but later archbishops were buried in the north *porticus* whilst King Aethelbert and his wife were buried in the south.[9] However, it should be stressed that burials of major figures could also take place within the main body of the church, and that there are at least two celebrated examples of founding fathers being buried to the east of the principal altar (Ceolfrid at Monkwearmouth, and Wilibrord at Echternach): on the analogy of the Monkwearmouth evidence, and particularly if one chooses not to put too much emphasis on the use of the term *porticus*, an equally plausible case can be presented for St John being buried to the east of the high altar.[10]

Timber churches of this period are certainly known,[11] and it is quite possible that the first church on this site was a wooden structure. Good stone, suitable for building, would have had to have been imported onto the site (the nearest source of freestone, as opposed to chalk, would have been the oolitic limestones from the Cave and Newbald areas, a few miles to the west), whilst timber may have been more locally available (depending on the size required). Nevertheless, many of the contemporary Northumbrian churches were built of stone from the outset. This is clear not only from the surviving archaeology, but also from contemporary documentary references – in his oft-quoted passage about King Nechtan's correspondence with Abbot Ceolfrid, Bede mentions that Nechtan requested that architects be sent to him, in order to build a stone church for his people in the Roman style.

Whatever the form of the original church, the presence of window glass fragments in Phase 4 contexts at Lurk Lane indicates that by the early 9th century the church at Beverley was certainly built of stone, and probably of comparable quality to its surviving contemporaries (e.g. Jarrow and Wearmouth). As such, it would presumably have had the round-headed doorways and small round-headed windows which are so typical of Anglo-Saxon church architecture of this period - compare Ledsham (Yorks., W.R.), Escomb and Jarrow (Co. Durham) or Brixworth (Northants.).[12]

Large quantities of carpentry debris (which were later to be discarded in the ditch after the site was abandoned) clearly show that most of the other precinct buildings would have been timber structures. The only building to be located within the eighth- and ninth-century levels (Phases 2–4) within the excavated area was a very peripheral structure, which was clearly industrial, and appeared to have been associated with metalworking. It is probable that most of the more important buildings would have been clustered nearer to the heart of the precinct,

8   An aerial view of the Minster from the north east showing excavation in progress to the south. The stone foundations of the building reconstructed in **93** are visible.

rather than being situated out on its edge; these might have included a refectory, a common dormitory, a novice house, an infirmary or hospital, a guest-house, and *cubicula* for the abbot, the prior, and some senior members of the community. There may also have been various domestic, industrial and farm buildings scattered around the rest of the precinct. The probability is that the great majority (if not all) of these structures would have been rectangular - like the excavated building - usually with an entrance set in one or both of the long sides. This basic plan form is found on both secular and religious sites of this period, and at most levels of society. At Jarrow and Wearmouth, the excavator has interpreted the buildings as being grouped into something resembling a formal cloister; but on a number of more extensively excavated sites (such as Whitby, Hartlepool, or Flixborough) the settlement plan can indeed be seen to incorporate some formal elements - such as rows or terraces of buildings loosely arranged on similar alignments - but these are accompanied by more random elements, including other buildings set at right-angles to them.[13]

The excavated building on the southern edge of the precinct was associated with both iron slag and very large quantities of charcoal; this suggests that its function was connected with some form of metalworking. Other finds from the excavation shed light on the quality of life enjoyed by this community. A range of pottery and glass vessels was in use, including imported Ipswich ware from East Anglia, demonstrating the trading connections of the monastery. Other evidence for trade is provided by finds of eighth- and ninth-century Northumbrian coinage - mainly sceattas and stycas. Building work is attested not only by the large quantities of wooden boards, joints and pegs which were recovered from the ditch, but also by a range of iron building fittings (such as hinges and wall-hooks). In addition, substantial quantities of lead spillage and offcuts indicate extensive lead-working - perhaps associated with the roofing and glazing of the church. Details of personal costume are provided by a range of copper alloy and lead alloy jewellery and dress fittings, worked bone pins and toggles, glass beads, and a number of antler combs; whilst a number of jet and worked bone amulets and pendants may also have had a symbolic significance, in addition to being decorative.

Weaving is indicated by a worked bone pin-beater, whilst a wooden mattock-head is a reminder of the agricultural regime which probably played a large part in the daily life of this community. A number of whetstones show that iron tools were being regularly sharpened, and a millstone shows that corn was being ground. Other finds include a worked bone gaming counter, and a simple lead cross and disc.

Local tradition has always maintained that this monastery was sacked by the Danes in c. 866. Some support for this was found in the excavations, which demonstrated that this site was indeed abandoned in the middle of the 9th century. However, there was no definite evidence for destruction in this part of the precinct. A purse-hoard containing twenty-three copper stycas, and dating to c. 851, was buried close by the precinct rampart. This might suggest that the monastery was in fact abandoned some fifteen years earlier than previously thought - in the first year that the great Viking army over-wintered in England. The hoard was probably deposited in a climate of panic and confusion caused by the dramatic appearance of that army. It may even be that the monastic community felt sufficiently under threat to abandon its precinct on two separate occasions - first in 851, and then again in 866.

The site was abandoned for over half a century, and the precinct ditches became overgrown and fell into disuse. The site was reoccupied in the 10th century. Tradition has it that the site was refounded under King Athelstan, after his visit to St John's shrine at the beginning of his campaign against the Scots in 937. The archaeological evidence is less precise, and could be used to support either of two interpretations. The first would be that the refoundation took place in the early years of the 10th century, and that Athelstan (if, indeed, he had any connection with this monastery) merely endowed or enriched a community which had already reoccupied the site. The second is that the house was indeed refounded in the 930s, or even later, under Athelstan. Given that the form of the new house (as a college of secular canons, similar to that of Beverley's sister minster at Ripon) was markedly different from its predecessor, the latter interpretation might be preferred; it is interesting to note that Ripon too was reputedly associated with gifts from Athelstan, following his visit – though any major building here is more likely to have post-dated the English army setting it alight in a punitive raid in 948.

The onset of occupation was marked by the clearance of the site of John's monastery, and large quantities of old building timbers and debris were cast into the former precinct ditch. A new layout of enclosures and buildings was quickly established. Although far more evidence was recovered for some of the buildings of the new college than for its predecessor, there were no indications as to the overall size of its precinct, as no clear precinct boundary was located within the excavated area. As with St John's monastery, all that can be safely stated is that it is unlikely to have occupied a larger area than its medieval successor.

Once again, all the more important buildings of the college lay outside the excavated area – presumably, to the north, much closer to the present Minster – and the area which was examined contained an industrial quarter of workshop buildings. The latter were rectangular timber structures, represented by a mixture of shallow earth-cut linear slots and post-holes, enclosing working areas and industrial hearths which were associated with lead-working debris: amongst the items recovered were a lead ingot, lead spillage, and fragments of lead sheeting, which demonstrate that lead was certainly being used for roofing within the precinct. In addition, lead window came (the grooved strips of lead which held the glass) was recovered from contexts of this period, along with numerous fragments of window glass. Chemical analysis of the latter shows that its composition compares closely with examples of pre-Conquest window glass recovered from the monasteries at Wearmouth and Jarrow. Lastly, the incidence of these glass fragments in the same contexts as the lead-working debris, and the finding of a fragment of glass slag adhering to part of a pottery crucible, tend to suggest that one of these buildings was being used as a glazier's workshop.

From this incontestable evidence for the use of glazed windows and lead sheeting on the roofs within the precinct, it is reasonable to infer that the tenth-century church was built of stone. Hence, when Archbishop Cynesige added a high stone tower to the church in the 1050s, he would have been extending and adapting an existing stone building.

Other finds shed light on the wealth of activities being carried out within the new precinct. Craft activities are represented not only by the lead-working and glazing mentioned above, but also by textile production, leather-working and the manufacture of objects out of antler. The preparation, spinning and weaving of textiles is indicated by fragments of wool or flax combs, spindle whorls, and pin beaters; leather-working or hide preparation is evidenced by finds of leather slickers and awls; antler-working by fragments of discarded antler tines. Agricultural activity is attested by finds of millstones, whetstones, and horseshoes, as well as by grains of oats, barley and wheat. Building work is demonstrated not only by the aforementioned lead roofing-sheets and glazing evidence, but also by finds of tools (such as a woodworking file), building ironwork (including a cranked tie, clench bolt, hinge, hinge strap, binding strip, padlock, key, lock plate and staple), and wooden planks and pegs.

Trade with other centres in eastern England (mostly within the Danelaw) is suggested by the presence of pottery vessels from Stamford and Northamptonshire, and coins from Lincoln and York. Foreign trade is shown by fragments of imported lava querns from the Rhineland, and a phyllite whetstone (possibly from central Europe). Many of the objects clearly demonstrate strong Anglo-Scandinavian influences, which cannot be attributed to a single production centre, but which can be paralleled by finds from other towns within the Danelaw. Certainly, this assemblage represents one of the largest stratified collections of Anglo-Scandinavian material to be found in the north-east of England, outside York itself. Trading connections are also shown by a folding copper alloy balance, which would have been used for weighing items. Coinage, as on many sites of this period, is less frequently found in tenth- and eleventh-century contexts: of the three coins recovered, the earliest is a St Peter penny of the Viking kingdom of York (possibly in circulation until c. 925), whilst the latest is a cut halfpenny of Harold II (struck in 1066).

The diversity of personal dress fittings and household equipment is shown by a broad range of buckles, brooches, bracelets, dress pins, toggles, pendants, combs and comb-cases, worked bone skates, an antler spoon, iron knives, a combined fork and spatula, and leather shoes. A small offcut of gold is a reminder that precious metals were used extensively for ritual vessels, adorning sacred objects, and even (as gold leaf) for illuminating manuscripts.

Cow, sheep, pig, roe deer, red deer, horse, goose, domestic fowl, and also a surprisingly large range of fish (including herring, pike, eel, sturgeon, carp, horse mackerel, salmon, smelt, and burbot) were all being eaten; the last of these is a freshwater species belonging to the codfish family, now extremely rare, if not extinct in England, but was once common in lowland rivers and large lakes. Other animal and bird remains recovered from the site offer evidence about the nature of the surrounding landscape and its environment: these include crane, mallard, red kite, blackbird, wagtail, field vole, common shrew, frog, snake and stickleback.

9 A twelfth-century stone corbel, carved in the shape of a helmeted head, re-used as a padstone in the southern area of the Lurk Lane excavation.

The new foundation was to prosper during the later 10th and 11th centuries, particularly under the last three Saxon archbishops of York – Aelfric (1023-51), Cynesige (1051-60) and Ealdred (1061-9). Documentary references to their improvements to the fabric of the college show that substantial building work was being carried out in the precinct. This programme of expansion and renewal was made possible by a general improvement in the fortunes of the college, shown particularly in the acquisition of new lands.

Excavations at the Lurk Lane site show that a wholesale re-planning of this part of the precinct took place in the middle or late 11th century. Not only were all the ditches and structures which had characterized the tenth-century monastery levelled and cleared away, but a major programme of earth-moving was initiated to create a site for a new timber aisled hall. Dendrochronological (tree-ring) dates for the timbers used in this new building suggest that its construction began shortly after c.1070. Thus, the re-planning of this part of the precinct would seem to have begun shortly after the arrival of the Normans. The decision to embark on this campaign may even have been taken in the last years of the episcopacy of Archbishop Ealdred, though the actual work is more likely to have taken place under his successor.

This was the first of three such halls to occupy the Lurk Lane site for the rest of the Middle Ages, and marks a distinct change in the usage of this part of the precinct. As such, these buildings - though they are of great interest and importance from an archaeological stand-point – clearly belong to the medieval pattern of claustral buildings associated with the Minster, and lie beyond the scope of the present essay.[14] They will be discussed further in chapter 13 below.

The first Minster church, which was badly damaged by the fire of September 1188, is dealt with elsewhere in this volume; but it is worth noting, in closing this chapter, that masonry from this building was subsequently reused in large quantities as building material on other sites throughout Beverley, and has been recognized on a number of archaeological excavations [**9**].

NOTES

1   For example the post-medieval infill of a well located in the south transept: W. Stephenson, 'On the discovery of a well in Beverley Minster', *YAJ*, 5 (1877-8), 126-33.

2   For the detailed report on the Lurk Lane excavations, see P. Armstrong, D. Tomlinson, and D.H. Evans, *Excavations at Lurk Lane, Beverley, 1979-1982*, Sheffield Excavation Reports, 1 (1991).

3   Excavations on the east side of the railway station located a curving ditch which was radiocarbon-dated to around 2,900 BC; excavations at Annie Reed Road in the Grovehill industrial estate revealed a stake and wattle fence on the edge of the Beck, which was radiocarbon-dated to around 600 BC: *East Riding Archaeologist*, 9 (1997).

4   Excavations at Wylies Road in 1985 and 1990, by the Humberside Archaeology Unit.

5   Three substantial sections of oak trees were recovered from the spring, and were dated by dendrochronology (tree-ring dating) to 3,891 BC: J. Hillam *et al.*, 'Dendrochronology of the English Neolithic', *Antiquity*, 64/243 (1990), 210-16. For a general summary of this site, see *A Roman Settlement in Woodmansey*, Humber Archaeology Information Sheet 26.

6   D.W. Rollason, 'Lists of saints' resting-places in Anglo-Saxon England', *Anglo-Saxon England*, 7 (1978), 61-98, especially 68.

7   For comparative plans, see C.D. Morris and N. Emery, 'The chapel and enclosure on the Brough of Deerness, Orkney: survey and excavation 1975-1977', *Proceedings of the Society of Antiquaries of Scotland*, 116 (1986), 301-74, especially illustrations 26-7.

8   R. Daniels, 'The Anglo-Saxon Monastery at Church Close, Hartlepool, Cleveland', *Archaeological Journal*, 145 (1988), 158-210.

9   B. Cherry, 'Ecclesiastical architecture', in D.M. Wilson, ed., *The Archaeology of Anglo-Saxon England* (1976), pp. 151-200, especially pp. 162-6. The best-known example of a Northumbrian church with a *porticus* is at Escomb (Co. Durham) – a two-cell church with a northern *porticus* entered from the church: *ibid.*, fig. 4.4b. Ledsham (Yorks., W.R.) still incorporates the nave walls, west porch and south *porticus* of a building which may well date from c.700: P. Ryder, *Medieval Churches of West Yorkshire* (West Yorkshire Archaeology Service, Wakefield, 1993), pp. 15-16. A further example of a *porticus* has been suggested at Bywell St Peter (Northumb.): H.M. Taylor and J. Taylor, *Anglo-Saxon Architecture* (Cambridge, 1965), pp. 122-6.

10 R. Morris and E. Cambridge, 'Beverley Minster before the early thirteenth century', in C. Wilson, ed., *Medieval Art and Architecture in the East Riding of Yorkshire*, British Archaeological Association Conference Transactions for 1983 (1989), pp. 18-19 and fig. 1; it should be noted that this 1983 paper had been prepared and published before the full results of the excavations at Lurk Lane had appeared in print, or were known to the authors. For definitions of *porticus*, see N. Pevsner and D. Neave, *The Buildings of England. Yorkshire: York and the East Riding*, (1995), p. 791; and Ryder, *Medieval Churches of West Yorks.*, p. 186.

11 A.C. Thomas, *The early Christian archaeology of North Britain* (Oxford, 1971); C.P. Loveluck, 'A high-status Anglo-Saxon settlement at Flixborough, Lincolnshire', *Antiquity*, 72/275 (1998), 146-61.

12 R. Gem, 'Church architecture', in L. Webster and J. Backhouse, eds, *The Making of England: Anglo-Saxon Art and Culture AD 600-900* (1991), pp.185-8, figs 15-16.

13 For plans of Jarrow, Wearmouth and Whitby, see R. Cramp, 'Monastic sites', in Wilson, *Archaeology of Anglo-Saxon England*, pp. 201-52; for Hartlepool, see Daniels, 'Anglo-Saxon Monastery at Hartlepool'; for Flixborough, see Loveluck, 'High-status settlement'.

14. P. Armstrong et al., *Lurk Lane*. A detailed summary can be found in *Lurk Lane, Beverley - Excavations 1979-82*, Humber Archaeology Information Sheet 20.

D. M. PALLISER

2 · The Early Medieval Minster

ORIGINS AND DEVELOPMENT TO C.1000

The Minster's foundation is usually credited to John, bishop of York, later known as St John of Beverley. We have very little reliable information about him except for five precious chapters in *The Ecclesiastical History of the English People* by St Bede. Fortunately, Bede was a great scholar who knew John personally, and who carefully collected stories about him from priests who had served under him. As a result, Bede's chapters on John give us information about him and his church which is unusually well authenticated and very nearly contemporary.

Many traditions about John, by contrast, derive from much later sources, such as Folcard's *Life* (1060s) and the Chronicle of Alfred (Alured) of Beverley (c.1140), and the traditions they record must be read with reservations. They include, for instance, his aristocratic ancestry, his birth at Harpham on the Yorkshire Wolds, and his education at Canterbury. What we learn from Bede is brief, and is furnished only incidentally as background to relating five of John's miracles of healing [**pl.3**]. John, he says, was one of five future bishops trained under St Hild (Hilda) in her monastery of *Streanaeshalch* (probably Whitby), and was later successively bishop of Hexham and York. Four of the five miracles were related to Bede by Berhthun, 'once his deacon but now abbot of the monastery called *Inderawuda*, that is, "in the wood of the men of Deira"', a place identified by nearly all later commentators with Beverley. Bede concluded his account of John by recording that when, owing to his age, he could no longer administer his diocese, he resigned the bishopric of York and retired to 'his monastery [*monasterio suo*] in the wood of the men of Deira', where he was buried in the chapel [*porticus*] of St Peter in 721 AD. [1]

It should be added that Bede, who popularized the Christian dating system and used AD dates frequently in his *History*, gives no other dates whatever for John's life: what mattered most to him were John's miracles, not his exact career. Since John's dates as bishop have to be taken from later, and sometimes contradictory, annals and chronicles, it may be worth noting the currently accepted chronology. According to this, John became bishop of Hexham in 687, was translated to York in 706, and probably retired around 714. [2] The chronology is worth stressing because many otherwise excellent accounts of Beverley date its origins to about the year 700, an impossibly early date if John was its founder.

A plausible interpretation of John's later life is that he was considering a retreat for some time before he retired, and hit upon *Inderawuda* as a suitable spot while travelling round his diocese. A miracle story of his Hexham period shows him accustomed to finding a remote retreat in the Tyne valley, for prayer and reading, as often as possible, and a marshy spot in the Hull valley may have had similar attractions. Certainly two, if not three, of Berhthun's stories show John active as a bishop not far from *Inderawuda*: twice he is described as healing the sick while dedicating churches on the estates of local landowners, one of them within two miles of *Inderawuda*, and on a third occasion he cured a nun while visiting a nunnery at *Wetadun*, almost certainly Watton. [3] He may have founded *Inderawuda* partly as a religious community to which he intended to retire, though Bede does not explicitly call him its founder; and the possibility is worth exploring archaeologically as to whether there may have been an earlier holy site, Celtic or English, which John adapted.

10 The twelfth-century font, of black Frosterley marble, in the south nave aisle. The font cover was carved by the Thorntons in the early 18th century.

The relevance of all this to the Minster depends, of course, on the identification of *Inderawuda* with Beverley. Bede never uses the name Beverley, and there are almost no contemporary sources referring to John's monastery after the death of Abbot Berhthun, or to a minster at Beverley before the 11th century. 'The burden of proof', wrote A.F. Leach in 1898, 'is on those who assert the identity of two places of wholly different names'.[4] However, the weight of scholarly opinion has now reverted to accepting the traditional view that the two were identical. The section of the *List of Saints' Resting Places* discussed in chapter 1 above, probably compiled before 900, locates John's tomb at *Beferlic*, and there is no record of his body ever having been translated from one church to another.[5]

Unfortunately, nothing is known of John's church except that it possessed at least one *porticus* of St Peter, in which he was buried. This might seem to imply a side chapel, but the commonest early location for the principal burials in a monastic church was to the south of the high altar, and it is possible that this was what Bede meant, and that the whole church was originally dedicated to St Peter. By the later middle ages it was certainly dedicated to St John the Evangelist, but that may have originated from the fact that Ealdred's new high altar of the 11th century was dedicated to that saint.[6] It is likely to have been a stone building, judging from other Northumbrian churches of this period, but it has not yet been located. The excavations of 1979–82 south of the present Minster found earthworks which were tentatively identified as part of a monastic boundary ditch, but no trace of a church or of other major precinct buildings.

After Bede completed his *History* in 731, we have no further references to the monastery except for the deaths of Abbot (St) Berhthun in 733 or 740, of an Abbot Wynwald in 751, and of Abbot Wulfeth in 773.[7] When it re-emerges into recorded history in the 11th century, it is described as a minster staffed by secular priests and not monks. The traditional explanation is in two linked parts, that John's monastery was destroyed by the Viking army which invaded Yorkshire in 866, and that it was refounded as a college of secular canons by King Athelstan in the 930s. These two stories have, as Richard Morris observes, 'tended to dominate discussion of Beverley's origins and early history', and are mutually reinforcing;[8] but both depend entirely on sources of the 12th and later centuries and may be nothing more than guesses to account for the disappearance of the monastery and the later appearance of an apparently very different church.

The archaeologists who excavated the Lurk Lane site believed that occupation ceased in the mid-9th century, and used the evidence of a coin hoard deposited about 851-2 to suggest that the site was abandoned 'in the first year that the Viking army overwintered in England'.[9] They added, however, that there was 'no definite evidence for destruction', and R.A. Hall has not only emphasized that doubt but adds that 'the supposed break in occupation ... is not altogether convincing; and even if this particular area was derelict, it does not follow that the nearby monastery was abandoned'.[10] It is, in fact, unnecessary to postulate a break in continuity of occupation at all. It is not unusual to find English churches recorded as *monasteria* in the 7th and 8th centuries, but re-emerging as secular 'minsters' in the 10th and 11th centuries, and Viking disruption need not be – indeed, cannot always be - the explanation, for the same phenomenon can be found far to the south of Viking-controlled territory, as at Bosham in Sussex. Nevertheless, the Lurk Lane excavation covered only a part of the probable monastic precinct, and it is only fair to add that at present the archaeological evidence is capable of more than one interpretation.

Tradition is also invoked for a refoundation and generous endowment of the church by King Athelstan of Wessex (924–39), who in 927 became the first southern English ruler to take control of Yorkshire, and who in 937 beat off a great coalition of his northern and Scottish enemies at an unidentified place, possibly somewhere in northern England, called *Brunanburh*. The two earliest collections of John's miracles both relate how Athelstan, passing through

Lindsey *en route* to this battle, met pilgrims who had been cured by St John, visited the shrine himself, and on his victorious return made lavish gifts to his church.[11] Later accounts elaborated this, making Athelstan responsible for the foundation of a college, for its privileges of sanctuary, and for its right to a render of grain (thraves) from the whole of the East Riding of Yorkshire. However, no known source before King Stephen's charter of 1136 mentions Athelstan in connection with Beverley, and it is likely that the endowment of the Minster was a more gradual process, credited afterwards to the king who had united England for the sake of the prestige conferred by such a founder.

Indeed, not only may the Minster's privileges have been acquired gradually, but there is no need to postulate any break in continuity, or any refoundation once the ninth-century break is questioned. If, as Morris argues, 'evidence for the continuous presence of a religious community at Beverley from c.720 is at least as strong as any argument to the contrary', then we can postulate on the eve of the Norman Conquest a settled community, the tomb of John enshrined in its midst, with no need to invent a foundation myth to account for its origins.[12]

It is true that there is no contemporary or near-contemporary reference to Beverley in the 9th and 10th centuries, apart from the possibly pre-Viking section of the *List of Saints' Resting Places*, but it is not unusual to have churches mentioned by Bede and not recorded again until the 11th century. Satisfactory documentation for Beverley does not recommence until the period of the three last Anglo-Saxon archbishops of York (1023-69) and the reign of King Edward the Confessor (1042-66), and when it does, it reveals a settled and privileged community with no claim to any founder except St John. Before considering this evidence, however, it may help to review the nature of monastic and minster communities, and to analyse some special features of Beverley first recorded in the 11th and 12th centuries, but suggesting a very archaic origin. By thus reasoning backwards from the known to the unknown, we may glimpse the likely nature of the early community before it is described in detail.[13]

MINSTER AND PAROCHIA

Beverley, like many important churches of pre-Conquest foundation and even some cathedrals, has always been called in English a 'minster'. They are especially numerous in the diocese of York, with York itself, its sub-cathedrals of Ripon and Southwell as well as Beverley, other major churches like Howden, and even lesser churches like Kirkdale and Stonegrave, all called minsters. Latin documents usually call Beverley 'the church [*ecclesia*] of St John', or *monasterium*, but Edward the Confessor's English charter of 1061 x 1065 calls it *Sancte Johannes mynstre*, and speaks of *mynstrelif* there.[14] What was a minster?

The Old English *mynster* was a translation of the Latin *monasterium*, 'monastery', but it had a wider connotation, allowing it to cover houses of priests as well as monks; and in the 11th century both *mynster* and *monasterium* could be used for any kind of religious establishment with a church. Minsters might house groups of monks, nuns, or secular priests, but they were all important as religious centres for their districts. Many of them originally controlled large mother parishes, often called *parochiae* in the modern literature to distinguish them from the later, smaller parishes which began to supersede them between the 10th and 12th centuries. Especially between about 1080 and 1120, there was a rapid decline both in the community life and in the pastoral importance of minsters, although some – chiefly those controlled by bishops and monasteries - retained significant rights over their ancient territories or *parochiae*. That model well fits Beverley with its episcopal lordship, though it should be added that Yorkshire

was a conservative area where a number of churches neither episcopal nor monastic also retained rights over large territories into the later middle ages, including important royal manors like Pocklington and Pickering.[15]

The eleventh-century records show clearly that the *mynster* at Beverley was a college of secular priests with wide estates, great privileges, and a popular shrine and cult of Bishop John (canonized in 1037). In the light of Morris' suggestion that the community had unbroken continuity back to John's time, it may be rewarding to look at the special features of the Minster's constitution and privileges, and to consider how far they may reflect very archaic arrangements antedating the surviving records. The doyen of historians of the medieval English church, Hamilton Thompson, considered that the organization of Beverley Minster before its suppression in 1548 'had a peculiar constitutional interest second to none', while more recently R.T.W. McDermid has argued that 'to a greater degree than perhaps any other comparable institution, the late medieval church of Beverley preserved within its constitution clear traces of its Anglo-Saxon origin'.[16]

Beverley is best studied therefore, not in isolation, but as a particularly conservative example of what may well once have been a much more widespread type of church, and some of the fragmentary evidence has to be interpreted in the light of analogies, or contrasts, with minster churches elsewhere. This involves some comparisons with collegiate churches and minsters elsewhere in England, but also, more immediately, with three other churches in the medieval diocese of York with which Beverley was closely connected. It is clear that the last three pre-Conquest archbishops of York, Aelfric, Cynesige and Ealdred, treated Beverley, Ripon and Southwell as sub-cathedrals of their vast diocese, and tried to reorganize their communities of priests on similar lines, with a common fund, buildings for communal living (refectory and dormitory), and an episcopal residence.[17]

There may, indeed, have been an assumption that all three sub-cathedrals shared the privileges of their mother church. A description of the rights and privileges of York Minster, as accepted at an inquest in 1106, survives only because it was copied into a similar response by Southwell in the 1330s, and was copied because the York liberties were presumably assumed to apply to Southwell as a dependent church of York. No such copy survives at Ripon or Beverley, but the 1106 inquest specifically refers to the sanctuaries of those churches as well as that of York itself, and it is legitimate to assume that all three sub-cathedrals expected to enjoy a similar range of privileges.

The York privilege of sanctuary, as described in 1106, gave the highest degree of sanctuary to anyone taking refuge 'in the stone chair [*cathedra*] near the altar, which the English call Fritstol [frithstool], that is, chair of peace'.[18] That York chair no longer survives, but both Hexham and Beverley have surviving Anglo-Saxon stone chairs, that at Beverley also called *Frithstool* and connected with sanctuary rights [**11**]. All three, however, may originally have functioned as episcopal thrones, which would originally have been placed in the east apse of a pre-Conquest church behind the high altar, an arrangement still preserved at Norwich. York and Hexham, of course, were pre-Conquest cathedrals, and would therefore need episcopal thrones, and an early Norman list suggests that Beverley, together with Ripon and Whitby, was a suffragan cathedral.[19]

Beverley also resembles York in its pre-Conquest constitution, so far as that is known. All four greater churches of the diocese were staffed by canons, originally seven in number at York, and probably also at the other three. They may just possibly have originated as groups of priests on a Celtic model: according to a tradition recorded later in York, the seven canons were originally called *Colidei*, 'Culdees', a term recorded from the 8th century for a Scoto-Irish religious order.[20] No such tradition is recorded at Beverley, but it is interesting that the known number

11 The Frithstool, which now stands in the sanctuary. Behind is the restored reredos. The statues, added by Hitch in 1897, show Lucius (the mythical founder of Beverley), St Hilda, St John of Beverley, St Berhthun, St Bede and King Athelstan.

of canons in Norman Beverley was seven, and it is probable that before 1066 there were already seven, deriving their income, like the canons of York, from a common fund.

After the Norman Conquest, to trespass on the later and better-recorded period, successive archbishops introduced to the York diocese the reformed continental model of secular chapters of canons, presided over by a dean, and with prebends (sources of income) assigned to each canon, who enjoyed a separate income and jurisdiction over their estates and parishes. This system, however, was implemented fully only at York itself (with, ultimately, thirty-six canons or prebendaries) and at Southwell (with sixteen). At Ripon the canons remained seven in number, and although each canon had a separate prebend from which his stall was named, he had no jurisdiction separate from the chapter collectively. Beverley remained even more conservative. As at Ripon, no canon enjoyed a separate jurisdiction, and until the later 12th century the canons maintained communal life and property holding. Even when prebends were created, they had little or no territorial basis, and each canon was identified by the Minster altar to which he was attached (e.g. the prebendary of St Martin's altar), whereas in the other three great churches of the diocese, and indeed in nearly all other English cathedrals and colleges, canons were named from one of their manors or parishes (e.g. at York, the prebendaries of Monkton or Newbald). Finally, although the Beverley canons were later increased in number to nine, a clear distinction was drawn between the seven 'ancient' prebendaries and the other two: only the original seven had stalls in chapter as of right. In short, the modest changes in post-Conquest Beverley seem to reflect a tardy and only partial reform of a very ancient constitution.

Even more interesting were the nature and functions of the canons' deputies at Beverley. In most collegiate churches the majority of canons became non-resident by the 13th century, and appointed substitutes (vicars choral) to deputize for them in services. At Beverley, however, the prime duty of the seven vicars attached to the 'ancient' prebends was to exercise cure of souls (i.e. parochial duties) on behalf of the canons. Contemporary documents very rarely describe the vicars of Beverley as vicars *choral*, and 'though attendance at the main choir offices was strictly enjoined upon all of them, ... each canon was officially represented in choral duties by a second clerk, usually in minor orders, who never aspired to the title of vicar whilst holding that office'.[21] These were the clerks later called *berefellarii* or parsons.

The written evidence for this unusual arrangement is very late – notably a description of their duties by the canons in 1325 at an archiepiscopal visitation, and a similar description by the chantry commissioners in 1548 – but it is emphatic that the Minster was effectively a multi-parish college, with the vicars of eight of the prebends having cure of souls (there is no evidence that the ninth prebend, that of the archbishop, ever did so). The 'parishioners' of each prebend came to the altar assigned to that prebend, and there received the sacrament, while the vicars took the eucharist to the houses of the sick, aged and infirm. The system receives corroboration from the wills of Minster parishioners between 1480 and 1548: many of them named particular vicars as their 'curates', that is, parish priests, and the evidence would indicate that five of the nine had parochial responsibilities in the town, and three others in the outlying townships.[22]

What we seem to have here, surviving in the late middle ages, is a very early system of pastoral care, where a team of clergy in a 'head' or 'old' minster had collective parochial responsibility for a wide area, but had at some stage divided the responsibility without creating extra church buildings (though it must be remembered that St Mary's church, and possibly also St Nicholas', began as chapelries to the Minster). In most districts such provisions gradually fell into disuse with the proliferation of local parish churches between the 10th and 12th centuries, but in some cases authority or tradition were strong enough to retain the primitive system, at least in part. It was relatively common for cathedrals and other churches to house at least one parish community with its own chapel or altar, but it may be significant that the closest parallels to Beverley's archaic structure seem to have been other major churches in the York diocese, Howden and (the closest parallel of all) Ripon.

Other features than the pastoral arrangements set Beverley apart from most other greater English churches, and suggest primitive survivals. One was the extensive and privileged area encompassing not only the Minster but what became the whole medieval town. The 1106 York inquest spelled out the privilege of sanctuary at York, and testified that neighbouring churches 'having a similar privilege of sanctuary' included Beverley, Ripon, Durham and Hexham. It went on to admit, however, that the privilege was greater at Beverley and Ripon than at York itself, for both had a liberty extending one mile from the church, within which there was a series of concentric zones with successively greater protection for fugitives.[23] The limits of the Beverley sanctuary were defined by crosses, of which three of the four on the outer one-mile ring survive, though they may have been moved from their original positions.[24]

Furthermore, the one-mile zones at Beverley and Ripon were exempt from all royal dues and taxes, including geld, a rare privilege which was recorded in Domesday Book c. 1086.[25] These zones of privilege echo those of much earlier 'circuits of miles' of English and continental churches, including Lindisfarne. Although, therefore, the privileges of sanctuary are linked in the surviving documents to the cult and shrine of St John, their unusually generous terms suggest an origin long before John's canonization in 1037, responding either to an unofficial cult of the 8th or 9th centuries, or possibly even to a ritual focus in existence before that time.

The other most striking privilege of the canons was their right to renders of grain from a wide area, first recorded in the 12th century but again almost certainly of much earlier origin. According to Alfred (Alured) of Beverley, it originated with King Athelstan, who in 937 'gave perpetual alms to St John, namely four thraves from each plough throughout the whole of the East Riding for coulter and ploughshare'. Since a northern English thrave comprised twenty-four sheaves, that amounted to ninety-six sheaves per plough or, when converted to grain, some 316 lb (143 kg.).[26] No other such grant is known for any other Yorkshire church except for York's 'Petercorn', a levy of one thrave per plough from the whole diocese of York, also credited to Athelstan (though Lincoln similarly enjoyed 'Marycorn' from a large area in Lindsey and Kesteven).[27] In both cases the association with Athelstan may be uncertain, but they may well have represented royal dues granted away in the 10th century or even earlier.

12 A pilgrim and dragon in the north aisle dado. The carving is a warning against pilgrimage undertaken for worldly motives.

THE MINSTER IN THE 11TH AND 12TH CENTURIES

Three hundred years after the death of Bishop John, the Minster re-emerged into recorded history. For almost the first time since Bede we have near-contemporary documents establishing the constitution and privileges of the church, and even some indications of its physical structure. An anonymous *Chronicle of the Archbishops of the Church of York*, written in the mid-12th century, provides detailed information about the benefactions and building works of the last three Anglo-Saxon archbishops, probably derived from now-lost Beverley sources, while a series of collections of miracles of St John compiled from the 12th century onwards, and recently augmented by a rediscovered manuscript, is also an important source of incidental information about the churches which preceded the present Minster.[28]

It was in 1037 that Bishop John was canonized by Pope Benedict IX, probably at the request of Archbishop Aelfric of York (1023–51); and it was Aelfric who then translated John's remains to a new shrine, placing the bones in a casket of gold, silver and precious stones; he also began building a new refectory and dormitory.[29] He was the first of three successive prelates who between them reconstructed the Minster and its associated buildings, regulated the college's common life, and enhanced the Minster's standing as the mother church of the East Riding. His successor, Cynesige (1051–60) added a high stone tower with two bells, continued the refectory and dormitory, and 'adorned the same church with books and ornaments'.[30]

Archbishop Ealdred (1061–9), according to the anonymous chronicler, was an even greater benefactor, and was perhaps inspired by the architecture and craftsmanship he had seen while acting as royal ambassador to Germany and elsewhere. He completed the canons' dormitory and refectory, added a new presbytery to the church, and installed over the entrance to the choir a *pulpitum* of bronze, gold and silver, (probably a combined screen and reading desk) topped by a cross of German work (*opus Theotonicus*). He also added a painted and gilded ceiling over the whole church from his presbytery to Cynesige's tower, which would best make sense if the tower was a western and not a central one.[31] A writ of Edward the Confessor, datable 1061 x 1065, acknowledged Ealdred to be the lord of Beverley under the king, and Edward is also said to have granted him the right to an annual fair on 24 June; taken together, they suggest that the archbishop was sponsoring a town adjoining the Minster.[32] That town grew up largely because of the shrine and cult of St John, to which Ealdred contributed by commissioning Folcard, a monk of St Omer, to write both a *Life* of John, and responsories in his honour.[33]

It was Ealdred (not Stigand of Canterbury) who crowned both Harold II and William I in 1066, the year of the Norman Conquest, and he was the beneficiary of two writs from William giving privileges and protection to the lands of the church of St John. It is clear from the second one that Ealdred had granted more lands to the Minster after the Conquest.[34] That Conquest, indeed, seems not to have been a serious disruption at Beverley, even in 1069–70, when William put down a northern rebellion with much brutality. Tradition held that Yorkshire was so ravaged that it was almost depopulated, and that 'Beverley was the only place in Yorkshire that escaped'; and Alfred of Beverley attributed the town's escape to supernatural intervention by St John. However, the story is not contemporary, and there are good reasons to think that the devastation has been exaggerated, so that Beverley need not have been so exceptional.[35]

There is no documentary or archaeological record of building at the Minster between the 1060s and 1188, and the extent of the Normans' contribution is not known. It is possible that Ealdred's new presbytery was an up-to-date Romanesque structure influenced by the Confessor's Westminster, and was retained by the Normans. There are indications, however, that at least part of the Minster, including the nave, was rebuilt in the 12th century. This can be suggested not only from the surviving font [10], and from fragments of Norman work re-used

13 The south transept and crossing from the north west. It was the collapse of the central tower in c.1213 which led to the complete rebuilding of the Minster in the following two centuries.

in the walling over the south-eastern transept, but also from the large quantities of Norman re-used stone recovered from excavations at Lurk Lane and elsewhere in the town. Most strikingly of all, four large decorated rere-arches, datable before c.1160, survive re-used in the present nave triforium. One early thirteenth-century miracle story also suggests that the upper parts of the Minster fabric were, at the earliest, of Romanesque style, since a boy who ascended a stair and fell to the nave floor was apparently in an internal wall passage.[36]

The Minster must have become wealthier after the Conquest, largely because of the growing cult of St John. Folcard's *Life* of the 1060s already mentioned a tradition of miracles occurring at his tomb, and the cult was, of course, officially encouraged by the very commissioning of that *Life*. By the time that the earliest extant manuscript of the *Life* was copied around 1175, a collection of John's miracles had been added to it by a Beverley clerk called William Ketell, and to this three further collections of miracles were later appended. None except the first can be closely dated, but there are sufficient indications within the stories to show that the bulk of the recorded miracles must have occurred between the Conquest and the early 13th century.[37] They reveal a cult which had achieved widespread fame, for miracles datable to the 12th century include cures of pilgrims from Lincolnshire, Norfolk, Northumberland, Scotland and Ireland, as well as from many places in Yorkshire [12]. The focus of the cult was naturally John's tomb, but physical presence in Beverley was not necessary for his power to be effective. Some stories involve his power being invoked at a distance, as with York merchants caught in a storm while sailing to Scotland.[38] Furthermore, a banner of St John, of unknown origin and kept in the Minster, was believed to aid victory in battle, and was frequently sent out with royal armies. The earliest recorded such loan was in 1138, when an English army defeated a Scots invasion near Northallerton; it became known as the Battle of the Standard from the ship's mast round which the army rallied, to which were fixed the banners of St Peter of York, St Wilfrid of Ripon, St Cuthbert of Durham and St John of Beverley.[39]

It must also have been the cult of John which encouraged the growth of an important town under the lordship of the archbishop. Expansion of the town to the north was well under way by the first half of the 12th century: there were buildings around at least one of the two market places by the time of Archbishop Gerard (1101–08), and the chapel of St Mary (the later parish church) was apparently founded by the second quarter of the century.[40] And it must have become already a thriving trading town, since at some uncertain date Archbishop Thurstan (1114–40) granted to 'his burgesses of Beverley' all the liberties enjoyed by the burgesses of York, including a *hanshus* or guildhall.[41]

The reverence in which John and his church were held is also attested by the grants and confirmations of privileges obtained by the Minster and its canons in the 12th century, not only from their archbishops but also from successive kings of England and at least three popes. They included two writs of king Henry I of 1103-04 and 1100-15 conditionally confirming that the church and land of St John were exempt from paying geld, confirmation by Pope Honorius II of the property of the provost and canons, including thraves (1125 x 30), a detailed confirmation by King Stephen of the Minster's privileges, including the sanctuary and thraves (1136), and a similarly detailed confirmation of the rights to thraves, sanctuary and tax exemption by the English-born pope Adrian IV (1155).[42]

This degree of privilege may have encouraged the canons to resist the growing trend in the church, from 1059 onwards, to disapprove of secular chapters, and to make communities of canons into quasi-monastic convents. Thus, between 1089 and 1092 the bishops of Salisbury and Lincoln, and the archbishop of York, seem to have collaborated in reorganizing their cathedral chapters on the reformed continental model, with the canons given separate prebends instead of living communally, and their organization into a chapter ruled by a dean, precentor, treasurer, and master of the schools. At Beverley, however, Archbishop Thomas of Bayeux instituted a provost to resolve problems over the canons' communal assets, probably in 1092, and the canons continued to live communally in their dormitory and refectory, and to hold their possessions in common, for another century. Henry Murdac, the Cistercian monk who was archbishop of York from 1147, was said to have intended to replace Beverley's secular canons with quasi-monastic Augustinian canons regular, and was prevented only by his death in 1153.[43] Be that as it may, soon after that the thraves and other endowments were formally partitioned among the canons, who became prebendaries and ceased to live in common. The order effecting this major change does not survive, but Canon McDermid gave good reasons to think that it was the work of Archbishop Roger (1154–81).[44] Even then, as we have seen, the Beverley chapter remained until its dissolution in 1548 a conservative body, never fully assimilated to the reformed continental model for secular chapters: the provost was never replaced by a dean, and he was not himself a member of the chapter unless he was also appointed a canon, while the other dignitaries – sacrist, chancellor and precentor – always ranked below the canons.

Scarcely was the new organization in place than the Minster fabric itself was twice severely damaged. On the night of 21–22 September 1188 the church was 'burned', and the fire is recorded both in chronicles and in two lost inscriptions copied in the 16th and 17th centuries.[45] One was a plaque found in St John's tomb in 1664, recording that after the fire the bones and relics of John were lost, only to be rediscovered and reinterred in 1197. That would suggest extensive damage, though it is impossible to know how far the work after 1188 involved the patching-up of the old structure rather than wholesale rebuilding. In any case, within a generation – in or about 1213 – the crossing tower collapsed, and it was that catastrophe which overtook whatever restoration or rebuilding was in progress, and which led to a complete replacement by the present church.

NOTES

1 *Historia Ecclesiastica*, iv. 23, v. 2-6, the best edition is that by B. Colgrave and R.A.B. Mynors, eds, *Bede's Ecclesiastical History of the English People* (Oxford, 1969), pp. 408-09, 456-69; J. McClure and R. Collins, eds, *Bede: The Ecclesiastical History of the English People* (Oxford, 1994), pp. 211-12, 237-44, 410-11.

2 See e.g. E.B. Fryde et al., *Handbook of British Chronology*, 3rd edn (Royal Historical Society, 1986), pp. 217, 224. There is no good evidence for the traditional date of 718 for his retirement.

3 *Historia Ecclesiastica* , v. 2-5; Colgrave and Mynors, eds, *Bede's Ecclesiastical History*, pp. 456-7, 460-5.

4 Leach, *Memorials*, i, p. xix.

5 D.W. Rollason, 'Lists of saints' resting-places in Anglo-Saxon England', *Anglo-Saxon England*, 7 (1978), 68, 87; R. Morris and E. Cambridge, 'Beverley Minster before the early thirteenth century', in C. Wilson, ed., *Medieval Art and Architecture in the East Riding of Yorkshire* (British Archaeological Association Conference Transactions, 9, 1989), p. 10.

6 Morris and Cambridge, 'Beverley Minster', p. 18.

7 *Acta Sanctorum*, May (1866 edn), iii. 500-01; Leach, *Memorials*, ii, p. 343. The date of 723 for Berhthun's death in the latter source must be an error, since Bede in 731 wrote of him as still alive.

8 Morris and Cambridge, 'Beverley Minster', p. 10.

9 P. Armstrong, D. Tomlinson and D.H. Evans, *Excavations at Lurk Lane Beverley, 1979-82*, (Sheffield Excavation Reports, 1, Sheffield, 1991), p. 243 (dating c.851: but the numismatic evidence is no closer than c.851-2: p. 164).

10 R.A. Hall, review in *YAJ* , 65 (1993), 182.

11 J. Raine, ed., *The Historians of the Church of York and its Archbishops* (3 vols, Rolls Series, 1879-94), i, pp. 263-4, 294-8. Other, later, traditions speak of a visit by Athelstan in 934 rather than 937, or of two visits.

12 Morris and Cambridge, 'Beverley Minster', pp. 9, 11.

13 The retrogressive method has its dangers, and its application to minsters has been strongly attacked: E. Cambridge and D. Rollason, 'The pastoral organization of the Anglo-Saxon Church: a review of the "minster-hypothesis"', *Early Medieval Europe*, 4 (1995), 87-104. The following analysis, however, draws upon two replies to that attack, the latter based on Beverley evidence: J. Blair, 'Ecclesiastical organization and pastoral care in Anglo-Saxon England', *op. cit.*, 4 (1995), 193-212; D.M. Palliser, 'The "minster hypothesis": a case study', *op. cit.*, 5 (1996), 207-14.

14 W. Farrer, ed., *Early Yorkshire Charters*, i (Edinburgh, 1914), no. 87.

15 For minsters generally, see J. Blair, ed., *Minsters and Parish Churches: the Local Church in Transition 950-1200* (Oxford, 1988); for Yorkshire minsters, R. Morris, *Churches in the Landscape* (1989), pp. 133-9.

16 A.H. Thompson, *The Cathedral Churches of England* (1925), p. 25; R.T.W. McDermid, ed., *Beverley Minster Fasti* (YASRS 149, 1993 for 1990), p. xviii.

17 The clearest explanations of the relationships of the four churches are still those by A.H. Thompson in *Cathedral Churches*, pp. 15, 18, 22, 121; and in his accounts of Beverley, Ripon and York in W. Page, ed., *VCH Yorkshire*, iii (London, 1913), pp. 353-9, 367-72, 375-83.

18 D. Rollason, ed., *Sources for York History to AD 1100* (The Archaeology of York, i, York, 1998), p. 221.

19 R. Morris, *Cathedrals and Abbeys of England and Wales* (1979), p. 18.

20 Rollason, ed., *Sources for York History*, pp. 200-01, for a thirteenth-century reference to Culdees of York, and for further references to the status and character of Culdees.

21 R.T.W. McDermid, 'The constitution and the clergy of Beverley Minster in the Middle Ages,' University of Durham, MA thesis, 1980, i, p. 313.

22 Leach, *Memorials*, ii, pp. 56-60; W. Page, ed., *The Certificates of the Commissioners appointed to Survey the Chantries ... in the County of York*, pt. ii (Surtees Soc., 92, 1895 for 1893), p. 525; D.J. Lamburn, 'Politics and religion in sixteenth century Beverley', University of York, D Phil thesis, 1991, pp. 274-5.

23 Rollason, ed., *Sources for York History*, pp. 224-5. Later references to the Beverley and Ripon sanctuaries are often in terms of a league (*leuca*) rather than a mile, but in Norman England the two terms were often interchangeable and the Ripon 'league' seems to have measured about one and a third modern statute miles: D.M. Palliser, 'An introduction to the Yorkshire Domesday', in *The Yorkshire Domesday* (Alecto Historical Editions, 1992), p. 17.

24 K. Miller et al., *Beverley: an Archaeological and Architectural Study* (HMSO, 1982), p. 34.

25 Domesday Book, I. ff. 303v, 304; Palliser, 'Introduction to the Yorkshire Domesday', p. 28.

26 Thraves are discussed by McDermid, 'Constitution and clergy of Beverley Minster', i, pp. 75-110; also in McDermid, ed., *Minster Fasti*, pp. xvi, etc. with a valuable map facing p. 139. This indicates that the privilege covered the pre-1974 East Riding except for Howdenshire and for Ouse and Derwent wapentake.

27 Sources cited in Palliser, 'The "minster hypothesis"', 211, n. 25.

28 Raine, ed., *Historians of the church of York*, ii, pp. 312-87 (Chronicle); i, pp. 261-347 (miracles). See also Morris and Cambridge, 'Beverley Minster', pp. 12-27, for a valuable commentary and additional miracle material not known to Raine.

29 Raine, ed., *Historians of the Church of York*, ii, p. 343; Leach, ed., *Memorials*, ii, p. 351. Cf. J.M. Cooper, *The Last Four Anglo-Saxon Archbishops of York* (Borthwick Paper, 38, York, 1970), pp. 16-17; F. Barlow, *The English Church 1000-1066*, 2nd edn (1979), p. 73.

30 Raine, ed., *Historians of the Church of York*, ii, pp. 344, 353.

31 Raine, ed., *Historians of the Church of York*, ii, pp. 353-4, partly translated in Morris, *Cathedrals and Abbeys*, p. 28.

32 Farrer, ed., *Early Yorkshire Charters*, i, no. 87; Raine, ed., *Historians of the Church of York*, ii, p. 354.

33 Barlow, *English Church*, pp. 89-90. The *Life* is printed by Raine, *Historians of the Church of York*, i, pp. 239-60.

34 Farrer, ed., *Early Yorkshire Charters*, i, nos 88, 89.

35 W.H. Dixon and J. Raine, *Fasti Eboracenses* (1863), p. 146; Raine, ed., *Historians of the Church of York*, i, pp. 266-79; D.M. Palliser, 'Domesday Book and the Harrying of the North', *Northern History*, 29 (1993), 1-23.

36 J. Bilson, 'Norman work in the nave triforium of Beverley', *The Antiquary*, 27 (1893), 18-23; I. & E. Hall, *Historic Beverley* (York, 1973), p. 8; Morris and Cambridge, 'Beverley Minster', pp. 15-16; N. Pevsner & D. Neave, *The Buildings of England: York and the East Riding* (Harmondsworth, 2nd edn, 1995), p. 283; P.S. Barnwell, *Beverley Minster, Minster Yard, Beverley* (RCHME Survey Report, York, 1999), pp. 2, 3.

37 Morris & Cambridge, 'Beverley Minster', pp. 13, 29, n. 53.

38 e.g. Raine, ed., *Historians of the Church of York*, i, pp. 272, 274, 279, 287-91, 308-09, 313-15.

39 The numerous chronicle references are collected in Dixon & Raine, *Fasti Eboracenses*, p. 198 n., and in Leach, *Memorials*, i, pp. lxxxix f.

40 J. E. Burton, ed., *English Episcopal Acta V: York 1070-1154* (Oxford, 1988), no. 26; *VCH Beverley*, p. 50.

41 ERAO, Beverley Borough Archives, BC I/1: several times printed, but the best edition is now in Burton, ed., *English Episcopal Acta V*, no. 31, where it is dated 1121 x c.1128.

42 Usefully collected in Farrer, ed., *Early Yorkshire Charters*, i, nos 90-113, though for royal charters, 1087-1154, the best edition is now C. Johnson, H.A. Cronne and R.H.C. Davis, eds, *Regesta Regum Anglo-Normannorum* (4 vols, Oxford, 1913-69), and for archiepiscopal charters Burton, ed., *English Episcopal Acta V*. Stephen's charter survives as ERAO, Beverley Borough Archives, BC I/2.

43 Leach, *Memorials*, ii, pp. 332-3; J. Raine, ed., *The Priory of Hexham* (Surtees Soc., 44, 1865), p. 166; McDermid, ed., *Minster Fasti*, pp. xviii f.

44 McDermid, 'Constitution and clergy', i, pp. 30-43; McDermid, ed., *Minster Fasti*, p. xix.

45 Leach, *Memorials*, ii, p. 350; Morris & Cambridge, 'Beverley Minster', pp. 15, 30 (nn. 60, 61).

ROSEMARY HORROX

3 · The Later Medieval Minster

The Minster as it was rebuilt after the collapse of the central tower in c.1213 was in essentials the building that we see today. As usual in a major rebuilding of a church, work started at the east end and moved west towards the transepts so that the first part of the building to be completed would include the high altar and allow formal celebration of mass. Fund raising for this stage of the work had begun by 1221 and the work itself was completed by about the middle of the century. Although there have been later changes, most dramatically the insertion of the Perpendicular east window in the second decade of the 15th century, the choir of Beverley, up to and including the transepts and the crossing, is an architectural unity. This phase of the building came to an end in the first and second bays of the nave, far enough west, presumably, to 'lock' the new crossing securely into the Romanesque nave which had been patched up after the fire of 1188. There was then a break in construction, but by the last decade of the 13th century plans were afoot for the continuation of the work, and the rebuilding of the nave began in the first decade of the 14th century. The style of the work is quite different, although pains were taken to ensure that it was in harmony with what had gone before. John Leland, who visited Beverley in 1541, was the first of many writers to praise the Minster's 'fair uniform making'.[1] The builders had reached the clerestory level by the middle of the century, but there may then have been another break in the building campaign. Work on the west front and its twin towers was under way in the closing decade of the century and probably well advanced, since the glazing scheme of the great west window honoured Richard II and Anne of Bohemia and can probably be dated to 1388-96.[2] The rebuilding was completed by the end of the first quarter of the 15th century. The north porch, facing up Highgate, was perhaps the last element of this phase of construction [14].

Thus for much of the middle ages worship at the Minster, as in many medieval churches, was carried out on the edge of a building site. In 1313 the altar of St Nicholas was out of action due to the new work on the nave, and the traditional celebration of the saint's feast by the schoolmaster (St Nicholas was the patron saint of children) was ordered to be held at the altar of St Blaise instead. Work stopped and started as funds permitted. Money for major rebuilding was raised by sending out collectors authorized by the chapter to solicit alms on the Minster's behalf. Possible donors were encouraged by the offer of an indulgence – the remission of a period of penance – in return for their contributions. Such indulgences could be granted by the pope or by the local bishop – in Beverley's case the archbishop of York – and were carefully recorded in the Minster cartulary. In 1290, for instance, when the resumption of work on the nave was in contemplation, Archbishop John le Romayn granted an indulgence of forty days to anyone contributing to the repair of the building. Such a system was not without its abuses, and dishonest or fraudulent collectors were a recurrent headache. In 1310 the bishop of Lincoln announced throughout his diocese that false collectors had been taking alms for the shrine of St John (then under construction) and that the only accredited collector for the chapter was William Hambleton. In the following year the chapter secured a royal order for the arrest of the false collectors, whose defalcations, they claimed, were delaying the completion of the fabric.[3]

14 The north porch, facing up Highgate, completed in the 15th century as the last stage of the nave rebuilding.

The offer of spiritual benefits for donations remained the corner stone of Minster fundrais-ing until the eve of the Reformation. In the 16th century a printed flysheet was produced item-izing the benefits which would accrue to donors. As well as listing the available indulgences, which implausibly included an indulgence from the tenth-century John XII (perhaps a printer's error for John XXII), the leaflet appears to envisage the existence of a sort of fraternity of benefactors (rather like a modern guild of friends) which it claims was established by St John himself. Benefactors would be rewarded by a share in the suffrages of the thirty priests praying daily in the Minster. Every day, potential donors were told, three solemn masses were said, including a mass of Our Lady and a mass of requiem 'by note' (with music). The exhortation ended with assurances of royal support for the enterprise.[4] By this date the Minster, with no major building work on hand, had resorted to farming the right to collect money. Under this system the farmer paid the Minster an annual sum (which was therefore guaranteed) and

15 The tomb of the fourth earl of Northumberland (d. 1489), drawn for William Dugdale in 1661 (College of Arms MS RR 14.C f. 89). The tomb canopy was taken down in the early 18th century. For the tomb as it appears today see **pl. 6**.

retained anything he managed to raise over that. In 1445–6 the annual farm was £10, and in 1531–2 John Wilkinson paid the same sum for the right to collect in the dioceses of York and Lincoln.[5]

Alongside such 'public' campaigns, individuals associated with the Minster made donations to particular projects. Master Walter of Gloucester, prebendary of St Andrew (d.1310), made himself responsible for the wooden frame supporting the four bells in the northern bell tower. Usually donors sought to be associated with a part of the fabric more securely in the public eye. William of Waltham, another of the canons, bequeathed £40 for work on the great east window in 1416 [pl. 4]. Such donations had a clear commemorative function, which is most explicit in the building of chantry chapels where mass could be said for the soul of the benefactor. In Beverley the major example is the chapel built at the end of the 15th century to house the tombs of the fourth earl of Northumberland (d. 1489) and his wife Maud Herbert [15]. The chapel is at the east end of the north choir aisle, and the medieval glazing scheme of the north window commemorated the earl's life and death. As well as representations of the earl and his family at prayer, there was an image of the earl's body being prepared for burial by weeping relations.[6] There was also a spectacular array of heraldic glass, of which only a single panel now survives [pl. 5]. By the time of the earl's death, this part of the church had already become something of a Percy mausoleum, with the burial there of Idonea and Eleanor Percy in the 14th century and of George, a younger son of the second earl of Northumberland, in 1474. Their tombs are discussed in more detail in chapter 9.

Part of the attractiveness of Beverley to donors was, of course, the Minster's possession of the relics of St John. These were associated with two locations in the Minster: the tomb, which stood at the east end of the nave, and the shrine at the high altar to which John's relics had been translated by Archbishop Aelfric in 1037. After the collapse of the tower, and the temporary abandonment of the east end of the church, the east end of the nave became the choir, with an altar erected above the tomb serving as the high altar. During this period the saint's relics were returned to his tomb, a retranslation which it was believed had been miraculously forecast before the tower's collapse by a great light shining from the tomb. It is not entirely clear how long the relics remained in the tomb. They may have returned to the high altar in the mid 13th century, when Archbishop Godfrey rededicated the altar to St John of Beverley (although the church itself remained dedicated to St John the Evangelist). If so, they were moved again with the completion of a sumptuous new shrine for them in the early 14th century. The shrine had two elements: the inner reliquary, the *feretrum*, which held the relics themselves and an almost equally opulent outer casing, the *capsula*, panelled with silver, which was winched up to display the *feretrum* by an arrangement of wheels and pulleys. In 1322, when a Scottish attack was feared, arrangements were made to move the inner shrine and the relics secretly to the treasury if an attack seemed imminent and to strip the silver plates off the outer shrine and take them to safety. The *feretrum* was described as 'new' in an indulgence of Archbishop Walter Giffard issued in 1275. The *capsula* was produced rather later. In 1292 the chapter contracted with a London goldsmith to make the new casing. The work was evidently still not finished in 1299, when Edward I visited the Minster and made offerings at the tomb of St John and at the high altar, but not to the shrine. In 1302 there was an appeal, repeated in 1305, for funds to complete the work. It was finished by July 1308, when it is mentioned in an indulgence issued by Archbishop Greenfield to those visiting the church, and in 1312 Edward's widow Margaret offered a gold ornament to the shrine (rather than the tomb) when she visited the Minster[16].[7]

The new shrine's eclipse of the tomb as a focus of devotion was apparent as early as 1314 when Archbishop Greenfield ordered that a recently erected altar at the head of the tomb be removed, to allow free access for the faithful flocking to the church. On Ascension Day 1474 the tomb attracted offerings of just 11s 8d, compared to £11 4s 2d offered to the *feretrum*.[8] But the tomb was never entirely overlooked. Little is known about its appearance in this period, apart from a reference to its marble columns in an early thirteenth-century miracle story – a detail which has led one commentator to suggest that it may have been rebuilt following the 1188 fire. It was evidently being refurbished in 1419, when the provost, Robert Manfield, bequeathed £20 to the new fabric of the tomb then begun if the work was not completed in his lifetime. In 1394 the keeper of the fabric had taken delivery of a load of stone for the repair of the vault over the tomb, but it is not clear whether this was an integral part of the tomb's structure or refers to its setting within the church.[9]

The appearance of the shrine is almost equally problematic. There is no doubt that it was associated with the high altar in some way, and it has been persuasively argued that the uncompleted tower above the eastern crossing [3] was to have been a lantern tower which would have bathed both in light. In the event, the shrine was lit instead throughout the middle ages by lights placed on a beam described variously in bequests as before the high altar in the choir and before St John. The *exact* location of the shrine relative to the altar remains uncertain. Shrines were usually set on a stone plinth behind the high altar, in the retrochoir, where they could be viewed from the west but where access was possible for the laity (who were not normally permitted into the choir) via the ambulatory. The difficulty at Beverley is that the rebuilding of the screen behind the high altar in the second quarter of the 14th century, which was surely designed to provide an appropriate setting for the shrine, would have blocked the view of the shrine from the west if the shrine was behind the altar. The most likely solution is that the shrine was actually placed on the platform on top of the reredos (the screen behind the altar) [20, 25]. The shrine would then be visible from the west, but access could still be from the east, through the choir aisles and Lady Chapel which occupied the extreme eastern end of the church. The most recent writer on the subject is clearly unwilling to concede this location, which would make Beverley unique, as far as is known, among English shrines, but admits that such a placing would be physically possible.[10] It certainly seems to have been the site of the relics before the rebuilding of the east end, for a miracle story of the 12th century mentions 'the presence of the relics of the man of God over the altar'. The problem is that shrines usually had an altar attached to their west side, which would not be possible in the case of a shrine mounted on the reredos – where the high altar, inaccessible to the laity, would become in effect the shrine altar. This does indeed seem to have been the arrangement at Beverley, where the high altar was rededicated to St John of Beverley in the 13th century. But pilgrims made their offerings to the reliquary [*ad feretrum*] as well as to the high altar, and it is possible, although the evidence is ambiguous, that the red chest in the Lady Chapel (to the east of the reredos) served as an offertory box for the shrine. Certainly offerings to the red chest are treated separately from the offerings at St Mary's altar in fabric accounts, although the chest explicitly stood at or near the altar.

Various days were associated with St John in Beverley's liturgical calendar. The saint's main feast day was 7 May, and the feast of his translation was 25 October. Archbishop Godfrey had rededicated the high altar to him on St Mark's day (25 April) and granted an indulgence to pilgrims attending mass on that day as well as on the saint's day 'in winter' (presumably October).[11] But much the most important celebration of the saint occurred not on one of his own feasts but during the Cross Days (Rogationtide). On Rogation Monday (the Monday before Ascension Day) the saint's relics were taken out of the Minster and carried in procession around the Minster's daughter chapels before returning to the Minster on Ascension Day. According to tradition, this procession was instituted by Archbishop Aelfric, although the earliest extant references are from the 12th century. The portage of the shrine was then the hereditary respon-

16 A label stop in the south aisle, perhaps representing Margaret of France, the second wife of Edward I, or Isabel de Valois, the wife of Edward II. Both queens visited the Minster in the early 14th century.

sibility of eight men, who were also responsible for guarding it in times of danger, sleeping in the Minster if necessary. Before carrying the shrine they underwent a period of purification, and were subject to various restrictions, including abstention from ale, during the period of the shrine's procession. Only when the shrine was safely back in the Minster did they celebrate with a feast in the refectory, a custom still in force in the 15th century.[12]

This procession was the highpoint of the liturgical year in Beverley for residents and pilgrims alike. The clergy formed up at the high altar to receive the reliquary, left the choir through the north door, followed the ambulatory round the east end of the church and then passed down the south choir aisle into the nave and out through the great west door. The shrine was apparently carried past the gateway of the Bedern, where the provost or his representative made an offering, and then the procession made its way down Highgate to the Cross bridge and along Walkergate to St Mary's (a chapel of the Minster), watched by the craft guilds in their best clothes from their 'castles' (wooden platforms) lining the route. In the afternoon it set off on a longer progress, with the guildsmen riding behind it, to visit the Minster's other subordinate chapels, including those at Hull Bridge, Thearne and Molescroft. When it returned to the Minster on Ascension Day, the reliquary was restored to its place and mass was sung, while outside, in Highgate, one of the town's main fairs opened for business.

Although the tomb and shrine of St John were central to the Minster's status and finances, the church contained other foci of devotion. St John's immediate successor as abbot, St Berhthun (who was Bede's main source for St John's life and miracles), certainly had a shrine of his own, which was rebuilt in the first decade of the 14th century. So, probably, did a subsequent abbot, St Wynwald, and the shadowy St Polfrida, whom later tradition claimed had been placed in charge of a house of nuns founded by St John in an oratory south of the minster.[13] In 1318 Queen Isabel [16] made offerings to the 'small shrines' as well as to the high altar, and to the shrine and tomb of St John. At the Ascension Day celebrations in 1474 the 'little tombs' received offerings of 18s 6d. But there is little evidence that these subsidiary shrines had much hold on local affection. Local devotion in the late middle ages focussed rather on the statue of St Mary above the red ark or red chest [*supra rubeam cistam*] which was mentioned by late-medieval testators more regularly than St John himself. This was presumably the great image of the

17 St Martin among thieves
(detail), thirteenth-century
glass now in the great east
window at the left hand end
of the second row of panels
from the bottom.

Virgin which was repainted in 1307 and two fifteenth-century references to it as an image of the *glorious* virgin suggest that it may have represented Mary's Assumption or Coronation. An account roll of 1531–2 has a separate entry for offerings at St Mary's altar on the day of the Virgin's Assumption, which perhaps implies a particular association with that feast.

There were other images of the Virgin, perhaps associated with other aspects of her life, in the middle of the nave and at the south door. In 1414 Thomas Wilton endowed the singing of a Marian antiphon by the choristers before the latter.[14] A little chapel of the Virgin and a porch were among the buildings destroyed in the reign of Edward VI, and the implication seems to be that the south porch of the medieval Minster housed a subsidiary chapel of the Virgin; a not-uncommon arrangement in the late middle ages. Another object of local devotion was the crucifix or great cross inside the north door mentioned by several fifteenth-century testators. It had been there since at least the 12th century, when it is mentioned in one of the miracle stories. Less frequently mentioned, but attracting offerings in the 15th century, was an image of the Saviour at the west end of the church.

As this implies, Beverley Minster, like any great medieval church, was not a single place of worship, but subsumed a whole range of devotional sites. It had at least sixteen altars as well as the high altar. Each of the nine prebends was named after an altar in the church, and those associated with the seven canons of the old foundation served as the parish altars for the residents for whom they were responsible. In addition, there are references to altars dedicated to the Holy Trinity, St Anne, St Thomas of Canterbury (once provost of the Minster) and St William, each of which was associated with a perpetual chantry, and to St Blaise, St Nicholas and St Christopher. The last was the altar 'adopted' by the Beverley creelers (porters) – presumably because they felt an affinity to a saint whose main claim to fame was carrying the Christ child - and also by the guild of painters and goldsmiths. Other crafts which looked to the Minster as the focus for their corporate devotion included the tailors, who held their annual obit for the souls of deceased members at St Andrew's altar, and the cooks, who maintained a light before the image of St Katherine the virgin and the martyrs in the chapel of St Katherine. The tilers and dyers maintained lights before the crucifix inside the north door.

The location of relatively few of these altars is known, and the situation is complicated by the fact that existing altars could be relocated and new ones created. The altar of St William, for instance, was described as 'newly made' in 1493, after the precentor, William Coke, had endowed a perpetual chantry in the Minster.[15] Among those that can be securely located is St Martin's altar, which carried the heaviest parochial responsibilities. It had originally been sited on the north side of the nave, near the great crucifix, but in 1324, as part of the reordering of the nave, this became the site of one of the other prebendal altars, that of St James, and St Martin's was relocated in the chapel above the charnel house in the churchyard. The charnel was the place where bones turned up by grave diggers could be honourably preserved and most medieval churches had one, although usually, as at St Mary's, in the crypt rather than in a separate churchyard building. The charnel house abutted the south-west corner of the Minster and was pulled down in the reign of Edward VI, although traces of its crypt survived. The fact that St Martin's, the chief parochial altar, occupied a building outside the Minster must have encouraged the tendency among fifteenth-century parishioners to think of it as a separate church. In 1435 one testator made a bequest to support the 'high altar' in the charnel: presumably St Martin's altar in contradistinction to the altar of St Nicholas, which, as mentioned above, had been affected by the nave rebuilding in 1313 and had also been relocated to the charnel.[16] The vicar of St Martin's, generally described as the parish priest or chaplain of the charnel, apparently shared these separatist tendencies, and in the mid 15th century Archbishop John Kempe had to remind the chaplain of his duty to attend processions in the Minster.[17]

Of the altars within the Minster itself, St James' altar probably stayed near the north door, to judge by the bequest of an alabaster of St Christopher to the altar in 1476. This at first sight seems a rather surprising gift, given that the saint had his own altar in the Minster, but it was widely believed that looking upon an image of St Christopher would give protection from sudden death that day, and representations of the saint were often placed opposite or near doors, where they could be readily glimpsed. The only other altar that can be located with some confidence is that of St Katherine, which occupied the south-east bay of the south transept. St Anne's altar was perhaps at the west end of the nave. An image of St Anne near the font was mentioned in 1485, when the font (moved to its present position in the early 18th century) still stood near the west door, and may have been associated with her altar. St Christopher's altar was probably also somewhere in the nave since Thomas Autyn, who explicitly sought burial in the nave, wanted prayers to be said at St Christopher's altar.[18]

As mentioned in the previous chapter, the original seven canons (associated with the altars of Sts Andrew, James, Martin, Mary, Michael, Peter and Stephen) had been augmented by this date by an eighth, associated with the altar of St Katherine. When the canons ceased to live communally, and were given their own endowments or prebends, a ninth prebend (that of St Leonard) was assigned to the archbishop of York, but he was never a canon and was not entitled to a place in chapter. Nor, technically, was the eighth prebendary, although he might attend by invitation. Each prebendary had a vicar, who, in the case of the vicars of the original seven canons, took on their parochial duties. The nine vicars were thus a far more immediate presence in the lives of the Minster's parishioners than the generally absentee canons. Their parochial duties distinguished them from vicars choral elsewhere, whose primary role was to sing the daily offices. In Beverley in the later middle ages this task devolved mainly upon the seven *berefellarii*. The etymology of their curious name is unknown. The irreverent evidently took it to mean bare skins, and in 1391 Archbishop Arundel outlawed the disgusting (*turpe*) name, which was a source of unseemly mirth, and insisted that they be known in future as parsons.[19]

Arundel's renaming of the *berefellarii* was part of a more general overhaul of the arrangements at the Minster, prompted almost certainly by the notorious breakdown in relations between the Minster clergy and the archbishop during the episcopate of Arundel's predecessor, Archbishop Alexander Neville, whose career has been characterized as displaying 'a dangerous combination of high ambition, exceptional litigiousness and an apparent lack of application to detailed business'.[20] The crisis grew out of Neville's claim that as the ninth prebendary he was entitled to preside over the chapter, and it came to a head with his announcement, in February 1381, that he planned to make a formal visitation of the canons and clergy the following month. When he arrived on 26 March he was met only by the precentor, the clerk of the Bedern and two chantry priests. The vicars turned up three days later, but refused to accept Neville's authority without the permission of their masters, the canons. Two canons did subsequently submit to the archbishop, but only one vicar did so, and in April the rest of the vicars left Beverley and were promptly excommunicated by the furious archbishop, who imported vicars choral from York to maintain divine service.

Not surprisingly, given the intransigence displayed on both sides, no resolution was found while Neville remained archbishop. But at least the conflict did not descend to physical violence, as it reputedly did in Hull, where the mayor was said to have been so exasperated by the archbishop on one occasion that he seized his crozier and relieved his feelings by clouting one of Neville's attendants. It was not until Neville's exile and deposition in 1388 that harmony could be restored at the Minster, and the old wounds were perhaps not fully healed until 1402. In that year the chapter agreed to pay an annual pension to the chaplain of the chantry of St Anne, founded to commemorate Archbishop Neville and his predecessors by the provost Robert Manfield and Roger Flex, who were licensed by the crown to endow the chantry with land in the same year. Manfield had been Neville's protégé, forced by him into the provostry at the height of the quarrel of 1381, and the endowment was presumably Manfield's tribute to his patron.[21]

Arundel's statutes were not the only documents to come out of the restoration of order after 1388. Both the Minster chapter and the vicars produced cartularies (collections of documents recording and justifying their privileges and endowments) at around this time. But the statutes offer the best guide to the organization of the Minster before the Reformation, although at least one of Arundel's requirements (that the archbishop should preside over the chapter) remained a dead letter. They begin by listing the ministers of the church: nine canons, the precentor, chancellor and sacrist, the seven *berefellarii*, nine vicars, the precentor's clerk, the clerk of the charnel, the clerks of the *berefellarii*, two thurifers, eight choristers, two sacrist's clerks and two vergers, who doubled as bell-ringers. Arundel ruled on their seating within the choir and their precedence, and the right of presentation to the various offices, together with their duties and entitlements. The archbishop also attempted to tighten up residence requirements. By this date the canons had their own houses around the Minster and Arundel made no attempt to alter that arrangement. But he did insist that the vicars should live in common in the Bedern. Arundel carefully specified the provision to be made for them there, including four bushels of wheat a week and tablecloths for their communal table. Shared meals, at least, were still expected in 1470 when John Ferriby bequeathed one silver salt cellar to the vicars and another to the parsons if they would formally promise to say a prayer for himself and his parents after dinner and supper.[22] But although a communal life remained the ideal for both vicars and parsons (who were given land on which to build their own clergy house within the Bedern close in 1399), the ideal was perhaps always fragile. Clergy wills show that some vicars had their own houses and servants within the town. In 1459 Archbishop William Booth sharply accused the vicars of turning away from ancient custom to the offence of God and the peril of their souls and reminded them that they were required by statute to dine and sup within the Bedern. He also added that Marion Scotswoman was not to be received within the gates of the Bedern.[23]

The collegiality of the lesser Minster clergy was reinforced, as in any spiritual or secular community, by a series of domestic festivals and celebrations. Although Arundel famously sought to abolish 'the ancient custom, or rather corruption, of the king of fools', he allowed the

18 A fool with a bladder-stick, the left-hand supporter of misericord 68.

continuance of a range of other traditional festivities, including the custom called *les Fulles*, the dinner for the bearers of St John's shrine and the drinks given to carol singers on Whit Monday. His statutes also endorsed the practice of giving the various categories of lesser Minster servant a special meal once a year during the Christmas season. The deacons had their dinner on St Stephen's day (26 December), appropriately, since the saint himself had been a deacon. The choristers and thurifers, all young boys, celebrated the Feast of the Holy Innocents (28 December), while the subdeacons and clerks had to wait until the Feast of the Circumcision (1 January) for their special dinner. Although an entirely common life was evidently impossible to achieve, clergy wills reveal that the Minster clergy did form a community, and the sense of association (at least within each category of clergy) is captured by the 1342 will of the vicar Giles of Hornsea, who bequeathed books to the 'fellowship of vicars'.[24]

Arundel's statutes were primarily concerned to regulate the ecclesiastical side of Minster life, over which the chapter traditionally claimed jurisdiction. They have nothing to say about the schoolmaster except to note the place of the under-master of the scholars in Minster processions – a formulation which implies that the precentor was officially in charge of what was seen primarily as a choir school. Other sources make it clear that the school catered for more than just the training of choristers, and was doing so at least by the 14th century. Certainly the Minster was sensitive to any local competition from unlicensed schools, and the archbishop also took action against such schools on occasion.[25]

The statutes also have relatively little to say, except in passing, about the role of the provost: the official appointed by the chapter to look after the Minster's secular assets, meet the costs of the officers and run the Bedern. In spite of the 'hands-on' management that this job specification seems to imply, the office was held throughout the middle ages by powerful ecclesiastics, sometimes of national importance and generally non-resident. The provost had no *ex officio* place in the chapter (he was, as the Provost's Book put it, a dignitary *of* rather than *in* the church), but most of the fourteenth- and fifteenth-century provosts subsequently acquired a prebend which gave them a voice in chapter.[26] Typical in these respects, although unusual in being a Beverley man by birth, was Robert Rolleston, who was provost from 1427–51 and combined the office with the prebend of St Katherine throughout that time. Rolleston was slightly unusual too in making his career in secular rather than ecclesiastical administration. He had been a clerk of Henry IV, for whom he also acted as master of the works at the palace of Westminster, and was keeper of the wardrobe of both Henry V and Henry VI. Rolleston was buried in the centre of St Katherine's chapel, where he had endowed a chantry, and bequeathed a window showing the miracles of the Virgin Mary and the life of St Katherine. The glass has all gone, but Rolleston's arms survive on the window's label stops (in the south-east bay of the south transept).

Rolleston's foundation is among the best documented of the Minster's chantries. The territorial endowment is recorded in a surviving cartulary and Rolleston's will itemizes the goods he left to the chapel, including a silver gilt pax, carved with a representation of the crucifixion with Sts Mary and John, and a silver vessel for holy water with a silver sprinkler – a glimpse of the riches acquired by great medieval churches.[27] The number of chantry priests was growing in the later middle ages and they probably provided welcome liturgical reinforcement for the Minster clergy. In 1444 there were nine of them, by the time of the Dissolution fifteen. Their primary responsibility was to say mass for the soul of the chantry's founder and for other souls specified in the terms of the endowment. But they were sometimes explicitly required to take part in the general liturgical round, and it is likely that they did so even when this was not an obligation.[28] Arundel's statutes had stipulated that they take the seats of absent vicars or parsons in choir, which implies participation in the daily office, albeit perhaps on a slightly *ad hoc* basis.

The chantry priests too may have been expected to live a communal life, as was certainly the

19 A late-fourteenth-century
drawing of Athelstan and St
John from the vicars' cartulary
(Bodleian Library, Oxford,
University College MS 82 p. 7).

case at York in the late middle ages. Their group identity was perhaps further reinforced by
their membership of the guild or fraternity of Corpus Christi, which had its focus at the altar of
St Nicholas in the charnel (where it maintained a priest). The guild, which was in existence by
the mid 14th century, seems to have acted as a sort of professional association for the lesser
clergy of Beverley, although laymen of honest conversation and employment were also admitted. It organized the Corpus Christi Day procession each year and the clergy members of the
guild marched at the procession's head, although the associated plays were the responsibility of
the borough rather than the guild. The clergy members of the fraternity were frequently
chosen to provide requiem masses or obits (an annual commemorative mass) by testators without the resources to endow a perpetual chantry of the sort founded by Robert Rolleston.
Thomas Wilton, for instance, who made his will in 1444 and sought burial before the altar of
St James, asked the chaplains of the guild to say a requiem mass for him in the charnel a week
after his death.[29]

The vicars were also much in demand for obits. Their cartulary gives details of some fifty
endowments of this kind, specifying the date, form of commemoration and benefaction. The
donors range from William Lulleman, who granted an annual rent of 12d from his house at the
Beck in return for a mass with three readings on the feast of St Hilary (13 January), to Master
John de Nassington, prebendary of St Martin's altar, who bequeathed £20 with which the vicars
purchased three houses to endow a sung mass on 1 February.[30] Parishioners of yet more modest
means might make a bequest to the Minster to earn their inclusion in the parish bede roll, the

list of benefactors for whom parishioners were encouraged to pray.

Approaching the Minster and its clergy through the wills of its parishioners gives an impression of harmony which is not quite the whole story. Inevitably, relations were always smooth between the church and its neighbours. For the borough of Beverley the archbishop was in some ways a more potent force than the Minster clergy, since he was the lord of so much of the town and its environs. But the Minster was arguably a more immediate force, and certainly liked to think of itself as having a certain primacy over the archbishop. Local opinion was firmly of the view that it had been to the church of St John of Beverley, not to the archbishop of York, that Athelstan had made his famous (if apocryphal) promise: 'As free make I thee as heart can think or eye can see'. Indeed, in the popular mind, the grant had been made to St John, and this is how it appears, for instance, in a drawing in the vicars' cartulary [19]. In the same cartulary a note of Athelstan's obit describes him simply as the king 'who gave and bestowed the liberties of the church of St John of Beverley'. The obit was celebrated on 19 March. All the clergy were expected to be present, on pain of being fined, as were all sanctuary men – whose attendance was one of the conditions of receiving sanctuary, as Archbishop Rotherham reminded them in 1488.[31]

Although much of Beverley was within the lordship of the archbishop, the Minster possessed extensive property on the north side of Beverley Beck, in Norwood and at Grovehill. There was another block of Minster property west of the church, including land in Minster Moorgate and Keldgate, and scattered tenements elsewhere. The provost's jurisdiction within these lands was complete. As well as his own steward and court, he also had his own coroner. Offenders were committed to a gaol within the Bedern. This was the responsibility of the Bedern porters, who were in trouble in 1377 for the escape of William Watson.[32] On the whole such jurisdiction was uncontentious, but there were intermittent disputes between the provost and townsmen over pasture rights on Swine Moor in the late 13th and early 14th centuries, which culminated in one of the prebendaries besieged in his own house. Relations were strained again at the turn of the 14th and 15th centuries, when the provost Robert Manfield seems to have been deeply unpopular in some circles. Opposition to him was led by the Rolleston family, and in 1408 the provost claimed that men under William Rolleston's leadership had attacked his house and assaulted his servants, in spite of an earlier promise by William to do no harm to the provost or his servants. What seems to have rankled most, however, was that William had had the general pardon recently granted to Manfield by the Crown translated into English and posted up on the doors of the local inns. Royal pardons consisted of an exoneration from every conceivable offence (all of which were listed) and it is easy to imagine how local men might have affected to believe that Manfield was guilty of all the crimes stated, 'to [his] no small scandal and despite'.[33] Relations calmed down after Manfield's death in 1419 and the appointment of William Rolleston's son Robert as provost in 1427 gave the town a valuable ally in royal and ecclesiastical circles.

The Minster's sanctuary rights also produced some tensions, bringing an element into the town which was not always welcome. Beverley was one of the major sanctuaries of the middle ages, and was unusual in that the whole town and its environs, not just the Minster precinct, comprised the sanctuary, although it was from the Minster that the sanctuary (known from the 12th century as the peace of St John) derived. The sanctuary drew men and women from all over England, although most, predictably, came from adjacent regions. In 1478–99, 132 fugitives were recorded as taking sanctuary, including fifty-two from Yorkshire, fourteen from Lincolnshire, thirteen from the north midlands and eleven from East Anglia. The assumption was that the fugitive would be allowed sanctuary for thirty days, to allow time for a canon to negotiate with their pursuers. But provision was made for fugitives to return more than once and it is clear that some settled permanently in Beverley. For much of the middle ages this source of new blood in the town seems to have been accepted, but in the 15th century sanctuary men were made progressively less welcome and from 1460 were forbidden to become burgesses. The oath imposed on them in the late middle ages also forbade them to carry weapons, an indication that they were seen as a potentially disorderly element in urban society.[34]

But in spite of such areas of friction, Beverley on the whole profited from the Minster. The shrine of St John drew pilgrims to the town throughout the year, particularly during the Rogationtide celebrations. Many of the pilgrims were humble folk, like the Norfolk peasant mentioned in one of St John's miracles. But the rich and famous were also drawn to Beverley. When Henry IV's son visited the town in 1407 it was to the Minster that the twelve keepers (Beverley's equivalent of the mayor and aldermen elsewhere) sent wine for his refreshment.[35] Kings themselves sought the saint's favour. By 1266 it was accepted that when the men of Yorkshire were summoned to the king's army, Beverley's contribution was to be one of the Minster clergy bearing the saint's standard. Edward I had the banner with him on his Scottish campaigns of 1296 and 1300. In the former year he signalled his gratitude by endowing a priest to celebrate mass at the high altar daily, and lights to burn before the tomb and the banner itself. The banner was also lent to Edward II, Edward III and Henry IV. The saint's military reputation received a further boost in 1415 when the battle of Agincourt was fought on the feast of St John's translation (25 October). Both Henry V (in 1420) and his son (in 1448) visited the shrine to pay their respects.[36] As late as the reign of Henry VIII collectors for the Minster fabric could claim that the king had exhorted 'his true lovers and subjects' to give the collectors a favourable hearing. Things were very soon to change for ever.

NOTES

1   J. Leland, *The Itinerary*, ed. L. Toulmin Smith (5 vols, 1906-10), i, p. 46.

2   D. O'Connor, 'The Medieval Stained Glass of Beverley Minster', in C. Wilson, ed., *Medieval Art and Architecture in the East Riding of Yorkshire* (British Archaeological Association Conference Transactions, 9, 1989), pp. 72-3.

3   Leach, *Memorials*, i, pp. 2-3, 280-1; Lincolnshire Archives Office, Reg. Dalderby, iii, f. 179v (a reference I owe to the kindness of Michael Robson); Poulson, *Beverlac*, ii, p. 550.

4   Bodleian Library, Arch. Ab 8(2), a xerox of the original which is tipped in between pages lxxxvii-lxxxviii of the appendix of F. Drake, *Eboracum* (shelf mark: Gough Yorks 57).

5   A.F. Leach, 'A fifteenth-century fabric roll of Beverley Minster', *TERAS*, 6-7 (1898-9), 6, 50; BL, Additional Charter 27324, m. 3 dorse (printed by Poulson, *Beverlac*, ii, p. 636).

6   O'Connor, 'Stained Glass', pp. 73-4.

7   Leach, *Memorials*, i, pp. xcii-xcv, ii, pp. 20, 299-300; BL, Additional MS 61901, ff. 82v-83; Poulson, *Beverlac*, ii, pp. 592-4.

8   BL, Lansdowne Charter 381.

9   C. Wilson, 'The early thirteenth-century architecture of Beverley Minster: cathedral splendours and Cistercian austerities', in P.R. Coss and S.D. Lloyd, eds, *Thirteenth Century England*, iii (Woodbridge, 1991), p. 183, n. 11; J.W. Clay, ed., *North Country Wills* (Surtees Soc., 116, 1908), p. 21; A.F. Leach, ed., *Beverley Town Documents* (Selden Soc., 14, 1900), p. 24.

10 B. Nilson, *Cathedral Shrines of Medieval England* (Woodbridge, 1998), pp. 56-8, 66-7; N. Coldstream, 'English Decorated Shrine Bases', *Journal of the British Archaeological Association*, 129 (1976), 21-22.

11 BL, Additional MS 61901, f. 83.

12 *VCH Beverley*, pp. 10-11.

13 Corpus Christi College, Cambridge, MS 298, p. 188; Leach, *Memorials*, i, pp. xciv, 173, 313.

14 Poulson, *Beverlac*, ii, p. 636; BIHR, Prob. Reg. 2, ff. 309v, 368; 4, f. 137; 5, f. 361.

15 BL, Landowne Charter 389; Leach, *Memorials*, ii, p. xciii.

16 BIHR, Prob. Reg. 3, f. 432.

17 BIHR, Reg. 19, f. 481v.

18 BIHR, Prob. Reg. 5, ff. 135, 258v, 362.

19 All the references to Arundel's statutes which follow are taken from Leach, *Memorials*, ii, pp. 265-79.

20 R.B. Dobson, 'Beverley in Conflict: Archbishop Alexander Neville and the Minster clergy', in Wilson, ed., *Medieval Art and Architecture in the East Riding*, p. 152.

21 M.J. Hebditch, *Yorkshire Deeds*, ix (YASRS, 111, 1948), p. 20; BL, Additional Charter 5757; *Calendar of Patent Rolls, 1401-5*, p. 118; *North Country Wills*, p. 23.

22 BIHR, Prob. Reg. 4, f. 166.

23 BIHR, Reg. 20, f. 139-v.

24 BL, Lansdowne Charter 305.

25 Leach, *Memorials*, i, pp. lvi-lxv; BIHR, Reg. 20, f. 133v.

26 R.T.W. McDermid, *Beverley Minster Fasti* (YASRS, 149, 1993), p. xviii.

27 The cartulary is in the Library of Congress, Washington; the will is printed by J. Raine, ed., *Testamenta Eboracensia*, ii (Surtees Soc., 30, 1855), pp. 138-41.

28 Leach, *Memorials*, i, p. 207.

29 BIHR, Prob. Reg. 2, f. 309v.

30 Bodleian Library, University College MS 82, pp. 34, 36.

31 *Ibid.*, p. 39; Leach, *Memorials*, ii, p. 272; E.E. Barker, ed., *The Register of Thomas Rotherham*, i (Canterbury and York Soc., 69, 1976), p. 226.

32 ERAO, PE 129/150, f. 63.

33 *VCH Beverley*, pp. 16-19; *Calendar of Patent Rolls, 1405-8*, p. 482.

34 *VCH Beverley*, pp. 8-10.

35 J. Raine, ed., *The Historians of the Church of York and its Archbishops* (Rolls Series, 3 vols, 1879-94), i, p. 309; ERAO, Beverley Keepers' Accounts 5.

36 *VCH Beverley*, pp. 7-8.

D.J. LAMBURN

4 · The Minster and the Reformation

The 16th century saw many drastic changes in English religious life which affected Beverley Minster in common with all other English minster establishments. The alterations to the Minster as an institution, to the religious experience it provided and to the character of popular religious practice during this period were of a magnitude and degree which would have been inconceivable in 1500. As a result of the Reformation process the Minster was transformed from one of the largest ecclesiastical institutions in the north to a mere parish church. Stripped of the assets which had made it easily the wealthiest ecclesiastical establishment in the East Riding and the third or fourth richest in Yorkshire, it became financially dependent on the town's corporation. Parts of the Minster complex were demolished and by the end of the century there were repeated complaints that the church was in decay and neglected. A total staff at the Minster of seventy-four was reduced to just two by the end of the century, to serve the spiritual needs of the parish. The rich and complex structure of the old faith had given way to one which was more simple, sober and precise. The refashioning of religious life necessitated changes to the structure, organization and clergy of the Minster which directly affected its relationship with the town and its governing body. Beverley's corporation came to play a more prominent role in the religious life of the Minster: appointing its clergy, bringing the parish more securely under its control, administering former ecclesiastical property, controlling educational provision and ensuring compliance with measures affecting morals and conduct. By the end of the 16th century a new form of religion had replaced the old, the emphasis being less on sacramental observance than on preaching, the bible and personal faith. The Minster and its clergy had succeeded in making the town a notable centre of protestant preaching. How this transformation came about is the theme of this chapter.[1]

In order to appreciate fully the impact of the Reformation upon the Minster, attention should focus first on one salient characteristic of its constitution, namely that it was both a college and the parish church of St John. Indeed, it was the fact that it was a centre for pastoral care which ensured that the Minster did not suffer the same fate as many other colleges of secular canons in the dissolutions which took place in 1548. At the dissolution, it comprised seventy-four offices: a provost, nine prebendaries (including the archbishop of York), a precentor, sacrist and chancellor, nine vicars, seven parsons, twelve chantry priests, a master of works, chamberlain, seventeen clerks, two incense bearers, four sextons and eight choristers. Of these the chantry priests and the vicars were the individuals who enjoyed most contact with the town and its inhabitants. The carving of the choir stalls, discussed in chapter 10, was the last major pre-Reformation addition to the Minster. But it is notable that between 1515 and 1540 only £1 4s 4d is recorded as having been bequeathed to the Minster fabric, and there is little sign that the clerical establishment or the collegiate status of the Minster generated much affection or concern in the town, leading to a general state of neglect. Leland reported that 'the prebendaries' houses stand round about St John's church yard: whereof the Bishop of York hath one ... but all in ruin'. In 1552 it was reported that the church 'is in great decay, and in a short space is very likely to fall into utter ruin and decay'.

20 The east end of the Minster. Before the Reformation, the shrine of St John is believed to have been located on top of the reredos.

21a A fox bishop attacked by his flock, in the north aisle. The head and the top of the staff is restoration work by Baker.

In the main, this lack of regard for the collegiate aspects of Minster life seems to have come about as a result of an absence of diligent oversight or concern on the part of the prebendaries, themselves appointed by archbishops who had little genuine interest in either the town or its ecclesiastical life and traditions. Perpetual absenteeism was rife; no senior cleric was obliged to reside and none kept meaningful residence in the town. At the dissolution only two canons seem to have been present, Robert Babthorpe and William Clifton, both of whom were likely to have been there to supply information to the commissioners as to their other preferments. Moreover it is clear that, on the eve of the Reformation, appointments to the Minster were regarded by Thomas Wolsey, cardinal archbishop of York and effectively Henry VIII's chief minister from 1515 to 1529, as a means of rewarding those likely to be useful in his service or who already enjoyed his personal favour. Wolsey's son Thomas Winter became provost, and his steward Robert Carter, his secretary Peter Vannes, his confessor Thomas Larke and his vice-general William Clifton all acquired prebends on their steps up the ladder of ecclesiastical preferment. Thomas Goodrich, prebendary of St Stephen's, and George Day, prebendary of St Andrew's, subsequently became bishops. Archbishop Lee had more regard to the needs of the northern church, but not of Beverley, with appointments of such men as William Holgill, who was precentor and a prebendary of York Minster, and William Strangeways, who also held a prebend there. It has been observed rightly that 'little active concern could be expected of prebendaries chosen on account of their closeness to the seat of government, academic associations, or, not least, their kinship with the archbishop of the day'.[2]

On the other hand, the Minster as a parish church and those who undertook pastoral care were held in much greater affection, and it was to be this aspect of the Minster's role which ensured its physical survival at the dissolution. Serving a parish population of around 3,000 souls, both within and without the urban centre, the parish church was the main focus of religious life. By the time of the Reformation, although St Mary's was regarded very much as the 'town' church, possibly diminishing further the role of the Minster, the parish church still had most claim on the religious interests of its parishioners. Almost all testators of the parish specified burial in the Minster or its churchyard, which was also favoured by some from the parish of St Nicholas. Henry Sanderson, a baker, desired to be buried before Our Lady of the Red Ark in the Minster; the images of St John the Evangelist and St Mary were favoured burial places, and Katherine Garret directed that her body should be interred in St John's churchyard 'before the picture of Our Saviour'. Some testators specifically bequeathed money to saints' images and shrines. For example, Cecily Lepington left 6s 8d to the shrine of St John along with her blue girdle, as well as her best bed covering to the Easter sepulchre, 'as an ornament to the sepulchre of our Saviour at the feast of Easter'. Others bequeathed items of silver and William Lerifax, a draper, specified the purchase of two copes and a further two velvet copes with the images of St John of Beverley and St George embroidered in gold should he die without heirs. As discussed in the previous chapter, some of the trade and craft guilds in the town maintained lights at the Minster, and the guilds (as well as the townspeople at large) shared in the Rogation or Cross Days festivities, when the shrine of St John of Beverley was carried through the town from the Minster to the other town churches.[3]

The pastoral care provided at the Minster contributed to that available elsewhere in the town. With only three parishes, serving a population estimated in the middle of the 16th century at around 5,000, parochial provision was far from lavish. In fact the provision was more extensive than at first sight it appears, for within the Minster parish the cure of souls was the responsibility of the vicars, whose duties were summarized in the Chantry Certificates prepared on the eve of the dissolution in 1548 as 'being bound to daily service in the choir of the said church and to have cure of souls, and to minister all manner of sacraments at nine several altars to all the parishioners of the forenamed prebends'. These vicars were the effective pastors to their parishioners, having deputies who dealt with their choral obligations. St Leonard's seems not to have had a separate cure of souls, being the prebend of the archbishop of York, but the three vicars attached to the altars of St Andrew, St Peter and St Michael had cures in the surrounding townships, where sacraments were received at one of the outlying chapelries. Vicars at the altars of St Stephen, St Katherine, St James and St Martin all had parochial responsibilities in the town and parishioners resorted to the appropriate altar within the Minster. St Martin's, valued at £39 12s 1d in the *Valor Ecclesiasticus*, seems to have been considered almost a distinct parochial unit in its own right. It possessed a separate chapel, built adjoining the south-west corner of the church 'in manner of an outshot'. After the dissolution the parochial responsibilities for St Martin's were assigned to the vicar of St Mary's, though as late as the 1590s parishioners still considered themselves to be part of a separate parish. Some of those resorting to the vicars in the Minster remembered them in their wills, along with some of the priests serving the twelve chantries there. In some parts of the north, chantry foundations and additional endowments to existing chantries continued to take place up to the eve of their dissolution. This was not the case at the Minster, where the chantries were supported only by their initial

21b A preaching fox with his congregation of geese, from misericord 51. The right hand supporter shows the proverbial folly of shoeing the goose.

benefactions. However, obits and funeral masses continued to be ordered, though in reduced numbers, and there is little doubt that the services provided by the vicars and the chantry priests in the Minster continued to be appreciated right up to the dissolution in 1548. Generally recruited locally, appointed quite young and serving often for long periods, they give every appearance of having performed their duties according to the wishes of their parishioners, conducting the familiar rites of passage, carrying out pastoral duties and living in an appropriate fashion. It is significant that after the dissolution of the college it was from the ranks of the vicars that Thomas Mitchell was chosen as the first incumbent of the parish of St John, along with another of his colleagues, Thomas Dring, who served as his assistant, and that a third former vicar, William Grigges, became one of the assistants in the 1550s. Two former chantry priests were also appointed as assistants to Mitchell at the dissolution.[4]

Although it was the dissolution of the college in 1548 which had the biggest impact on the Minster, the process of religious change had begun in the 1530s. The alterations to the fabric and structure of religious life introduced by Crown and Parliament are a familiar story. Henry VIII's desire for a male heir led him to seek a divorce from Katherine of Aragon, which led him to break from the Church of Rome. In 1534 the Act of Supremacy declared Henry to be Supreme Head of the English Church and in the 1530s protestant reformers and their views gained prominence. Injunctions of 1536 and 1538 promoted the spread of the bible in English and singled out for destruction images and shrines which were regarded as superstitious. In 1547 and 1548 the Edwardian government condemned images and commissioners went around seeking to ensure that action was taken. It was during Edward's short reign that a series of parliamentary statutes brought in doctrinal and liturgical change aimed at promoting Protestantism.

The question of how quickly the political and legislative acts which constituted the Reformation affected the Minster and its parishioners and transformed religious worship and practice is more difficult to answer. In particular, the absence of any surviving churchwardens' accounts for the 16th century makes it impossible to know how swiftly royal and diocesan injunctions were complied with. Although Beverley was mentioned in a campaign conducted by Nicholas Wilson against protestant heresy in 1533, the early evidence suggests opposition to religious changes in the 1530s. Some parishioners from the Minster participated in the Pilgrimage of Grace in 1536, though that may have had more to do with political than religious affairs in the town. Certainly there was opposition to cutting down the number of saints' days and in 1538 Robert Sherwood, the archbishop's suffragan and chancellor at the Minster, was reported for preaching in the town against the king's injunctions and against the word of God.

22 A surviving fragment of the west face of the medieval reredos. Religious images were removed in the reign of Edward VI. What remained of the altar screen was cut back and plastered over in 1663.

It was following this incident that the archbishop took steps to ensure that his injunctions of 1538, which in many ways marked the beginning of religious change in the York diocese, were openly proclaimed, relying on his own chaplain, Dr Downes, Robert Creke, one of his secular officers in the town, and William Clifton, prebendary of St James' altar in the Minster, to carry this out.[5]

The extent to which those injunctions made an impact at the Minster is not known. Whether bibles were purchased and the creed and ten commandments made available in English, and the degree to which the Minster clergy complied with the instructions relating to their conduct, pastoral and teaching duties or the provision of sermons is difficult to ascertain. But in three areas there are some indications of acceptance of and compliance with official injunctions, which may indicate the beginnings of changes in belief. First, some evidence suggests that orders against the worship of images, forbidding the offering of lights and stressing that saints were to be treated only as examples of holy life, and commands to remove images which attracted pilgrims did not go unnoticed. Most of the trade and craft guilds in the town, including those maintaining lights at the Minster, made provision for fines and contributions to be paid at least partly in wax for the maintenance of the guild lights. However, from 1537 onwards guild ordinances began to command members to make such payments in money rather than wax. The tailors then stipulated that contributions and fines from aldermen failing to present accounts should be paid in money and thereafter an increasing number of guilds followed suit. In 1541 the shoemakers ceased their payments to the guild of St Peter and ordered payments of fines in money not wax. Individuals too seem to have complied. Apart from the bequest of a soul to the Virgin and saints generally, references to individual saints in anything other than a burial context are non-existent in wills of the 1540s, in contrast to fifteenth-century wills when personal selections of saints were more common. After 1538 no testators mentioned pilgrimages. Offerings at the shrine of St John, oblations, gifts at Our Lady's altar at the Red Ark and those at the shrine on Rogation days, Whitsuntide and sundry festivals suffered a spectacular decline from over £120 in the 14th century to under £3 in 1532. Income from St John's shrine had always been credited to the prebendary of St Katherine's altar, but no mention was made of any income from that source in the Chantry Survey.[6]

Secondly, although wills and especially the bequest of the soul which begins them are notoriously difficult to interpret, it is noticeable that between 1541 and the end of Henry VIII's reign the only two inhabitants of the town to produce wills with unambiguously protestant dedications of the soul, Ralph Brown and John Butterfield, were from the Minster parish. Wills which were traditional in terms of soul bequests remained the norm. However, there was a clear decline in specific religious legacies. Between the same dates, masses, a clear indicator of catholic religious enthusiasm, were commissioned by only one testator from the Minster parish. Finally, there is some evidence that within the Minster there may have been some clergy who not only complied with Archbishop Lee's injunctions but went on to adopt protestant views. Thomas Mitchell, one of the vicars and the first curate of the Minster parish, later made a will showing protestant leanings; John Bonsaye, a former choirman, was to go on to deny transubstantiation, whilst his colleague Robert Thwing, who had witnessed the will of Ralph Brown, was to find himself before the Chancery court in Mary's reign. Scant though the evidence may be, later developments suggest that the basis of the Minster's later unequivocally protestant reputation may have been laid in this period.[7]

However, it is likely that most of the clergy and officers at the Minster, along with most of the laity, remained religiously conservative. The changes in religion - material, institutional and theological – instituted by the Edwardian government must have caused real spiritual dislocation, discontinuity and deprivation. Though they evoked no recorded public protest, they were radical and far-reaching. In accordance with an act of parliament in 1547, the college was suppressed along with its dozen chantries and any surviving religious guilds. Three chapels-of-ease in the outlying townships of Storkhill, Thearne and Molescroft, but within the Minster parish, were lost at the same time. Most of the plate, weighing 1,200 ounces, belonging to the collegiate church was seized and much of what remained was probably taken in the later Edwardian confiscations. The Minster itself and many of its associated buildings were granted to Sir Michael Stanhope, the governor of Hull, and the Crown surveyor John Bellow. In 1548 Stanhope offered to sell the church, chapter house and charnel to the town, together with the daughter church of St Nicholas. A group of wealthy residents, led by the merchant Robert Grey, raised the necessary £100 to save the Minster as their parish church – subsequently recouping the money by demolishing the chapter house and charnel and selling off the materials. The double staircase in the north choir aisle, which once led to the chapter house, still survives [**pl. 8**], as do traces of the charnel (home to the parochial chapel of St Martin) at the foot of the wall of the south-west tower.

If the Edwardian injunctions were observed there would have been other drastic changes to the internal and external appearance of the Minster, with the removal of statues, images and altars, along with the whitewashing of walls and removal of wall paintings. It was probably at this time that the figures were removed from the niches on the west towers. A lone survivor is the carving of the first earl of Northumberland on the north-west tower [**23**] – a tribute perhaps to the continuing influence of the Percy family in the area. Changes in the form of worship also continued apace. As the increasingly protestant doctrine and liturgy embodied in the First and Second Prayer Books of 1549 and 1552 and the Forty-Two Articles of 1553 were introduced, the magnitude of the changes cannot have gone unnoticed in the parish. From now on the Minster was merely a parish church, served initially by four clergy, two drawn from the ranks of the former vicars and two from among the chantry priests.[8]

There are three aspects of the dissolution which would have had a major impact on the lives of parishioners. First, the conventionally phrased wills of many parishioners before the dissolution leave little doubt that most still believed in purgatory. The abolition of the chantries and seizure of funds left to ensure the safe repose of the souls of the departed must, therefore, have come as a shock. Secondly, there was the immediate impact on pastoral provision. It was not just the loss of the cantarists, who often served as assistant parish clergy, but particularly the removal from office of the vicars within the Minster and the subsequent removal of the preben-dal altars where the laity were accustomed to resort, although separate arrangements for services were made for those from the quasi-parish of St Martin within the borough. Later in the century the number of assistants was reduced to one, so that two clergy served the needs of the parishioners. How this affected parishioners and their levels of religious commitment is difficult to assess, but it was clear during the early part of Elizabeth's reign that the Minster clergy were unable to control effectively the conduct of the laity, whether within or without the church. Some parishioners were brought before the ecclesiastical courts for irreverent behaviour during divine service and in 1569 William Richardson, then one of the assistants at the Minster, found himself unable to comment on the conduct of one parishioner during services 'for that the disorder in the said church is almost general'. Finally, the school attached to the Minster was another victim of the dissolution and it is clear that its loss was keenly felt. In 1552 inhabitants petitioned for its refoundation and for a grant of land towards the upkeep of the Minster. The latter was successful and although the fate of the Grammar School is uncer-tain, evidence examined later indicates that it had probably been refounded by 1554; payments by the town for repairing the school and to the schoolmaster were recorded from the 1560s onwards [**24**].[9]

23 Henry Percy, first earl of Northumberland (d. 1408), from the north-west tower. Very little of the medieval programme of statuary on the towers survived the iconoclasts, this is a rare exception.

Whilst the material effects of Edward's reign on the Minster and its parishioners are obvious, less is known about the impact on spirituality or religious opinion. Of the eleven surviving wills made during the reign only four refer to the Virgin or saints, the remainder entrusting the soul simply to Almighty God, or to 'Almighty God my creator and redeemer'. No wills made any allusion to funeral ceremonies or sought to commission masses. And although communion services for the dead were authorized by the 1549 Prayer Book, none was requested. Neither is there any evidence of passive resistance to the Edwardian changes. When Catholicism was restored under Mary, there is little sign that it evoked any real response. Although there was a clear move back to wills mentioning the Virgin and saints, there were no attempts to establish chantries or obits, no testators in the parish requested masses and only two individuals specifically asked for prayers: Robert Gray, a tanner, requested Robert Hill, the former friar and chantry priest, 'to pray for my salvation', and John Willy left money to the poor to pray for him, the last occasions that prayers of this nature were commissioned in either the parish or the town.[10]

It was during Mary's reign that firm evidence emerged that Protestantism had made real inroads at the Minster and that some amongst the upper echelons in the town were displaying an attachment to literate and informed Protestantism. Amongst them were former members of the Minster establishment and some laity of the Minster parish. The cases have been fully and accurately described by Dickens and in consequence only a brief outline will be given here. Two of the cases involved clerics, both pensioned choirmen of the Minster, Robert Thwing and John Bonsaye. In 1554 Thwing, who had taken advantage of Edwardian legislation allowing clerical marriage, was brought before the Chancery court. Declining an offer to be restored to the priesthood, he observed that 'he had rather continue with his wife and live like a layman if it might so stand with the law'. Although there is no direct reason to connect this case with the holding of protestant convictions, such a link may be made. Thwing had witnessed the protestant will of Ralph Brown in 1545 and also had connections with other Protestants in the parish. In 1556 John Bonsaye, another pensioned former choirman, confessed to speaking against transubstantiation and it emerged that he and John Pesegrave had three protestant books, *Vox Populi or the People's Complaint* written by Nicholas Grimald, chaplain of Nicholas Ridley, bishop of London, *The Governance of Vertue* by Thomas Becon and *The Image of God or laie Man's book*, which had been circulated in the town. The books were ordered to be burned. The remaining cases involved the laity. In 1554 Robert Bigott of the Minster parish, who ran an alehouse in the town, was charged with 'rail[ing] against the holy and blessed sacrament of the altar' and accused of permitting many others to do the same. Six named individuals, including at least three from the Minster parish, faced similar charges in the same year, being variously accused of 'oft and sundry times [speaking] unreverently of the sacrament of the altar' or of 'mocking, jesting and scoffing the same'. Finally, in 1557 Gawin Brackenridge was alleged to have said that the priest brought the devil when he came to administer the sacrament to him.[11]

Other evidence suggests that the penetration and continuance during Mary's reign of protestant views at the Minster and within the town was a cause for serious concern. In 1554 Robert Robinson, a former monk from Meaux who had held St William's chantry at the dissolution and who was then a schoolmaster, probably at the refounded Grammar School, wrote that some local boys 'were counselled by evil persons not to haunt my school, because I was, as they termed it, a papist...'. Later evidence indicates that from an early date the town's governors were concerned to install sound Protestants as schoolmasters at the Grammar School, which may well account for the strength of Robinson's comments. In any event, after 1554 Robinson was used by the ecclesiastical authorities at York to secure compliance with their attempts to stamp out heresy. Pesegrave, for example was ordered to do penance before either Thomas

Mitchell, the incumbent, or Robinson, possibly reflecting doubts as to Mitchell's reliability.[12]

It is significant that the individuals from the Minster parish named in these various court proceedings were wealthy and important individuals. Two, Thomas Settrington and Arkinwald Shepherd, were governors of the town at the time they were brought before the court. Others served on the common council and one was the son of a governor. They were in a good position to influence the character of the religious life of the town. Three of them later expressed clear protestant sentiments. Although less is known of John Pesegrave, he had links with other known Protestants, such as Robert Pickering, Alex Guye and John Atkinson, a former chantry priest, and later assistant and vicar at the Minster, who refused to wear the surplice in 1566. When taken with the evidence of protestant leanings amongst the Minster clergy it is clear that it was during Mary's reign that evidence of religious divisions first appeared. While curate at the Minster, Mitchell was described by one parishioner with protestant leanings as a 'crafty priest', and abused more vehemently as a 'whore master, harlot master, naughty harlot, and false harlot', probably for the role he was called upon to play in disciplining Protestants. The evidence is too fragmentary to suggest that by the end of Mary's reign the Minster could be regarded as a protestant stronghold, but it is clear that protestant views had made a significant advance, were well entrenched, and had attracted the support of an important and influential section of both lay and clerical opinion.[13]

The accession of Elizabeth and subsequent changes to the religion established by law were greeted calmly at the Minster, but the religious divisions which had become evident under Mary continued to affect both clergy and laity. In 1566 John Atkinson was embroiled in the vestiarian controversy for his failure to wear a surplice and possibly for failing to use the prayer book. He was commanded 'at all times from henceforth when he cometh into the choir in St John's church in Beverley as well at morning prayer and communion and also at evening prayer [to] come into the same church with a surplice and so minister in the same church upon pain of the law and … minister all kinds of divine service in such sort as is appointed by the book of common prayer…'. Atkinson evidently demonstrated his conformity and continued his ministry. The following year three other members of the Minster clergy demonstrated their attachment to traditional popish practices. Thomas Levett, his brother John, another former member of the dissolved college, and Thomas Saunders were all arraigned for contumacy, keeping prohibited books and equipment and using 'certain idolatrous and superstitious monuments'. The Levetts were ordered to undergo penance, by parading through the streets of York wearing paper mitres on their heads, standing at the Pavement in York for a quarter of an hour before parading again, followed by an open declaration and confession of their crimes, and were suspended from the priesthood. Although they were later restored to their sacerdotal office, they were barred from ministering in Beverley or holding a cure of souls within ten miles of the town.[14]

Amongst the laity there is little sign of open opposition to Protestantism. However, the preambles to wills may reflect the confusion and divisions so evident elsewhere. Bequests of the soul may well reflect the beliefs of the scribe rather than those of the testator, though of the thirty-one wills surviving from the Minster parish between 1560 and 1570 only a handful show evidence of clerical authorship. The majority of the preambles show no signs of the type of catholic piety evident at the beginning of the century. Only six employed phrases mentioning the celestial company or the saints, none asked for prayers for the soul and only two referred to the Virgin Mary. William Adamson, a clothier, who made his will in November 1567, bequeathing his soul to 'Almighty God my only saviour and redeemer and to the fellowship of the celestial company', was the last parishioner to employ traditional phrases of that nature until the early 17th century. Specific bequests for the church fabric practically ceased, totalling no more

24 The early-seventeenth-century Grammar School, which stood in the south-west corner of the Minster churchyard.

than 13s 4d in the same decade. As time went on some testators increasingly made more personal declarations of their faith. Robert Pickering bequeathed his soul to 'Almighty God the creator of the same having my full confidence to be saved only by the redemption wrought of his son our lord and saviour Christ Jesus'. Henry Bushell expressed the trust that he was one of God's 'elect and chosen children', and in 1572 Anne Browne, in a lengthy and personal declaration of her faith, left no doubt as to her protestant convictions.[15]

In spite of the spread of Protestantism, the Minster parish retained a small but important number of Catholics. In the main these seem to have been drawn from the rural sections of the parish. The household of Michael Warton figured prominently in prosecutions of those who deliberately absented themselves from the services of the Established Church, though other important individuals in the parish were suspected of holding catholic views. Suspected Catholics, such as Thomas Wilberforce, Edward Truslove and Ralph Freeman held civic office as governors of the town. In an unusual return to expressions which appeared to have died out in the parish in the 1560s, Freeman made reference to the 'celestial company of heaven' in his will in 1604 and Truslove expressed the hope that his soul would be received into 'the company of the blessed saints'. The influence which such individuals were able to wield in the town may well have resulted in the outbreak of political factionalism in the corporation in the 1590s, in the course of which the Council of the North intervened, resulting in the removal and resignation from office of some governors, including those suspected of having conservative religious sympathies.[16]

However, there is little evidence of rejection of the church. John Poor, a papist from Molescroft, was unusual in deliberately avoiding the protestant preaching of John Atkinson and William Richardson at the Minster, finding the atmosphere at St Mary's more congenial. Some parishioners preferred drinking in alehouses or playing at cards or other games during divine service. But at the same time others expressed the strength of their religious feeling. The importance of catechizing was taken seriously by the laity who complained when it was not available and expected the clergy to examine parishioners before admitting them to communion. Those who considered themselves to be parishioners of St Martin's, but who were served by the vicar of St Mary's, grumbled when Thomas Utye, who doubted that it was his responsibility, failed to catechize. William Crashaw, the vicar of the Minster at the end of the century, certainly appreciated the importance of catechesis in parish life and was later to write two catechisms, the first of which, *Milke for Babes*, was a 'north country catechism made plain and easy, to the capacity of the north country people', which ran to six editions. He observed that, 'by preaching I prepare meat for men. By catechizing I provide milk for children and endeavour to perform ... the duty of a faithful and wise steward in the house of God'. He advised householders to ensure that children and servants received instruction at both church and home, 'without which all our labour in preaching is utterly lost, as lamentable experience shows ...where after long preaching many are found miserably ignorant for want of catechizing'. Moreover, it seems that good levels of formal religious attendance at the Minster were attained. In 1599, anxious to keep down the cost of bread and wine, the town governors ordered the communicants within the parish of St John and St Martin to defray the costs. The figures suggest that around 600 households were represented at the Easter communion, probably representing most of the households in the parish, and around 200 at other times.[17]

After the uncertainties of the 1560s the two most notable developments affecting the Minster during the last third of the 16th century related to the control which the town corporation began to exercise and the establishment of a preaching ministry. Well before the grant of its charter of incorporation in 1573, which considerably increased the authority and self-confidence of the governing body, Beverley's governors had been actively participating in affairs at the Minster. As the century progressed, their influence was increasingly wielded financially, personally and through patronage. Probably by the 1560s the governors were nominating, or at least approving, the churchwardens for the parish. In 1566 all four churchwardens, whose names were recorded in the Minute Book of the town, were governors, well able to influence the financial regulation of the Minster, as well as the discipline of parishioners at visitations. Later appointments of churchwardens suggest that the governors maintained a close control, and in the 1590s they were to claim similar rights of nomination and veto at St Mary's. The concern which had been expressed in 1552 over the fate of the Grammar School and the maintenance of the fabric of the Minster had resulted in the grant of lands to the town for the upkeep of both institutions. Further grants were to follow. By 1575-6 the gross income from the Minster rents

25 The east face of the altar reredos. The space under the vaulting – one of the most sacred sites in the medieval Minster – was appropriated in the 17th century for the monument of Sir Michael Warton (d. 1655).

(without making allowance for unpaid rents, arrears and vacant holdings) was approaching £70 a year and the net figure rarely fell below £60. The governors made regular payments for the support of the Grammar School and its staff, ensuring the appointment of fervent Protestants, such as John Hunt and William Richardson, as masters. Richardson's services were especially appreciated, earning him a salary of £21 18s.[18]

Attention to the needs of the Minster's fabric was less assiduous. The amount spent on its repair fluctuated widely, from only £1 8s in 1576-7, to over £30 in 1584-5. Payments were regularly less than £20 a year in the 1590s, until over £80 had to be disbursed in 1602-3. The latter payment undoubtedly reflected the extent to which the fabric of the Minster had been allowed to fall into decay in the preceding decades. Minster finances were treated as part of those of the town. The surplus of income for the support of the church over expenditure had not been ring-fenced or allowed to accumulate, but had been treated as accruing to the town. It may be that the absence of any surviving churchwardens' accounts for St John's during this period, apart from such records as appear in the town's account rolls, reflects the fact that they were not kept diligently. There were constant and repeated complaints of decay and neglect. In 1595 the mayor was accused of being 'in default for two homily books wanting and for not causing their surplice to be washed according to their old custom'. Decay was alleged in 1590 and in 1595 the body of the church was said to be in great decay and windows broken 'in Mr Mayor's default'. In 1600 the mayor was blamed again, this time for the lack of repair to the chancel. The parishioners too seem to have shown no real concern for the Minster's fabric. No testator directed funds for its upkeep in the 1580s or 1590s, perhaps considering that arrangements for its maintenance through the grant of lands should have been adequate.[19]

The governors did play a more positive role in establishing a preaching ministry at St John's. From the beginning of Elizabeth's reign the burden of evangelization, spreading the protestant faith in the town, was undertaken principally by the Minster clergy. The influence of John Atkinson, who succeeded Thomas Mitchell in 1558, and William Richardson, his assistant (and also schoolmaster) and later successor should not be under-estimated. Though not a graduate, Richardson was described by the governors in 1581 as a 'learned man and good preacher' and his services were clearly appreciated. It was his death which caused the governors to realize the inadequacy of the stipend and the consequent difficulties in attracting a suitable successor. The stipend for the incumbent, sometimes styled vicar but more usually curate (or, later, preacher), was fixed by the Crown at £13 6s 8d and £8 for each of the three assistants. In 1581 the governors petitioned to be granted the advowson and in consideration for agreeing to augment the stipend received the right to appoint, discipline and if need be dismiss the clergy at the Minster. Using the characteristically puritan language of such petitions, they expressed the desire to obtain a 'learned and able person to preach and set forth God's word to the people of the said town and parish'. The stipend was increased to £21 6s 8d and subsequently raised to £30 and then £40 during the 1580s. Such a salary was on a par with that enjoyed by corporation-sponsored preachers at Hull. The number of assistants was reduced gradually to one. It is hard to assess the effect of this further reduction in clerical provision on the quality of pastoral care, but it seems as though the curate's main duties consisted of preaching, with the assistant being responsible for other aspects of pastoral life.[20]

A number of significant points emerge from the grant of 1581. First, it enabled the governors to secure the appointment of learned men who were able to advance the boundaries of the protestant Reformation. After 1581 the incumbents at St John's were always graduates. The first, Thomas Wincop, held an MA and his successor William Crashaw additionally held the degree of BD. Before his appointment Crashaw had been a fellow of St John's College at Cambridge – a college in whose foundation the Beverley-born John Fisher had played a major role at the beginning of the century. One of the official editors of William Perkins, later a preacher at St Paul's Cross, and a prolific writer of polemical works attacking popery, Crashaw ended his career as preacher at the Temple. Secondly, in the long term the grant gave the urban authorities not only considerable freedom of choice in the selection process, but also enabled them to respond to the needs of the town and parish. Although later an element of election came into the process, early appointments seem to have owed more to the exercise of patronage. It is likely that Wincop owed his appointment to the earl of Huntingdon, Lord President of the Council of the North, who praised his preaching, and Crashaw to William Gee, then recorder in the town. By securing the bond of patronage between magistracy and ministry, the 1581 grant enabled the development of the moderate puritan godly preaching tradition which was to characterize the Minster throughout the late 16th and 17th centuries. Both Wincop and Crashaw sought, as zealous Protestants, to maintain the unity of the church, oppose popery and introduce strict control of moral life. In 1586, after Wincop's arrival, presentations at the visitation increased from eight to sixty-three before falling back to around twenty in subsequent years. Crashaw adopted the same policy, presentments jumping to sixty-four in 1604. Drunkenness, sexual impropriety, gaming, absences from divine service, scolding and sabbath breaking all figured prominently in the lists of offences. These levels of presentment demonstrated the determination of newly arrived clergy to impose their stamp on the religious and moral life of the parish and town. Despite these measures, the parishioners at the Minster were not all godly by the end of the century. There were still adulterers and fornicators like William and Katherine Thomson, and drunkards such as John Peece, William Greenleaf, 'an accustomed drunkard', and John Westerall and Christopher Scales who were 'common frequenters of the alehouse', but there was now no doubting the religious complexion of the parish and town.[21]

The impact of the preaching ministry which had been brought to the town markedly changed the character of religious life at the Minster, the town and its surrounding countryside. Wincop, for example, was prominent in organizing exercises, at which attendance was enforced by the ecclesiastical courts, where sermons were preached and discussed by assembled ministers, partly as a means of providing in-service training to clergy from surrounding villages. By the end of Elizabeth's reign, a godly ministry, supported at times by a godly magistracy, had implanted in Beverley a new form of religion which was to prosper in the 17th century. As the traditional vehicles for influencing the character of religious life were abandoned, so new avenues were opened up to provide for the essential work of evangelization, making both the Minster and the town notable for moderate puritan preaching.

NOTES

1   W. Page, ed., *The Certificates of the Commissioners Appointed to Survey the Chantries, Guilds and Hospitals etc. in the County of York*, ii (Surtees Society, 92, 1895), [hereafter *Chantries*], pp. 524, 542, 552; Leach, *Memorials*, i, p. xxxvi; *VCH Beverley*, p. 77.

2   *Chantries*, pp. 524-52; Leach, *Memorials*, ii, p. 345; D.M. Woodward, *Descriptions of East Yorkshire: Leland to Defoe* (EYLHS, 39, 1985), p. 8; R.T.W. McDermid, 'The Constitution and Clergy of Beverley Minster in the Middle Ages', Durham University MA thesis (1980), pp. 296-312 and Appendix VII; *idem*, *Beverley Minster Fasti* (YASRS, 149, 1993); D.J. Lamburn, 'Politics and Religion in Sixteenth Century Beverley', York University DPhil thesis (1991), pp. 272-314.

3   References to wills in this study are based on an analysis of surviving wills explored in more detail in my 'Politics and Religion'; the registered wills are in the Borthwick Institute of Historical Research, York. BIHR, Prob. Reg. 9, ff. 432 (Sanderson), 278v (Lerifax), 44 (Doufe), 337v (Lepington); Prob. Reg. 10, f. 82 (Lerifax); Prob. Reg. 11A, f. 72 (Garret); ERAO, BC/II/3, ff. 80v, 58, 44v.

4   *Chantries*, p. 528; McDermid, *Beverley Fasti*, pp. xxv-xxvii; J. Caley, ed., *Valor Ecclesiasticus*, v (Record Commissioners, 1825), pp. 130-6; BIHR, CP.G. 2667; *ibid*. V.1590-1/CB f. 98; Lamburn, 'Politics and Religion', pp. 274, 308-9; BIHR, Prob.Reg. 11A, f. 13.

5   *L. & P. Hen. VIII*, vi. 247, vii. 953, viii. 990, 1011, 1026, ix. 704, xiii (1). 1247, 1317, xiii (2). 108; W.H. Frere and W.M. Kennedy, eds, *Visitation Articles and Injunctions of the Period of the Reformation*, ii (Alcuin Club Collections, 15, 1910), pp. 44-52.

6   ERAO, BC/II/3, ff. 92v, 74v, 75v; A.F. Leach, ed., 'A Fifteenth-Century Fabric Roll of Beverley Minster', *TERAS*, 6 (1898), 62-103; ERAO, BC/III/33, 34.

7   BIHR, Beverley Peculiar Probate Register, ff. 18v, 32; Leach, *Memorials*, ii, p. ci; BIHR, Prob. Reg. 13B, ff. 710, 835. For Bonsaye and Thwing see below. Lamburn, 'Politics and Religion', pp. 272-394, 461-2.

8   Stat.1 Edw. VI, c.14; *VCH Beverley*, pp. 77-8; *Chantries*, pp. 524, 529, 531-2, 552-3; W. Page, ed., *The Inventories of Church Goods for the Counties of York, Durham and Northumberland* (Surtees Society, 97, 1897), pp. 58-9, 64-5; A.G. Dickens, *Lollards and Protestants in the Diocese of York* (1982 edition), pp. 168-235; D. & S. Neave in *Friends of Beverley Minster: Report for 1996-7* (1997), pp. 12-13.

9   *VCH Beverley*, p. 231; ERAO, BC/I/74; BIHR, CP.G 1434; *Chantries*, pp. 540-53; A.F.Leach, ed., *Early Yorkshire Schools*, i (YASRS, 27, 1899), pp. li-liii, 113-9.

10 Lamburn, 'Politics and Religion', p. 255; BIHR, Prob. Reg. 15B, f. 99 (Gray), 15C, f. 148v (Willy).

11 Dickens, *Lollards and Protestants*, pp. 191-2, 223-4, 227-30; BIHR, Ch.A.B.6, ff. 37v, 38-38v, 26; Lamburn, 'Politics and Religion', pp. 357-364; A.G. Dickens, *Marian Reaction in the Diocese of York* (York, 1957), part I, pp. 11-12, 27.

12 BIHR, Ord. 1554/1/10 & 11; *Chantries*, p. 534.

13 Lamburn, 'Politics and Religion', p. 361 and table 5; *VCH Beverley*, p. 201; ERAO, BC/II/7/2, ff. 2, 15, 25; *ibid*. BC/II/6/18; BIHR, CP.G 3560.

14 Leach, *Memorials*, ii, p. ci; BIHR, HC.AB. 3 1566-67/8, f. 34; J.S. Purvis, *Tudor Parish Documents of the Diocese of York* (Cambridge, 1948), p. 119; BIHR, CP.G. 883; *ibid*. HC.AB.3, ff. 112, 114, 118, 143; H. Aveling, *Post Reformation Catholicism in East Yorkshire 1558-1790* (EYLHS, 11, 1960), pp. 12, 31.

15 BIHR, Prob. Reg. 17B, f. 778 (Adamson); Prob. Reg. 18, f. 192; Prob. Reg. 28B, f. 846 (Bushell); Prob. Reg. 19A, f. 267 (Browne).

16 Aveling, *Catholicism*, p. 63; Lamburn, 'Politics and Religion', pp. 268-9, 372-80; BIHR, Prob. Reg. 29B, f. 611; Prob. Reg. 31, f. 228.

17 BIHR, CP.G.1434: *ibid*. HC.AB. 4, ff. 75, 80, 99v; *ibid*. V.1567-8/CB2, f. 28v, V.1578-9, f. 197v, V.1586/CB, ff. 131v, 133, 134v, 135, V.1594/CB, f. 153; *ibid*. V.1582, f. 198; *ibid*. V. 1578-9, f. 198, V. 1590-1/CB, f. 98, V. 1594/CB, ff.154, 154v, V. 1600/CB f. 89; *ibid*. CP.G. 2667: *ibid*. HC.AB 11, ff. 233v, 234v, 237v, 241v, 245v, 247, 257v. W. Crashaw, *Milke for Babes* (1622), unpaginated; Lamburn, 'Politics and Religion', pp. 367-9; ERAO, BC/II/7/4/1, ff. 23, 54v, 69; *ibid*. BC/II/6/37-8, 42.

18 ERAO, BC/II/7/2, f. 77; BIHR, HC.CP. 1594/4; *VCH Beverley*, p. 78; ERAO, BC/II/6/33-43; *ibid*. BC/I/74.

19 ERAO, BC/II/6/33-43; BIHR, Chanc. AB. 8A, f. 60; *ibid*. V. 1590-1/CB, f. 98, V.1595-6/CB, 1 f. 122v, v.1600/CB, 1 f. 91v.

20 ERAO, BC/I/74; *ibid*. BC/7/4/1, ff. 6, 24, 24v; *Calendar of Patent Rolls 1557-8*, p. 401; PRO, CP 25(2)/259/8 Eliz. Trin. [no. 2]; Leach, *Memorials*, ii, p. ci.

21 *DNB*, *sub* Crashaw, William; P.J. Wallis, *William Crashawe, the Sheffield Puritan*, (Transactions of the Hunter Archaeological Society, 8, pts 2-5, 1960-3); ERAO, BCII/6/37; *ibid*. BC/II/5/1 (second part), f. 7; *ibid*. BC/II/7/4/1, ff. 6, 24, 24v, 33, 55v. BIHR, V. 1582, ff. 196-198v, V. 1586/CB, ff. 130v-135v, V. 1600-1/CB, ff. 89-93v, V. 1604, ff. 96v-109; K.G. Murray, 'Puritanism and Civic Life in York, Newcastle, Hull, Beverley and Leeds, 1590-1640', Durham University PhD thesis (1990), pp. 170-3.

W. J. SHEILS

5 · The Minster in the 17th and 18th centuries

By the time of William Crashaw's departure in 1605 the Minster was firmly established in its role as a parish church serving the united parishes of St Martin, which covered the area within the borough, and St John, which included those settlements outside the borough but within the liberty of Beverley. It was a parish which had already established a godly preaching tradition which stressed the importance of the word of scripture rather than the sacraments and which gave an important place to local or congregational initiative in the life of the parish. This was to be the chief characteristic of parochial churchmanship throughout the first half of the 17th century, built in part on the foundations of a locally funded lectureship in the patronage of the corporation. That the tradition was a moderate puritan one can be discerned in the regular presentation of parishioners to the diocesan courts for moral offences and sabbath breaking by the churchwardens of St John's. It was not one which commanded universal support, however, and in 1615 differences over religion within the godly camp became public, with some puritans adopting a more radical stance. On 23 July, at the end of the communion and sermon, a group of about sixty persons remained behind in the chancel of the Minster and sung psalms, as they had done on the two previous Sundays. They would have embarked on discussion of the sermon had it not been for the intervention of the assistant curate, Thomas Brabbes, who challenged the legitimacy of their proceedings which, he alleged, took place without the consent of 'any save themselves'. When the psalm singing came to an end he demanded to know what was going on and was told by one of the leaders 'to make no reckoning'. He offered to join the company but was told that his presence was not required and the group refused to acknowledge him as their minister. Threatening to report the event to the church courts, Brabbes withdrew to taunts from the congregation that 'there are too many such dumb dogs as you are', a reference to the fact that he was a non-preaching curate, and therefore failing to perform the central ministerial function of the reformed clergy as understood by puritan theologians. This sort of puritan activity and the confrontation that ensued can be traced in many northern towns at this time, during the archiepiscopate of the strongly Calvinist and committed preacher Tobie Matthew, but in this case matters did not rest. Within a fortnight twenty-two individuals were summoned to the ecclesiastical courts, among whom were sons of former governors of the town and some related to the present governors. The leader of the meeting was identified as John Garthwaite, master of the Grammar School, and it was probably the case that the curate, Richard Rhodes, was also involved. Clearly there was significant support among parishioners for puritan practices which were more radical than those countenanced by the town governors at this time, and indeed, from the names of those involved, it seems that these religious disagreements reflected a split within the community between the governors and those governed whose roots lay further back. Many of those presented before the court in 1615 had been involved in criticism of the town government during the previous decade or, like Marmaduke Attmar, had taken their criticism further and been imprisoned for an assault on the town's officers. Just as in other towns in Yorkshire, religious tensions at this time were often mingled with political faction and disturbance.

It appears that the meetings which had occasioned the dispute were suppressed in the short

26 The west doors, carved by the Thorntons in the 18th century and showing the four Evangelists and their emblems. The surrounding statuary was carved by the Bakers in 1909-10.

term. They certainly no longer took place in the Minster after Rhodes, the curate, was admonished by the court. The radicals, however, may simply have removed their activities to less public places, for similar gatherings once again attracted the attention of the diocesan authorities in the early 1630s when Rhodes was reported for holding illegal 'conventicles', which he maintained were no more than evening catechizing classes for the youth of the parish and 'sermon sessions' for the schoolboys. Rhodes was supported in his churchmanship once again by successive masters of the Grammar School who, like him, were appointed by the corporation which, by this time, was more disposed to support their puritan clergy against the Laudian churchmanship advocated from York by Archbishop Richard Neile.[1] The school itself, which had new premises built about 1610 in the Minster Yard [24], had developed close links with St John's College, Cambridge and sent a number of pupils there, some of whom, like Peter Clark, vicar of Carnaby in 1637, were to emerge as puritan preachers during the Civil Wars and as dissenters thereafter. The links between the school and the university were strengthened further during the Interregnum as the result of a bequest from an old scholar, Robert Metcalfe, who had subsequently been a fellow of St John's College, Regius Professor of Hebrew and finally vice-master of Trinity College, and by his will of 1653 left money for three scholarships to be held at Cambridge for pupils of the Grammar School.[2]

The events of 1615 apart, the prevailing puritan religious temper of the parish was not one which disturbed the church authorities further, except for some entirely conventional complaints about neglect of the fabric which were common throughout the diocese at this time. Notwithstanding these complaints the corporation appears to have taken some pains to maintain the building, paying Christopher Smeadley, plumber, £40 to repair the leads and windows in 1629 and an annual fee of £5 thereafter, increased to £8 in 1637.[3] Puritanism was not the only form of religious departure from the Prayer Book in these years, the parish also contained a small but significant number of Catholic recusants around the household of the principal inhabitant Sir Michael Warton, lord of the manor of Beverley. Never large in number, this group did include substantial inhabitants who had links with the recusant gentry of the neighbouring villages, and their potential for disruption was thought sufficient by Archbishop Tobie Matthew for him to direct his visitation sermon at Beverley in 1611 specifically against Roman Catholics. Warton was to become a royalist supporter during the Civil Wars and probably acted as host to Charles I when the king moved his headquarters to Beverley for a period of three weeks in July 1642. During his brief stay Charles attended a service at the Minster on at least one occasion but, after his withdrawal to York, the puritan traditions of the town came to the fore again.[4] Godly continuity was provided by John Pomroy, a graduate of Emmanuel College, Cambridge who had been master of the Grammar School since 1630 and served as lecturer at the Minster during the Cromwellian regime, but the most distinguished of the puritan lecturers in the town in these years was John Oxenbridge, a fellow of Magdalen Hall, Oxford who, after deprivation by Archbishop Laud, ministered in Bermuda before returning to England on the eve of the Civil Wars. He preached in Beverley from 1644 and commanded sufficient support to be made a burgess in 1648, removing from the town early in 1652. Oxenbridge went abroad again at the Restoration, first to Surinam and eventually to Boston, Massachusetts where he became pastor of the first church, dying there in 1674.[5] During Oxenbridge's time at Beverley the curate's income was increased in a number of ways, only the first of which became permanent. Under the will of Robert Metcalfe (d. 1653) the curate received an extra £10 a year for preaching a weekly sermon at St Mary's; in addition the corporation secured an increase to the income of the living by a grant of £50 from the Committee for Plundered Ministers, a body which redistributed income from wealthy and royalist livings elsewhere to more needy or more populous congregations, but this was lost at the Restoration. It was also suggested that the incumbent's salary from the decayed church of St Nicholas be used to augment the salaries of the clergy at the Minster or St Mary's, but it was the latter which received the endowment in 1667.[6] St Nicholas's church was demolished during the Civil Wars, when the Minster also suffered damage from military action which required expensive repairs to be undertaken. Nevertheless the building itself continued to impress visitors like John Evelyn who described it in 1654 as 'not much inferior to the best of our cathedrals', and an engraving of the church was produced in 1656 [27].[7]

27 An engraving of the Minster made in 1656 but based on a drawing made in the late 16th century. For all its manifest inaccuracies of scale, the picture is an important source for the appearance of the central tower.

The Restoration of the monarchy in 1660 brought substantial changes to the church and parish in the years immediately following. First and foremost the church had to be reordered for Anglican worship once again. The old pews were sold off and a new pulpit, and pews for the mayor, recorder and aldermen were purchased with the money; the plate and flagons were returned to the church from the safekeeping of the corporation; a table of the Creed, Lord's Prayer and Ten Commandments was set up in the chancel; the pillars and other parts of the interior were to be 'dressed and beautified', in the course of which the tomb of St John was rediscovered and its location marked with a brass plate; and the royal arms, still to be seen in the south transept, were placed in the church.[8] These improvements did not please all elements in the parish, however, and in 1662 factions appeared over the appointment of the curate. The official nominee, Elias Pawson, was opposed by a group of parishioners, including some aldermen, who sought to have appointed the puritan Joseph Wilson, who had earlier served at St Mary's and was described by his opponents as 'a person so scandalous in his life, factious and seditious in his practice in what concerns the civil government, and schismatical as to the ecclesiastical, that he scarce hath his equal'. A fracas took place in the Minster itself when Wilson's supporters tried to prevent Pawson from entering the church, and subsequently disturbed the congregation by banging on the chancel doors in a vain attempt to get access to the pulpit for their candidate. Thereafter Wilson preached for a time as an unlicensed minister in the town and the godly congregation of the Minster was divided between those who accepted the Restoration, and a sizeable minority, representing one-sixth of the parish or ten per cent of the adult population of the town, who chose to stay outside the church and form a dissenting congregation on presbyterian lines.[9] A few of these were members of the corporation and found themselves excluded from office under the Corporation and Test Acts of the 1660s and '70s, which required that all office holders in local and central government subscribe to the Thirty-Nine Articles and receive the Anglican communion at least once a year. Dissent thus became part of the life of the parish if not of the church. But just as the congregation was fragmenting in this way, the church party gained considerable support through the conversion to Anglicanism of the most substantial residents, the Warton family, whose principal members turned their back on Catholicism and began to play a major role in the life of St John's. Their intention was expressed in the fine renaissance monument put up to Sir Michael Warton (d. 1655) by his grandson which stands behind the choir of the church [25, 79]. The monument was probably the work of a London sculptor and shows Sir Michael kneeling in his armour within a black and white marble setting designed on the model of an Ionic doorway. From this date the Wartons not only lent their considerable social clout to the cause of the Established Church in the town, but were also to have the most significant financial impact on the physical appearance of the church for the next two centuries.[10]

Storm damage in 1676 brought down the pinnacles of the church, and the cost of maintenance was an increasing burden on a corporation whose chief income for this purpose was derived from rents of properties in the town which themselves required improvement and rebuilding in these years. The parish also covered the less prosperous part of the town and contained a sizeable nonconformist element which continued to cause concern to the curates. To judge from the comments made in the parish register by the curate Stephen Clark, the Act of Toleration of 1690 only served to revive those animosities recorded at the Restoration. He wrote dismissively of the conventicle which had been established earlier in the parish, in Well Lane, expressing the hope 'that it will please God to put it into the heart of the King and his council to take away from the presbyterians and all other dissenters this their beloved liberty of conscience, as those of that gang are pleased to call it', and referred disparagingly to the lowly origins of their minister, Mr Foster, as 'that *quondam* eminent tailor of Berwick', presenting him and some of the congregation to the consistory court at York.[11] Clark's words remind us that the religious divisions noticed in 1615 and 1662 remained live issues in the parish throughout the century. The divided nature of the parish and the difficulties of its endowment, which resulted in the salaries of both Clark and his assistant being in arrears at this time, meant that the Minster was less well represented on the corporation than its sister parish of St Mary's, which Celia Fiennes identified as the principal church of the town on her visit in 1696. Although the Minster impressed her and she gave it a much lengthier description than St Mary's, she noted that, in comparison, it appeared to be neglected. However, other visitors continued to be impressed by the building. The future bishop of London, Edmund Gibson, described it as 'a very fair and neat structure' and recorded its historic associations and monuments, not only major ones like the frithstool and the Percy tomb, but also lesser ones such as the painting of St John and King Athelstan which was then placed by the choir and is now in the south transept [pl. 9].[12]

By the end of the century both the state of the fabric and the administration of the Minster finances were the cause of some concern to the archbishop of York, John Sharp [28]. In his compendious survey of the parishes in the diocese his first conclusion was that there was sufficient to maintain the building if the income 'be rightly applied' by the corporation, but further enquiry convinced him that the revenue was not as great as first thought, and that after payment of taxes, repairs to the houses and shops, and additional salaries to the Minster clock keeper and bellringers, as well as money for wine at the communion, 'they have nothing in stock'.[13] As a result of his enquiry, and in response to a request from the corporation, Sharp

28 Archbishop John Sharp of York (d. 1714), from a portrait at Bishopthorpe Palace.

secured a Royal Brief in 1704 which gave the corporation the authority to make a national appeal for funds for the repair of the Minster. A trust was established and collectors appointed later that year when the corporation borrowed £60 for emergency use. The Brief was given a grant of £100 from the King's Charity and a similar one from the archbishop, whilst collections in the town raised £57 12s 6d from St Mary's and £24 9s 6d from the Minster parish, probably a fair reflection of the comparative wealth of each. Contributions were also forthcoming from the local gentry and from many of the canons of York Minster, but by far the greatest donation was that of £500 by Sir Michael Warton, MP for the town.[14] By 1717 major structural repairs had become a matter of urgency, as the gable wall of the north transept was falling away by some four feet and the church had been 'so much shaken of late that if immediate care be not taken to prevent its falling, the whole fabric will be in danger'. In this crisis the corporation embarked upon full restoration and engaged Nicholas Hawksmoor as architect. Doubts about the corporation's administration of the Minster fund continued to be aired, principally by John Moyser, the other MP for the borough, and the mayor felt it necessary to send a deputation to put the corporation's case to the archbishop in 1720. Moyser was eventually brought on to the trustees administering the Brief account which, by 1731, had raised the sum of £6132 15s 5d, a significant proportion of which had come as interest from investment in the South Sea Company.[15]

The details of the restoration are discussed in chapter 7. By 1722 over £3000 had been expended on the work, and its scope and scale, and in particular the woodwork of the doors [26] and galleries, attracted the admiring comments of visitors to the town during its progress. On 18 October 1725, however, the corporation noted that the money raised by the Brief was 'near disbursed, and there are yet several things wanting towards the repairing and beautifying the minster. It is this day ordered that such works as they are going forward with shall be perfected'. By this date the corporation was aware that the Minster finances were likely to be transformed by the bequest of Sir Michael Warton (d.1725), who left £4000 to various charitable purposes in the town, principally to the fabric of St John's. This bequest must have been very welcome to the hard-pressed corporation, which at this time was also engaged in financing a number of projects: the building of a new workhouse, upgrading those houses it owned around the town, undertaking works to make Beverley Beck more navigable to keep trade up, and providing municipal amenities such as a town fire engine. Secure in the knowledge of Warton's generosity, the members felt confident enough in June 1726 to borrow £600 in order to finish off the work in progress on St John's.[16]

By the time of Warton's bequest there had also been some augmentation of the curate's salary. A grant from Queen Anne's Bounty was used to buy 10 acres of glebe land in Sutton on Hull in 1722, and in the same year an annual pension of £2 from a property in Toll Gavel was left to the curate by Anne Routh, who also set up an almshouse in the town. But all of this was eclipsed by the terms of Warton's will, which marked a watershed in the history of the Minster.[17] Thereafter the problem was not so much one of finding enough money to fulfil the responsibility of maintaining the fabric as of ensuring that the funds were spent wisely. The sum of £4000 was to be vested in trustees, and the earlier doubts about the corporation's responsibility for the poor state of the fabric meant that the archbishop and dean of York were determined to ensure that the town governors did not get sole control of the funds, especially as the mayor of Beverley was more often a parishioner of St Mary's than of St John's. The corporation, on the other hand, was not keen to have the churchwardens of St John's parish involved in managing a sum of this magnitude, they being 'chosen out of the several small villages or hamlets that are within the Minster parish but not within the town of Beverley, and who at the best are generally poor farmers and very often poor labouring men and therefore unfit to be entrusted with the produce of the said £4000'. The matter went to Chancery and a decree was issued on 6 July 1726 setting up four trustees, the archbishop and dean of York, and the mayor and recorder of Beverley, who were empowered to use the capital sum to purchase land, and nominating the wardens for St Martin's, who came from the borough part of the parish and were therefore among the more prosperous inhabitants (and more likely to be in sympathy with the corporation), as the administrators of the income which those lands produced.[18] The income accruing was in excess of the sums now needed for the fabric and the capital sum increased so that, in 1747, an estate in Lincolnshire, the manor of Dalby Darthorpe, was purchased. Despite spending £1304 4s on the fabric between 1743 and 1765 the trustees found it impossible to spend all the income from the estate on the church, and an additional 39 acres were purchased at Dalby in 1763. It is possible that Warton's bequest had a significant impact on the appearance not only of the Minster but of the townscape more generally for, released from the burden of maintaining the fabric out of the original Elizabethan endowment, the corporation appears to have ploughed a large proportion of that income back into what became known as the 'Old Minster Fund' to distinguish it from Warton's bequest, called the 'New Minster Fund'. Between 1743 and 1765, at a time when the fortunes of the town were high and its leaders were actively promoting new developments and amenities, the corporation spent the considerable sum of £1757 3s 3d farthing on rebuilding and restoring the tenements and houses in the town which formed the Old Minster Estate.[19]

Thus the impact of Warton's bequest went beyond the Minster itself, and helped to create the landscape of that prosperous, if small, Georgian town which remains a striking characteristic of modern Beverley. That prosperity was shared among a relatively small commercial elite within the town, and the close social and kinship relationships which emerged can be discerned within the Minster itself in the numerous monuments which proliferate on the floor and walls of the transepts and choirs and recall the names of prominent residents of Beverley, such as the benefactress Anne Routh (d. 1722), the curate Thomas Lewthwaite (d. 1769), and various members of the Strickland family.[20] Warton's own contribution to the recovery of the Minster's fortunes was recognised in the elaborate monument to him by Peter Scheemakers [29]. Scheemakers was the son of an Antwerp sculptor and is reputed to have lived in poverty as a young man in Copenhagen before walking to Rome, where he completed his studies. He came to England a little before 1720 and designed the monument shortly after Sir Michael's death in 1725. It comprises female seated figures flanking a Roman sarcophagus and urn beneath a garland of flowers surmounted by a pediment, and dominates the east end of the church where one would normally expect to find the Lady Altar, turning the part of the Minster behind the high altar into something of a Warton family chapel. The only other sizeable eighteenth-century monument was that to Sir Charles Hotham (d. 1722), also MP for the town, but its appearance was greatly altered by the restoration of 1874 which left only the tip of the obelisk surrounded by trophies of Roman armour [78].[21]

While these additions and restorations were taking place in the building itself, parochial life was also undergoing change. The Grammar School in Minster Yard went from strength to strength under Joseph Lambert, master there from 1674 until 1716, and one of his successors, John Clarke (master, 1736–1751), and over 150 of its pupils went on to Cambridge in the first half of the 18th century. About one-fifth of these were natives of Beverley, including John Green the future bishop of Lincoln, the rest being made up of the sons of 'many gentlemen of the best quality' who were recorded as pupils there c.1710, and whose presence reflects the importance of the town as a place of resort by the local gentry at this time. The school building had to be enlarged in 1702-3, involving the replacement of part of the churchyard wall, and repaired extensively in 1736 [24]. By the latter date the Grammar School had been joined by a Charity School established in 1710, and pupils at both attended services in the Minster.[22]

Here lieth the Body of Sir MICHAEL WARTON late of Beverley Parks Knight, eldest Son of MICHAEL WARTON Esq who departed this Life 25th March 1725 aged 73.
He gave in his Life Time in Charities and other Gifts to this Town six thousand Pounds, and left by Will to be a perpetual Fund for the Repairs of this Fabrick four thousand Pounds, to augment the Hospital founded by his Father one thousand Pounds, to the Charity School five hundred Pounds, and ordered to be distributed at his Death to the Poor of the several Parishes of this Town two hundred Pounds.
He was descended from a Family always firmly attach'd to the publick Good, who, excepting some short intervals, represented this Borough in Parliament several successive Generations; a little before his Death he resigned his Interest to his Nephew the Honourable Sir MICHAEL NEWTON Knight of the Bath, his Executor, by whom this Monument was erected.

29   The monument of Sir Michael Warton (d.1725) by
Peter Scheemakers.

The curate of St John's for almost the whole of the first half of the 18th century was Thomas Mease, appointed in 1703 when his salary was £60 a year. It was during Mease's incumbency that the restoration of the Minster took place, and the building and its fittings received further enhancement during these years of renewed prosperity in the town by way of gifts from both the corporation and individuals. New furnishings, such as pulpit cloths and surplices, were provided; the bells rehung and new ones added, the great bell in the south-west tower in 1703 and a treble in 1747; a marble altar table was presented by John Moyser, MP, in 1717; and several items of new plate, much of which still survives, were donated. These all formed part of the revival of Anglicanism during these years. Mease adopted a more conciliatory attitude to the dissenters in the parish than his predecessor had, and brought some of the Presbyterians to baptism during adulthood, 'some nigh 60 years old' he reported in 1743. He ensured that the boys at the Grammar School attended church and that the master taught them the catechism on Saturdays, he visited the smaller dame schools in the parish and asked the teachers to catechize their pupils twice weekly. During Lent the young were catechized in the parish church on Sunday afternoon by Mease or his assistant, William Morrell, both of whom were resident in the parish. Public prayers were said twice a day in 1743, and the sacrament was administered monthly. The number of communicants at the monthly eucharist, sixty or seventy, was high for an urban parish in the diocese at this time, and on the great festivals it was even higher, with over 200 receiving the sacrament at Easter (125 on Easter day and eighty-four on Good Friday), and even more at Christmas (111 on the Sunday before and 177 on Christmas Day itself). In a parish of 340 families this level of participation was impressive and a testimony to the effectiveness of Mease's ministry.[23] He sought a more tangible testimony himself in the following year when he asked for an increase in his salary, and the corporation was sufficiently sympathetic to ask the archbishop of York to approach Queen Anne's Bounty, but nothing came of the proposal. Mease died in February 1750 at the age of 84 and his monument, on the wall of the south transept, tells something of the style and aspiration of his ministry [**30**]. It reads 'Your late pastor T.M. being dead yet speaketh. Be daily and devout in private, and (if opportunity serve) in publick prayer. Frequently receive the holy communion with humble, penitent, faithful, charitable, and thankful hearts. Live soberly, righteously, and godly. Fear God and keep his commandments. The peace of God be with you all in Christ Jesus. Amen.'[24]

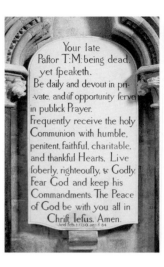

30 The monument of Thomas Mease (d.1750) on the wall of the south transept.

Mease was succeeded by Thomas Lewthwaite in 1751 at the same salary. This was now a matter of some contention as the income from Warton's bequest was proving too large for the stated purpose of maintaining the Minster fabric, but could not be used for other purposes of the church such as increasing the salaries of the curates. Various building schemes, like the proposal from John Carr, the well-known York architect, for a new steeple in 1757, were mooted but not acted upon, and the corporation continued to raid the fund to provide loan capital for other civic undertakings, including major works such as rebuilding the Flesh Shambles, and also more trifling items as supplying the cart and horse belonging to the corporation and paying the wages of the groom. Even so the capital continued to grow, and in 1761 it was decided to seek an act of parliament in order to widen the purposes of the fund so that other church needs could be met from it. This became a source of faction within the corporation, some of whom objected to the decision in 1764 to appoint Lewthwaite as both curate and assistant curate in the parish so that he could receive both salaries. On complaint to the archbishop, Lewthwaite was ordered to surrender one of the positions, and the dean of York, John Fountayne, determined that, whatever changes might be desirable in the new arrangements for Warton's Charity, on no account should control of the salaries of the Minster clergy be entrusted solely to the corporation.[25]

Although Lewthwaite's financial arrangements caused some concern in 1764, parochial life seemed to be thriving under his charge. He was resident in the parish, had provided a resident assistant, whether willingly or not, at an increased salary of £30 a year plus part of the surplice fees, which were payable to the clergy for the performance of baptisms, marriages and burials. Although he does not seem to have kept up Mease's tradition of daily worship, sermons were preached twice every Sunday, in the morning and the afternoon, and catechizing had become a year round activity, based on the much-used and comprehensive text of John Lewis, first published in 1701 but now available in an up to date edition. Most impressive of all were the figures for communicants; a communion service was held on the first Sunday of every month and at Easter there were 300 communicants recorded.[26]

The dissenting interest was also well represented in the town at this time. The presbyterian meeting house in the parish still drew a large congregation, though most of them were said to come from other parishes and the rural hinterland. By this date Wesley's ministry, still technically within the Established Church, had also reached the town. He first preached at Beverley in 1759, and on his visit in 1766 was drawn to record his admiration for the Minster, 'such a parish church as has scarce its fellow in England. It is a most beautiful as well as a stately building, both within and without and is kept more nicely than any cathedral I have seen in the Kingdom'. He followed these remarks with the sombre comment 'but what will it be when the earth is burned up and the elements melt with fervent heat', sentiments which reflected his sense of the urgency of revival within the establishment. The Wesleyan community continued to grow and by the time of John's final visit in 1780 it was a thriving society with its own meeting house. From that time onward Methodism became an important element in the religious life of the town.[27]

One way to try to stem the growth of nonconformity in the town was to strengthen the institutional framework of the Established Church, an outcome which the act of parliament concerning Warton's charity, finally passed in 1766, was designed to achieve. The bequest, which had accumulated an additional capital sum of £2,226 by 1766, was to remain in the control of the original trustees, so that the diocesan authorities retained a supervisory role in its administration whilst the running of day to day matters belonged to the corporation and churchwardens. Just under a quarter of the fund was turned over to the needs of the Charity School and Warton's Hospital, and the rest reserved for the use of the Minster, though no longer exclusively for the fabric. The sums were to be divided between the fabric fund, the salaries of the Minster clergy, the costs of building an organ, and the salary of an organist. The salary of the curate was increased by £50 a year as a result of the act, giving an income of approximately £100 a year to Lewthwaite, and the assistant now received an additional £25, bringing his annual salary to over £40 plus a share of the surplice fees, a source which was to become a matter of dispute later.[28] By this time work had also been done on the curate's house by the Minster, which was described a few years later as being built of brick with four good rooms, a little hall, a fore kitchen and back kitchen, a dining room 'wainscotted to chair height then papered above', and with a further two rooms on the first floor. No accommodation was provided for the assistant, however, who rented property in town.[29]

Much of the accumulated surplus in Warton's bequest was spent on the organ, which cost over £1500. It was built between 1767 and 1769 by John Snetzler with the assistance of a number of local craftsmen who were also employed on restoration work at Burton Constable in these years. Timothy Lightoler designed the case with the help of the York architect Thomas Atkinson, the plasterwork and modelling was carried out by Guiseppe Cortese and William Collins, the wood carving by Edmund Foster, and most of the joinery by Thomas Middleton [87].[30] A substantial annual salary of £40 was made available for an organist and Matthias Hawdon of Hull was appointed to the post. The completion of the work was celebrated in a music festival, said to be the first in the north of England, held on 20-22 September 1769. Performances began at 11am on each day and involved singers from York and Oxford as well as local choirs; the repertoire comprised Handel's oratorios, the *Messiah, Judas Maccabeus* and *Samson*, and tickets cost 5s for the nave and 2s 6d for the gallery. The event was part of the Beverley social season and attracted the local gentry as well as the leading townspeople. Music was not the only recreational opportunity available at Beverley in the middle decades of the century, when the town and the relative cheapness of its amenities attracted immigrants and visitors whose presence brought variety to the close-knit social organisation of the community. Most of these came from the rural hinterland, but Beverley also saw more exotic figures passing through, none more so than two Orthodox monks from the monastery of Pantocrator on Mount Athos, who sought help from the corporation following an invasion by the Ottomans and were granted two guineas in 1733. A more permanent visitor to the town was Brigadier Oliver Delancey, a native of New York and a soldier on the loyalist side during the American War of Independence, who retired to a house in Highgate where he died in 1785 and was buried in the north transept of the Minster.[31]

The music festival of 1769 marked the high point of activity within the Minster during the 18th century. The Warton bequest continued to produce a significant income for the church, and in 1781 William Collins made the statues of St John of Beverley and King Athelstan which now guard the door in the south aisle [41], but by that date tastes had changed and the eighteenth-century improvements no longer received universal praise.[32] When Arthur Young, the agricultural writer and traveller, visited the church in 1769 he described the building as 'very light and beautiful', but went on to decry the recent improvements. Starting in the churchyard, he went on 'its modern decorators appear to have ideas of neither beauty or propriety; for with true taste, they have given the venerable pile just such an entrance as you would imagine for a cakehouse; a new fashioned iron rail, and gate handsomely adorned with gilding, and a modern stone wall with two urns of white stone, which, with a few reliefs cut on them, would do tolerably well for a shrubbery. But these gentlemen, not content with this stroke of genuine propriety, have carried their Grecian ideas into the very choir of a Gothic cathedral. At the entrance, under the organ, they have raised some half dozen (if I recollect right) ionic pillars and pilasters; and built an altar piece in the stile of I know not what. It is an *imperium in imperio*; the bird of Jove certainly flutters her lofty wings to command the attention of the spectator, and call it off from the barbarism of Goths and Vandals to fix curious fluted Corinthian pillars, raised merely to support the pedestal whereon appears the king of birds. You will not quickly meet with a more capital piece of absurdity.'[33]

Pastoral duties were also subject to more criticism than had been the case earlier in the century. Parishioners complained to the corporation in 1774 about the negligence of Lewthwaite and his assistant, William Coulson, in visiting the sick of the parish 'the one pretending or insisting that it is the duty of the other, so that between them it appears that several people have died without either the prayers or sacraments administered', and of Coulson's refusal to bury the poor until the burial fee was paid, so that 'the corpses of such poor people have been left all night in the church to the great scandal both of the said curate as well as the parish'. The mayor upheld the complaints of the parishioners and both curates were reprimanded by the archbishop. By the end of the decade Lewthwaite was dead and Coulson had moved on, to be replaced by James Graves, whose ministry extended into the next century and who, by his will of 1807, left £1000 in stock for the teaching of poor boys and girls of St Martin's parish and a small sum for the purchase of bibles for their use, probably in the Charity School. Such concern for the proper performance of pastoral duties reflected the committed Anglican nature of the corporation at this time, and in 1790 the mayor and aldermen made the Common Hall available for a meeting of the Friends of the Established Church called to register objections to the proposed repeal of the Test and Corporation Acts, which had excluded dissenters from holding public office and thus been instrumental in reinforcing the Anglican nature of the corporation.[34]

By the end of the century both the physical structure of the Minster and the pastoral structure of the parish no longer commanded the same degree of respect that they had in the second quarter of the century, but the generosity of Sir Michael Warton, the long and conscientious ministry of Thomas Mease, and the distinguished headmasterships of Joseph Lambert and John Clarke during those years had provided enduring structures which secured stability and success to parochial endeavours in the succeeding years. As the 18th century gave way to its successor the corporation of Beverley sought another act of parliament to change the terms of Warton's will once again so that his generosity could be used to face the challenges of a new century. The act of 1806 marks the start of the next phase in the history of the Minster and of the parish it served.

NOTES   1   R.A. Marchant, *The Puritans and the Church Courts in the Diocese of York 1560–1642* (1960), pp. 37–8, 48, 248, 271; D.J. Lamburn, 'Religion and Politics in Beverley' in P. Collinson & J. Craig, eds, *The Reformation in English Towns* (Basingstoke, 1998), pp. 69–71.

2 *VCH Beverley*, p. 253; A.G. Matthews, *Calamy Revised* (Cambridge, 1934), p. 118; DNB, *sub* Metcalfe, Robert.

3 BIHR, V.1607/CB, ff. 136v-37v; 1627/CB, f. 249v; V.1633/CB, ff. 289-90v; ERAO, BC II/7/4/1, ff. 33v, 68.

4 H. Aveling, *Post-Reformation Catholicism in East Yorkshire* (EYLHS, 11, 1960), p. 63: *VCH Beverley*, pp. 92–3; York Minster Library, Additional MS 18 (Tobie Matthews' Preaching Diary), p. 87.

5 Matthews, *Calamy Revised*, pp. 349, 394.

6 *VCH Beverley*, p. 232; ERAO, BC II/7/4/1, f. 91v; J. Dennett, ed., *Beverley Borough Records, 1575-1821* (YASRS, 84, 1933), p. 140.

7 *VCH Beverley*, p. 95; Poulson, *Beverlac*, p. 723; D.M. Woodward, *Descriptions of East Yorkshire: Leland to Defoe* (EYLHS, 39, 1985), p. 27.

8 Dennett, *Borough Records*, pp. 120-9; C. Hiatt, *Beverley Minster* (1898), p. 10.

9 Dennett, *Borough Records*, p. 127; Matthews, *Calamy Revised*, p. 537; BIHR, V/1662-3/CB, f. 356 and v.

10 *VCH Beverley*, pp. 96-7; Aveling, *Catholicism*, p. 49: Warton's widow continued as a recusant, BIHR, V.1662-3/CB, f. 355v.

11 *VCH Beverley*, p. 264; Poulson, *Beverlac*, pp. 710-11.

12 Woodward, *Leland to Defoe*, pp. 48-9; ERAO, BC II/7/5, f. 208v.

13 BIHR, Bp. Dio. 3, pp. 42, 46.

14 ERAO, BC IV/14/1, Minster Brief Account Book.

15 ERAO, BC II/7/6, ff. 90, 119, 127, 130, 138; *VCH Beverley*, p. 234; BIHR, Bp. C. & P. XVIII/7.

16 ERAO, BC II/7/6, f. 231; IV/14/1; BIHR, Bp. C. & P. XVIII/8; *VCH Beverley*, pp. 123-4.

17 BIHR, TER. I, Beverley, 1727; Bp. Dio. 3, (East Riding), p. 41.

18 ERAO, BC IV/14/4.

19 BIHR, Bp. C. & P. XVIII/7.

20 I. & E. Hall, *Historic Beverley* (York, 1973), p. 3 and *passim*; Poulson, *Beverlac*, pp. 699-700; monumental inscriptions in the Minster.

21 Hall, *Historic Beverley*, p. 33.

22 *VCH Beverley*, pp. 132-3, 254.

23 BIHR, TER. 1764, lists the plate and furnishings provided earlier in the century, and see *VCH, Beverley*, p.235: S.L. Ollard and P.C. Walker, eds, *Archbishop Herring's visitation of the diocese of York, 1743*, i (YASRS, 71, 1928), pp. 103-4; Hiatt, *Beverley Minster*, p. 50; K. McMahon, ed., *Beverley Corporation Minute Book, 1707-1835* (YASRS, 132, 1958), pp. 24, 36; Poulson, *Beverlac*, p. 685.

24 McMahon, *Minute Book*, p. 26; inscriptions in the Minster.

25 McMahon, *Minute Book*, pp. 39-40, 68; BIHR, Bp. C. & P. XVIII/7, 8.

26 C. Annesley & P. Hoskin, eds, *Archbishop Drummond's Visitation Returns, 1764* (Borthwick Texts and Calendars, 21, 1997) pp. 50-1.

27 *VCH Beverley*, p. 243; J.Crowther, *Descriptions of East Yorkshire: De la Pryme to Head* (EYLHS, 45, 1992), p. 17.

28 Act of Parliament, 6 Geo III c.83 (Private Acts), printed in Poulson, *Beverlac*, pp. 714-20; BIHR, Bp. C. & P. XVIII/8.

29 BIHR, TER. I, Beverley, 1777.

30 Hall, *Historic Beverley*, p. 25; see also chapters 7 and 12.

31 Poulson, *Beverlac*, pp. 684-5; McMahon, *Minute Book*, p. 16.

32 Hall, *Historic Beverley*, p. 25 and figs 49, 181.

33 Crowther, *De la Pryme to Head*, p. 19.

34 McMahon, *Minute Book*, pp. 54, 59-60, 73; *VCH Beverley*, pp. 262-3.

DAVID NEAVE

6 · The Minster in the 19th and 20th centuries

On his appointment to the living of Beverley Minster in 1880 the Revd Henry Nolloth described it as 'one of the most arduous posts in the Church of England'.[1] Arduous because of the ever-present challenge of maintaining the fabric and services of what in scale was a cathedral whilst meeting the practical and spiritual needs of the disparate Minster parishes of St Martin and St John. In the 19th century St Martin's parish covered nearly half the town and many of its inhabitants were employed in tanneries, shipyards, mills and an iron foundry. The population of the parish rose from 2,407 in 1801 to 5,912 a century later. In contrast the parish of St John comprised eight outlying townships with a total area of 8,722 acres. Its widely dispersed population, which increased from 647 in 1801 to 1,534 in 1901, was almost entirely agricultural.

The difficult task facing the incumbent of the Minster parishes was acknowledged by the corporation in the act of parliament they obtained in 1806 to alter the distribution of money from the Minster Old and New Funds. This act increased the annual salaries of the curate and assistant curate and provided for an additional assistant curate. It also stated that the assistant curates must have been educated at Oxford or Cambridge, that prayers were to be said twice every day in the Minster and that the curate was to preach twice on Sundays. Five years later the corporation decreed that any person appointed curate or assistant curate should enter into a bond with a £1,000 penalty to 'reside and abide' in Beverley.[2]

Joseph Coltman (1777–1837) was the additional assistant curate appointed under the 1806 act and he was a wise choice. Coltman, non-resident rector of Hammeringham-cum-Scrafield, near Horncastle, Lincolnshire (a family living) was well connected at Beverley where he had been brought up. His brother-in-law Alderman William Beverley of Norwood House was mayor in 1806-7. A great man, in more than one sense of the word for he weighed thirty-seven stone [32], Coltman was a conscientious clergyman and his monument in the north aisle of the Minster records that 'he devoted much of his time and talents to education'. He was a supporter of Sunday schools, one of the founders and first secretary of the local branch of the National Society for the Education of the Poor in the Principles of the Established Church, and for his work with the Blue Coat school he was granted the freedom of the town in 1810. Coltman's commitment contrasted with that of his fellow assistant curates Bethell Robinson, who was dismissed for immorality in 1811, and Robert Ramsey, charged in 1815 with neglect of duty and of rushing into the Minster to take prayers whilst still wearing his shooting clothes.

In 1813 Coltman was appointed incumbent, or curate, of the Minster in succession to the Revd John Jackson. During the twenty-four years that Coltman held the living the Minster underwent its first major restoration and re-ordering for nearly a hundred years. The corporation, concerned about the state of the building, commissioned reports in May-June 1812 from John Cliff, a Beverley joiner and surveyor, and William Shout, the master mason of York Minster. Shout's report highlighted the serious state of the stonework and advised cleaning throughout and the removal of 'the great Corinthian columns' of the altar screen which had 'a gloomy appearance'.[3] On Shout's recommendation the corporation appointed his former assistant William Comins as clerk of works at the Minster in December 1812, a post he retained until his death in 1838.

31 The choir from the south-east transept c. 1870. The pews in the transepts and the galleries in the choir aisles were removed in 1873. The stone altar rails designed by William Fowler in the 1820s were replaced in 1876-7.

As well as repairing the Minster the corporation sought to improve the setting for worship. In 1823, at the request of the corporation, the builder, architect and renowned antiquarian artist William Fowler of Winterton, Lincolnshire, drew up a scheme whereby the choir became the location for all services, not just the monthly communion, and the nave was abandoned. The pews and galleries in the nave and side aisles were to be taken down and re-sited in the choir aisles 'with the backs of the choir stalls removed to enable the congregation to see'.[4] The proposal met with opposition from the churchwardens, and a meeting they called of the parishioners, under the chairmanship of Coltman, sent a petition to the archbishop of York which listed the disadvantages of Fowler's scheme. These included the destruction of 'the beauty of the choir', the inferior accommodation and its unhealthiness, being damp and airless after the cold but ventilated nave.[5]

This opposition delayed, but did not prevent, the implementation of the scheme and in May 1824 the corporation sought detailed designs from the established architectural firm of Rickman and Hutchinson of Birmingham. Thomas Rickman (1776–1841) was the author of the first systematic work on Gothic architecture in England and formulated the nomenclature for the styles of ecclesiastical architecture which is still used today. Rickman and Hutchinson's plans were approved in December 1824 and Fowler and his son were put in charge of implementing the changes. The nave was cleared of galleries and pews in September 1826 and soon afterwards the much-derided 'Grecian' altar screen was removed and the medieval stone reredos reconstructed by William Comins. The new fittings in the choir included a pulpit and a stone sanctuary wall designed by Fowler and sixteen cast iron pillars supplied by William Crosskill of Beverley which were painted to resemble marble [31]. The discarded materials including the columns from the galleries and Hawksmoor's altar rails (but not his cupola from the central tower which had been removed without opposition in 1824) were sold.[6]

A correspondent to the *Hull Advertiser* in November 1828, after praising the improvements to the interior of the Minster, complained that no attempt had yet been made to exclude the cold which was 'almost intolerable' and commented that 'during the latter part of the service here, it is truly distressing to witness the pallid countenances, the shrunk forms, and the shivering limbs of the congregation'. At their meeting on 2 March 1829 the corporation gave instructions to improve the heating of the choir 'by a slight alteration at small expense' but turned down Coltman's request for additional seating for children.[7]

Coltman was clearly out of favour with the majority of the corporation because of his support for the Catholic Emancipation Bill then before parliament. The corporation petitioned the goverment against granting rights to Roman Catholics on nine occasions in the years 1813–29 but Coltman, who was convinced that the 'concession of the Catholic claims, so far from injuring the Protestant interest, will tend materially to strengthen and consolidate it', proclaimed his views in a pamphlet issued in March 1829 and at a public meeting alongside William Beverley and his son Robert Mackenzie Beverley, the notorious pamphleteer. A much larger anti-Catholic meeting in Saturday Market was urged by the Revd William Hildyard, an assistant curate at the Minster, 'to resist to the utmost of our power the introduction of Roman Catholics into both houses of parliament'.[8] Less than five years later Coltman found himself on the same platform as vehement anti-Catholics when he spoke in defence of the Established Church then under attack from radicals and dissenters including R.M. Beverley, whose pamphlet *A Letter to His Grace the Archbishop of York, on the Present Corrupt State of the Church of England* of 1831 had gone through at least seventeen editions. In his speech Coltman claimed that it was 'essential to the best interests of society that there should be an Established Church' but he did accept that there was need for church reform.[9]

At the time of Coltman's death in 1837 it was municipal, rather than church, reform which

32 Silhouette of the Revd Joseph Coltman. He reputedly rode his dandy-horse, or velocipede, down the nave of the Minster and on reaching the choir would be helped to dismount by a group of sidesmen, who then hauled him into the pulpit 'which fitted him like a socket fits the candle'.

was having its impact on Beverley Minster. Under the Municipal Corporations Act of 1835 the corporation had been forced to give up its control of the Old Fund, and with it responsibility for the Minster fabric and services. It also had to sell the advowson, that is the right to present the curate and assistant curates. The advowson was purchased for £3,300 by the Simeon Trust which had been established by the evangelical Anglican Charles Simeon as a contribution to the reform of the clergy. Although the trustees were not sectarian they were committed to choosing evangelical clergy. At the time of Simeon's death in 1836 the trust had twenty-one livings including Beverley Minster and Bridlington Priory; a century later it had 150 livings.

The first incumbent presented to the Minster living by the Simeon Trustees was the Revd Charles Augustus Thurlow who stayed less than three years. His successor in 1840, the Revd Abel John Ram, also had a short stay at Beverley but it was far more eventful. Ram, who came from a wealthy Anglo-Irish family, was determined to assert his authority at Beverley, but, lacking in diplomacy, he did not endear himself to his fellow clergy, the churchwardens, and many parishioners. His banning of the traditional distribution of bread in the Minster at the end of the annual perambulation of the parish boundaries led to a near riot in 1842. A crowd forced their way into the church and when Ram arrived outside in his carriage he was hissed and hooted at and pelted with sods by some 500 children and several women. He was accused by the corporation of charging excessive burial fees and two parishioners were forced to apologize for circulating 'a grossly false, and defamatory report' against his character and reputation.[10]

Ram attempted to make changes to the interior of the Minster. He headed a committee formed in January 1841 which planned to make alterations to the organ screen to the designs of George Gilbert Scott [pl.13]. Stone was purchased but work had not begun by May 1842 when the 'new' organ screen is last mentioned.[11] Alterations he made in the choir were not approved of by Archdeacon Wilberforce, who had been a fellow student of Ram at Oriel College, Oxford. On a visit to the Minster in July 1844 the archdeacon took particular exception to a flight of steps that Ram had placed under the Percy tomb which he instantly destroyed with a mallet and chisel.[12] By then Ram had left Beverley for the more valuable Crown living of West Ham and had been succeeded by the Revd J. B. Birtwhistle.

John Burton Birtwhistle (1802–79), one of the great incumbents of Beverley Minster, was instituted in June 1844. A Yorkshireman educated at Glasgow University and Lincoln College, Oxford, he came to the Minster after twelve years in charge of the North Riding parish of Holy Trinity, Richmond. Described as 'very effective' by the rural dean in 1847 Birtwhistle had an uphill task to bring his church and parishes under control.[13] Initially he had to contend with neglectful assistant curates, brawling churchwardens, disrespectful parishioners and services considered unworthy of the building.

The senior assistant curate was the Revd James Eyre (1770–1855) who had been appointed in 1814. He was non-resident vicar of North Dalton and carried out few duties at the Minster. In 1850 he left Beverley to live with his son in London where he died five years later without having resigned his curacy. His colleague the Revd William Hildyard (1790–1872) who had been in post almost as long was chaplain to the East Riding House of Correction and had succeeded his old adversary Coltman as non-resident rector of Hammeringham. Although a dedicated teacher, at both the Grammar School and the private school he ran in Minster Moorgate, and an active supporter of the Mechanics' Institute, Hildyard's pastoral care left much to be desired. In 1848 he refused to read the funeral service for an unbaptized child and forbade a local Baptist minister to do so. As well as being accused by the churchwardens of becoming over-zealous in his exaction of marriage and burial fees he was reported to the archbishop and archdeacon in 1851–2 for arriving very late for funerals, for refusing to baptize and to conduct marriage services without having the fee first and for failure to take weekday evening prayers. At the end of 1852 Hildyard was declared insolvent and imprisoned for debt in York castle. On his release he retired to London where, pursued by his creditors, he died almost twenty years later, still drawing his salary as assistant curate.[14]

Although united in their hostility to Hildyard the four churchwardens of St Martin's parish and the four churchwardens of St John's were frequently at odds with each other. On one occasion in the 1830s they fought openly during a service over the right to sit in the churchwardens' pew. Gillyatt Sumner, the indefatigable collector of manuscripts and printed ephemera to whom all East Yorkshire historians owe a great debt, was at the forefront of this and most other disputes. In 1850, when senior churchwarden for St John's, Sumner was fined for breaking fourteen wine glasses in the Minster vestry, which he had once called a 'drinking shop', and for defacing prayer books by blotting out the names of the St Martin's churchwardens. The following year he took a large sledge hammer and broke open the iron poor box in the north aisle of the nave, removed the contents, 'one penny halfpenny' and reduced to firewood the charity board hanging above. This was because the St Martin's wardens would not share the alms with St John's parish.[15]

At this period the conduct of services was also far from ideal. In early March 1851 it was said that the choristers were the worst for many years and that they had been threatened with dismissal if they did not improve. In the light of such problems the attendances recorded at services at the Minster on Sunday 30 March 1851 appear impressive although not as great as at the Wesleyan Methodist chapel in Walkergate. There were 386 adults and 213 Sunday school children at the morning service at the Minster and 492 adults and 236 children at the afternoon service. Many parishioners, however, chose to attend services at the Minster chapel-of-ease of St John, Lairgate, which had a morning congregation of 300 adults and ninety Sunday school children and an evening congregation of 400 adults.

St John's chapel, situated a short distance from the Minster, had been built by public subscription in 1839–40. It was a typical Evangelical proprietary chapel run by trustees and supported by pew rents, with only 300 of the 850 seats free. St John's was for many years the fashionable Anglican church of Beverley particularly whilst the Minster services were in the choir and the church not heated and when the unrestored church of St Mary was said to be terribly damp. The chapel had its heyday during the early part of the twenty-eight year incumbency of the Revd William B. Crickmer, a former missionary in Canada, who was appointed to St John's chapel as an assistant curate of the Minster in 1864. The average Sunday evening attendance in 1865 was nearly 800, far greater than at the Minster or St Mary's. Crickmer was a leading light in the local Orange lodge and the crowds were attracted by the militant Protestantism of his sermons. Birtwhistle's Protestantism was less virulent although he was an early subscriber to the Church Association which was founded in 1865 'to uphold the principles and order of the United Church of England and Ireland, and to counteract the efforts now being made to assimilate the services to those of the Church of Rome'.[16]

As he was initially hindered rather than helped by his assistant curates, Birtwhistle secured funding for two stipendiary curates with whose support he began to improve the life and work of the parishes. He concentrated first on church extension and education. Within St John's parish a chapel-of-ease was built at Tickton in 1844, and by 1851 regular services were being held at private houses at Molescroft and Weel, the school at Aike and at a former Church Methodist chapel at Woodmansey. The last was replaced by a new school which was licensed for worship in 1856. Other church schools were opened at Tickton, and for boys and infants at Beverley. Soon there were seven church schools in the parishes each with a Sunday school attached. Evening classes for young men were started in 1863 and three years later Birtwhistle helped found the Beverley Church Institute which had a library, reading and news rooms and provided lectures in the arts and sciences as well as theology and ecclesiastical government 'as taught by the English Church'. Birtwhistle established a branch of the Church of England Temperance Society and in 1872 opened the British Workman coffee or cocoa house at Potter Hill, Beckside as a temperance venue for working men. Such ventures were supported by the Minster Church Work Association, an elected committee of laymen and church officials, and publicized in the parish magazine begun in 1866. Birtwhistle's achievements were recognized by his appointment as a canon of York Minster in 1867. A year later the living was styled a vicarage for the first time.

It was in the 1860s that special services became a feature of the Minster year and its role as the central church of the region began to be recognized. The annual harvest festival service, first held in October 1863, attracted congregations of up to 1,500 and was attended by the mayor, aldermen and councillors in full regalia. A report of the 1865 service comments on the lighting from the recently installed gas supply, the numerous candles and the coloured Chinese lanterns and the lavish decoration, with flowers, evergreens and sheaves of corn everywhere. In the 1860s and 1870s the Minster was the venue for the annual local festival of the York Diocesan Choral Association, one such gathering being condemned by an ultra-Protestant observer as out of keeping with the wishes of 'good old Mr Simeon'.[17]

At this time all the regular Minster services were held in the choir and with an average congregation of 600-700 it was often overcrowded. Sunday after Sunday men, women and children were reported to be seen sitting on the altar steps and 'rows of the female sex perched up above the reredos'.[18] The services on Sunday were matins at 10.30am, litany at 3pm and evensong at 6.30pm all with a sermon. The protestant tradition of the Minster gave prominence to the word over the sacraments. The number of communion services a year was doubled in the years 1865-68 from twelve to twenty-four, as well as the great festivals, but the sixty-five to seventy regularly communicating at the festivals was far less than a century before. Each weekday there was matins at 7.30am and evensong at 7pm and the litany was said on Wednesdays and Fridays at 11.30am. A Thursday choral evensong was first held in January 1863 but did not become a permanent fixture until October 1876 by which time the music of the Minster and its setting had greatly improved.

With the exception of the construction of clergy and choir vestries under the supervision of the architect J.L. Pearson in 1859 and the regular maintenance of roofs, stonework and windows there was little concern with the Minster fabric during Birtwhistle's incumbency until the mid-1860s. In December 1865 the trustees of the Minster New Fund asked George Gilbert Scott to inspect the Minster and recommend 'what may be necessary to be done'.[19] Scott at that time was overseeing the refitting of the nave of St Mary's Church, Beverley and working at Hull on Holy Trinity and his cousin's church of St Mary, Lowgate. A priority at the Minster was the removal of the dirt and yellow wash that covered the walls and pillars and gave the interior a drab appearance. Under Scott's supervision the whole of the interior stonework was cleaned and repaired in the years 1866-73. Layers of colourwash and the 'accumulated dirt of centuries' were scraped off, the Purbeck marble shafts were repolished and the roof redecorated. Work began at the west end in August 1866, the nave was completed in 1868, the main transepts in 1869-70 and the choir, lesser transepts and retrochoir in 1871-2. The decoration of the roof was 'a reproduction of the ancient painting, so far as the semi-obliterated remains could be any guide'.[20] Most of the painting was carried out by William Padget of Beverley who had repainted the chancel ceiling at St Mary's in 1863. The more elaborate painting at the intersection of the lesser transepts above the sanctuary with its richer mouldings was designed by Scott and executed by Clayton and Bell.

Because of the great success of the temporary use of the nave whilst work was under way in the choir it was decided in 1873 to use it permanently for all but Holy Communion and week-day services. The pews in the lesser transepts and the galleries in the choir aisles were removed and stalls and chairs provided in the nave. The curtains and boarding above the organ screen and the 1820s stonework above the entrances to the choir aisles were removed and for the first time the church was fully heated with stoves placed in the nave and lesser transepts. Changes were made in the sanctuary in 1876–7 when the stone wall was replaced by a brass rail, the wooden sedilia placed in their present position and a marble floor laid. When preparing for this floor workmen discovered a medieval well thirteen feet deep in which there were fragments of richly carved stonework decorated with colour and gilding.

One project, a scheme drawn up in 1875–6 in consultation with Hardmans of Birmingham for filling over forty of the Minster's windows with stained glass depicting scenes from the life of Christ, was fortunately only partially carried out. Hawksmoor's choir screen [41] which had been long out of favour was, however, taken down in October 1875. The statues of St John of Beverley and Athelstan were retained and placed by the south door of the nave on pedestals designed by Scott. The organ was temporarily placed in the north aisle whilst a magnificent oak organ screen was carved by James E. Elwell of Beverley. The screen, which took four years to complete and cost the Minster New Fund over £3,000, was said by Scott's son to be the most graceful work he ever achieved [83]. Neither Scott, who died in 1878, nor Birtwhistle, who died in 1879, lived to see the completion of the organ screen which, with the provision of a brass lectern in Birtwhistle's memory, marked the end of the restoration.

Birtwhistle's immediate successor, the Revd Charles Edward Lamb, was instituted in December 1879 but resigned three months later on accepting the living of St George's, Leeds. In contrast the Revd Henry Edward Nolloth (1846–1929), instituted on 16 May 1880, remained vicar of Beverley Minster for forty-one years. Nolloth, educated at Worcester College, Oxford, had been vicar of Christ Church, Chesham, Buckinghamshire since 1873. He was the son of a naval officer, single and seemingly quite well off. A year after his arrival he married Marian, a daughter of Thomas Crust, town clerk, prominent solicitor and clerk of the Minster Old and New Funds. The Nolloths had no children and they devoted most of their life and much of their fortune to Beverley Minster.

Nolloth, who became rural dean of Beverley in 1888 and canon of York in 1896, gathered round him a team of clerical and lay helpers [33]. In addition to the two permanent assistant curates he usually had two stipendiary curates and a varying number of voluntary and paid lay workers and as he admitted in 1900 'a very large proportion of the stipends [of the curates], as of other clerical and lay help' fell upon him.[21] In 1887 he purchased part of the nearby Old Friary and had it converted into a clergy house for his unmarried curates. In the years up to the First World War the Minster parishes were served by a succession of young university-trained curates, nine of whom had been at Oxford, six at Cambridge and two at Durham. A number had also been to the recently established Evangelical theological colleges of Ridley Hall, Cambridge, and Wycliffe Hall, Oxford. One who stands out is the Revd Reginald Pyne who was at the Minster 1899-1910. Described as 'a man of splendid physical powers ... overflowing with energy' he was renowned for his long walks and still longer cycling tours. He had rowed for Emmanuel College, Cambridge, and possessed two inscribed oars, 'mementoes of two victorious weeks rowing'. Put in charge of the Flemingate area and Woodmansey he tackled his duties 'with energy and decision'.[22] He could be found holding a bible class for boys, assisting at open air services at Beckside attended by 600–700 people, acting as secretary to the Woodmansey vegetable, fruit and flower show, which he founded, or taking nature study classes at Woodmansey school. He was a great organizer, putting together a grand missionary exhibition at the Assembly Rooms in 1901 and the following year running the first nature study confer-

33 (above) A church garden party, possibly the garden bazaar at Norwood House in 1907. Canon Nolloth is on the left and the Revd W.H. Savile, vicar of St Mary's 1905-16, on the right.

34 (above right) Minster Sunday School children processing along Highgate from the Minster, c. 1907.

ence for the East Riding which was attended by 600 delegates. In 1906 he organized the emigration of fifty local men to Canada, accompanying them to Liverpool and visiting them the following summer. Pyne was a man of unquenchable enthusiasm and optimism.

With a band of committed workers Nolloth took up the challenge of coping with his extensive parish. In 1884 in addition to the three or four services at the Minster it was usual for there to be as many as eleven other services held each Sunday at nine venues in the Minster parishes. At Molescroft the mission room was replaced in 1896 by a chapel-of-ease, now St Leonard's church, at Woodmansey services were transferred in 1898 from the National School to the new church of St Peter, and at Tickton the church was thoroughly restored in 1896. Great efforts were also made to extend the church's presence within St Martin's parish. In 1883 Nolloth secured a former Wesleyan mission room at the west end of Keldgate and here were held a ragged Sunday school, a working men's club, a mothers' meeting, a sewing class and regular Sunday evening services for 'those classes especially needing such efforts'.[23] Ten years later this room was replaced by a mission hall and reading room built by Admiral Walker, who also provided a new reading room in Flemingate in 1894. The latter served as a replacement for the British Workman cocoa house, Beckside, which had closed down four years earlier. St John's chapel, Lairgate, was refurbished in 1893 but with the greater part of its pews still rented it continued to be a middle-class preserve and to Nolloth's regret was not a mission church. In 1920, when it was still attracting congregations of up to 200, he declared that St John's had 'outlived its usefulness'.[24]

Education was the foundation of work in the parish for Nolloth as it had been for Coltman and Birtwhistle [34]. Sunday schools flourished with some sixty-two Sunday school teachers in the Minster parishes in 1894 but Nolloth was much concerned about the threatened secularization of the day schools through the imposition of a School Board. To prevent this a new girls' school was built on the north side of the Minster in 1885 and greatly enlarged in 1899. Similarly on the eve of the implementation of the 1902 Education Act a large classroom was added to the boys' school to the south of the Minster. Although adult 'night schools' met with little success, one-off meetings and lectures in the parish room were well attended. Four hundred attended a temperance meeting there early in 1903 and a few weeks later the room was filled for a lecture on 'China and the Chinese' with dissolving views. Unfortunately the supply of gas gave out before all these could be shown. There were numerous parish organizations including a Boys' Brigade formed in 1902 and a branch of the Mothers' Union founded in March 1904.

Parish work was costly and although funds could be raised by events such as the Minster's first recorded 'jumble sale', which was held in April 1903 in aid of Molescroft chapel-of-ease, or the garden bazaar at Norwood House in 1907 [**33**], there was little surplus money in the parish. In 1920 Nolloth commented that although there was very little real poverty in St Martin's it was 'a poor parish, ... the *villa* population is mainly in the parish of St Mary'.[25] There were a few large houses in St Martin's most notably the Hall, Lairgate, the home for over forty years of Captain, later Admiral, Charles Francis Walker (1836-1925) a great benefactor of the Minster parish, not least by the provision of soup kitchens throughout the winter in the mission rooms he had built.

The great commemorative services which were regularly held in the Minster from the later 19th century, such as that for Queen Victoria's Golden Jubilee in 1897 with 3,300 present or that held on her death in 1901 with a congregation of 4,000, reinforced the building's role as the central church of the East Riding [**91**] and prompted thoughts of its elevation to a cathedral and the creation of an Anglican diocese of Beverley. A Roman Catholic diocese of Beverley, covering all Yorkshire, had been established in 1850 but it was divided to become the new dioceses of Leeds and Middlesbrough in 1879. Ten years later, on the appointment of Robert Crosthwaite as the first Anglican suffragan bishop of Beverley, Nolloth reported in the parish magazine that 'the scheme is intended to develop into the formation of a separate diocese with our Minster for its Cathedral'. Nothing more was heard of this scheme and on the retirement of Bishop Crosthwaite in 1923 the suffragan bishopric came to an end but not without the Parochial Church Council proposing yet again that the Minster should be the seat of a new diocese.

The work of Nolloth and his curates had an immediate impact on church attendance. By 1884 the average congregation was between 950 and 1,000, twice the figure of seven years before. Nolloth introduced weekly communion services and there was a consequent rise in communicants. In 1877 there were only ninety communicants at the Minster on Easter day, but there were 256 in 1883, 375 in 1897 and a peak of 514 in 1911. The increased sacramental element in the Minster services did not indicate a radical change in churchmanship on the part of the clergy or the bulk of the parishioners. Nolloth was staunchly Protestant, and as noted in his obituary he 'disliked elaborate ceremonial and did not care for ritual', and although 'courteous towards those who differed from him, he defended his convictions with tenacity and skill'.[26] One who differed from him was the senior churchwarden Lt Col George Cussons, a tannery owner from Keldgate. Cussons, related by marriage to Canon Birtwhistle, was vicar's warden for fifty years and he and his family were Anglo-Catholics. His brother John, chorister, secretary of the Minster Sunday Schools and trustee of the Old Fund, was also secretary and treasurer of the Beverley branch of the English Church Union, the leading Anglo-Catholic organization. When in 1922 the family offered a cross for the communion table in memory of Colonel Cussons it was declined by the newly established Parochial Church Council, being described by one member as 'the thin end of the wedge'. When offered again in 1925 it was accepted on a majority vote.

Because of the recent restoration Canon Nolloth was able to concentrate on beautifying the Minster rather than structural repair. His task could have been different if Caroline Hanks, the young headteacher of Flemingate infants' school, had not spotted a fire on the Minster roof in November 1889 and raised the alarm before it had spread. Some major works were necessary in the following years including extensive repairs to the north tower in 1892, the rebuilding of the embattled parapet between the western towers after it had blown down in a gale just before Christmas 1894 and the securing of the Percy Chapel with iron ties and concrete foundations in 1902, but the emphasis was on the embellishment of the Minster, inside and out. Handsome wrought-iron gates, designed by J. Oldrid Scott and made by William Watson of Landress Lane, were placed at the entrance of the choir in 1890 and four years later the sculptor John Baker of Kennington began replacing the 'debased' early nineteenth-century additions to bosses and capitals of the arcade of the north aisle of the nave. In 1897 the reredos was provided with twelve statues by N. Hitch of Vauxhall and thirty-six mosaic panels by Powell of Whitefriars, under the superintendence of J. L. Pearson [11]. This was paid for by Canon Nolloth in memory of his father. He later paid for the stained glass windows in the lesser transepts, two of the fifteen windows inserted in the Minster in his time.

Controversy surrounded Nolloth's plan to fill the 177 empty niches on the exterior of the Minster with statues which he launched at a conference at the Guildhall in January 1897. Many subscribed for statues but the project, which had great local support, was strongly opposed by the Society for the Protection of Ancient Buildings. Hiatt, the author of the excellent monograph on Beverley Minster in 'Bell's Cathedral Series', also doubted the wisdom of the proposal. Five of the eleven Old Fund Trustees objected to the use of trust funds for the Ketton stone for the statues and the fixing but they were overruled by the Charity Commissioners. The first statue, that of Queen Victoria carved by Robert Smith and paid for by the women of Beverley, was unveiled after the Diamond Jubilee thanksgiving service on 22 June 1897 [35]. Hiatt did not consider the figure 'altogether a success'. In all 105 statues carved by Smith were placed in niches on the exterior in the years 1897–1908. The workmanship of three statues was deemed unsatisfactory, Edward VII on the north tower and St Gregory and Wycliffe on the south tower. These were replaced in 1918–9 by new ones by Hitch who also carved the statue of Queen Elizabeth I on the north tower.[27]

35 Unveiling the statue of Queen Victoria on the north-west tower, 22 June 1897.

Inside the church the mason Percy Baker, son of John Baker, with the help of his son Bryant, carved the twenty-nine statues on the west window and west wall of the nave for the Minster Old Fund in 1909-10 [26]. The Bakers and Elwell and Son also provided bosses for the vaulting that was placed in the westernmost bays of the nave in 1910. An accomplished woodcarver Robert Peter Baker, another son of Percy Baker, was responsible in 1911-13 for forty-four statues placed in the niches over the choir stalls and the smaller figures in the cornices. Finally in 1918 Hitch carved sixteen statuettes for the pillars supporting Elwell's organ screen. Nolloth had provided the organ case.

One of Nolloth's greatest interests was church bells on which he was an authority. He was a principal benefactor of the bells of York Minster and at Beverley he planned, and paid for, two major overhauls of the bells and their fittings by Taylor of Loughborough in 1896 and 1901 [36]. When they were rehung in August 1901, the peal in the north-west tower was increased from eight to the present ten bells, four of which were new and four recast. The other two had been

36 Removal of the Great Bell, recast in 1900, which was replaced by Great John in 1902. After re-tuning the bell went to Downside Abbey.

recast in 1896. In the south-west tower was hung a new Bourdon known as Great John and the two remaining medieval bells, one of which became the prayer bell. New chimes were composed by the organist John Camidge. The hour is struck on Great John and the quarters upon all ten bells in the north-west tower. Another legacy of Canon Nolloth is the wall and iron fence around the churchyard which he paid for in 1905-6 to replace a brick wall 'of squalid ugliness'.[28]

Nolloth resigned in 1921 and moved to Oxford although he retained a close interest in the Minster until his death in 1929. He was succeeded at Beverley by his wife's nephew the Revd William Harrison Rigg. Soon after his appointment Mr Rigg let it be known to the Parochial Church Council that his financial position was very different from that of his predecessor. Nevertheless during Rigg's incumbency the Minster usually had four clergy, a Church Army sister and up to four licensed layreaders and every Sunday services were held at six places of worship in the parish. St John's chapel in Lairgate, now the Memorial Hall, lingered on but there were only about thirty people attending the Sunday evening services there in 1936.

There was a general decline in church attendance and communicants in the inter-war years. Those taking communion at the Minster on Easter day fell from 464 in 1914 to 345 in 1938 and the vicar attributed the neglect in attendance to indifference, the wireless and, in the summer, motoring which 'has done more than anything else towards emptying our churches'.[29] The wireless however filled the church with a 'very large and reverent congregation' on Sunday 15 April 1934 when evensong was broadcast from the Minster. Parish organizations and church-based leisure activities were seen as the answer to indifference. In the later 1920s the Minster parish could boast a Men's Fellowship, Mothers' Union, Minster Dramatic Club, Young People's Fellowship, Girl Guides, Girls' Friendly Society, Rangers, Boys' Brigade, a newly formed Scout troop and a ping pong club. Financial and other support continued to be received from Mrs Nolloth after the canon's death, including the gift of the field called Hallgarth south of the Minster. On her death in April 1935 she bequeathed £1,700 in trust towards the income for a senior curate at the Minster, £300 for the upkeep of the bells and £100 for the care of the churchyard. The greater part of the residue went to Canon Rigg, who soon after resigned and moved to Cornwall where he later became archdeacon of Bodmin.

He was succeeded in 1936 by the Revd Louis J. Baggot whose first year at Beverley was 'a strenuous self-sacrifice after a very pleasant life at Clifton' where he had been vicar and rural dean and lecturer in pastoral and moral theology at the local theological college. He stayed for six years during which the Minster was scaffolded for a year for stone renewal and an annual gift day introduced. Mr Baggot's lasting achievement was the founding of the Friends of Beverley Minster on 1 September 1936. Miss Mary Hewson was appointed secretary and treasurer and within a year there were 223 members. In the early years the Friends contributed to the maintenance of services at the Minster rather than to the fabric and fittings.

The war years were a difficult time with a greatly reduced staff and the need to keep a constant fire watch on the Minster. The Revd Daniel T. Dick who succeeded Mr Baggot in 1942 had only one curate and a lady worker and he found the Minster parish 'an extraordinarily heavy one to work' with 'peculiar problems with regard to administration'.[30] His five years at the Minster saw church attendance at a low point with an average of 50-100 at the Sunday morning service and 100-150 at evensong in 1947. This was barely a fifth of the figures at the end of Canon Nolloth's incumbency and the number of Easter communicants had fallen by half.

A revival began during the incumbency of the Revd Reginald C. Collwyn Hargreaves (1947–58) who had been trained at Cuddesdon College. He showed a great interest in the services, music and fabric of the Minster and enhanced the role of the building as the central church of the East Riding. In 1950 he inaugurated the annual St John of Beverley service and the week-long music festival which for many years followed it. Concerts and recitals became a feature of the Minster year with the annual performance of the *Messiah* by the County Choir as a highlight. The glory of the building was brought to the attention of a wider audience through its prominent role in the 1954 film *Lease of Life*, starring Robert Donat, and by the televising of a special service from the Minster on 6 January 1957.

In 1953–7 the tops of the western towers, which were in a bad state of decay, were restored and the whole interior was cleaned. The work was funded through a restoration appeal masterminded by Mr Hargreaves. With the ordinary maintenance of the fabric costing at least three times the pre-war sum the urgent repairs were beyond the resources of the Old Fund. An appeal for £25,000 was launched to which the Historic Churches Trust contributed £3,000, the largest sum they had yet given to a parish church. The Friends of Beverley Minster donated £550 towards the restoration, marking the commencement of their invaluable support of the fabric. Only twelve members had gathered at the vicarage for the AGM of the Friends in November 1956, when Tom Liddle was appointed the new secretary and treasurer, but at the next AGM held ten months later at the Guildhall under the chairmanship of Lord Hotham seventy members were present.[31] From this point both the membership and funds increased steadily enabling more ambitious projects to be undertaken. These included the interior screen for the Highgate porch in 1964, the movable round altar for the nave in 1970 [13] and a contribution to the new chairs provided in the same year by the Old Fund with the red leather donated by Hodgson's tannery in Flemingate.

Over the past fifty years the care of the Minster has been very much a partnership between the Trustees of the Minster Old Fund, the Friends of Beverley Minster, the Parochial Church Council, clergy, lay staff, churchwardens, architects, craftsmen and generous benefactors. In the late 1950s the Old Fund trustees began a rolling programme of cleaning the exterior of the Minster and repairing the roof and stonework. To complement this the Friends funded the cleaning and redecoration of the interior ceilings and stonework from 1972. The eastern end of the Minster was completed early in 1973 and the great transepts and aisles by 1975 when the project was interrupted by the urgent need for the restoration of the whole building. At the end of 1974 the Trustees, on the advice of the consulting architect, decided that unless a thorough scheme of repair and renewal, both inside and out, was carried out within the next five to ten years the decay to the stonework would be irretrievable. A committee was formed under the presidency of the Earl of Halifax and the chairmanship of Lord Middleton and an appeal for £500,000 was launched on 30 January 1976. Fund raising events included a flower festival in the summer of 1977 which brought in £12,000. Remarkably the target was achieved in less than two years, but inevitably with increased costs and the identification of additional work a second round of fund raising was needed.

Restoration work began early in 1976 when scaffolding was erected at the east end, and except for a fortnight early in 1980, the Minster was not free from scaffolding until the end of 1984. The last phase of the restoration, the bracing of the north transept roof and reglazing of its windows, was completed in 1987. Five years later the trustees began a long term project to replace the lead roof of the aisles and the central tower and west tower roofs. The major task of renewing the roof of the central tower was carried out in 1994–5; at the same time the organ was completely overhauled at a cost of some £200,000. Although it is fortunate that the Old Fund exists to carry out the maintenance of the Minster its finances need to be greatly supplemented if major works are required. It is here that the support of the Friends is so vital. Membership of the Friends exceeded 1,000 for the first time in 1981 and peaked at over 1,400 in 1992–3 after a vigorous membership campaign. Numbers have since declined but a membership of 2,000 is a realizable target early in the new millennium. The annual report of the Friends produced since 1957 is an invaluable source for information on the building and on parish life and worship.

During the past forty years there have been four incumbents: the Revd Ernest Bull 1958–67, Canon Peter Harrison 1968–91, Canon Peter Forster 1991–96, now bishop of Chester, and Canon David Bailey who was instituted in October 1997. Their contributions to the Friends' annual reports record the growth of the parish, the development of worship and the special events and services. These include the visits of the Queen Mother in 1960 and of the Queen and Prince Philip on their jubilee tour in July 1977 and the consecration of the bishops of Selby and Whitby in January 1971. The co-operation recorded between the three Anglican parishes and with churches of other denominations in the town, and the preaching in the Minster by two Roman Catholic bishops, Leeds and Middlesbrough, in 1979 and 1983, is a clear sign that the partisanship recorded in the 19th century has long gone.

Innovations in worship, although frequently leading to increased attendance, have caused most controversy. A family service on the first Sunday of the month was introduced in 1963 and the following year choral communion replaced matins on the third Sunday. The foundations for less formal family worship were laid in the 1970s but it was in the 1990s that the 10.30am parish communion service with special all-age celebrations became the central focus of worship. In Peter Forster's words there was a need for 'a sensitive combination of traditional beliefs and practices, with a modern forward-looking, and to a degree, experimental outlook'.[32] This has allowed for the reintroduction of the Book of Common Prayer for the 8.00am communion service each Sunday. Other developments of the past decade have been the establishment of a parish office with an administrator, the employment of a full-time youth officer and the expansion of the Minster shop.

The challenge of reconciling the Minster's role as a parish church with its position, in scale and function, as the 'cathedral' of the East Riding is as great as ever. But thanks to the dedication of laity and clergy who over the past fifty years have built on the foundations laid in the eras of Canons Birtwhistle and Nolloth, the fabric and life of the Minster at the beginning of the new millennium is as strong as it has ever been.

NOTES

1   HUL, DDMM/2/120, Beverley Minster parish magazine, May 1880. The principal sources for this chapter are the Minster parish magazines from 1872 in the MacMahon deposit in the archives at Hull University (HUL, DDMM/2/120-122), the parish records of the Minster in the care of the East Riding Archives and Records Service (ERAO, PE/129), the visitation returns for 1865-1947 in the Borthwick Institute of Historical Research, University of York (BIHR, Bp. V.), the records of the Minster Old and New Funds which in April 1999 were in the offices of Crust, Todd and Mills, Beverley and the annual reports of the Friends of Beverley Minster.

2   K. A. MacMahon, ed., *Beverley Corporation Minute Books 1707-1835* (YASRS, 122, 1958), p. 105.

3   HUL, DDMM/2/20, copy of Shout's survey, 1812.

4   ERAO, DDBC/23, section K/19.

5   ERAO, PE/129/128, Minster vestry meeting book, 1818-76.

6   I. Hall, 'The first Georgian restoration of Beverley Minster', *The Georgian Group Journal*, 3 (1993), 23-4.

7   MacMahon, *Minute Books*, p. 138.

8   Beverley Library, Gillyat Sumner Scrapbook A.

9   *Speeches of the Rev Joseph Coltman, the Rev John Scott and the Rev John King at a meeting of clergy at Beverley January 1834* (1834), p. 7.

10 *Hull Advertiser*, 6.5.1842.

11 HUL, DDCV/15/228.

12 *Hull Advertiser*, 5.7.1844.

13 BIHR, ER V/AE 1847, Archdeaconry of the East Riding Articles of Enquiry.

14 *Beverley Guardian*, 23.3.1872.

15 *Hull Advertiser*, 22.11.1850.

16 *Report of the Fourth Annual Meeting of the Yorkshire Church Association* (York, 1871), p. 40.

17 *Beverley Guardian*, 19.10.1867; G. P. Brown, *Minster Life* (Beverley, 1979). 'Mr Simeon' refers to the evangelical Anglican, Charles Simeon. The trust he established owned the advowson of Beverley Minster.

18 *Beverley Guardian*, 9.11.1867.

19 Crust, Todd and Mills, minute book of the trustees of the Minster New Fund, 1848-90.

20 *Beverley Guardian*, 6.7.1872.

21 BIHR, Bp. V. 1900/Ret. Beverley Minster.

22 HUL, DDMM/2/122, Minster parish magazine, March 1934.

23 HUL, DDMM/2/120, Minster parish magazine, February 1883.

24 BIHR, Bp. V. 1912-22/Ret. Beverley Minster.

25 *Ibid.*

26 HUL, DDMM/2/122, Minster parish magazine, December 1929.

27 For a detailed account of the statues see E. B. Bull, *The statues of Beverley Minster* (Beverley, 1967).

28 HUL, DDMM/2/122, Minster parish magazine, March 1929.

29 ERAO, PE/129/115, Vicar and churchwardens' meeting minute book, 1898-1913.

30 BIHR, Bp. V. 1946-7/Ret. Beverley Minster.

31 *The Friends of Beverley Minster Annual Report 1956-7* (typescript). Much of the rest of this chapter is drawn from the annual reports of the Friends.

32 *The Friends of Beverley Minster 58th Annual Report, 1993-94*, p. 4.

37 The west front of the Minster.

IVAN HALL

7 · Beverley Minster Observed

The creation of Beverley Minster involved the use of good building materials, carefully handled, a brilliant initial design, and the highest standards of decorative detailing. The thirteenth-century architects did, however, take risks that ultimately threatened the structural stability of much of the church. The thirteenth-century ideal was nonetheless maintained with great sensitivity during the 14th and early 15th centuries without unduly compromising the styles of their own day.

This left the underlying structural crisis unresolved until the early 18th century, when the centre of the church threatened to collapse. The extraordinary restoration that followed undoubtedly saved the Minster, giving it a new lease of life. What follows is an attempt to bring together those factors of design, construction, and decoration that have created the church we now see. Every age, and thus its commentators, has viewed Beverley Minster within its own perspective. Five names represent our particular concerns: Nicholas Hawksmoor (1661–1736), William Thornton (?1670–1721), Thomas Rickman (1776–1841), Sir George Gilbert Scott (1811–1878) and John Bilson (1856–1943). The first two were actively and intimately concerned to save the Minster from collapse and went on dramatically to re-order it. The third undertook a further no less drastic internal rearrangement, as did the fourth, but while Scott successfully corrected those structural weaknesses left untouched by his baroque predecessors, he was perhaps fortunately unable to do much more because of the lack of money. John Bilson, though never an architect to the Minster as such, brought to the history of its fabric intense and critical powers of observation in an attempt to elucidate the church's more than usually complex building history.

The Beverley Minster that so excited Hawksmoor, Thornton, and Timothy Lightoler in the 18th century and Rickman and Hutchinson, Pearson, and Scott during the 19th did so because of its unique aesthetic qualities. Its nearest rival would seem to be Westminster Abbey, but the work at Beverley preceded that in Westminster in each case of similarity. Both have a deceptive sense of unity, despite the fact that significant sections of each were built at different times. The later work acknowledged that of its predecessors whilst carefully avoiding mere duplication. Each architect in turn conscientiously followed the general lines of the earlier work but with clearly altered detail. To give but one example at Beverley: in the angles between the western aisles of the transepts and those of the nave the fourteenth-century architect, probably Oliver de Stainefield, left small portions of the plain thirteenth-century parapet sandwiched between the much richer Decorated ones. The latter were then continued round the eastern arm of the church to suggest a token unity between the old and the new. Such processes gave vitality to the new work because they represented an opportunity, fully taken by those working upon it, to express their personality and the currently prevailing style through new moulding profiles and sculptural enrichment. One can thus admire the 'classical' unity of the whole while being entranced by the subtle changes of the successive building periods.

Beverley Minster has long been recognized as one of the finest Gothic churches in Europe, even during those periods when classical architecture was at the height of fashion. Hence when parts of the Minster seemed to be on the point of collapse, sufficient money was raised not only to restore the building to a structural balance that has proved lasting until the present day, but also to permit a level of internal decoration only exceeded by great schemes such as those for St Paul's. The majority of Nicholas Hawksmoor's rich internal fittings of the 1720s and 1730s were to be destroyed or dispersed by public auction during the successive nineteenth-century campaigns of restoration, but sufficient survive to show the extraordinary care taken during the restoration of the first third of the 18th century.

It is significant that Beverley Minster is still a pilgrimage church, a class of building through which an uplifting of the spirit has always been sought. Regardless of the direction of approach, Beverley Minster can be viewed from afar and seen as a whole, and this initial impression was and is important. In consequence the roof ridges of the nave and choir were carefully brought up to the same level. This sense of high expectation must also be continued when viewed from the middle distance, and in every part subsequently seen by the pilgrim. In practice there has to be a complex mixture of those simple and repetitive elements such as the parapets or pinnacles that provide the vital rhythms that bind the whole structure, together with sufficient small-scale detail to hold the eye at close range. At Westminster Abbey, now the most visited of English pilgrimage churches, this is achieved in part through the visually close spacing of the columns, and the extreme height of the vault (at least by English standards). At Beverley the situation is wholly different because the building is far smaller. Here the primary effects are achieved by an even closer compression of the column spacing, coupled with an extraordinary attention to perspective effects, whether achieved by physical means or by a careful counter-play between highlights and shadows. The early architects of Beverley Minster took what are now known to be unjustifiable risks with the structural stability of the building, particularly by the omission of the flying buttresses needed to support the outward thrusting weight of the high vaults which gave the clerestory an uncluttered appearance, an aesthetic advantage for a comparatively small church.

The history of the successive phases of the building of Beverley Minster has been repeatedly told elsewhere but at least an outline is needed here. The Anglo-Saxon Minster was seriously damaged by fire in 1188 following which a determined attempt was made to restore rather than to rebuild it, but in 1213 a collapse of major parts of the structure brought matters to a head, and a decision was then made to begin anew.[1] As was the custom, work began at the east end and progressed steadily westwards, so that by 1260 the Lady Chapel, lesser eastern transepts, choir, and greater transepts had advanced sufficiently far for that part of the building to be conse-crated. Since at least the 1840s there has been a dispute as to the precise form of the easternmost parts, prompted by the survival of thirteenth-century ornamental stonework within the roof space. It has been argued that the great arch immediately behind the reredos was formed by the opening up of the original east wall. Others have claimed that the junction of choir, transepts, and Lady Chapel was to be crowned by a lantern tower, the lowest parts of which survive above the present vaulting [3].[2]

Beyond dispute, however, is the regular and consistent use of wrought iron tie-bars in an attempt to strengthen and stabilize the structure. They can clearly be seen at clerestory level where they help support the Purbeck marble shafts that frame the window openings [38]. Purbeck marble easily splits into its constituent layers under pressure, the more so when those layers are worked into slender columns set vertically, sometimes one end set upon another. In such cases the ties help prevent these much taller columns from buckling outwards into a potentially dangerous collapse. They are also present at column capital level within the famous double staircase in the north choir aisle [pl. 8]. It is almost certain that the thirteenth-century architect hoped that by a daring use of such bars it would not be necessary to provide flying buttresses externally. There are two reasons for thinking this. Firstly, they are absent from the

38 The choir clerestory (detail), showing the use of wrought iron tie bars. The bottom few dogteeth immediately above the abacus, invisible from below, have been left uncarved.

great north transept and secondly, the late Emil Godfrey discovered, when he was the architect to the Minster, that several of the existing flying buttresses had not been bonded into the wall they were supposed to support. Instead the shallowest of rebates had been made in the wall surface, and in them the upper ends of the flying buttresses had been housed. Presumably these buttresses had been added, perhaps as early as the 13th century, in response to a perceived structural failure. Perhaps there had been some movement following the construction of the choir vaulting, but at a time when there was no comparable failure in the great north transept; for if any failure had been visible there too, it would have been sensible to have added any necessary buttresses at the same time. Centuries later it was the great north transept that threatened to collapse, as the apex of its north wall increasingly overhung the street below until it was nearly four feet out of perpendicular. It may be significant that flying buttresses were not omitted from the fourteenth-century nave. Here there are also iron ties, but now they are to be found concealed within, for example, the thickness of the clerestory walls. The ties here are straight bars, twisted at intervals into short spirals to minimize the risk of the bar being pulled through the wall. Much later still, both the Georgian and Victorian builders inserted a variety of iron wall and roof ties in order to counteract real or potential structural weaknesses. The most notable are the series of cast and wrought iron roof ties devised by Sir George Gilbert Scott as an economical but effective resistance to the unmistakable outward movement of the uppermost parts of the nave walls. These supported the massive brick vault, as well as the barrel-vault-like wooden roof that is closely similar to those at Westminster Abbey. It was standard practice not to construct the vault while there was a risk of settlement. The chosen roof type appeared presentable in the interim between the construction of the roof itself and of the vault below. It should be noted that the thirteenth-century choir vault is of the cheaper, much lighter, locally available chalk.

One might also note the use of lead to anchor the stone or Purbeck marble capitals to their supporting columns, many of them wholly detached from the general walling. Here the masons feared not only a sideways movement of column under capital, but also, because of the weight they might carry, a squeezing out of un-set mortar at the relevant joint. To counteract this, a thin layer of mortar was placed on the upper surface of the column followed next by a thin layer of oyster shell and then a second layer of mortar. Should the capital and the stonework over it exert undue downward pressure, the oyster shell provided a strong enough resistance to prevent a significant loss of mortar. Care was also taken to work a small circular rebate into the top of the column to correspond with a similar hole in the underside of the capital. This was then linked to the outside of the capital by a hole cut on the diagonal and, at the appropriate time, molten lead would be poured via the diagonal hole into the two vertical ones to create a metal plug strong enough to resist any lateral movement of the column shaft. In Victorian practice the oyster shell was replaced by a thin layer of slate.

The attempt to dispense with components as vital as flying buttresses was matched by other if less obvious aesthetic calculations. One of them was the careful attention paid to the play of light and shade, very much a part of the thirteenth-century design process. The use of black Purbeck marble to contrast with the matt pale golden magnesian limestone is one obvious example. Another was the calculated use of the polished surface of the black marble to reflect light. The tallest colonettes in the clerestory were worked as octagons with each facet gently curved so as to reflect the most light and in so doing make those columns seem even more slender. Their number is greatest on the south side of the choir and they are virtually absent in the transepts. The progressive elimination of the Purbeck marble detailing was one of the fourteenth-century changes to the design of the nave.

Then there was the thirteenth-century calculation of perspective effects, a decision that involved an understanding of the functioning of the Minster as a pilgrimage church. Since perspective effects only 'work' from one direction, their use in favour of pilgrims who typically view from the west will correspondingly be to the detriment of the clergy viewing from the choir. This is most easily seen by examining the comparative sizes of the bosses in the high choir vault. These progressively diminish in diameter from west to east, thus apparently lengthening the choir when it is viewed from the nave. Likewise, when west of the crossing, it is possible to see the apex of the great west window, but because that apex is about six feet higher than the general level of the nave vault, it appears cut off when viewed from the choir. In a similar connection one can understand the extraordinary change in design between the upper parts of the arches of the crossing east of the reredos, and the quite different modelling of the supporting piers below. The arches themselves (but not their lower parts) can be seen from the nave, and this close spacing of powerful elements is another device to enhance the perspective effect. Here, in the eastern crossing alone, are there carved capitals at the higher level, in acknowledgement of the nearby shrine of St John. On a lesser scale, the designers knew that any projecting moulding will mask the base of a moulding immediately above it, and so there was no need to carve what the eye could not see. Thus the bottom few dogteeth were not finished off above the abaci at clerestory level in the south transept [38] and other small elements placed at a high level were similarly treated. Such an omission was economical in both time and money, but there is evidence that this was not always the prime consideration. The adjacent vaulting bosses are in fact pendants. The aim was to create a beautiful junction of the vaulting ribs whilst introducing a sculptured boss. The Beverley solution was to hang the thin disk-like boss from a concave stalk. The drop of about eighteen inches is invisible from below.

The Minster, like most of its major contemporaries, presents a skin of ashlar that comprises finely cut, finished and jointed stones outside, with a core of rubble and mortar within. At best there are few through stones, and in most areas none. But where the ashlars are of generous depth in relation to the rubble core, the system is sound when it is well maintained. Each building age has its own favoured size for ashlars. In general terms those of the Norman and Transitional styles, that is of the 11th and 12th centuries, have an outside surface that is approximately square. At Beverley, stones of this period were carefully salvaged and re-used in parts of the thirteenth-century choir. The thirteenth-century builders, however, preferred shallower but longer stones in each course, and their fourteenth- and especially fifteenth-century successors worked with stones that were far larger in surface area but only a few inches thick, as in the zone below the great east window. Those that have been observed during the course of recent restoration have been between five and six inches thick. Thus most of the wall thickness is made up of rubble. These characteristic changes in surface area can easily be seen if one examines either the inside or the outside of the walls, working from the earlier east end to the latest medieval work at the west end. The surface texture also varies from one era to the next. Earlier masonry tends to have a coarser finish while that of eighteenth-century date can have a ribbon of tooling round two or all four sides of each stone, such as can be seen on the north wall of the north transept. One should also note the survival of numerous medieval masons' marks. Two deserve special notice. The spandrels of the north choir arcade have a series of vertical and diagonal marks the full height of the stones. Are they oversized masons' marks, or do they represent the setting out of an unexecuted scheme of decoration? Secondly there is a group of masons' marks in the form of the monogram IR or JR within the arcaded east face of the reredos.[3] Since some are clearly upside down, the carving must have been done in the workshop rather than in situ.

The interior of Beverley Minster gains much of its character through a careful manipulation of vistas, some of which focus upon height, others upon spatial complexity or the play of light and shade. The latter is most noticeable if one stands at the west end of the north nave aisle and looks eastward. The areas of shade, and thus of mystery, are strongest in the north choir aisle especially in the area of the chapter house staircase, but beyond it the extra lighting afforded by the lesser eastern transept appears intensified because of its shadowed foreground. Most of the great cathedral churches of the earlier 13th century made lavish use of Purbeck marble, typically as part of the column shafts. At Lincoln and Salisbury they are detached or nearly so from the lighter coloured limestone central core, while at Westminster Abbey the whole shaft is of Purbeck. There the earlier columns have a large core with four attached shafts, at Salisbury or Lincoln there are eight. At Beverley the columns are composed of a series of lobes compressed together, with the alternate lobes differently detailed. Some are rounded, some obtusely pointed, some keeled and so forth. These variations produce both different combinations of verticals, and contrasting patterns of light and shade. This insistent repetition of verticals, together with the closer than usual spacing of the columns, stress height in a church where the actual height is comparatively low. At Beverley the vault height is approximately sixty-six feet, at Lincoln eighty feet and at York 100 feet. The plan of the quadripartite vaulting is uniform for both nave and aisles, but additionally the high vaults were given carved bosses. Ridge ribs were omitted presumably because their continuous lines would have had the unwanted effect of

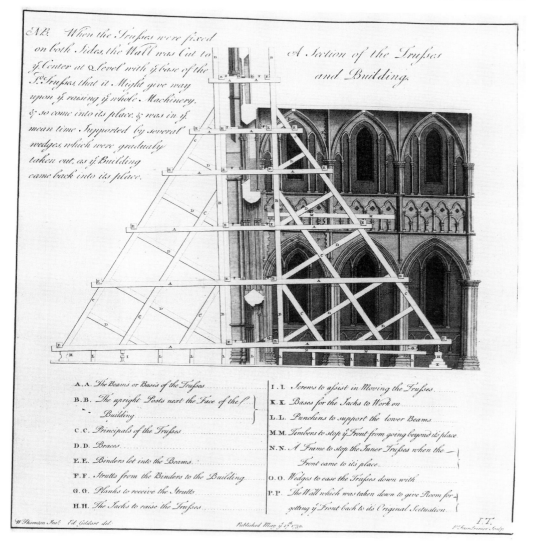

39 Engraving of the scaffolding truss used to push the north wall of the north transept back to the vertical during the eighteenth-century restoration.

diminishing the sense of height by intensifying the forward movement of perspective. The apparent uniformity of the vaults is, however, misleading, for they were not only built at different periods, but of different materials. Those of the choir and south transept are of stone and of the 13th century. That over the nave has webs of brick between the stone ribs, and is probably of the earliest 15th century. It may reflect, through the influence of the Baltic trade, the brick building experience of Northern Germany. The vault over the north transept, discussed in more detail below, is contrived from wood and stucco and dates from the 1720s.

Since too great an appearance of harmony can lead to boredom, the medieval designers of the Minster introduced the occasional note of dissonance within elements such as arcading where wilfully irregular spacing is occasionally noticeable. Thus the wall arcading toward the west end of the north nave aisle has a spacing of 32″ - 32¼″- 28¾″- 26″ whereas its more staid earlier Georgian counterpart in the south nave aisle is strictly regular. A little less obviously the arcading of the east face of the reredos was given arches of 87″- 81¾″ - 86¼″, with, in addition, a difference in overall arch height that is chiefly noticed because of the horizontal string-course immediately above. The eye then picks up the shattered pattern of the carved diaper work and the uneven spacing of the crowning open-work parapet. The changes in design between the beautiful canopies of the two statue niches are much more difficult to detect. Within the arcade, the northernmost blind window tracery has not only the standard quatrefoils, but one with three cusps and then one with only two. A glance at the ridge rib reveals, instead of the expected straight line, one that wavers disconcertingly, almost drunkenly, from north to south. None of these aberrations from normal practice can be attributed to careless workmanship, for here the workmanship is of a brilliance unparalleled elsewhere in the Minster. This can be easily demonstrated, firstly by studying the technical virtuosity displayed in the carving of the successive vaulting bosses [44, 52] and, secondly, by an examination (with the necessary help of a torch) of the sleeve of a small figure on the right hand edge of the capital of the northernmost column. Near the bottom of that sleeve there are twenty minute buttons fastening the opening. For someone in clear command of such levels of skill, the aberrations must surely be intentional rather than accidental. The design has long been attributed to Ivo de Raughton (fl. 1317-39) who became a freeman of York in 1317, and it is possible that the mason's marks in the form IR or JR on the east side of the reredos are his. He was a protégé of William de Melton, archbishop of York from 1317-40, for whom de Raughton carried out the great west window of York Minster (1332–1339) and work at Southwell Minster.

Three-quarters of a century later, but in much the same vein, one might note the variations in design of the groups of three canopies that flank the great west door. Here each is subtly different in design and decoration, with only the innermost being given panels of feigned vaulting as an additional enrichment. One might argue, however, that the different functions of the north and south doorways justified their different treatment, for the first had become the principal entrance on the town side, while the second was a convenient link to the Bedern. Externally only one tower was given a western entrance, an obvious asymmetry, while anyone who studies the uppermost parts of the towers will find numerous differences, especially in the treatment of the upper parts of the buttresses. It is the present writer's view that the successive designers of Beverley Minster, from the 13th century to the 18th century, have pursued a policy of including changes of design that enhance the interest of the building whilst not disturbing its unity. In the thirteenth-century parts these changes were matters of detail: thus the facetted columns of the south choir clerestory are virtually absent from the clerestories of the transepts, and there are changes of profile in the string-course and so forth. Where one might have expected changes of detail, in, for example, the foliaged capitals of the wall arcade, those capitals are singularly uniform in their design. The chief exceptions are a group of capitals on the west wall of the south transept. Their earlier fourteenth-century successors were far bolder, most notably in the asymmetrical design of the Percy tomb where a staircase turret infills the angle between the canopied tomb and the reredos, and in so doing pushes the centre line of that canopy westward.

Their turn-of-the-century successors were more ambivalent, for at aisle level west of the north porch the detail is overtly Perpendicular not Decorated, but the latter style was maintained by the same builders at clerestory level and one must look closely at its parapet to detect the changes in detail there. This same process was continued during the eighteenth-century restoration and refurbishment, but in addition to adopting an admixture of the medieval styles that the various craftsmen found at the Minster, there is an overlay of the contemporary late baroque. In the 19th century it was the wholly baroque elements that were sacrificed first; the remainder survive because, as Gilbert Scott acknowledged, they were too expensive to replace.

Nothing more clearly indicates the gap between the ideal and the practicable than two wholly unrelated elements of the Minster. The first was the desire of the thirteenth-century designer to try to eliminate the use of flying buttresses, an attempt that ultimately proved unsuccessful. The second was the insistence of the architect of the Perpendicular west front on achieving a magnificent great west window despite the fact that its apex was several feet higher than the crown of the nave vault immediately behind it. As a result the last bay of vaulting was left incomplete for many years. Thomas Rickman described the west front as 'by far the finest', set in 'a building much less known than its great value merits it should be.... In this front nothing but one style is seen, – all is harmonious'.[4] The towers as such are quite narrow at their base, though they rise some 200 feet, much the same height as the west towers of Lincoln Cathedral. The twin towers at Beverley differ from most of their great English counterparts in that for much of their height they are joined not only by the west window, and by the continuous deep band of panelling over it, but by what has been dubbed the 'sham gable' and the crowning parapet and tall pinnacles [37]. This type of west front is more frequent in continental Europe and can be seen in great churches as different as Magdeburg or St Wulfram at Abbeville. The pediment-like gable at Beverley and its eastern facing duplicate rise above the ridge of the nave roof and between them support their own shallow pitched roof. Below this is a room whose eastern wall is supported by superimposed arches. The lower one rises above, but does not touch, the crown of the heightened last bay of the nave vault. The upper arch was intended to serve as a relieving arch should the lower one fail. This box of masonry with its arches was intended to restrain any inward movement of the twin towers, which, like the rest of the Minster, are built upon a site with a high water table and possibly upon made up ground. There is thus a valid structural purpose for the 'sham gable', quite apart from the aesthetic aim of uniting the towers into a single grand composition.

Beverley Minster was built to the highest standards of design and decoration, whether viewed from a distance, or close at hand. Its major and minor elements have a classical beauty in their composition, show a fine balance between light and shade, make use of perspective effects, and display a significant variety in detail. Where richness was called for, superlative standards of craftsmanship were forthcoming, most strikingly during the second quarter of the 14th century. The Percy tomb and the adjoining reredos, discussed in more detail in chapters 8 and 9 below, have few equals.

In a building which, at a first view, shows a unity of design, there are in fact several quite separate eras of construction, and when repetition might be expected, there are enough small changes to counteract all feeling of boredom. Indeed, in general terms one might say that nothing on the left equals anything on the right. Anyone who has attempted to measure the components of the Minster will quickly realise its actual irregularity. It is the present writer's view that these subtle differences are intentional rather than accidental, and that they were thought through to achieve their designers' purposes, rather than being the result of a careless approach or an error of alignment. This view runs counter to those nineteenth-century authors who, against the background of the industrial revolution with its emphasis on precision, could not escape from seeking a mechanical regularity of parts. Thus John Bilson, an architect and a long-acknowledged authority on medieval architecture, says that the marked irregularity in the column spacing of the nave was due to the impossibility of laying out 'any through cross lines' when work on the nave was recommenced circa 1308, and that the initial 'error' was compounded as the work proceeded westwards toward the north and south doorways when some correction was undertaken during the final building phase.[5] Moreover, illustrators of Beverley Minster either omitted the irregularities, or sought to correct them. Thomas Rickman omits a small eccentrically placed window in his south elevation of the great transept, while Crowther, in his view of the east side of the reredos, deliberately regularizes its diaper work. In the previous century Nicholas Hawksmoor sought to suggest overtones of classical regularity by suggesting the figure eleven as a significant multiplier in some of the Minster's dimensions.[6] He was not attempting to demonstrate that the Minster was designed upon classical principles of proportion, but he was nevertheless struck by its unity of effect. Equally, as Bilson knew, there were measurable irregularities beneath that palpable sense of unity.

Several possible reasons may be mentioned. Firstly, some contraction in column spacing near the central tower would help the latter's stability. Secondly, it may have been considered advisable to re-use existing foundations where these had proved sound. Thirdly, it was presumably important in a pilgrimage church such as Beverley to maintain the access to the burial place of St John of Beverley for as long as possible, a consideration that might have influenced the survival of an earlier spacing of bays. Fourthly, the typical bay widths of the nave are somewhat less than those in the transepts and choir, a reduction from approximately 140″ to 127″-129″, a contraction that will allow a greater than usual number of bays per given length, thus intensifying the overall perspective effect. There are eleven arches in the nave of Beverley compared to eight in the nave of the much larger minster at York. In diameter the column shaft is roughly half the space between the column bases, whereas in other great churches it can be 1:3½ or 1:4. At Beverley this close spacing has the immediate effect of diverting the eye from the

40 Hawksmoor's dome on the central tower, from Thomas Gent's *History of Rippon* (York, 1733). Gent was an enthusiastic admirer of the dome and the gilt ball and cross surmounting it. The arms in the top left-hand corner, with their rather canine 'beaver', are those of the town of Beverley.

width of the church to its height. Thus if one stands in the centre of the west doorway one cannot see into the aisles beyond the third bay [2], while, if the nave is viewed from the choir through the cusped arch of Scott's screen, it is a vista of column overlapping column. One can only get a full sense of Gothic space by standing in a side aisle close to the central crossing, from where sequences of arches open out in different directions.

It was just here that the greatest potential danger lay. The medieval central tower had developed serious signs of structural stress, and it was presumably to counter these deep-seated cracks that a new much lower vault (generally thought to be of the 15th century) was constructed beneath the lantern, visually cutting it off from the interior. If the tower had collapsed, the adjoining already weakened north transept would almost certainly have been brought down with it. This was the situation by 1700, and the townspeople must have been mindful of the fates of the choir of Howden, and the central tower of Selby.

The corporation of Beverley had the obligation to maintain the structure, but they hesitated to incur the substantial cost and others stepped in to raise the money. An illustrated broadsheet was issued in 1716, perhaps the first of its kind, to aid their public appeal. It was signed by Nicholas Hawksmoor, to whom an appeal for technical help had presumably been made. Hawksmoor was one of the greatest of English eighteenth-century architects, working in a powerfully idiosyncratic style that was to have few parallels either here or on the continent, but in turn he was to be reliant upon the extraordinary skills demonstrated by the carver-architect William Thornton of York, whom Hawksmoor would have met during the design and construction of Castle Howard. A precise distribution of credit between these two very different men is now almost impossible. It is certain, however, that neither could have succeeded without the other. On the one hand we have the inventive genius of Hawksmoor, then at the height of his powers designing his extraordinary group of London churches. He visualized the Minster as a whole. On the other hand we have William Thornton, a joiner-carver by training, who sought and found the necessary technical means to save the fabric of the building itself, before going on to invent an extraordinary intermixture of the classical and Gothic detail that is virtually without English parallel.

There were three obvious courses of action to deal with the impending crisis. One was to demolish the affected parts of the transept and make good thereafter. This would have involved the construction of a new north wall, whether to a new design or a reconstitution of the old one. It could have left the central crossing and tower inadequately supported and would have been expensive. A much cheaper but uglier alternative was to demolish as before, but simply wall up the severed parts to secure them. Thirdly there was Thornton's audacious scheme to push the leaning wall back to the vertical and reconstitute the adjacent internal stonework. Obviously the walling up of the sounder parts prior to the demolition of the defective ones was common to all three schemes, and so that particular cost would not vary. The demolition of the defective parts would in itself be both expensive and dangerous, requiring substantial scaffolding and also incurring the further cost of disposing of very large quantities of rubble of limited value. Thornton's scheme was therefore an ingenious fusion of the practical and the economical. The walling up and the associated scaffolding were unavoidable necessities, as was the removal of the existing roof structure, but the element of demolition of the transept itself was confined to the two bays of stonework immediately adjacent to the north wall. The ashlar work was numbered, carefully taken down piecemeal, and stored ready for re-erection, as were all of the sound or re-usable parts of the roofing. At the same time, both sides of the north wall were cradled in scaffolding, firstly to hold it in position, and then, the most hazardous part, to push the entire wall inwards back to the vertical [39]. Once this had been achieved, the stonework of the demolished bays would be as fully restored to their former appearance as the new conditions would allow. The visible evidence suggests that at least the moulded thirteenth-century masonry was reset, while much of the plain walling was renewed. Some of the necessary additional stone was acquired from the ruins of St Mary's Abbey, York, by royal licence and shipped direct to Beverley.[7] It was, however, considered that the weight of a new stone vault would be unsustainable, and so it was reconstituted in timber and plaster. The curved ribs that support the stucco were built up by lamination rather than using single timbers. The visible underside of the vault was ingeniously reproduced in moulded stucco by the York plasterer Joseph Bagnall and few now realize that the vault is of Georgian not medieval construction. Bagnall's work of 1722-6 was the culmination of the first phase of the Georgian restoration which was one of the most daring achievements of its day.

Not everything was to be so carefully restored, however. The richly carved and canopied monument to the fourth earl of Northumberland was apparently also structurally unsound. The tomb and its chapel had been the last parts of the medieval Minster to be built. The earl was murdered in 1489 and the monument was erected soon thereafter. It was sketched in the mid-seventeenth century for the antiquary William Dugdale, a drawing now in the College of Arms [15].[8] The canopy was demolished and its remains re-dressed for use in masonry repairs to the choir, where fragments, one bearing armorial badges, were discovered some years ago.

The long campaign to raise the necessary money led by the borough's two members of parliament, Sir Michael Warton and Sir Michael Newton, together with John Moyser, proved unexpectedly successful. Hawksmoor's appeal had been for £3,500 but by 1725 a total of £6,132 had been subscribed, offering an opportunity for further building work on the exterior, and a drastic re-ordering of the interior. The central tower was replaced by a new tower and ogival dome designed by Hawksmoor [40].[9] These quickly fell out of favour, but although John Carr of York was asked to suggest an alternative in 1758,[10] nothing was done until 1824 when the dome was demolished.

The south aisle of the nave between the south door and the south-west tower was also substantially reconstituted, again presumably to Hawksmoor's design. The problems presented by the south aisle were partly structural, partly aesthetic. In the reign of Edward VI the charnel house and chapel of St Martin, which had abutted the west end of the south aisle, had been demolished and the scars roughly made good. But the lesser church had served to buttress the greater. There were thus no flying buttresses to the last three bays of the Minster nave and this was a potential but remediable source of weakness. In 1722, 7s 6d was paid for '$2\frac{1}{2}$ days making Centres for Flying Buttresses and Scaffolding', which is probably (although it is not explicitly stated) a reference to this site.[11] Aesthetically, the renovation posed a problem. The medieval masons had cut blind tracery in the Perpendicular style above the south doorway to match that of the contemporary north aisle. The dilemma was whether to repeat that tracery westwards to match that directly opposite in the north nave aisle, which was presumably the intention of the medieval designers, or to go for that external unity so characteristic of the Georgian period. This would involve the reproduction of fourteenth-century detail westward along the remainder of the south aisle. The latter route was chosen and this created the anomaly of Perpendicular tracery above the inside face of the south door and Decorated tracery without. At the same time the wall arcading was wholly renewed, copying much of the Decorated detail found in the arcading east of the south door. The carved label stops are however wholly Georgian in their character and subject matter. This duality of approach was repeated in the design of much of the new Georgian carved woodwork. Thus the Thornton workshop seized upon the gadroon-like decoration of the late twelfth-century font bowl and cleverly incorporated that motif in the lowest part of their astonishing new font cover of 1726, the remainder of which is luxuriantly baroque [10]. The quality of the Thornton firm's hybrid intermixture was recognized during the 19th century when successive architects left it virtually intact, while destroying or dismantling for sale by public auction those fittings that were wholly classical and therefore considered in unpardonably bad taste.

For almost a century, from the 1720s to the 1820s, Beverley Minster possessed more Georgian carved woodwork than any other church except St Paul's Cathedral. Most of it was to be sold off during the successive restorations, the first of them by Rickman and Hutchinson. Until then the Georgian Minster had been two churches separated by a stone choir screen, and Hawksmoor had expensively re-fitted them both. The choir was dominated by a huge Corinthian-columned reredos that rose far higher than the adjoining Percy tomb. Its upper

41 Hawksmoor's choir screen, with William Collins' statues of Athelstan and St John (1781). The screen was taken down in 1875 and the figures moved to their present location by the south door, where Athelstan can be glimpsed in the background to **63**.

42 The early eighteenth-century box pews and galleries in the nave, drawn by Thomas Duncum before they were taken down in 1826.

parts can be glimpsed in John Carter's drawing of the tomb, but its full appearance is not known [55]. The Beverley reredos was of greater complexity than the one Hawksmoor suggested for York minster, which remained unexecuted. It was set off by his London-made wrought iron altar rails, and the boldly geometrical coloured marble pavements with which he filled the choir and presbytery [66]. The choir stalls themselves were carefully repaired and extended, with new bench ends in the style of the old, and over eighty new figures to replace those missing from the underside of the choir stall canopies. Their subject matter, presumably chosen by the Thorntons, is a random admixture of the religious and the secular. Included among the former are the Virgin and Child, St Katherine, St John of Beverley, the four Evangelists, and King David. Prayer is a frequent subject, alongside the seasons, signs of the zodiac, and the social hierarchy from the king to the farm labourer with his flail. The mix is unconventional, skilfully avoiding the more familiar baroque winged cherub, and is in a style wholly different from the baroque of Grinling Gibbons or more light-hearted touch of the rococo. The Thorntons received £9 in part payment for more than eighty heads. Their bench end showing a sphinx beneath the poppyhead was banished for some time by the Victorians but is once again in its rightful place [pl. 12].

The altar rails virtually duplicated those in Hawksmoor's London church of St Mary Woolnoth and were subsequently bought at auction by Henry Ellison who incorporated them into his new staircase at St Mary's Manor, Beverley. (Their successors of the 1820s were to be replaced by Scott and served for many years to ornament the garden of 15 Highgate nearby, only for them to be destroyed during the recent restoration of that house.) This sumptuous re-fitting of the choir was concluded by the provision of a new pair of wrought iron gates to the choir screen. The gates, which resemble a Hawksmoor design for iron gates at All Souls College, Oxford, were later to be re-sited in the north choir aisle. The choir screen itself apparently survived, at least there is no record of its demolition, but the west side was refaced in the later 1720s, with carvings by Mr Pate [41]. The style adopted by Hawksmoor and Pate was partly classical, partly Gothic (in the manner later made famous by Batty Langley), and is clearly related to that of Hawksmoor's contemporary drawings for proposed new work at All Souls, and to his design for the western towers of Westminster Abbey.

The Georgian changes in the appearance of the nave were dramatic. At least five bays in each nave arcade were infilled with galleries which were so contrived as not to touch the medieval walls or piers. In consequence each bay of the gallery was supported on a quartet of Doric columns. Thomas Gent in his History of Ripon says that the new columns resembled those in the church of St Alban in Rome,[12] but this is probably an error and Hawksmoor's source was an antique fragment found at Albano near Rome. He was to use the same model of the Doric order for his huge marble doorcase in the long gallery at Blenheim. Since Hawksmoor never visited Italy he must have gained his knowledge of the Albano example from engravings, possibly one published by John Evelyn.[13] The original model was unfluted but the columns supporting Hawksmoor's galleries have flutes that meet in a point rather than with a flat fillet, a more apt choice because its pronounced verticality flows more easily with the Gothic columns adjacent. The entablature was more conventional, its carved metopes displaying cherub heads alternating with the palms and starry crowns of martyrdom. The gallery fronts themselves were singularly plain, curving back behind each pillar. Thomas Duncum's drawing of 1826 gives no hint of the access staircases whose balusters took the form of fluted miniature Doric columns, or of the gallery seating. He does however show the continuous banks of seating that rose between the Doric columns and the wall arcading [42]. The underside of the gallery was raked to allow the aisles to be lit from the lower parts of the medieval windows. The galleries were sold by public auction and four sets of their columns have been identified. The most completely preserved now stand at the New Hall, Barton upon Humber. The columns themselves were thin shells of oak, concealing the balks of reused timber which provided the actual support. It was the policy of Beverley corporation to appoint a small committee of aldermen or councillors to view a demolition site in order to arrange for the salvage of oak or other re-usable building materials needed for the repair of the Minster or other properties for which they were responsible. A pair of the gallery columns was therefore purchased for re-use within the Guildhall.

The height of the galleries determined that of the great pulpit. This with its tripod base, twin columns, and wide circular tester or sounding board was mounted on sets of brass wheels so that the whole could be trundled to within convenient earshot of the principal members of the congregation. A similar though not identical pulpit was provided for St Alphege, Greenwich, thus establishing that its design was from Hawksmoor, rather than from the Thorntons who carved it. Its most extraordinary feature was the huge very rich vertical scroll surmounted by an eagle, on whose head and outstretched wings Hawksmoor rested the reading desk. The pulpit too was sold by auction but survived into the age of photography [43]. It was said to have been taken to the stables at Nostell Priory, and to have been sought by J.T. Micklethwaite for St John's church, Wakefield, when he was restoring that church. It is not known whether any part of it now survives. The baroque boldness of the pulpit was matched by the towering font cover also carved by the Thorntons. If the lowest stage of the design cleverly echoes the gadrooning of the bowl of the late Norman font, the remainder is an extravagance of cherub heads and scrolls clasping an octagonal core. A flourish of wrought iron was subsequently added to the finial [10].

The font stands close to one of the many doors that were refurbished if not wholly renewed by the Thorntons. All are Gothick, but overlaid by an admixture of contemporary classical detail, some of which corresponds to the Thornton woodwork at Beningborough Hall near York. As a series the Beverley doors are unique and far removed from the standard Georgian door with its graduated raised and fielded panels. The great west door is much the most elaborate [26]. Its upper tracery is based upon that of the fourteenth-century Decorated windows of the side aisles. Beneath this stand four large figures of the Evangelists, in full relief, while their respective symbols stand on similar pedestals in the lower tier of panels, which also contain four small classical heads emblematic of the seasons. The adjacent tracery here however is of a Perpendicular character. Neither Hawksmoor nor Thornton saw any displeasing incongruity in the intermixture of the classical and Gothic, or between the Gothic styles themselves. Hawksmoor's classical mausoleum at Castle Howard contains a burial chamber with a ribbed Gothic vault, while his All Souls College, Oxford has classical interiors within its Gothic walls. The same is true of Thornton whose wayward detail gives such pleasure at Beningborough.

This sense of freedom was to be rejected by the next generation, which took its Gothic more seriously. One may note that Horace Walpole visited Beverley in the 1770s, and that he was among the first to seek a greater authenticity of Gothic detail in his designs for his house at Strawberry Hill. Then followed the antiquarian-painter John Carter (1748-1817) who in his series of paintings illustrating Walpole's Gothic novel *The Castle of Otranto* gives an unmistakable rendering of the Percy tomb.[14] At Beverley itself this rococo phase of the Gothic Revival found a less antiquarian expression in the schemes to replace Hawksmoor's central tower and dome, and in the provision of a new organ. John Carr's proposals for the tower were not accepted, but great care was taken to provide Snetzler's new organ with an appropriately Gothick case. The chosen architect was Timothy Lightoler (1727-69), a Lancashire carver-architect and a man usually unafraid to mix the classical and the Gothick in either his house designs or those for churches. He may have become known in the locality for his work at nearby Burton Constable, for two of his fellow craftsmen at Beverley, William Collins (of London) and Edmund Foster (of Hull) were also being employed by William Constable. At Beverley Collins modelled the Gothic ornament for Foster to carve. Mid nineteenth-century photographs show how the new case towered above the Hawksmoor-Pate screen, filling its wide central bay [**87**]. Fragments of Lightoler's case survive and have been re-set at the extremities of the south choir aisle. On its eastern face, the composition was dominated by a broad cusped arch, perhaps derived from that of the Perpendicular great west door, but ending in a rich finial such as that crowning the Decorated Percy tomb. There were galleries above the return choir stalls, which were arched over to avoid any mutilation of the medieval work. The stylistically mixed Gothick of the organ case also bears some resemblance to two of the engravings for fashionable organ cases in Thomas Chippendale's *The Gentlemen and Cabinet Makers Director* where plate 104 is dated 1760 and plate 106, 1761.

Thereafter, until the 1820s, work on the Minster was chiefly confined to its repair, but in that interval pressure developed to remove the more overtly baroque features, now so hopelessly out of fashion. The immediate result of the Rickman and Hutchinson restoration of the 1820s was to concentrate worship within the eastern half of the church, a process that was to continue under Sir George Gilbert Scott and culminated in one of his last works, the new choir screen (see below).

No contemporary had a better grasp of medieval detail than Rickman, though as an architect he felt obliged to design in the classical manner if the occasion demanded it. Nor was he averse to mutilating medieval work, for in his refitting of the choir at Beverley he removed the backs of the choir stalls so that the occupants of his new seating in the side aisles could see into the chancel. Here, as in his Liverpool churches, Rickman was prepared to use cast iron in a most unmedieval way, for as the late Mr G. P. Brown discovered, the decorative parts of the new bench ends were of cast iron, painted and grained to resemble oak. Just as Hawksmoor had had the able assistance of the Thorntons, so Rickman benefited from the exceptional skills of the carver William Comins. He renewed the whole of the west face of the medieval reredos that had been initially defaced during the Reformation and perhaps further damaged during the erection of Hawksmoor's Corinthian baldachino [**22**]. He was also responsible for the new pulpit for the choir.

In c.1842 George Gilbert Scott's schemes for the Minster were published, but remained

43 The eighteenth-century pulpit, designed by Hawksmoor and carved by the Thorntons. As the photograph shows, it was on wheels and could be moved into position.

unexecuted. They included a massive new stone choir screen of the richest character [**pl. 13**]. Then came the campaign of 1866-80. The existing stone choir screen was wholly demolished on the instructions of Scott, and its remains transported to various gardens in Lincolnshire, where fragments may still be seen, most notably in the Avenue at Healing near Grimsby. It is possible that Scott destroyed not only the undoubtedly Georgian west front of the choir screen but also what may have been medieval work behind it. As well as a new choir screen, Scott's work included new altar rails, the repaving of the sanctuary, and a new organ as well as a series of repairs to the structure. Scott was however hampered by the Minster's loss of income during the great agricultural depression and this resulted in the survival of the remaining Georgian fittings. He did however succeed in securing the removal of all but the tip of the obelisk that had been erected in the north-east transept to the memory of Sir Charles Hotham who was one of the chief promoters of the Hawksmoor restoration [**78**].

The building and restoration of Beverley Minster form a very special chapter in the history of English architecture, for here as perhaps nowhere else one can study a sequence of harmonious changes in which widely separated generations of architects and craftsmen have worked creatively together. No less important is the surprising fact that the original materials which they wrought still largely survive, and it is this combination that gives the Minster its special character.

NOTES

1 The post-1213 rebuilding included partly finished elements from the previous restoration, such as inverted capitals re-used as bases on the north side of the Lady Chapel. The present writer also uncovered carved fragments re-used as rubble infill in the upper parts of the lesser south transept.

2 C. Hiatt, *Beverley Minster; an illustrated history of its history and fabric* (1898), pp. 98-100.

3 Perhaps to be identified with Ivo de Raughton, to whom the design of the reredos has been attributed. In discussion with the present writer, Dr John Harvey would go no further than to say that the connection between the monogram and Raughton was plausible.

4 T. Rickman, *An Attempt to Discriminate the Styles of English Architecture from the Conquest to the Reformation* (1817), p. 105.

5 J. Bilson, 'Beverley Minster', *Architectural Review*, 3 (1898), 252.

6 Nicholas Hawksmoor, Engraved Survey of the West Front of Beverley Minster, dated 27 February 1716.

7 F. Drake, *Eboracum or the History and Antiquities of the City of York* (1736), p. 577.

8 There is another drawing of the tomb in the Bodleian Library, MS York.Top.C.14, f. 258v.

9 K. Downes, *Hawksmoor* (2nd ed., 1979), p. 260.

10 A drawing attributed to Carr by the present writer is in the British Museum, Atlas 1.c.77.

11 ERAO, BC IV/14/1, Minster Account Book 1718-31, *sub* 1722, June 9.

12 T. Gent, *The Antient and Modern History of the Loyal Town of Rippon* (York, 1733), p. 91.

13 J. Evelyn, *A Parallel of the Antient Architecture with the Modern* (1664), pp. 20-1.

14 J. Mordaunt Crook, *John Carter and the Mind of the Gothic Revival*, Society of Antiquaries occasional paper 17 (1995), pl. 10.

NICHOLAS DAWTON

8 · Gothic Sculpture

The fourteenth-century sculpture of Beverley Minster is one of the principal glories of the Decorated style – remarkable both for its high aesthetic quality and for the light it sheds on the history of the building and its people. Despite the inevitable losses of the 16th and 17th centuries, the abundant and varied nature of the sculpture enriching the nave and east end provides a valuable insight into the appearance and character of a great English pilgrimage church in the later middle ages.

Home to St John of Beverley, a saint renowned for his miracle-working powers, Beverley Minster retained its status as one of the most popular pilgrimage centres in the north of England throughout the medieval period. At Beverley, as at York, the saint's tomb was situated at the east end of the nave, while a separate shrine containing his relics stood to the east of the high altar. Little is known of the appearance of the tomb, although its position in the centre of the second bay west of the crossing was established in 1664.[1] The shrine, on the other hand, was described in considerable detail in the contract for its manufacture drawn up in 1292 between the chapter and the London goldsmith, Roger of Farringdon. Five and a half feet long and resplendent with a multitude of gilded images and pinnacled canopies, the new shrine is generally considered to have been finished by 1308, when Archbishop Greenfield dedicated the high altar to St John of Beverley.[2]

THE ARCHITECTURAL CONTEXT

The completion of the new shrine was followed by an ambitious programme of reconstruction and renovation, which saw both the replacement of the twelfth-century nave and the refurbishment of the east end. Work on the new nave is unlikely to have begun before 1308, but may already have been under way in 1311, when John of Boynton was required to pay a fine 'to the new work' at Beverley.[3] Construction was repeatedly interrupted, however, and it was only after a series of campaigns spanning the 14th century that the monumental west front was finally undertaken. The lost heraldic glass from the great west window dates the completion of the façade to the years between 1388 and 1399.[4]

Building began with the eastern bays of the south aisle, but to minimize disruption to the lucrative flow of revenue from pilgrims visiting the tomb of St John in the nave, the old building was left standing for as long as possible. The first campaign was thus limited to the wall of the south aisle, which could be erected without disturbing the wall of the narrower twelfth-century nave. Work on the new wall progressed westward as far as, but excluding, the bay containing the lateral doorway in the south wall.

As in the thirteenth-century work to the east, the inner face of the new aisle wall was enriched with blind arcading. Faithfully reproducing the dog-toothed mouldings of the earlier design, the south aisle dado arcading demonstrates the canons' desire to harmonize the new work with the Early English choir and transepts. In line with the prevailing taste for greater ornamental richness, however, sculptured heads and small figures [16, 45, 46] were introduced to support the label mouldings over the arcading, initiating the decorative scheme pursued throughout the rest of the nave.

44 Gathering acorns. The altar reredos, boss no. 6 (see fig. 2 for a plan and listing of the bosses).

107

This phase of building activity in the south aisle appears to have advanced little further than the aisle wall and exterior buttressing. The remainder of these bays, including both their vaulting and fenestration, belongs to a separate campaign, datable to the 1330s. At this time, the wall of the north nave aisle was erected as far as, but excluding, the north porch - stopping at a point corresponding to that reached by the wall of the south aisle. Only then, it seems, was the old nave demolished. This is suggested by the fact that the bays of the north aisle are slightly shorter than their southern counterparts. The effects of this initial miscalculation were cumulative, with the result that, on reaching the lateral doorways, the two walls were a good two feet out of alignment. Such a discrepancy could hardly have occurred if the old nave were not still standing when the north aisle wall was built.

45   The pedlar in the south aisle.

46   A dragon in the south aisle.

After the demolition of the twelfth-century nave, work on the eastern portion of the new nave was continued, most probably as a series of horizontal layers - the method described by Gervase in his account of the rebuilding of the choir of Canterbury cathedral.[5] Advancing from east to west in this fashion, the two aisles were vaulted as far as the fifth bay from the west. A change in the coursing of the stonework in the spandrels of the nave arcades confirms that construction stopped before it was possible to vault the fourth bay from the west.

The impact of the new campaign is seen most clearly in the six bays of the north aisle, east of the north porch. The niches for statuary on the exterior buttresses have nodding ogee canopies which are clearly more advanced in design than their counterparts on the south, and the windows are filled with a spectacular display of flowing tracery - a form of decoration at which the new architect excelled. The leaf-stem design used for the south aisle windows shows a comparable mastery of curvilinear composition and clearly comes from the compasses of the same architect. Unlike their northern counterparts, the south aisle windows do not course with the masonry of the buttresses outside and evidently date from the later campaign.

At this time, too, the design used for the south aisle dado arcading was superseded by a richer scheme - incorporating crocketed ogee arches, carved cusping and a series of label stops remarkable for their dramatic increase in scale [12]. The south-aisle sculptor is nowhere in evidence and the sculpture in the north aisle is by a new master. Best known for his carvings of musicians [84], this sculptor is referred to throughout as the Clifford Master, after the knight with the arms of Clifford on the Percy tomb, which is also from his hand.[6] In addition to his work in the north aisle, the Clifford Master was responsible for carving capitals for both the north and south nave arcades [47, 48a], demonstrating that it was only at this stage that the eastern bays of the south aisle could have received their vaults. The Clifford Master was also a member of the workshop responsible for the presbytery furnishings, playing a minor role in carving the Percy tomb, whose heraldry precludes a date before 1340. It seems clear, therefore, that the second campaign was marked by the arrival of a new architect and a new team of sculptors, whose activity at Beverley extended from the 1330s into the 1340s.

In order to construct the aisle vaults, the walls of the central vessel of the nave would have to have been erected at least up to the bottom of the triforium storey. This level of the nave, which includes both the arches of the main arcade and the walling in their spandrels, contains two further fields of architectural sculpture. The label mouldings of the arcades are terminated by a series of figures, all of whom represent musicians of one kind or another. Some of these were carved by the Clifford Master, but a greater number, depicting angels playing musical instruments [86], can be attributed to a different sculptor, referred to below as the Angel Master. Another opportunity for sculptural enrichment was provided by the corbels supporting the vault shafts. Set into the spandrels of the nave arcade, just above the level of the angelic orchestra, these were decorated with a mélange of human heads, grotesques and animal subjects. Construction work must have made rapid progress, for stained glass was already being produced for the aisle windows around 1340.[7]

Although the second nave campaign progressed no further than the fifth bay from the west, the revised dado design seen in the eastern bays of the north aisle was retained when the remainder of the nave was tackled in the latter half of the century. This is consistent with the remarkable desire for homogeneity seen throughout the interior of the nave - a reflection of the affection in which the Early English building was held. The result was to line the nave from end to end with a dazzling display of sculpture and arcading, creating a richness of effect commensurate with the high standing of St John of Beverley, and appropriate for a part of the church sanctified by the presence of his tomb.

When building activity resumed, apparently after a break of many years, the atelier responsible for the second campaign had departed. The sculpture decorating the dado arcading of the three westernmost bays of the north aisle [20, 49] is very different in style and was evidently carved by a new group of sculptors. By the time these bays were completed, moreover, building operations would have been in the hands of the architect responsible for the Perpendicular west front, which was not commenced until c. 1380 [37].[8]

Modelled on the earlier west front of York, the Minster's majestic two-tower façade dominates the landscape for miles around. A masterpiece of Perpendicular design, its walls and deeply projecting buttresses were covered with tiers of settings for statuary. Before its imagery was removed - probably during the reign of Edward VI - the west front of the Minster would have constituted one of the most extensive programmes of façade sculpture in the country.

It seems clear, therefore, that the western bays of the high vault could not have been erected before the latter half of the 14th century. This is supported by the label stops of the three westernmost arches of the south nave arcade, two of which depict sword-carrying shawm-players.[9] Possibly representing town waits, these figures are stylistically very different from their counterparts in the eastern nave.[10] To the same sculptor - here called the Bottle-bell Shawm Master - may be attributed the corbel heads supporting the vault shafts above the two shawm-players, which have similar 'baby-faced' heads. Angels with the same type of head occur on the capital of the pier beneath the more westerly shawm-player, which may also be ascribed to this sculptor. The south-east angle of this capital is decorated with a heavily veined kind of foliage unlike any found on the pier capitals east of the north porch. The same style of foliage carving is found on the bosses of the first four bays of the nave vault to the east of the tower bay.[11] The foliage on the bosses of the eastern bays of the high vault is noticeably different - finding close comparisons in the leaves ornamenting the pier capitals of the eastern bays of the nave. This suggests that the nave was vaulted in two campaigns, and that the second of these followed immediately upon the completion of the south aisle.[12] Since none of the figure-sculpture on the north side of the nave can be attributed to the Bottle–bell Shawm Master, it is probable that the western bays of the north aisle were undertaken before their southern counterparts. Indeed, it is possible that the campaign to complete the south aisle and vault the western bays of the nave was left until the façade was sufficiently well advanced to buttress these elements from the west.

Interestingly, the label stops over the three westernmost piers of the north arcade are attributable to the Clifford and Angel Masters, suggesting that a considerable quantity of sculpture for the western bays had already been prepared when the second nave campaign - perhaps still in full swing - was suddenly cut short. The most likely cause of this significant interruption to building operations was the Black Death of 1349. However, it is also possible that the campaign ground to a halt some years earlier for lack of funds, in which case the intervention of the plague would merely have prolonged the delay.

While the second nave campaign was in progress, the canons embarked on an ambitious programme of refurbishment at the east end of the Minster. A magnificent screen [25], consisting of three vaulted bays, was set up across the eastern limit of the presbytery, its richly carved western face functioning as a reredos for the high altar. Resting on the vault behind, and accessed by an integral staircase at the northern end of the structure, was a broad platform which served to support the shrine of St John of Beverley. Raised above the high altar in this manner, the new shrine would have formed a dramatic visual focus for the liturgy in the choir.

As part of the same scheme, a set of intricately carved wooden sedilia was set up along the southern boundary of the sanctuary to accommodate the clergy officiating at services. The installation of the Percy tomb [53] to the north of the high altar completed the new presbytery arrangement. The Percy tomb and altar reredos both incorporate sculpture by the Clifford Master, establishing beyond doubt that the presbytery fittings are contemporary with the second nave campaign. In their combination of figure-sculpture and small-scale architectural ornament, they rank among the most elaborate examples of the Decorated style ever produced. Together with a group of related buildings, tombs and shrines elsewhere in Yorkshire and the north of England, they represent a final flowering of the richly ornamental manner seen in the Lady Chapel of Ely cathedral.

THE SCULPTURE OF THE NAVE

In a manner reminiscent of York, the nave of the Minster was encrusted with a wealth of figure-sculpture and foliage carving. Supporting architectural elements, such as corbels, capitals and label stops, were exploited as fields for carved decoration, giving rise to a colourful display of sculpture deployed at various levels around the building. When still radiant in its original polychromy and gilding, the sculpture would have contributed greatly to the chromatic richness of the interior.

The work of carving this remarkable corpus of sculpture began with the dado arcade in the eastern bays of the south aisle. The label stops are a striking example of the invasion of architectural sculpture by the kind of popular and didactic imagery found in the margins of illuminated manuscripts, in which biblical themes occur side by side with subjects drawn from secular and scientific literature - very much in the spirit of the anecdotal *exempla* used by contemporary preachers to illustrate and enliven their sermons.

47 A couple embracing, north nave arcade. Attributed to the Clifford Master.

The series bears witness to the effects of iconoclasm - missing heads and limbs - while the surface of many of the figures was severely scraped by later restorers, evidently in an attempt to remove the vestiges of painted decoration. Fortunately, however, the carvings are otherwise unrestored.

Ostensibly a group of disparate and unrelated subjects, not all of which can be precisely identified, the series nevertheless expresses through its very heterogeneity the medieval conception of the human condition. Central to this was the belief that mankind had been redeemed through Christ's willingness to sacrifice himself for the sins of humanity. Not until the Crucifixion did it become possible for the souls of mortals to ascend to heaven - a point emphasized by the carving depicting Samson wrestling the lion at the eastern extremity of the series.[13] One of the few specifically biblical subjects in the aisle, Samson and the lion uses the language of Old Testament typology to symbolize the fight between Christ and the Devil that took place at the Harrowing of Hell. At the moment of his death, Christ descended into Limbo, broke open the doors of Hell and overcame Satan, thereby liberating the souls of Adam and the patriarchs of the Old Testament. Thenceforth, a place in paradise became a possibility for the souls of the Christian dead.

In order to reap the rewards of Christ's sacrifice, however, the individual had to avoid the plentiful array of vices which the Devil was wont to place in his path. At York, where the sculpture in the chapter house has much in common with the Beverley south aisle programme, many of the carvings were intended to be read as moral allegories. Here at Beverley, the pedlar [45] at the eastern end of the second bay suggests an analogous concern with virtue and vice.[14] Several misericords, including one at Beverley, illustrate an expanded version of the subject, in which a troupe of monkeys rifles the pedlar's pack and makes free with the contents [76].[15] Typically these include ribbons, combs, hairbrushes and mirrors - all symbols of vanity. The coarse, strongly modelled features of the Beverley pedlar may well have been intended to make a pointed contrast between the physical ugliness of the man and the exotic finery hidden away inside his pack, drawing attention to the absurd futility of human vanity.

Other subjects in the aisle served to warn the faithful in no uncertain terms of the frightening strength of the Devil's army. Among the forces of darkness ranged against mankind are three nasty-looking dragons, seemingly poised in readiness to ensnare the unwary and devour the sinful. One of the best preserved - a lively winged monster with a hairy torso and a long scaly

48 Two of the Minster's fine collection of 'Green Men'. (a) is from the north nave arcade, attributed to Clifford Master. (b) is boss no. 12 from the altar reredos, attributed to the Reredos Master.

tail - is found at the west end of the third bay [**46**].[16] These dragon-like creatures are accompanied by half-human hybrids, such as the bony-backed monster with a cowled human head located at the west end of the sixth bay from the east.[17] Interspersed with these denizens of the demonic underworld are four carvings of musicians, showing a fiddler, a bagpiper, a harpist, and a man in a turban playing the pipe and tabor while nonchalantly carrying a lion over his shoulder.[18]

At the western end of the second bay, and continuing into the eastern end of the next, the moralizing carvings are interrupted by a group of four 'portrait busts'. The series begins with a pair of crowned heads, depicting a queen in a veil and wimple [**16**] and, to her right, a king dressed in a close-fitting tunic buttoned down the front. The head to the queen's left has also been taken for a royal figure, although he is not shown wearing a crown and his headgear resembles the brimless caps worn by academics. The fourth member of the group, looking very distinguished in his fashionable, dome-shaped hat, wears a cloak fastened over his shoulder with a row of large buttons and sports the drooping moustache then in vogue with the noble classes. Differentiated from the other carvings by virtue of their subject matter, format and grouping, the busts seem to constitute a micro-programme of their own.[19]

Often assumed to be purely decorative features, head stops and busts were sometimes used to commemorate important donations towards the cost of construction work. At York Minster, for instance, the south-eastern crossing pier has a bust of Richard II, known to have contributed 100 marks towards the completion of the new choir. The Beverley busts could well have performed a similar function, commemorating members of the laity who had earned themselves a place in the Minster's martyrologium by contributing towards the fabric and estate of the church.

The war with Scotland brought Edward I, Edward II and their French queens to the north of England on numerous occasions. All four visited Beverley and made significant benefactions to the church and shrine, none more generous than that made by Edward I on his victorious return from Scotland in 1296.[20] The town and Minster of Beverley thus had good cause to remember the first two Edwards and their wives, two of whom are almost certainly commemorated by the 'portrait busts' in the south aisle. The virtuous nature of their actions would have been emphasized by the neighbouring subjects devoted to the ongoing struggle between good and evil, implying a duty on the part of the secular world to contribute towards the increase of Christ's Church on earth.

Although not a portrait in the modern sense, the king to the queen's right is smooth-featured and clean-shaven, contrasting in this respect to the figure on her left, whose furrowed brow and prominent beard suggest a man of more mature years. Since work on the south aisle is unlikely to have been commenced before 1308, the youthful appearance of the king's head suggests that it is more likely to represent Edward II (d. 1327), the reigning monarch, than his father, Edward I, who died in 1307. The queen could be either Isabel of France (d. 1358), the consort of Edward II, or Margaret of France (d. 1317), Edward I's second queen.

The moralizing theme of the south aisle label stops was continued in the sculpture decorating the dado arcading of the eastern bays of the north aisle, although in this case the series was fully restored by John Percy Baker during the vicariate of Canon H.E. Nolloth (1880–1921).[21] Six of the label stops are entirely restoration work,[22] while many of the other figures have had their heads, limbs or attributes repaired or replaced.

Carved in the 1330s by a new sculptor - the Clifford Master - the north aisle figures are notable for their significant increase in size, affording an opportunity to realize with greater precision the full horror of the demons and dragons dedicated to the corruption of mankind. One of the most memorable evocations of evil is the gargoyle-like figure at the east end of the third bay.[23] Naked to the waist, he is gripped by a bald-headed devil emerging from his nether regions, who seizes him by the chin and yanks open his mouth. His deformed features and the tufts of hair sprouting from his arms leave no doubt about his demonic nature, while his gaping mouth and protruding tongue suggest that he was intended to symbolize Luxuria, the sin of lust.

No less impressive is the long-eared dragon coiling its bony-backed tail around the neck of the hapless person depicted two stops further to the west [12]. The figure wears the broad-brimmed hat of a pilgrim, while the dragon's tail ends in a second head, a feature associated with the semi-mythical amphisbaena. According to the sixteenth-century writer, Ulysses Aldrovandus, the amphisbaena symbolized the two-faced deceiver whose actions were based entirely on self-interest.[24] In the opinion of the Church authorities, this would have been an apt description of those deceitful pilgrims who arrived at their destinations with bulging purses, intent more on eating, drinking and singing bawdy songs than on the purification of their souls.

In contrast to the overtly moralizing nature of the majority of the carvings in the north aisle, the figures in the three bays east of the north porch mostly depict secular musicians. A treasure trove of information for musicologists, the Minster musicians are also valuable evidence of the form of dress associated with minstrelsy. Some of the musicians - those playing the psaltery and portative organ,[25] for instance - wear a short hooded cape with a long point or cornette hanging down to the shoulders or below. The bagpiper [84] is shown wearing the same garment, but with the hood rolled down to form a thick, cord-like collar around his neck. Other members of the band, such as the guitarist and fiddler, wear a turban-like hat, which may in fact be the same article of dress, rolled up rather than down.[26] The two figures at the west end of the sixth bay have had their attributes renewed, but wear the same kind of hooded cape as the bagpiper, and in all probability formed part of the troupe.[27] The instruments held by the minstrels playing the horn, geminate horn and so–called serpent are also restoration work, but the costume of all three figures corresponds to that of the other musicians, and it is clear from their puffed-out cheeks that they must have been playing wind instruments of some kind.[28] Towards the eastern end of the fifth bay one encounters a female figure, her long tresses tidied away within a hair-net.[29] Her legs are folded behind her in a pose recalling that commonly found in dipictions of Salome, suggesting that she represents a dancer. The tambourine-player in the sixth bay is entirely by Baker, as is the man playing the hurdy-gurdy in the next bay to the east, although both are surrounded by musicians, and there is every reason to suspect that the lost figures were also minstrels.[30]

It thus seems evident that the label stops in the two and a half bays immediately to the east of the north porch were given over entirely to musicians and entertainers. The only other musicians in the north aisle east of this point are the man playing the lute, who is entirely restoration work, and King David playing the harp, who is separated from the other minstrels by the bare-footed cripple at the eastern end of the fourth bay.[31] Within the context of the north aisle, there-fore, the minstrels constitute a localized group, analogous in this respect to the portrait busts at the east end of the south aisle.

As well as documenting the importance of music at Beverley, the Minster musicians draw attention to the diverse and contradictory attitudes with which music and minstrels were regarded. For the secular world, minstrels and entertainers were an indispensible feature of great occasions, such as feasts, weddings and public celebrations. For pilgrims and important lay guests entering by the north porch, the musicians would have constituted a permanent welcoming committee, whose very presence would have emphasized the status of the saint whose house they were visiting. In the eyes of the Church, however, the itinerant minstrel was a marginal figure, whose life-style posed serious ethical questions. The Dominican preacher John Bromyard included minstrels in the Devil's army that ventured forth at Eastertide to undo the good work achieved during Lent with an excess of dancing and merry-making. In this springtime 'congregation of the Devil's parishioners', the piper usurps the bell-ringer's role of calling the faithful to worship.[32] Some of these negative associations of music may well have found expression in those musicians playing instruments associated with dancing, who not infrequently occur in mixed programmes of a broadly moralizing or didactic nature. The bagpiper and the pipe and tabor player in the south aisle, for instance, could well have been intended to represent two of these rabble-rousing agents of evil, intent on leading good men into error.

In the north aisle, however, it is significant that the musicians are not dotted about in this manner, but rather form a cohesive group. And while some visitors may have found their pres-ence inappropriate, their sheer number suggests that they were not intended primarily as examples of worldly temptation or moral turpitude, which would surely have been a case of iconographical overkill. Moreover, in contrast to the pig-faced bagpiper in the south aisle, no attempt has been made to satirize the physiognomies of the north aisle musicians, who have regular features and neutral expressions.

The Church was willing to accept some forms of secular entertainment, and it was not uncommon for minstrels to participate in the processions which took place at Rogationtide and Pentecost.[33] It is known from a transcript of the sixteenth-century ordinances of the confraternity of Beverley minstrels that it had been the time-honoured custom of musicians between the Trent and the Tweed to repair to Beverley at Rogationtide, when the shrine of St John was carried through the town and around the Minster's various daughter chapels. This was also the time when the confraternity elected their alderman and stewards.[34] The minstrels may even have met for this purpose in the porch of the Minster, church porches being frequently used for conducting municipal business and holding elections. However, it is debatable whether this alone would have been sufficient to warrant depicting so many of their number in the north aisle. In order to qualify for representation within an ecclesiastical build-ing it was normal for members of trade guilds to pay for the privilege by donating money towards the fabric. Thus when the nave of the church of St Mary at Beverley had to be rebuilt following the collapse of the crossing tower in 1520, the easternmost pier was paid for by the guild of musicians, five of whom were represented standing on corbels beneath the capital.[35] One imagines that the Minster, too, may have materially benefited from the presence of so many minstrels in the town, and it is by no means inconceivable that the north aisle musicians were intended to commemorate their services to the church.

The capitals of the wall arcading in these bays of the north aisle are decorated with stylized leaf ornament, remarkable for its sense of linear rhythm and subtlety of carving. The same softly undulating style is seen in the foliage on four of the pier capitals at the eastern end of the north nave arcade, populated by figures or animals which can be ascribed to the Clifford Master.[36] Here, as in many of the capitals of the nave arcade, leaf-sculpture alternates with figure subjects which extend the moralizing programme of the carvings in the aisles. A medley of devils, monsters, animals, hybrid creatures and mouth-pulling figures, the capitals of the Minster nave constitute a gallery of the grotesque fit to rival any Romanesque cloister or pilgrimage church.

The theme of Luxuria is handled with captivating wit and sensitivity in the pair of embracing lovers on one of the capitals of the north arcade [47], clearly from the hand of the Clifford Master.[37] While kissing couples are open to more than one interpretation, the moralizing nature of the Beverley lovers is made clear by their ungraceful features and differing facial expressions, the look of determination in the eyes of the left-hand figure contrasting somewhat comically with the far-away gaze of his companion.

On the next capital to the west,[38] staring menacingly into the central nave, is a representation of the Green Man - the name given to a human head which is either composed of leaves, or else surrounded by a garland of foliage sprouting from the mouth, ears or nose. This example, like the many other Green Men and Women at Beverley, belongs to the latter variety. A large undulating leaf emerges from either side of the mouth and spreads out across the flanking areas of the capital. The deep-set eyes, boldly arched eyebrows and broad, smiling lips give the head a decidedly sinister look [48a].

The Minster is especially rich in carvings of the Green Man, although there is currently no consensus of opinion regarding their meaning. Lady Raglan, who first used the term 'Green Man' to describe the theme, identified the carved foliate head with the figure of Jack-in-the-green and his counterparts in European folklore.[39] However, later research has tended to distance the foliate head from folkloric tradition, emphasizing instead the religious significance of the theme. Kathleen Basford, who drew attention to the sources of the image in classical antiquity, suggested that by the 10th century the foliate head had been conscripted into the Christian pantheon of demons.[40] The glowering grin of the Green Man in the nave at Beverley suggests a malevolent nature not far removed from that of his pre-Gothic precursors, and his proximity to another image of Lust - an embracing pair of half-human hybrids on the other side of this capital – suggests that he, too, was in some way a demonic personification of sin and temptation.

In complete contrast to the didactic tone of the sculpture in the aisles, the musicians punctuating the rhythm of the main arcades define the upper level of the nave as a place of unmitigated joy. Some of these are secular minstrels and, on stylistic grounds, can be attributed to the Clifford Master.[41] Others depict music-making angels [86] and were evidently carved by a different sculptor - the Angel Master.[42] Angelic orchestras were rare before the second half of the 13th century, but thereafter became increasingly common as a method of suggesting heaven in manuscript illumination and wallpainting, as well as in architectural sculpture.[43] Angel musicians are often to be found in churches with important shrines, where their main purpose was to signal this fact by symbolizing the state of celestial bliss enjoyed by the soul of the saint whose mortal remains lay within the church. In the Angel Choir at Lincoln, for instance, the point at which the angels associated with the Last Judgement give way to angels playing musical instruments coincides exactly with the presumed site of the shrine of St Hugh. The music-making angels at the Minster could have served a similar function, drawing attention to the heavenly status of St John of Beverley, whose tomb was in the nave, and emphasizing the sanctity of this part of the building.

The distribution pattern of the musicians by the Clifford and Angel Masters at this level has implications for the chronology of construction. The series begins at the east with two pairs of secular minstrels by the Clifford Master.[44] These are followed by three pairs of angel musicians by the Angel Master,[45] suggesting a change in both iconographic plan and personnel. This is supported by an analogous change in authorship evident in both the pier capitals and the heads beneath the corbels supporting the vault shafts. In addition to the four capitals at the eastern end of the north arcade, the Clifford Master was also responsible for two capitals at the eastern end of the south arcade, both of which have figures, animals or monsters carved in his inimitable manner.[46] The next three capitals of the south arcade all feature figures or creatures which are stylistically attributable to the Angel Master.[47] The foliage carving on these capitals is also distinguishable from that ascribed to the Clifford Master, lacking the delicate veining of the latter. Since the same type of leafage occurs on the two capitals immediately to the west of the Clifford Master's capitals in the north arcade,[48] it is reasonable to attribute these, too, to the Angel Master. A similar story is told by the vault-shaft corbels: the Clifford Master carved the easternmost head of the north arcade and the two heads at the eastern end of the south arcade, but all the remaining heads down to those above the seventh pair of piers west of the crossing were carved by the Angel Master.[49] The corollary of this is that the Clifford Master may be presumed to have ceased working on the nave before the erection of the arches joining the second and third pairs of piers west of the crossing. At this stage, no more than three of the twelve aisle bays completed during the second campaign – one on the north and two on the south – could have been vaulted, although capitals for at least three more piers would have already been prepared.

By this time, the north aisle wall must have been substantially complete, since the figures lining the parapet, although weathered, retain sufficient definition to be recognizable as the work of the Clifford Master. The same is true of the large gargoyles projecting from beneath the north aisle buttress niches, which, to judge from what remains, must have been uproarious masterpieces of demonic lewdness and crudity. The figures on the parapet of the south aisle are also badly decayed, but seem nevertheless to be the work of a different sculptor, very possibly the Angel Master. If, as seems likely, all or most of the north aisle wall was already standing when the old nave was demolished, the Clifford Master would have been free to begin work on the altar reredos very soon afterwards.

The date at which the second nave campaign commenced cannot be established with complete precision. On 21 August 1334, William Melton, archbishop of York, instructed his receiver at Beverley to donate twenty marks towards the fabric of the nave and a further ten marks to the fabric of the high altar.[50] New evidence for the date of the nave was published by M.R. Petch in 1981, following the discovery of the name 'Malton', together with a mason's mark in the form of a St Andrew's cross, scratched into the stonework of the north nave aisle.[51] These, Petch argued, could be connected with William of Malton, master mason of Beverley from 1335. Taken together with Melton's donation, this suggests that work on the north aisle wall was under way in the mid-1330s, contemporary with the completion of the upper stage of the west front of York minster. If stained glass was being prepared for the aisle windows around 1340, it is reasonable to assume that by this time the work of vaulting the aisles was already under way. The Clifford Master would no longer have been engaged on the nave, and one assumes that he was already at work on the altar reredos. This should date his work on the nave to the period c. 1330–40.

The plan to surround the interior of the nave with a 'sermon in stone' was continued in the later 14th century, when the three westernmost bays of the north aisle were completed. The figures in the wall arcading of these bays are a remarkable mélange of moralizing subjects, fully consonant with the didactic spirit of their counterparts to the east. Carved by a new team of sculptors, the figures show a greater concern for realistic representation, although in many instances the differences between the two groups of figures are blurred by Baker's extensive restoration work.

Nearly half the figures represent minstrels. The degree to which they were satirized is difficult to assess as most of the heads are restoration work. Diabolical allusions are present in two cases, however, underlining the ambiguous position of musicians in the medieval scheme of things. The man playing the tambourine on the north wall of the tower bay is shown sitting astride a monstrous beast which has its claws firmly locked around his ankles.[52] Another member of the troupe – shown wearing the same hooded garment seen in the Clifford Master's figures - plays merrily on a portative organ, apparently unaware of the fact that he is kneeling on the broad neck of an abominable grotesque head.[53] The bagpiper in the westernmost bay is of particular interest for its stylistic similarity to the figures in the eastern bays of the aisle, and may represent a further example of the use of sculpture prepared during the earlier campaign.[54]

The minstrels are not concentrated in any one bay, and are mostly arranged in pairs. Two such pairs are placed next to figures depicting ladies with lap-dogs [**49**], while a third instance of the latter theme is found at the southern end of the arcading on the west wall of the tower bay.[55] Pets, when they came in for comment, were rarely viewed as a sign of sanctity. In 1387 the bishop of Winchester felt compelled to caution the abbess of Romsey regarding reports that some of her nuns were bringing to church 'birds, rabbits, hounds and such like frivolous things, ... with frequent hindrance to their own psalmody ... and to the grievous peril of their souls'.[56] Not uncommonly found at the feet of effigies commemorating high-born ladies, lap-dogs had an iconographic value insofar as they denoted affluence and social status. For John Bromyard, however, they are the pampered pets of the wealthy, turning up their noses at the daintiest of morsels while the peasantry is condemned to starvation and destitution. Those who care more for their dogs than for the poor, he accuses of breaking Isaiah's injuction, 'Deal thy bread to the hungry', emphasizing that 'the latter does not say - "to the dog" ... but to the poor man'.[57] The preacher's use of 'dog didacticism' to castigate the aristocracy for their lack of charity suggests that the 'lady with the lap-dog' images at Beverley were a conscience-pricking device, intended primarily as an exhortation to alms-giving.

49 A lady and a lap-dog, north aisle. Carved by the Lap-dog Master. The dog's head is restoration work but the lady is original.

The close proximity of these ladies to images of musicians raises the interesting possibility that there may have been a connection between minstrelsy and munificence. Together with lap-dogs and prostitutes, musicians were condemned by Bromyard for their ill-deserved rewards, when the poor of the world petitioned Christ the Judge with the words:

> Oh just Lord, the minstrels and the rich and shameful persons who received from them [their lordly masters] food and robes cried, 'For largesse! For largesse!'; and we, the poor, their subjects and creditors, cried, 'Flee away! Flee away!'; for such help themselves freely as often as they like, they borrow and pay back unwillingly.[58]

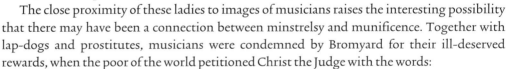

Giving to people such as these, Bromyard emphasized, 'is not largesse, but vice'. Coming at the end of a stream of indictments levelled against the aristocracy, however, this passage was intended primarily as a commentary on the meanness of the ruling classes - forever reluctant to help the poor but never slow to bestow largesse on those who sustained their own pleasures. Giving vent to sentiments akin to those expressed by John Ball in his sermon at Blackheath, he compares the behaviour of the nobility to that of 'sea monsters that give suck to their young'.[59] Like the ladies with their lap-dogs, it may be suggested, the minstrels echo the widespread social discontent that boiled over in the Peasants' Revolt of 1381. Their message, one imagines, was directed mainly at the ears of those more affluent pilgrims visiting the shrine of St John of Beverley, underscoring the ethical and charitable duties that should accompany the possession of power and position.

Other themes of note include a hen-pecked fox at the eastern extremity of the second bay from the west, and, on the next stop to the west, a pair of women - one of whom is shown holding a rosary, while her companion appears to comfort her with a crucifix.[60] The cross is not original, however, and rosaries were sometimes used to imply hypocrisy. Moreover, the two women are bagged up in a winding sheet held by a large, hairy-armed creature - evidently not on their way to heaven!

The fox [21a] is especially interesting as a variant of the 'preaching fox', an image whose broad social appeal stemmed partly from the popular proverb - 'When the fox preaches, beware your geese!' - and partly from a version of the Reynard fable, in which the fox deceives Chantecleer by pretending to be a priest of the 'Order of the Repented'. Preaching foxes occur in many guises: pilgrims, priests, friars, monks, bishops and abbots could all find themselves satirized for hypocrisy in this manner. Since the head of the Beverley fox and the top part of his staff are both replacements, his exact identity is unclear. Kenneth Varty suggested that he may represent the 'pilgrim fox'.[61] However, the side of an elaborate chair is depicted running down the left edge of the carving, suggesting that in this case the fox has assumed the identity of a bishop, standing in front of his throne. Also noteworthy is the fact that none of his 'flock' has fallen asleep - generally the prelude to an unsavoury end. On the contrary, all present are wide awake, and apply themselves to giving the fox a vigorous pecking. This is an unusual feature, and it is tempting to connect the image with the famous confrontation between the canons of Beverley and Archbishop Alexander Neville, as a result of which the Minster clergy effectively went on strike from 1381 to 1388. As Barrie Dobson has pointed out, one of the principal causes of friction was the archbishop's appetite for a greater proportion of the Minster's exploitable clerical wealth.[62]

The social commentary of the label stops is reinforced by the carvings in the cusps of the arcading. Those along the west wall of the tower bay contain an assortment of animals from the Bestiary, the popular medieval book of moralized natural history, which underline the ultimate victory of good over evil. Here one encounters the pelican in her piety - the much favoured allegory of Christ's sacrifice, in which the pelican feeds her young with her own blood.[63] The cusp on the other side of this arch is home to a curious creature with a bumpy back and a long, toothed snout.[64] Shown with a smooth object protruding from its mouth, it represents the Bestiary crocodile swallowing the hydrus. Once inside the belly of the crocodile, the hydrus - a water snake - proceeds to vanquish its assailant by eating its intestines, eventually emerging unharmed. This contest was taken to symbolize Christ's victory over Satan at the Harrowing of Hell, and makes the same point as the carving of Samson wrestling the lion in the south aisle.

The dado sculpture in these bays of the north aisle was not all carved at the same time and includes the work of several different sculptors. The four label stops on the west wall of the tower bay – depicting a figure playing the lute, a fiddler, St George and the dragon and a lady with a lap-dog - have broad-folded, softly modelled draperies and are all clearly from the same hand,[65] here called the Crocodile Master after the above-mentioned Bestiary animal, located in the cusp next to the fiddler. Figures attributable to the same sculptor occur alongside carvings by other sculptors in the arcading lining the north side of all three bays, and include the figures at the beginning and end of each bay.[66] It is reasonable to conclude, therefore, that the activity of the Crocodile Master was coeval with the Perpendicular campaign responsible for erecting the west façade and completing the bays of the north aisle west of the north porch. This should date his figures to the 1380s or early 1390s.

As already mentioned, there is evidence to suggest that the wall arcading of these bays incorporates elements left over from the second nave campaign. However, the style seen in the above-illustrated lady with a lap-dog [49] is unrelated to either group of sculpture. In contrast to the softly modelled draperies of the Crocodile Master's figures, the draperies of the lady are handled in a more staccato manner, falling between her knees in a prominent V-fold. Evidently the work of a different sculptor – here called the Lap-dog Master - the lady finds close stylistic comparisons in the bell-ringer two stops to the east and the harpist in the next bay to the west.[67] These figures by the Lap-dog Master suggest that an abortive attempt to tackle the western bays of the north aisle was made at some time during the period c. 1350–80.

EXTERIOR STATUARY

While most of the statues now decorating the exterior of the west front and towers are modern, put up between 1897 and 1901 to commemorate Queen Victoria's Diamond Jubilee, the knight in armour on the north face of the north tower [23] is medieval. The figure caught the attention of the herald, Sir William Dugdale, on his tour of Yorkshire in 1641, and a drawing of it appears in *Dugdale's Yorkshire Arms*.[68] Then, as now, the knight's jupon was emblazoned with the arms of Percy, as modified by Henry Percy, first earl of Northumberland, following his marriage to Maud Lucy in 1386.[69] Earlier authors identified the knight as Henry's grandson, the second earl (d. 1455), but the redating of the west front strongly suggests that the figure represents the first earl himself - Henry of Lancaster's accomplice in the conspiracy which resulted in the deposition of Richard II in 1399.

The Percies are now best known as lords of Alnwick and earls of Northumberland. However, their connection with Yorkshire was much older, and even after the acquisition of their lands in Northumberland the Percies maintained a strong interest in Yorkshire – Leconfield and Wressle remaining favourite family residences throughout the 15th and 16th centuries.[70]

The Percies' affection for Beverley is reflected most clearly in the remarkable collection of monuments that accumulated around the shrine of St John, turning the east end of the Minster into a veritable family mausoleum. The Percy statue on the north tower would have served as a further public reminder of the family's close ties with the Minster. Situated close to the north porch, it suggests that the earl of Northumberland may have provided significant material assistance in connection with the building campaign at the west end.

Finally, mention should be made of two early fifteenth-century statues, situated in niches on either side of the great east window, datable to the years c. 1416–20.[71] Drawings of both figures were made by Sir William Dugdale's artist in the 17th century.[72] Depicting King Athelstan and St John of Beverley, they afford additional testimony to the wealth of statuary that formerly enriched the exterior of the building.

THE SCULPTURE OF THE ALTAR REREDOS

The altar reredos [25] and Percy tomb [53] constitute the two principal elements in an ambitious programme of refurbishment designed to embellish the presbytery and complement the splendour of the new shrine. With the decoration of these two structures, sculpture at Beverley attained a peak of perfection equal to anything produced in northern Europe during the second quarter of the 14th century. The dignified solemnity of the Percy tomb statues, the grotesque beauty of the reredos bosses and the rhythmic sinuosity of the foliage carving adorning both monuments - all are eloquent testimony to the mastery of three-dimensional expression achieved at the height of this golden age of English sculpture.

The Percy tomb, which is discussed in detail in chapter 9, was carved by a workshop of five sculptors.[73] Two of these also worked on the altar reredos: the Clifford Master – the sculptor responsible for the musicians in the eastern bays of the north nave aisle – and another sculptor, referred to below as the Reredos Master. Clearly close in date to the reredos, the Percy tomb must nevertheless have been begun slightly later, since it was built against the west face of the screen staircase, whose mouldings had to be cut back to accommodate it. The difference in date can only have been minimal, however, and the Percy tomb could well have been commenced while the reredos was still under way.

The armorial shields decorating the arches of the Percy tomb include the quartered form of the royal arms adopted in 1340 by Edward III in order to promote his claim to the French throne. Although the tomb cannot, therefore, have been erected before 1340, it ought to have been in existence by 1347, since its influence can be seen in the sculpture of the tomb of Sir John Harrington at Cartmel (Cumbria), thought to have been begun shortly before his death in that year.[74]

The altar reredos, chronologically sandwiched between the Clifford Master's work in the nave (c. 1330–40) and the Percy tomb (c. 1340–7), can thus reasonably be dated to the late 1330s or early 1340s. It fulfilled the roles which would normally have been served by two separate structures – an altar screen and a shrine base. In the more usual arrangement, the saint's shrine was placed behind the high altar in an enclosed area, the feretory or retrochoir. Open to the faithful on great feast days, the feretory was separated from the presbytery by a screen, thereby reducing the disruption to services caused by the throng of pilgrims visiting the shrine. However, it was also considered important that the shrine could be seen by the priest celebrating mass at the high altar. This was achieved by elevating the shrine on a tall base, thus making it visible from the choir. At Beverley, where there was insufficient space for a feretory, a processional path and an eastern Lady Chapel - each of which would normally have required a separate bay - the solution adopted was to place the shrine on top of a raised platform projecting eastward from the top of the altar screen. The space under the vault, which is open to the east, would have given the faithful a place to pray and an opportunity to touch the hallowed lower storey of the saint's 'house'.

As a backdrop for the high altar, the west face of the reredos would have been the setting for the most important programme of imagery inside the Minster. Regarded as idolatrous by protestant reformers, the sculpture became a prime focus of iconoclasm at the Reformation and, in its present form, the west face of the screen is the product of two nineteenth-century

50 (left) Christ blessing, from the south arch of the Percy tomb, attributed to the Annunciation Master. The carving is probably based on the same design as the figure of Christ in 51.

51 (right) Coronation of the Virgin, boss no. 2 from the altar reredos. Attributed to the Reredos Master.

restorations. As at York, the religious figures were probably removed during the general destruction of altars ordered by the Privy Council after the introduction of the Book of Common Prayer in 1549.[75] In 1663, whatever remained of the medieval reredos was plastered over and inscribed with the words of the Apostles' Creed, the Lord's Prayer and the Ten Commandments.[76] The screen remained in this state until the 18th century, when a massive wooden screen was erected in front of it as part of the programme of restoration carried out between 1716 and 1740.[77]

The Georgian screen was taken down during the campaign to fit up the choir for services in 1824, when the seventeenth-century plaster was also removed - revealing the remnants of the fourteenth-century screen. The projecting parts of the canopy-work had been cut away, but a considerable amount of the original carved stonework remained, described by a contemporary source as 'painted and gilded in the gorgeous style of the earlier ages'.[78] This is confirmed by a number of fragments discovered in 1872–3, reused in a supporting wall beneath the galleries erected in the choir aisles in the 1820s.[79] These fragments, now on display in the south transept, show the west face of the screen to have incorporated a wealth of small-scale figure carving, very much in the spirit of the tomb of St William of York and the shrine of St Werburgh at Chester.

Casts of the surviving fragments were made by William Comins, master mason of the Minster, and used as the basis for a complete re-make of the west face, the intention being 'to restore the ancient Altar Screen to its original form in all its details'.[80] Completed in 1826, the renewed west face comprised an unbroken row of twenty-four canopied niches with bases for standing figures, surmounted by a row of smaller canopied settings. At the end of the 19th century, mosaic panels and statuary were added during the vicariate of Canon H.E. Nolloth [11].[81]

As it stands today, the west face of the altar screen can give no more than the most general impression of its original appearance. However, in view of the spirit of authenticity in which the restoration of 1825–6 was carried out, there is good reason to believe that the overall layout was closely based on the remains of the original screen discovered in 1824. This is supported by a fragment from the west face of the reredos [22] which came to light in the 1990s during the clearance of an outhouse belonging to the former Minster vicarage.[82] Inscribed on the verso: 'This Stone was removed from the old altar Screen in the Minster when the new one was erected A.D. 1825 [–] The Rev Jos Coltman Curate', it shows the battered remains of a miniature buttress rising vertically between a pair of crocketed gables. The stonework on either side of the gables is enriched with rose diaper, while the gables themselves contain two of the most entertaining grotesques in the church. Attributable on stylistic grounds to the Clifford Master, they depict a figure with outlandishly styled facial hair poking out his tongue in an attitude of blasphemous contempt, and a man wearing a pilgrim's hat, whose bloated features and fashionable attire are redolent with satirical implications. Beneath these figures, the surface of the slab is cut back to form a pair of shallow niches – the entire arrangement corresponding closely to that of the renewed west face put up in the early 19th century. The fourteenth-century screen, it seems reasonable to conclude, incorporated an extensive programme of statuary surmounted by elaborate canopies decorated with small-scale figure-carving, the whole being richly painted and gilded.

The east face of the screen [25] is in a much better state of preservation. Accessible images regarded as idolatrous were removed or defaced, but figures depicting 'non-religious' subjects were left untouched, and the remaining medieval sculpture, although stripped of its original polychromy, is otherwise unrestored. As the entrance to the vaulted space beneath the shrine platform - a place associated with miracles of healing - the east face of the reredos came in for special embellishment. Resting on freestanding piers of Purbeck marble, its three arches support a wall covered with carved diaper decoration. In its originally gilded state, this variegated surface would have created a dazzling impression of reflective richness. The cornice above is lined with foliate motifs interspersed with an assortment of figure subjects, including heads, angels and a representation of the Virgin suckling the infant Christ. Supporting the southern end of the cornice is a reclining figure resting his head on his hand and gazing to one side, seemingly expressing resignation at the tedium of his task. At the other end, the cornice rests on the back of a wonderful hybrid creature, composed of the upper body of a man joined to the hind quarters of a winged lion.

The awkward junction between the upper wall of the reredos and the eastern piers of the eastern crossing is disguised, on the left, by a figure playing the bagpipes, and on the right, by a fiddler whose open mouth and farouche expression suggest a ballad of the more bawdy kind [85]. The bagpiper may be attributed on stylistic grounds to the sculptor responsible for the north aisle musicians, although the treatment of the head shows a greater interest in the expressive potential of facial features.[83] In contrast to the more passive look of the north aisle musicians, the puffed-out cheeks and knitted brows of the reredos bagpiper reflect the strenuous physical effort required to play the instrument. The effect of extreme exertion is almost comical, the figure's broad, stumpy nose combining with his swollen cheeks to give him a coarse, pig-like look. Similar features are found in the south aisle bagpiper, and also in the man dicing for Christ's garments on one of the brackets of the Percy tomb [62] – both carved by different sculptors. Given the generally pejorative view of secular music on the part of the Church, this suggests that the treatment of the facial features of the reredos bagpiper may have had negative connotations that went beyond their purely descriptive function.

The fiddler at the northern end of the reredos [85] is by a different sculptor – the Reredos Master - although here again the emphasis appears to be on the negative associations of music. Evidently singing with gusto, the musician is shown with his mouth open in an attitude which focuses attention on his teeth. While it could be argued that this was a natural by-product of the act of vocalizing, the gesture of showing the teeth is especially common in figures symbolizing rudeness, lust or anger. In the case of the reredos musician, this gesture is combined with a heavily furrowed brow and a cross-eyed stare, giving the figure a frighteningly demonic expression. Given the frequent use of musician imagery to allude to the animal passions that music could inspire, it is quite probable that the Beverley fiddler was intended to represent another of those music-making servants of Satan whose corrupting activities were so roundly condemned by contemporary preachers – a true 'demon fiddler' in fact. Located at the margins of the structure, the reredos musicians may thus have had a conscience-pricking role, similar to that of the subjects lining the nave aisles. In the context of medieval notions regarding the sinful origin of physical illness, figures reminding pilgrims of the dangers associated with excessive merry-making would have had a special relevance.

If sin was regarded by many as the chief cause of disease, divine absolution was popularly believed to be the most reliable cure. The relics of the saints were considered especially efficacious in bringing about healing. In part this was a function of the general belief that earnest prayers addressed to the saints in heaven could dispose them to intercede with God on behalf of the suppliant. The granting of divine grace in response to the saint's intercession was the direct 'cause' of the miracle. Relics were not a necessary requirement of this, but it was generally accepted that bodily relics, through their association with the soul of the saint, possessed an intrinsic merit which made them particularly effective in the process of intercession, making them in some sense a direct line of communication between heaven and earth.

The clearest statement of the miracle-working potential of the relics of St John of Beverley would have been the shrine itself. However, the power of saintly intercession would also have found expression in the statuary associated with the reredos. The present statues are modern

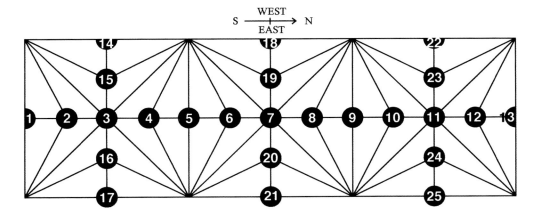

fig. 2   Bosses in the vault beneath the shrine platform of the altar reredos.

Identification of subjects:

1 Figure wearing a dome-shaped hat	9 Green Man biting vault rib	17 Tongue-poking head
2 Coronation of the Virgin	10 Foliage	18 Grotesque head
3 Foliage	11 Foliage	19 Foliage and rosettes
4 Foliage	12 Green Man	20 Bird, bat and cow
5 Green Man biting vault rib	13 Foliage	21 Foliage and flowers
6 Gathering acorns	14 Foliage	22 Lion's head
7 Foliage	15 Tongue-poking head, wearing a cowl	23 Angel with horn
8 Foliage	16 Winged dragon	24 Foliage
		25 Foliage

but St John of Beverley appears with King Athelstan (924–39) on the bracket for a statue on the north face of the screen staircase [**pl. 7**], while a figure of the Virgin almost certainly stood in the niche over the southern pier of the eastern face of the reredos. This is suggested by the carvings supporting the miniature buttresses on either side of the niche, which depict the Legend of Theophilus - one of the most widely represented of the miracles of the Virgin. Theophilus, steward of the church of Ada in Cilicia, signed an agreement with the Devil in order to gain professional advancement, and as a result secured his appointment to the bishopric. Later, however, gripped by remorse at the gravity of his crime, he prayed for forgiveness to the Virgin, who intervened on his behalf and wrested the contract from the Devil.[84] This legend, a fore-runner of the Faust story, highlights the ability of the Virgin to secure absolution for repentant sinners, no matter how serious their offence. Surmounted by their spectacular openwork or traceried canopies, the statues on the east face of the reredos would have given the programme a focus, providing pilgrims with a message of hope to counterbalance the concern with sin seen in so much of the surviving sculpture at the Minster.

Only the most illustrious visitors to Beverley would have had the privilege of ascending the spiral staircase that led to the platform supporting the shrine. For the majority of the faithful, the vaulted space beneath the platform was the closest they could expect to come to the shrine. On approaching this area and raising their eyes towards the vault, their gaze would have been met with a series of twenty-five bosses, depicting subjects which extend the themes of sin and salvation seen in the sculpture on the eastern face of the reredos. Carved by both the Clifford and Reredos Masters, the reredos bosses are masterpieces of English boss sculpture, remarkable both for the excellence of their design and the variety of their subject matter.

The Coronation of the Virgin [**51**], represented on boss no. 2 in the southern bay of the vault [fig. 2], is central to the overall significance of the programme. In contrast to ordinary mortals, whose souls alone could make the journey to heaven in the period of time preceding the Last Judgement, the Virgin was considered to have ascended to heaven in bodily form. The image of the Coronation of the Virgin - in part derived from a mariological interpretation of the Song of Songs - reflects her exalted position in the heavenly hierarchy. Her ability to intercede on behalf of sinners was closely connected with her corporeal presence in heaven. For Amadeus of Lausanne (d. 1159), for instance, the bodily nature of the Virgin's celestial existence gave special force to her entreaties on behalf of the spiritual salvation and physical health of mortals. Thanks to her prayers, not only are sinners pardoned, but the blind, lame and insane recover their powers of sight, mobility and reason.[85] In the present context, the Coronation of the Virgin may be said to affirm the power of the Virgin to intercede on behalf of the sick, and, by implication, to emphasize the basic importance of penitence and prayer in the process of miraculous healing.

The struggle between Christ and the Devil for the souls of men and women is succinctly symbolized by boss no. 6 [44], in which a figure with a basket is shown climbing through the branches of an oak tree, collecting acorns. Another figure, evidently standing on the ground, tries to dislodge the acorns by taking swipes at them with a long club. This recalls the scene commonly used to represent November in cycles depicting the occupations of the months, in which the acorns that fall to the ground are gobbled up by hungry pigs. However, this is no ordinary tree, for perched among its branches is a large dove, symbolizing Christ or the Holy Spirit.[86] Interpreted in this way, the tree becomes a symbol for the Church of Christ, with the souls of the faithful represented as acorns. The man climbing through the tree, his face framed by an arc of curls recalling the angels of the Percy tomb, gathers these souls into his basket, much as the angels on the tomb bear aloft the soul of the deceased in a napkin [53]. The man with the club is very different in appearance, his frowning expression leaving no doubt as to his evil intent. The implication is that the acorns dislodged from the tree will be eaten by pigs - a gruesome reminder of the fate awaiting those unable to resist the temptations of the world.

The virulent, ever-present power of evil is a theme that runs through many of the reredos bosses, where one finds a mixed collection of subjects, including tongue-poking heads, dragons, demonic animals and Green Men. Boss no. 16 [52] shows a winged dragon perched in a fruiting tree, biting into the stem with its sharply pointed teeth. The dragon has the knotted tail of the salamander, whose various characteristics are mentioned in the Bestiary.[87] Reputed to have the most venomous bite of all creatures, the salamander was held responsible for climbing through apple trees and poisoning the fruit.

The relevance of this subject to its location turns on the thaumaturgical function of relics and the medieval belief that illness was the consequence of sin. Many of the people visiting the shrine would have been suffering from diseases and conditions which they believed were either punishments from God or brought on through possession. Sin, it was thought, delivered the person's soul into the hands of the Devil, enabling evil spirits to take up residence in his body. Gluttony, for instance, enabled demons to enter and dwell in the body of the glutton. Frequently choosing to occupy the bowels and stomach cavity, they were popularly regarded as a cause of flatulence. The power of sin to 'poison the system', it may be suggested, is paralleled in the way in which the venomous bite of the dragon poisons the fruit on the tree.

In their haunting beauty and aggressive malevolence, the reredos Green Men rank among the most memorable examples of the theme to survive from the Middle Ages. The emphatically furrowed eyebrows, glaring eyes, gaping mouth and bared teeth of the head on boss no. 12 [48b] give the figure a chillingly diabolical expression, revealing the sentiment of horror that lay hidden beneath the fantastic flights of Decorated Gothic. The reason for their presence in such close proximity to the shrine would appear analogous to the use of gargoyles outside the building: they symbolize the power of the saint to drive out the demons that caused illness and death.

The two main sculptors responsible for the altar reredos had very different personal styles. The drapery of the figures attributed to the Clifford Master tends to flow smoothly around the figure, without sharp folds. The drapery of the figures ascribed to the Reredos Master [85], on the other hand, is more angular in treatment, behaving more like real material and responding more subtly to the underlying form of the body.

The heads of the Clifford Master's figures [84] are distinguished by their ovoid regularity of form, and bold, strongly modelled features. Hair is frequently treated as a flat, almost depthless layer, inscribed with a pattern of parallel incisions whose unbroken linearity emphasizes the curvature of the crown of the head. Eyes are outlined with graphic precision, their elongated, leaf-shape form adding to the mask-like appearance of the face as a whole.

The Reredos Master's heads [48b, 85] are very different, being more finely drawn and more confident in their use of undercutting to produce a richer range of effects. Hair, for instance, breaks free from the surface of the head, forming elaborate arrangements of intricately modelled curls and ringlets. Facial features are more naturalistically proportioned and show greater subtlety of modelling. And whereas the heads of the Clifford Master's figures tend to be neutral in expression, the Reredos Master's heads demonstrate a particular interest in the use of facial expression to portray extremes of emotion.

While the artistic background of the Clifford Master remains to be traced, the Reredos Master can be shown to have worked at several locations in Yorkshire and Lincolnshire. He may be identified as one of the sculptors responsible for completing the new choir of Selby Abbey in the years around 1330. Here, in a manner reminiscent of the exterior parapet of the Minster nave, figures were placed along the parapet of the clerestory passage inside the choir.[88] The two figures on the south side of the westernmost bay, together with their two counterparts opposite, have the thick limbs and stocky proportions of the Beverley fiddler [85], and can with confidence be attributed to the Reredos Master. The Reredos Master also played a leading role in

52 A dragon biting at the tree of life, boss no. 16 from the altar reredos.

carving the tomb of St William of York, the richly decorated cenotaph erected in the nave of York Minster around 1330 to mark the site of the tomb of William Fitz Herbert, the twelfth-century archbishop of York canonized in 1227.[89] A similar style, rendered less distinct by the effects of weathering and restoration, can be seen in some of the archivolt figures surrounding the centre portal at York, which may also be from his hand. Already a well-established figure in Yorkshire when he joined the Beverley workshop, the Reredos Master appears to have origi-nated in the Lincolnshire area. His distinctive style of carving recalls that found in the statue of a female saint in St Andrew's church, Pickworth, dated to c. 1320 and related to a group of sculp-ture in Lincolnshire by Veronica Sekules.[90] An early example of this elegant style are the statues of Eleanor of Castile, Edward I's queen, on the Geddington cross. Like the cloister bosses in Lincoln cathedral – which offer further comparisons with the work of the Reredos Master – they show an awareness of artistic developments in northern France and Picardy.[91]

The sculpture of the nave and altar reredos testifies to the strength, variety and uniqueness of English sculpture during the remarkable flowering of creative activity that took place in the years preceding the Black Death. Imbued with a robust sense of humour and reflecting the concerns of contemporaries for their physical health and spiritual well-being, it epitomizes the role of medieval sculpture as a public art form, capable of giving expression to many of the central fears, beliefs and aspirations of the age.

NOTES

1 J. Bilson, 'Beverley Minster', *Architectural Review*, 3 (1898), 198.

2 Leach, *Memorials*, ii, pp. xxxiii, 299-300.

3 W. Brown and A. Thompson, eds, *Register of William Greenfield*, iii (Surtees Society, 151, 1936), p. 203.

4 J. Bilson, 'Beverley Minster: Part Two', *Architectural Review*, 3 (1898), 250–9; N. Coldstream, 'York Minster and the Decorated Style in Yorkshire', *YAJ*, 52 (1980), 102; D. O'Connor, 'The Medieval Stained Glass of Beverley Minster', in C. Wilson, ed., *Medieval Art and Architecture in the East Riding of Yorkshire* (British Archaeological Association Conference Transactions, 9, 1989), pp. 72–3.

5 R. Willis, *Architectural History of some English Cathedrals* (2 vols, Chicheley, 1972), i, pp. 48–62.

6 N. Dawton, 'The Percy Tomb Workshop', in C. Wilson, ed., *Medieval Art and Architecture in the East Riding*, p. 127.

7 O'Connor, 'Medieval Glass', pp. 68–71.

8 C. Wilson, *The Gothic Cathedral: the architecture of the great church* (1990), p. 216.

9 Located above SP 8 & 9. The piers of the north and south nave arcades are here referred to as NP and SP respectively, and numbered from east to west, beginning with NP 1 and SP 1, the first pair of piers west of the crossing.

10 G. & J. Montagu, 'Beverley Minster reconsidered', *Early Music*, 6 (1978), pls 26, 46.

11 NV 7–10. The bays of the nave vault are numbered 1 to 11, beginning with NV 1, the first bay of the main vault west of the crossing.

12 The sentimentalized figures decorating the dado arcading of the western bays of the south aisle are not medieval. They date from the extensive campaign of restoration and refurbishment carried out in the 18th century. See chapter 7 above and G. Cobb, *English Cathedrals: the forgotten centuries* (1980), p. 57 n. 18.

13 SA bay 1, no. 1. In the numbering system used to locate the sculpture in the aisles, the bays are numbered from east to west, beginning at the junction of the aisle wall with the main transept. Bays of the south aisle are prefixed with SA, bays of the north aisle with NA. The label stops in each bay are numbered 1 to 6, again proceeding from east to west.

14 SA bay 2, no. 1.

15 C. Grössinger, *The World Upside-Down: English misericords* (1997), pp. 101–2, and see chapter 10, below, for the Beverley example.

16 SA bay 3, no. 6.

17 SA bay 6, no. 6.

18 SA bay 1, nos 5 & 6; SA bay 4, no. 1; SA bay 5, no. 1.

19 SA bay 2, nos 4, 5 & 6; SA bay 3, no. 1. See B. Allsopp, 'A Note on the Arcading and Sculpture in the South Aisle of Beverley Minster', *Architectural History*, 2 (1959), figs 5–8.

20 Leach, *Memorials*, i, pp. xxviii, lxxxviii–lxxxix, xci–xcii, 17, 21–2, 72, 294–5, 362, 364, ii, pp. 196–7.

21 Montagu & Montagu, 'Beverley Minster reconsidered', 402.

22 NA bay 2, nos 3 & 5; NA bay 3, no. 5; NA bay 4, no. 2; NA bay 5, no. 5; NA bay 6, no. 2.

23 NA bay 3, no. 1.

24 G. Druce, 'The Amphisbaena and its Connexions in Ecclesiastical Art and Architecture', *Archaeological Journal*, 67 (1910), 299–300.

25 NA bay 5, no. 3; NA bay 4, no. 4. The former's hands and arms, and the latter's left foot, are modern.

26 NA bay 6, no. 3; NA bay 5, no. 4. The guitarist's arms, left hand and left foot are restoration work, as are the fiddler's right forearm and bow.

27 NA bay 6, nos 5 & 6. The brazier held by the former, and the baton held by the latter, are both restoration work.

28 NA bay 6, no. 1; NA bay 5, no. 6; NA bay 4, no. 6. The serpent-player's hands are also modern, as are the horn-player's left hand, right arm and left foot, and both arms of the man playing the geminate horn.

29 NA bay 5, no. 2. Both hands and forearms have been renewed.

30 NA bay 6, no. 2; NA bay 5, no. 5.

31 NA bay 3, nos. 5–6; NA bay 4, no. 1. The upper part of David's harp and his hands and right forearm have all been replaced, probably before Baker's time, but the cloth 'bucket' at the base of the instrument is medieval; Montagu & Montagu, 'Beverley Minster reconsidered', 408.

32 G. Owst, *Literature and Pulpit in Medieval England* (Oxford, 1961), pp. 393–4.

33 R. Hutton, *The Stations of the Sun: a history of the ritual year in Britain* (Oxford, 1997), pp. 277–87.

34 BL, Lansdowne MS 896, 'Warburton's Collections for Yorkshire', VIII, f. 153.

35 R. Hope, 'Notes on the Minstrels' Pillar, St Mary's Church, Beverley', *TERAS*, 3 (1895), 67–8; J. Bilson, 'St Mary's Church, Beverley', *YAJ*, 25 (1920), 414–9.

36 Those above NP 2, 3, 4 & 5.

37 Located above NP 3.

38 Located above NP 4.

39 Lady Raglan, 'The Green Man in Church Architecture', *Folklore*, 50 (1939), 45–57.

40 K. Basford, *The Green Man* (Ipswich, 1978), pp. 12, 24 n. 35.

41 Those above NP 2, SP 2, NP 3, SP 3, NP 7, NP 9 & NP 10.

42 Those above NP 4, SP 4, NP 5, SP 5, NP 6, SP 6, SP 7 & NP 8.

43 R. Hammerstein, *Die Musik der Engel: Untersuchungen zur Musikanschauung des Mittelalters* (Bern and Munich, 1962), pp. 195–238.

44 Those above NP 2, SP 2, NP 3 & SP 3.

45   Those above NP 4, SP 4, NP 5, SP 5, NP 6 & SP 6.

46   Those above SP 2 & 3.

47   Those above SP 4, 5 & 6.

48   Those above NP 6 & 7.

49   Those above NP 3–7 and SP 4–7.

50   J. Bilson, 'Beverley Minster: some stray notes', *YAJ*, 24 (1917), 221–2 n. 6.

51   M. Petch, 'William de Malton, Master Mason', *YAJ*, 53 (1981), 37, 39.

52   NA bay 10, no. 6. The instrument is restoration work, as are the figure's left hand and right forearm.

53   NA bay 10, no. 2. The portative organ is mostly modern, although the bellows seem original.

54   NA bay 10, no. 5. The figure's hands, the chanter and the blowpipe have all been renewed. See also the tongue-poking head in the arch cusp to the right of the minstrel playing the pipe and tabor, NA bay 8, no. 6.

55   NA bay 8, no. 4; NA bay 10, no. 4; NA bay 10 (west wall), no. 4. The label stops on the west wall of bay 10 are numbered 1 to 4, reading from north to south. The front half of the dog held by the lady in bay 8 has been renewed, as have both the dog and the head of the lady on the north wall of the tower bay. The head of the lady on the west wall of the tower bay is also restoration work.

56   E. Power, *Medieval English Nunneries* (1964), pp. 306–7.

57   Owst, *Literature and Pulpit*, pp. 327–8.

58   *Ibid.*, pp. 10–13, 300–1.

59   *Ibid.*, p. 328.

60   NA bay 9, nos 1 & 2. The fox's head and the upper section of his staff are replacements, as are the goat-like head of the creature on the neighbouring label stop, together with the left-hand lady's right arm and her companion's left arm.

61   K. Varty, *Reynard, Renart, Reinaert and Other Foxes in Medieval England: the iconographic evidence* (Amsterdam, 1999), pp. 55–60, 63, 65.

62   R.B. Dobson, 'Beverley in Conflict: Archbishop Alexander Neville and the Minster Clergy, 1381–8', in C. Wilson, ed., *Medieval Art and Architecture in the East Riding*, pp. 149–58.

63   NA bay 10 (west wall), cusp to right of no. 3.

64   NA bay 10 (west wall), cusp to left of no. 2.

65   NA bay 10 (west wall), nos 1–4 respectively. The lutenist's head and right arm are restoration work, as are the fiddler's head, right arm and bow. Much of the body of the latter's instrument has also been replaced. St George's head and right arm are evidently by Baker, as is the dragon's snout. The lady has had her head renewed, but otherwise both she and her lap-dog appear unrestored.

66   NA bay no. 8, nos 1, 3 , 5 & 6; NA bay no. 9, nos 1, 2, 3, 4 & 6; NA bay no. 10, nos 1, 2 & 6.

67   NA bay 8, no. 2 & NA bay 9, no. 5. The bell-ringer's head, hands, book and bell are all restoration work, as is the harpist's head.

68   College of Arms, MS RR 14.C, 'Dugdale's Yorkshire Arms' (1667), f. 90.

69   Quarterly, 1 and 4, *Or a lion rampant azure*, 2 and 3, *Gules three lucies haurient argent*.

70   G. Oliver, *The History and Antiquities of the Town and Minster of Beverley* (Beverley, 1829), pp. 472–80; E. Barrington De Fonblanque, *Annals of the House of Percy* (2 vols, 1887), i, pp. xix–xx; G. Batho, 'The Percies and Alnwick Castle, 1557–1632', *Archaeologia Aeliana*, 35 (1957), 49.

71   C. Foster, 'Lincolnshire Wills proved in the Prerogative Court of Canterbury 1384–1468', *Associated Architectural Societies Reports and Papers*, 41, i (for the year 1932), 75–6.

72   College of Arms, MS RR 14.C, f. 90.

73   Dawton, 'Workshop', pp. 121–32.

74   M. Marcus, '"An Attempt to Discriminate the Styles" - the sculptors of the Harrington Tomb, Cartmel', *Journal of the Church Monuments Society*, 11 (1996), 7.

75 G.E. Aylmer and R. Cant, *A History of York Minster* (Oxford, 1977), p. 200; J. Phillips, *The Reformation of Images: destruction of art in England, 1535–1660* (California, 1973), p. 96.

76 The sum of £1 6s 8d for setting up these texts was paid on 23 March 1663: J. Dennet, ed., *Beverley Borough Records 1575–1821* (YASRS, 84, 1932), p. 129.

77 Cobb, *English Cathedrals*, p. 54, and see chapters 5 and 7 above.

78 K.A. MacMahon, ed., *Beverley Corporation Minute Books 1707–1835* (YASRS, 122, 1958), p. 129; W. Fowler, *An Engraving of the Restored Altar Screen in Beverley Minster* (Winterton, 1826).

79 *The Beverley Guardian* (5 July 1873).

80 Fowler, *Engraving of the Restored Altar Screen*.

81 C. Hiatt, *Beverley Minster: an illustrated account of its history and fabric* (1898), pp. 90–1; H. Nolloth, *Beverley and its Minster* (1910), p. 22.

82 Details of the find were kindly supplied to the writer by Mr David Wilson, Head Verger of the Minster.

83 L. Stone, *Sculpture in Britain: the Middle Ages* (Harmondsworth, 1972), pl. 130(B).

84 Bilson, 'Stray Notes', 221–5.

85 H. Graef, *Mary: a history of doctrine and devotion* (1963), pp. 135–6, 247.

86 Although the dove was most commonly used as a symbol of the Holy Spirit, the red dove of the Bestiary was identified with Christ: R. Baxter, *Bestiaries and their Users in the Middle Ages* (Stroud, 1998), pp. 53–4.

87 M.R. James, ed., *The Bestiary: being a reproduction in full of the manuscript Ii.4.26 in the University Library, Cambridge* (Oxford, 1928), p. 47; M. Tisdall, *God's Beasts* (Plymouth, 1998), p. 205 and pls 409–13.

88 N. Pevsner and E. Radcliffe, *The Buildings of England: Yorkshire: The West Riding* (Harmondsworth, 1967), pl. 28(b).

89 See the present writer's account in J. Alexander and P. Binski, eds, *Age of Chivalry: art in Plantagenet England 1200–1400* (Royal Academy of Arts, 1987), p. 422 nos 513–6.

90 Ibid., pp. 420 no. 507, 422 nos. 513–6 and pl. 507.

91 E.S. Prior and A. Gardner, *An Account of Medieval Figure-Sculpture in England* (Cambridge, 1912), fig. 386. Cf C. Brighton, *Lincoln Cathedral Cloister Bosses* (Lincoln, 1985), figs 12, 91, with K. Gould, *The Psalter and Hours of Yolande of Soissons* (Cambridge, Mass., 1978). fig. 10 and *L'Art au temps des rois maudits* (Paris, 1998) p. 84.

9 · The Medieval Monuments

To the late-medieval observer, the Minster's funerary monuments would have been overshadowed by its extensive series of tombs commemorating various members of the powerful Percy family. Many of the earlier Percies, it may be noted, were buried either at Whitby Abbey, refounded by William de Percy in 1078, or at Sawley Abbey, founded by his grandson in 1147. Henry Percy, first lord of Alnwick (d. 1314), was buried at Fountains, and his two successors at Alnwick Abbey. This preference for monastic burial reflects the pioneering role of the monasteries in developing the art of praying for the dead.[1] By the mid–14th century, however, it was becoming increasingly common for the highest in the land to found chantries in collegiate churches, leaving an endowment for a priest to say masses on behalf of their souls in purgatory. The effectiveness of such intercessionary prayers was greatly enhanced by the presence of an important saint. Located close to Leconfield and home to St John of Beverley, the Minster was ideally suited to catering for the sepulchral needs of the Percy family.

The Percies were not the only people to be buried at the Minster, however, and the varied nature of its medieval monuments draws attention to the importance of the church as a crossroads for people from many different social and professional backgrounds.

THE TOMB OF NICHOLAS OF HUGGATE, PROVOST OF BEVERLEY

On a tomb chest in the eastern aisle of the north transept lies the effigy of a priest dressed in full mass vestments [54]. His hair is neatly groomed, terminating at ear-length in a row of small curls, while around his head he wears an almuce, the hooded cape traditionally worn by canons, wardens and masters of colleges. Clasping his hands in prayer, he rests his feet on the back of a lion in an attitude of dignified tranquility. His costume is especially interesting for its lavish use of embroidered heraldry – the coats of arms of many leading Yorkshire landowners, together with three royal shields, are represented on the alb, maniple and amice. Other items of dress, such as the orphrey and stole, are richly ornamented with rose diaper. Clearly commemorating a man of some standing, the effigy has been identified as that of Nicholas of Huggate, provost of Beverley for much of the period covered by the second nave campaign.[2]

The long sides of the tomb chest are decorated with panels of blind tracery surmounted by crocketed gables. There is no provision for attaching 'weeper figures' representing the deceased person's relatives or associates, and Richard Gough - the eighteenth-century antiquary - stated that the tracery lights were painted with figures of saints.[3] Faint traces of polychromy still remain, suggesting the outlines of standing figures, and recalling the scheme of decoration seen in the tomb of Sir Richard de Goldsborough V (d. c. 1331–4) in St Mary's, Goldsborough (North Yorkshire) – where the long side of the chest was painted with standing nimbed figures, possibly representing the twelve apostles.[4] The tracery itself is in the flowing style which flourished in Yorkshire throughout the mid–third of the 14th century, and of which the Minster nave and reredos are outstanding examples.

However, while the monument that we see today corresponds in all essentials to that recorded by Dugdale when he visited Beverley in 1641, this arrangement is clearly the result of

53 The Percy tomb, south side. The view is from the top of the reredos into the north lesser transept. The early eighteenth-century ironwork gates into the north choir aisle, glimpsed through the arch of the tomb, were originally part of Hawksmoor's screen and gave access to the choir.

alterations carried out in the post-medieval period.[5] The short ends of the tomb chest are devoid of decoration and were evidently designed not to be visible. This would accord with the kind of canopied arrangement seen, for instance, in the tomb of Archbishop William Greenfield (d. 1315) at York. The irregular coursing of the base beneath the tomb chest is clearly not medieval, suggesting that the tomb was repositioned or reassembled in later times. The tomb, moreover, has lost its original lid. Monuments of this type commonly incorporated a tomb lid - a separate stone slab, whose function was to seal the tomb chest and support the effigial slab above. This intermediary slab - the tomb lid - was presumably discarded when the tomb chest was dismantled and reconstructed, probably in the 16th century.

The effigial slab, as W. Longstaffe noted, is considerably shorter than the tomb chest,[6] and in the drawing made for Gough by the architectural historian and draughtsman, John Carter, there is an empty space at the feet of the effigy, through which the interior of the chest can be seen.[7] While this could be explained by the loss of the tomb lid, the monument has been interfered with to such an extent that one cannot be certain that the effigy was originally associated with the tomb chest on which it now lies.[8]

Thanks largely to the researches of Canon Richard McDermid, no such uncertainty surrounds the identity of the man commemorated by the effigy. Most of the identifiable shields on the vestments are those of prominent baronial houses with lands near the provostry, or else belong to lesser families from the area to the west of Beverley where the Huggates had lived for generations. Taken together with the other evidence considered by McDermid, this argues strongly in favour of the effigy being that of Provost Nicholas of Huggate.

A Yorkshireman hailing from the village of the same name, Huggate appears in documents dating from the first decade of the 14th century, which show him to have been a royal clerk, receiving payment for his services in the form of a number of ecclesiastical benefices.[9] Evidently an able and trusted servant, he had risen by 1317 to become treasurer to the Prince of Wales - the future Edward III - and by 1324 had taken over as the royal receiver for Aquitaine and Gascony. In 1332, clearly with retirement in mind, he obtained a royal exemption for his debts to the Crown - granted 'in consideration of his manifold services to the king from boyhood'.

Appointed provost of Beverley in 1318, Huggate spent much of the earlier part of his period of office engaged on the king's business in London, simultaneously using his position to increase his personal wealth through the acquisition of a string of preferments. His release from royal service in the early 1330s precedes by less than two years the donations of the archbishop of York which signal the revitalization of work on the Minster nave, and it is reasonable to suspect that the provost, freed from the burden of his royal duties, played a key role in forwarding the campaign. Huggate died on 24 June 1338. In his will, proved the following month, he directed his body to be buried in the Minster, leaving £100 (many thousands of pounds by today's standards) to cover his funeral expenses, and making provision for sixty priests to celebrate continuously on behalf of his soul for the following year.

As a canon of Beverley, Huggate was entitled to wear an almuce, the hooded garment shown in his effigy. This is actually highly unusual, as McDermid noted.[10] Examples of effigies showing canons wearing the almuce over mass vestments are not uncommon on the Continent, but in England this article of dress was normally worn only with processional vestments. Effigies of English ecclesiastics wishing to proclaim their canonical status are thus shown wearing an almuce in combination with a processional cope. These, however, do not appear in any numbers until the end of the 14th century. Nicholas of Huggate's effigy is in fact the earliest surviving example of an English ecclesiastic portrayed as a canon, pre-dating by over twenty years the two miniature effigies at Bitton (Gloucestershire), in which the almuce is worn over choir dress.[11] The most likely explanation is that Huggate wished to emphasize the fact that he

54 The tomb of Nicholas of Huggate, provost of Beverley, viewed from above. The tomb is in the north transept.

was a canon – hence the almuce – but was confined by the prevailing conventions of monumental representation – hence the mass vestments.

Huggate's status as a prominent servant of the Crown is reflected in the presence of the three royal shields among the coats of arms on his vestments. One of these shows England quartering France with England in the dexter (top left quarter) – an uncommon form of the royal arms, not to be confused with the quartering adopted by Edward III in 1340, in which the arms of France were placed in the dexter. The former quartering, referring to Edward's descent from his French mother, is found from 1327 until 1340, but thereafter seems to have disappeared until reintroduced by Henry IV in the early 15th century.[12] There is thus a presumption in favour of dating examples of this shield to the years before 1340, suggesting that the provost's effigy was carved between 1332 and 1340.

THE PERCY TOMB

The Percy tomb [53], a spectacular 'ciborium tomb' in the tradition of the monument of Edmund Crouchback in Westminster Abbey, is of exceptional interest due to the fortunate survival of its full programme of canopy sculpture.[13] Built between the screen staircase and the north-west pier of the eastern crossing, it forms the northern boundary of the presbytery, traditionally the preferred location for tombs on account of its proximity to the high altar.

Until the general refurbishment of the choir in the 1820s, the monument contained a tomb chest made of a dark, marble-like stone [55], whose upper slab bore an indent for a lost brass. The tomb chest was removed at that time in the belief that it was a later addition, installed to protect an assumed earlier interment beneath what is now the floor of the tomb.[14] This fanciful conjecture is entirely without foundation, however. There are, on the contrary, sound archaeological reasons for believing that the canopy was always intended to house a tomb chest

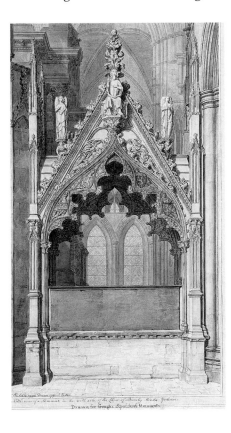

55 (left) Drawing by John Carter of the Percy tomb from the north in 1791 (Bodleian Library, Gough Maps 227). The drawing shows the tomb chest in situ. Behind the tomb to the left can be glimpsed the massive Corinthian columns of Hawksmoor's altar screen.

56 (right) Carter's drawing of the indent for the lost brass on top of the tomb chest in the Percy tomb (Bodleian Library, Gough Maps 227). The outline suggests that the brass was that of a cleric.

comparable in size and placement to that removed in 1824. The Percy tomb is not a free-standing structure. Its canopy is supported to the west by the north-west pier of the eastern crossing, and to the east by the wall of the staircase leading to the shrine platform on top of the reredos. In order to provide a flat end wall for the tomb, the projecting mouldings of the screen staircase were cut back, but only *above* the level of the lost tomb chest. The mouldings that were formerly hidden by the chest were left in place, suggesting that a tomb chest formed an integral part of the original design.[15] This is supported by the design of the lost brass, which, to judge from the drawing of the indent made by Carter in 1791 [**56**], was consistent with a date in the second quarter of the 14th century. Aside from the arrangement of the heraldic shields, which is difficult to parallel anywhere, the design suggests a London origin, as pointed out by Sally Badham.[16] As we see it now, the Percy tomb is a tomb without a tomb chest.

Using the metaphorical language of sculpture, the canopy encapsulates the concern of the tomb owner for the fate of their soul after death. The sequence of events begins on the south side of the canopy, with the group depicting Christ receiving the dead person's soul in heaven [**53**]. The soul, represented as a naked figure in prayer, gazes up towards Christ, who raises his right hand in blessing and tenderly supports the arms of the soul with his left. Since the days of Gregory the Great (540–604), the prevalent view in the West had been that the soul of the deceased was subjected to an individual judgement at the moment of death, which the Last Judgement would confirm at the end of time. During the interim, the souls of the blessed resided in heaven, where they were able to experience the beatific vision – the state of bliss that accompanied seeing God in both his nature and essence.[17] The beginning of this state of bliss,

57 Christ showing his wounds, from the apex of the north side of the Percy tomb. Attributed to the Soul Master.

58 The angel with the cross and nails, from the north side of the Percy tomb, standing on the left hand of the image of Christ in **57**. Attributed to the Soul Master.

marked by the arrival of the soul in heaven, is the moment symbolized by the sculpture above the south arch of the Percy tomb.

The statuary on the north face of the canopy [**57, 58, pl. 14**] depicts Christ showing his wounds, flanked on either side by angels carrying the instruments of the Passion. This is an image of the Last Judgement, at which time it was held that the bodies of the dead would rise from their graves to be reunited with their long-departed souls. With this reunion of body and soul, the joy of the blessed would be immeasurably increased. In the words of Dante:

> When our flesh, sanctified and glorious
> shall clothe our souls once more, one person then
> will be more pleasing since it is complete.[18]

Symbolizing the place to which the soul is taken after death, and from which Christ descends at the end of time, the canopy is defined by its statuary as an image of heaven. The throng of music-making angels flying around the arches [**59, pl. 16**] strongly recalls accounts of paradise in visionary literature, while Christ [**50**] and the Virgin appear as the crowned rulers of heaven in the cusping of the south arch, reinforcing the impression that the canopy as a whole was intended to represent a vision of the heavenly Jerusalem.

Many of the angels on the outer face of the north arch carry scrolls, whose lost inscriptions in all probability prophesied the Second Coming, depicted in the statuary above. In contrast, many of the angels on the inner faces of the arches are shown diving downwards, suggesting that they formed part of the heavenly host which descended to earth at the moment of the Last Judgement. This is supported by the crown held by the two angels on the easternmost boss of the vault [**back cover**]. Following the general resurrection, crowns of righteousness were bestowed on the perfected bodies of the blessed to mark their arrival in heaven.[19] Angels holding crowns for the blessed were a standard feature of the Last Judgement in French portal sculpture, and there can be little doubt that the crown held by the two angels on the Percy tomb was the crown which the tomb owner hoped to receive at the end of time. Unlike the well-ordered treatment of the theme in French Gothic, however, the way in which the multitude of angels on the bosses and cusping of the Percy tomb [**pl. 16**] threaten to break free from their architectural settings has a distinctly visionary quality, as if one were witnessing an actual event taking place at this particular spot.

The illusion of reality is heightened by the atlas figures beneath the angels on the roof of the canopy [**60**], whose anguished expressions leave no doubt as to their displeasure at their task and recall Dante's description of the punishment awaiting the proud in purgatory:

> Sometimes one sees a corbel, holding the weight
> of roof or ceiling, carved in human shape
> with chest pressed tightly down against its knees,
> so that this unreality gives real
> anguish to one who sees it – this is how
> these souls appeared, and how they made me feel.[20]

Atlas figures, personifying the supporting function of the architectural members which they decorate or replace, were frequently invested with an allegorical significance which in some way paralleled their structural role. The Percy tomb atlantes, which include both secular figures in contemporary dress and figures whose bare feet and ferocious expressions mark them out as demons, emphasize the crushing power of Christ and the heavenly host to overcome evil and punish evil-doers.

The mood of ecstasy evoked by the angels inhabiting the canopy [**59, pl. 16**] is underpinned by an assortment of other subjects strategically placed in the minor cusps at the bottom of the arches. St Michael, shown vanquishing the dragon on the outer face of the cusp at the base of the west side of the south arch, was closely associated with the souls of the dead. He was often shown supervising the weighing of souls at the Last Judgement, or rescuing the souls of the newly dead from the demons popularly thought to be waiting to snatch them. His role on the Percy tomb is thus to exercise his martial prowess to protect the soul on its journey to judgement.

St Katherine of Alexandria, identified by her emblem, a spiked wheel, is represented on the inner face of the cusp above the eastern springer of the south arch. Having protested against the worship of idols and refused to renounce her faith, she was finally beheaded, but not before converting fifty of the emperor's religious advisers and 200 of his soldiers. Learned, beautiful and evidently gifted with remarkable powers of persuasion, St Katherine was a popular intercessory saint and is frequently found on tombs of this period. According to the Golden Legend, God had promised that all who honoured her martyrdom would be granted the comfort of heaven.[21]

The Annunciation [61] is depicted on the outer face of the same cusp, while the inner face of the cusp above the eastern springer of the north arch is carved with the Nativity. Both visible from the presbytery side of the monument, these scenes emphasize the importance of the Incarnation, prior to which the souls of the dead had been excluded from heaven. Located at the bottom of the arches, they form a prelude to the images which formerly stood on the brackets on the short sides of the canopy, in which the redemption of mankind was completed.

These images no longer exist, but the subjects on the brackets which supported them point to a series of narrative scenes showing the Passion of Christ. The casting of lots for Christ's garments [62], represented on the southern corbel at the eastern end of the tomb, is a clear reference to the Crucifixion, strongly suggesting that this theme was depicted in the lost panel above. The lion and dragon, carved on the neighbouring corbel to the north, are the animals which Christ traditionally tramples underfoot to signify his victory over sin and death. Here, however, they are shown locked in combat, a subject frequently used to refer in general terms to the struggle between good and evil. In this context, given the connection with the Crucifixion, the fight between the two beasts may have been an allusion to the Harrowing of Hell, and this could well have been the subject depicted in the lost relief.

Although the Percy tomb is traditionally believed to belong to a member of the Percy family, the exact identity of the person commemorated is far from clear. The documentary source most frequently cited is the account of the Minster monuments written by Henry VIII's antiquary, John Leland, who visited Beverley in 1541. Brief yet imprecise - it is not always clear which tomb he is talking about, or who exactly he thought it commemorated - Leland's account is nevertheless extremely valuable as the only eye-witness description of the monuments prior to the Reformation. He wrote:

> ... besides the tombs of saints [there] be 3 tombs most notable on the north side of the choir: in one of them with a chapel arched over it is buried Percy earl of Northumberland and his son, father to the last earl.
>
> In another is buried Eleanor, wife to one of the Lord Percies. And in another of white alabaster Idonea Lady Percy, wife to one of the Lord Percies.
>
> Under Eleanor's tomb is buried one of the Percies, a priest.[22]

From this account it is clear that in Leland's day the east end of the Minster was home to a number of tombs commemorating various members of the Percy family. His location of the tombs 'on the north side of the choir' needs to be interpreted as a general reference to the northern part of the east end, since the tomb which he ascribed to the earl of Northumberland can only be that of Henry Percy, fourth earl of Northumberland (d. 1489), which has always stood in the Percy Chapel, in the angle between the Lady Chapel and the north-east transept. The Percy

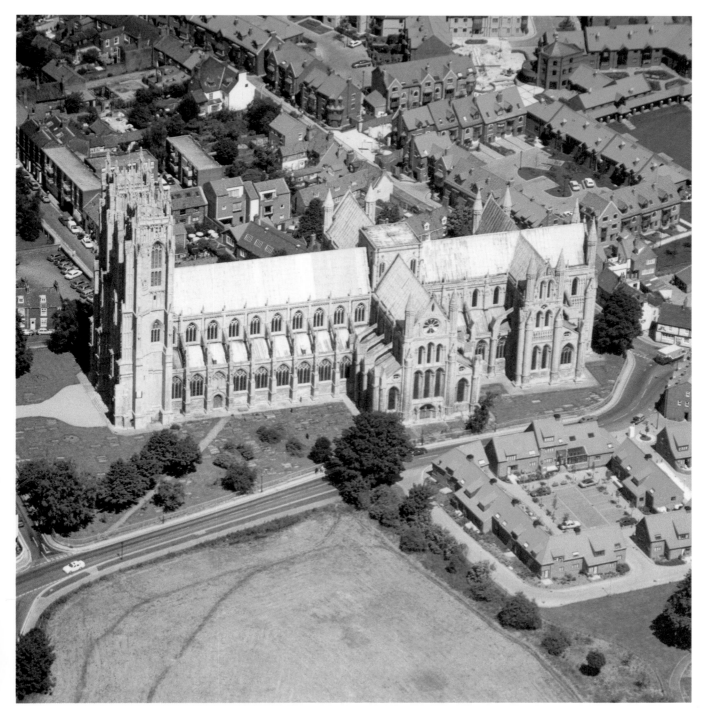

Plate 1   An aerial view of the Minster and its setting
from the south. Although most of the building to the south east and north east is modern,
the sense of enclosure would have been
matched in the Middle Ages, when the circuit
was completed by the archbishop's manor
house on the now-empty site to the south
west. Compare fig. 4 for the location of the
medieval buildings of the precinct.

Plate 3   A late-eleventh-century crozier head of walrus ivory showing St John of Beverley healing the dumb youth. On the other side, not shown, Sts John the Evangelist and Peter heal a cripple – a miracle which Bede compares with that of St John of Beverley.

Plate 2   C.H. Tate, the nave in 1849, watercolour wash over ink. Note the verger on the right. In the distance is Hawksmoor's screen surmounted by the Snetzler organ. See also **87** for a view of the screen and organ from the east.

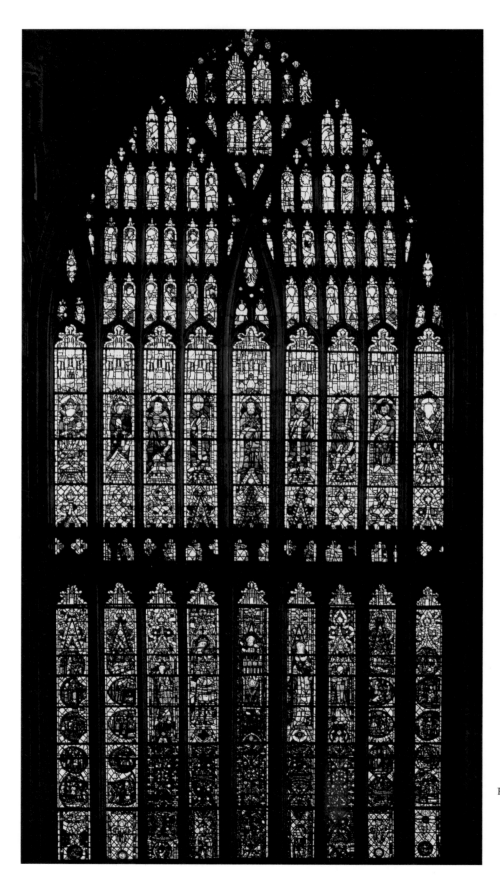

Plate 4   The great east window, glazed
in c.1416–20 and now also home
to the Minster's other surviving
medieval glass, which was moved
into the lower lights in 1725
and 1882.

Plate 5   The Percy Chapel, the only surviving panel of the original glazing, now in the chapel's east window. It depicts the arms of the 4th earl of Northumberland (d. 1489). A decorative surround has been made from fragments of medieval glass. A fragment above the shield combines two of the family's badges: *a shaklebolt or, within a crescent argent*. The shaklebolt, also known as a pair of manacles, was a variant of the fetterlock.

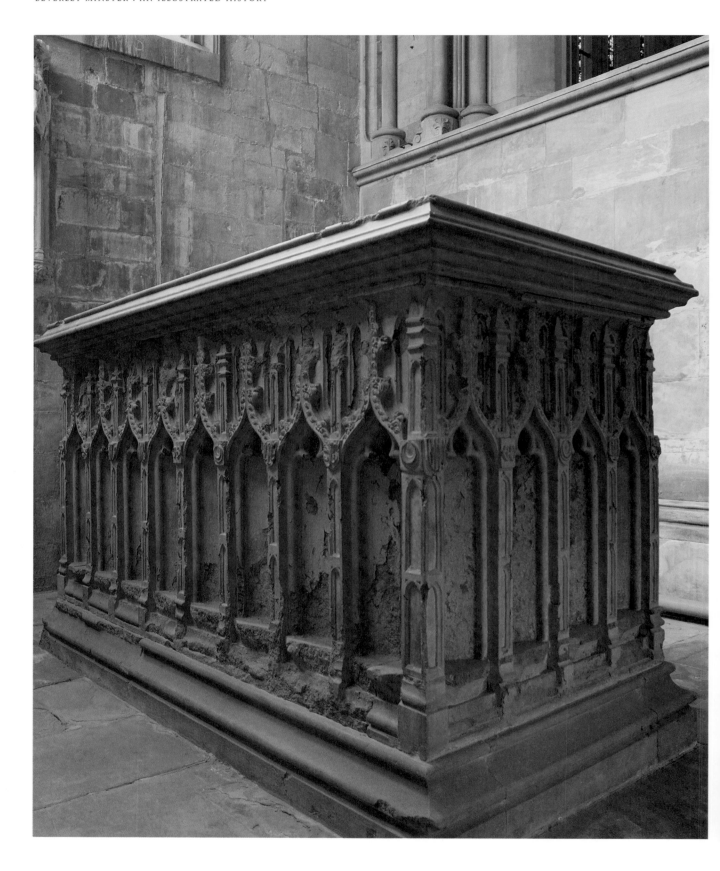

Plate 6   The Percy Chapel, the tomb chest of the 4th earl of Northumberland. For the canopy, which was taken down in the 18th century, see **15**. The arches around the sides of the chest originally housed figures. Their destruction before the 1640s suggests that they may have been angels or saints rather than 'weepers', who were more likely to survive religious iconoclasts.

Plate 7   A fourteenth-century corbel in the north choir aisle representing St John of Beverley and King Athelstan. The king is handing over a sealed document (representing his grant of liberties to Beverley), the bishop raises his right hand in blessing.

Plate 9   St John and King Athelstan. The date of
this panel painting, tersely dismissed as
'late C15, bad' by Pevsner, is uncertain.
It is apparently first mentioned in the
early 18th century, when it hung near
the entrance to the choir. It is now in
the south transept.

Plate 8   The stairway in the north choir aisle,
originally leading to the medieval
chapter house which was destroyed at
the Dissolution. The chapter house was
built over an undercroft, to which the
door below the stairs gives access.

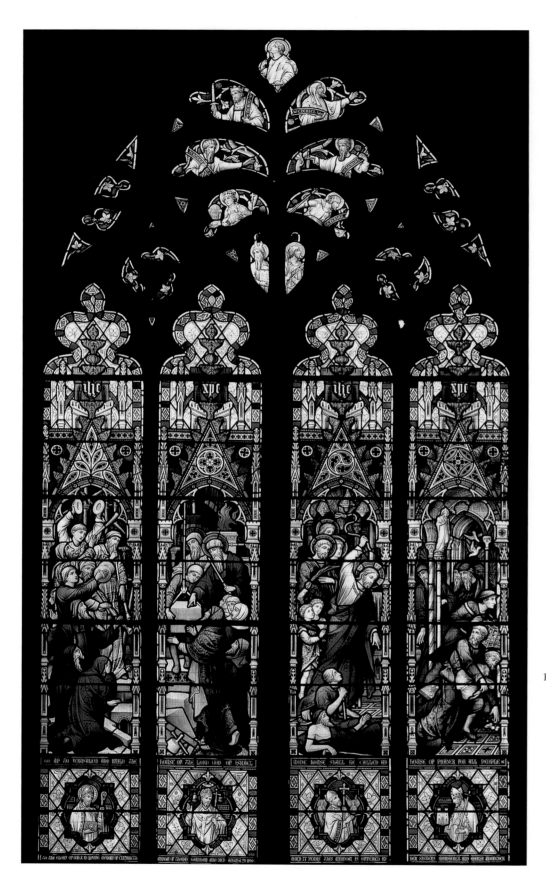

Plate 10   Stained glass from the third window in south nave aisle by Hardman and Co. Over forty of the Minster's windows were to have been reglazed by the firm but the project was never completed. The two panels on the left show the building of the Temple, the two on the right Christ driving out the moneylenders.

Plate 11   Stained glass from the
            northern window at the
            west end of the nave, by
            Hardman and Co.,
            Birmingham.

Plate 13   Design for a choir screen by George
Gilbert Scott, c. 1842. This design was
never executed and can be compared
with the final version shown in **83**.

Plate 12   Thornton's sphinx. The eighteenth-
century restoration included repairs
and additions to the choir stalls,
including many new bench ends. The
bare-breasted sphinx was temporarily
banished in the 19th century but is
now back in place.

Plate 14   The Percy tomb, north side
(detail). The angel with the
cross and nails, attributed
to the Soul Master.

Plate 15   The Percy tomb, north side
(detail). A knight holding
the Percy shield, traces of
the original colouring can
still be seen. Attributed to
the Evangelist Master.

Plate 16   The Percy tomb, south side (detail). An angel with a portative organ. 'Portative' is something of a misnomer – only angels can casually hold the instrument in the crook of one arm while fingering the keys with the other hand. Attributed to the Annunciation Master.

tomb, situated on the north side of the presbytery, was within the area Leland was talking about, and it has generally been assumed that it should, therefore, have been one of the other two 'notable' tombs mentioned in his account.

Most modern writers have connected the Percy tomb with Eleanor, the wife of Henry Percy, first lord of Alnwick (d. 1314). Eleanor's exact parentage is unclear, but she is generally believed to have been the daughter of Richard Fitz Alan, earl of Arundel (d. 1302). She died in 1328 and arrangements for the celebration of her obit at Beverley were made in 1336.[23] However, the provision of an obit at the Minster does not necessarily signify that she was buried there. It is evident, moreover, that the tomb which Leland believed to commemorate 'Eleanor, wife to one of the Lord Percies', was in reality that of Eleanor Neville, the wife of Henry Percy, second earl of Northumberland (d. 1455), which stood further to the east. The tomb itself has disappeared, but it is referred to in the will of George Percy, one of her younger sons. George was a cleric, the rector of the churches of Caldbeck (Cumbria) and Rothbury (Northumberland), and in his will, drawn up in 1474, he expressed the wish to be buried in the north aisle of the Minster, next to the tomb of Lady Eleanor Percy.[24] The will does not actually specify which Lady Eleanor he is referring to, although he mentions his mother earlier on, and it can reasonably be assumed that her tomb is meant. Since Leland stated that George was buried 'under Eleanor's tomb', it is clear that the tomb which he identified as Eleanor's was in fact that of Eleanor Neville.

There is more than one position in the north choir aisle where George's tomb could have been next to another major monument. One is in the bay adjoining the Percy tomb, in which case one would have to assume that Leland was simply mistaken in his identification, since the ascription of the Percy tomb to Eleanor Neville is ruled out on chronological grounds. Another possible location is on the north side of what in George's day was the easternmost bay of the aisle. For then, if Eleanor's monument stood on the southern boundary of the adjoining bay of the north-east transept aisle, the two tombs could reasonably be described as lying next to each other. The north-east transept aisle, although subsequently appropriated for use as a vestry, is traditionally believed to have been a place of burial for the Percies, with an altar at which masses were performed for deceased members of the family.[25] Antiquarian sources, moreover, have recorded the existence of two lost Percy and Neville shields in one of the vestry windows.[26] This strongly supports the view that the tomb of Eleanor Neville was associated with a chapel there. While not disproving that the earlier Eleanor (Fitz Alan) was buried at Beverley, this clearly demonstrates that Leland did not believe that anyone called Eleanor was commemorated by the Percy tomb - which, by process of elimination, ought to have been the tomb he assigned to Idonea.

Idonea (d. 1365), whose family arms appear on the north arch of the tomb, was the daughter of Robert de Clifford, and wife of Henry Percy, second lord of Alnwick (d. 1352). Idonea, it may be noted, was the person to whom the tomb was ascribed in the 18th century.[27] She would certainly have known Beverley well, since she received the manor of Leconfield as part of her dower on the death of her husband.[28] There is a reference to her tomb in the sixteenth-century metrical pedigree of the Percies by William Peeris, who relates:

> Lady Ydondye his wife, which was circumspect and wise,
> In Beverley minster is tombed in right costly wise.
> And at the same Minster she founded a chantry men may see,
> Of which the Percies patrons perpetual be.[29]

This is supported by an ordinance issued to the canons of Beverley by Archbishop Arundel in 1391, specifying that the observance of the exequies of Lady Idonea should continue according to ancient usage.[30] There is thus every reason to believe that Idonea was buried at Beverley.

However, the tomb chest removed from the Percy tomb in 1824 was made of a dark, marble-like stone, whereas we know from Leland's account that Idonea's tomb was made of 'white alabaster'.

Alabaster, a form of gypsum quarried in the Midlands, came into use as a fashionable material for both tombs and effigies in the 1330s. Ideally suited to the contemporary taste for achieving subtle monochrome effects through the combination of black, white and grey stones, alabaster was employed for the effigy of Edward II at Gloucester – his tomb chest being composed of a light-coloured freestone ground enriched with dark Purbeck panelling. In order to reconcile Leland's description of Idonea's tomb with the tomb chest seen in Carter's drawing, the latter would have to have been faced with a revetment of alabaster panelling - similar, perhaps, to that seen in the monument of John of Eltham at Westminster, where the tomb chest is encased with open-work panelling incorporating alabaster weeper figures set off against a dark ground imitating the appearance of Purbeck marble.

Such an arrangement does not seem very probable, however. The material used for the tomb chest removed in 1824 was in all probability Purbeck marble - a dark, shell-limestone with well-established funerary associations. Quarried at Corfe and worked both there and in London, Purbeck marble required specialized cutting and polishing. It was not a cheap alternative. The side of the tomb chest visible in Carter's drawing appears uniformly flat and plain, suggesting that the whole slab was originally worked to a mirror-smooth finish. It is hard to justify the expense that this would have involved, if the sides were to have been faced with alabaster. Even if the intention were to employ a system of open-work panelling to create a 'white against black' effect, one imagines that a less costly method would have been adopted, as it was for John of Eltham's tomb at Westminster.

While an unadorned Purbeck tomb chest would be highly unusual in England at this period – a fact which may well have contributed to the view that the chest was a later addition - it finds a supremely respectable precedent in the monument of Edward I (d. 1307) in Westminster Abbey. Here, too, the tomb chest was essentially a plain, polished marble box. At a time when English artists were becoming increasingly adept at creating spectacular visual effects, sometimes using base materials to mimic the appearance of more expensive ones, Edward may have deliberately chosen to reassert the deep-rooted medieval belief in the intrinsic nobility of fine materials – emphasizing substance over artifice. In so doing, he may well have been inspired by his knowledge of the similarly austere tombs of the Norman kings of Sicily, as Paul Binski has suggested.[31] In the tomb of Roger II (d. 1154) at Palermo, for instance, a comparable effect of *gravitas* was achieved through the use of porphyry, a material with strong imperial associations. Edward, the conqueror of Wales and Scotland, may have hoped to evoke similar associations by using the nearest English equivalent – Purbeck marble.

The tomb of Edward I not only provides a prestigious precedent for the plain Purbeck chest formerly associated with the Percy tomb, it also suggests that whoever commissioned the tomb chose this particular type of chest specifically to emphasize their own status and *gravitas*. Any additional decoration in the form of alabaster panelling would have been counter-productive, and this hypothesis can reasonably be rejected. The corollary of this is that the Percy tomb could not have been the tomb which Leland ascribed to Idonea. For whatever reason, Leland simply failed to include the Percy tomb in his account.

In the opinion of Sir William Dugdale, the Percy tomb commemorated Maud, the wife of Henry Percy, fourth earl of Northumberland.[32] However, Maud was a late-fifteenth-century figure, who had not even been born when the Percy tomb was erected! Indeed, since none of the ladies mentioned by Leland, Dugdale and Gent is likely to have commissioned the Percy tomb, it may be asked whether there remains any basis for considering the Percy tomb to be a *Percy* tomb at all.

59 (left) An angel with a viol, from the north side of the Percy tomb. Attributed to the Evangelist Master.

60 (right) Atlas figure, from the south side of the Percy tomb. The figure is supporting the angel on Christ's right hand, shown in 53. Attributed to Evangelist Master.

However, the heraldic shields in the cusping of the canopy [**pl. 15**] – while not all positively identifiable – do point strongly to a connection with the house of Percy. The two main antiquarian sources – James Torre and Richard Gough – have left us with partially conflicting accounts of the tinctures, but four of the shields can nevertheless be identified, with reasonable or complete certainty, with the lordship of Clun, the families of Warenne and Clifford, and the royal arms of England. While the royal arms have traditionally been viewed as a sign of loyalty to the Crown, the arms of Clun, Warenne and Clifford have been interpreted as references to the wives of three consecutive Percy barons: Eleanor Warenne (d. after 1281), Eleanor Fitz Alan (d. 1328) and Idonea Clifford (d. 1365).[33] Torre and Gough disagreed over the four remaining shields. Briefly summarized, Gough – acting on information supplied by John Carter – blazoned all four shields as *or, a lion rampant azure*, the famous blue lion of Percy. As blazoned by Torre, on the other hand, none of the shields can be identified with Percy. However, the lion on the shield at the top right of the north arch [**pl. 15**] retains extensive traces of blue polychromy, the dull red diaper work being the remains of a red lead or bole ground for either gold or silver. The field was blazoned gold by Carter, silver by Torre. Both could have been reasoned guesses based on the rules of heraldry, which require colours to be placed next to metals. If Carter was right, the arms would be those of Percy. If Torre was right, they would most probably have been those of the Fauconberg family. P.J.P. Goldberg, the most recent writer to discuss the heraldry, believed that the arms were most probably those of Percy – a not unreasonable assumption, given that the Percies were linked by marriage to three of the families represented by the undisputed shields, whereas no similar connections can be demonstrated for the Fauconbergs, a family of lesser rank who chose their marriage partners from the local Yorkshire nobility.[34] A Percy connection thus seems assured.

The other important Percy lady at this time was Mary, the daughter of Henry, earl of Lancaster. A great-granddaughter of Henry III, Mary married Henry Percy – Idonea's son and the future third lord of Alnwick – in 1341. Mary died in 1362, predeceasing her mother-in-law by three years. It is known from the Alnwick Chronicle that she was buried at Alnwick Abbey, but this – it could be argued – may not have been her original intention. Her father-in-law, the second lord of Alnwick, had stated in his will that he wished to be buried at Sawley Abbey. As things turned out, even the second lord's last wish was disregarded, and he, too, was buried at Alnwick.[35]

The case for a connection with Mary is supported by Torre's account of the heraldry, according to which the arms on the shield at the bottom right of the south arch were those of the Lacy family. Alice (d. 1348), the daughter of Henry de Lacy, earl of Salisbury and Lincoln, had been married to Thomas, second earl of Lancaster, and was thus Mary's aunt. The Lacies bore *or, a lion rampant purpure*, and clear traces of gold still remain on the ground – sufficient at least to rule out Longstaffe's much-favoured identification of the arms with Fitz Alan, viz. *gules, a lion rampant or*. Moreover, Mary's illustrious ancestry could help explain the presence of the royal arms on the tomb – her own arms were those of England, with a label of five points – while the tomb of her

61 The Annunciation, from the south side of the Percy tomb. Mary stands on the right, the Holy Spirit above her head. The pot of lilies between her and the angel symbolizes her virginity. Carved by the Annunciation Master.

grandfather, Edmund Crouchback (d. 1296), would provide a family precedent for a prestigious canopied monument of this type.

Mention, however, should be made of an effigy commemorating a lady in the church of St Michael and All Angels at Alnwick. The effigy, attributable on stylistic grounds to one of the Percy tomb sculptors, now lies on a post-medieval tomb chest against the south wall of the chancel. Immediately to the east of the lady, on a tomb chest of identical design, lies the effigy of a fourteenth-century nobleman.[36] The latter is dressed in a tight-fitting tunic buttoned down the front, with a gathered skirt falling to the level of the knees. This form of dress, amounting to a revolution in male fashion, was adopted by the English aristocracy from around 1340, its introduction being closely dated to the years 1337–42 by the royal accounts. Seen also in the Percy tomb atlantes, it preceded the fashion for straight, tight-fitting skirts, which did not come in until the early 1350s – suggesting that the effigy was carved during the period c. 1340–55. The nobleman is unmistakably from the hand of the Clifford Master, whose work at Beverley affords convincing comparisons for the oval head, tightly curled hair and bulbous, leaf-shaped eyes. A nobleman of this date at Alnwick, carved by a Percy tomb sculptor and resting on a post-medieval tomb chest, can with near certainty be identified as the effigy of Henry Percy, second lord of Alnwick, who died in 1352. It was presumably moved to its present location after the dissolution of the monasteries.

The Alnwick lady is carved from the same local sandstone as the nobleman, and both effigies have similar nodding ogee canopies. Given the *prima facie* case for identifying the nobleman as the second lord of Alnwick, these considerations suggest that the lady is another Percy memorial brought from Alnwick abbey. Since the first Percy lady documented as having been buried at Alnwick is Mary, the effigy ought to be her's, suggesting that she may have always intended to be entombed at Alnwick. However, before assuming that the Alnwick lady commemorates Mary, and concluding that the Percy tomb, by process of elimination, must commemorate Eleanor (Fitz Alan), the evidence of the matrix for the lost brass effigy needs to be taken into account.

The indent [56] suggests that the brass depicted a figure in long robes that reached to the feet. Clearly this could not have been a knight in armour, and it has been assumed that the figure was that of a lady. In fact, this is far from certain. Carter's drawing shows the outline of what appears to have been a bare-headed figure, but effigies of high-born fourteenth-century ladies almost invariably show the deceased wearing a head-dress of some kind. A lady's head-dress was a mark of her social status, and the absence of one on the lost brass suggests that the person commemorated by the Percy tomb may not have been a woman at all. Neither is the figure likely to have represented one of the noble lords dressed in courtly attire. Quite apart from the fact that the first three Percy lords of Alnwick are known to have been buried elsewhere, the garment is too long to qualify as a mantle. On the other hand, the combination of an uncovered head with full-length robes would suit an ecclesiastic. In this case the stepped right-hand edge of the indent makes sense as either a maniple or the outer edge of a chasuble, while the projections on either side of the neck can be read as the silhouette of an almuce - the hooded garment seen in the effigy of Provost Huggate. Indeed, these curious projections are difficult to interpret satisfactorily in any other way. On this evidence, the Percy tomb would commemorate not a lady, but a canon dressed in mass vestments.

It was not uncommon for the younger sons of noble families to take holy orders, although the only Percy known to have achieved high ecclesiastical office at this period was Idonea's son, Thomas. Created bishop of Norwich by papal provision in 1355, Thomas died in 1369 and was buried at Norwich. While it is theoretically possible that he commissioned a tomb before his consecration, his age makes this somewhat unlikely. Born in 1333, he was only fourteen years old in 1347, by which time the Percy tomb should already have been in existence.[37] Who the Percy tomb commemorated, and why they should have been buried at Beverley, are thus questions which remain to be answered. However, the strong likelihood that the tomb was made for an ecclesiastic helps to contextualize its single most notable feature – the overwhelming richness of its religious imagery.

The sculpture of the Percy tomb can be ascribed on stylistic grounds to a workshop consisting of five sculptors. Two of these can be identified as the Clifford and Reredos Masters, the sculptors responsible for the altar screen. However, the bulk of the figure-sculpture was divided between the three other members of the atelier, each of whom is here named after one of his carvings on the tomb. A single sculptor, henceforth referred to as the Soul Master, produced the statues for the roof of the canopy, comprising the two seated figures of Christ and their attendant angels [53, 57, 58, pl. 14]. Another sculptor, here called the Annunciation Master, was primarily responsible for the sculpture decorating the cusping of the south arch [50, 61, pl. 16], all of which is from his hand. Most of the remaining sculpture can be attributed to the fifth member of the workshop, referred to below as the Evangelist Master. To his hand may be ascribed the bosses in the vault [**back cover**] and the brackets on the short sides of the canopy [**62**] – one of which depicts St John the Evangelist accompanied by his symbol, an eagle. The Evangelist Master was also responsible for three of the four atlas figures on the roof [**60**], and, together with the Annunciation Master, carved most of the cusping of the north arch [**59**].

The Soul Master, the sculptor responsible for the statuary, was clearly a master of high standing. Indeed, to be given the job of carving the main figures for such a prestigious monument ought to mark him out as one of the most important sculptors of his age. His style is highly distinctive and represents a very English interpretation of the aristocratic image of courtly refinement inherent in the artistic conventions of the Gothic style. Sculpture attributable to him is found over a broad area of middle and northern England, and includes two effigies of prominent northern ladies at Staindrop (Co. Durham) and Alnwick (Northumberland). Carved in the local sandstone, the Staindrop lady has been identified as Euphemia de Clavering, the mother of Ralph, second lord Neville. A very similar effigy, possibly commemorating Mary of Lancaster, now lies in the south aisle of the chancel of the church

62 Casting lots for Christ's garments (detail), the south-east bracket of the Percy tomb. The dice are clearly visible on the garment stretched out between the gamblers. Attributed to the Evangelist Master.

of St Michael and All Angels at Alnwick. The statue of the Virgin and Child over the door to the chapel of St Mary and the Holy Angels at York, probably carved in the years around 1320, could well be an earlier work by the same sculptor.[38]

The solid proportions and upright attitude of the Percy tomb Christ [57] echo the treatment seen in the seated Christ found on the site of the abbot's house at Rievaulx, a figure datable on stylistic grounds to the third quarter of the 13th century.[39] The verticality of the folds falling from the knees of the Percy tomb figure is especially reminiscent of the handling seen at Rievaulx, as is the preference for acutely pointed drapery forms, such as the folds falling to the side of Christ's right leg. These similarities go well beyond what one would normally expect to find in sculpture separated by an interval of seventy to eighty years, and suggest that one is dealing with a single stylistic tradition at different stages in its evolution. The style of the Rievaulx Christ itself reaches back to the sculpture of the Lincoln Judgement Portal, carved by the atelier responsible for Henry III's work at Westminster Abbey, but also looks forward to the style seen in the statue of the Virgin and Child at the entrance to the York chapter house.[40] By the time the Percy tomb was executed, the tradition to which the Soul Master was heir had been a vital force in the development of English sculpture for over 100 years. Despite being successively modified by exposure to outside influence, it constituted a continuity of approach to sculptural problems, passed from one generation to the next through the process of training and apprenticeship.

In contrast to the Soul Master's tendency to conceal the figure behind the formal perfection of their pendulous draperies, the Evangelist Master's handling of drapery shows a greater sensitivity to the form of the body beneath. The material itself seems thinner and more responsive, falling in rippling cascades and clinging more closely to the surface of projecting limbs [**59** and **back cover**]. The Evangelist Master has been identified as one of the workshop responsible for the statues of secular benefactors in the nave triforium of York Minster, probably dating from the years around 1320, and there is reason to believe that he may have been the sculptor who carved the weeper figures on the tomb of Aymer de Valence in Westminster Abbey, executed in the later 1320s.[41] He has also been credited with the figure of Christ on the Easter Sepulchre at Hawton (Notts.).

The style seen in this group of sculpture suggests a knowledge of the softer, more graceful form of Gothic seen in Parisian art around 1300 – the style seen in the statues of the children of Louis IX at Poissy and in illuminated manuscripts associated with Master Honoré.[42] An awareness of this stylistic tradition is evident in the work of English artists associated with the court of Edward I, including the Westminster Retable and the statues of Queen Eleanor on the Waltham Cross.[43] Echoes of this anglicized version of the French style can still be recognized in the work of the Evangelist Master at Beverley, and it is reasonable to believe that it was within this artistic milieu that his style was formed.[44]

A desire to achieve greater realism through the accurate observation of detail is evident to varying degrees in the work of all the members of the Percy tomb workshop. However, this tendency is especially pronounced in the sculpture attributed to the Evangelist Master. The costume of his atlas figures [**60**] is described with astonishing exactitude, buttons and other minutiae of dress being realized with near-microscopic precision. The same attention to detail is seen in the delineation of facial features [**59**], suggesting a heightened awareness of the small-scale topography of the human face. Equally important is the way in which the Evangelist Master applied his enhanced powers of description to accentuate the character and iconographic significance of his figures. His angels, for instance, have delicately proportioned features which give them a self-consciously 'angelic' beauty. On the other hand, the studied ugliness of the figures in the casting of lots for Christ's garments [**62**] emphasizes the baseness of the actions in which they are engaged. In this small scene, the Evangelist Master's spectacular talent as a story-teller is dramatically revealed. The animated narrative style recalls the wall-paintings of St Stephen's Chapel, Westminster, the earliest surviving example of English monumental painting to show the influence of Italian Trecento art.[45] Here, too, a new level of naturalism in the depiction of faces, hands and the details of contemporary dress was combined with a more traditional, north-European drapery style, suggesting that these aspects of the Evangelist Master's style may have been inspired by a knowledge of recent Italian painting.

The Annunciation Master, the sculptor responsible for most of the cusping of the Percy tomb, shared the Evangelist Master's interest in the minutiae of costume. This is especially evident in his knights, whose armour and accoutrements are described with the greatest attention to detail. His formula for representing hair [pl. 16] is especially distinctive: flying out in a halo of flame-like locks, it gives his angels a dramatic intensity which enhances the visionary quality of the monument as a whole. His treatment of drapery [61] closely parallels the miniatures in the Egerton Genesis, illuminated by an artist familiar with Giottesque painting and almost certainly based on a lost cycle of wall paintings.[46] Had English wallpainting of this period survived better, the Annunciation Master's style might seem less isolated. He was also responsible for carving the tomb of an ecclesiastic in St Mary's church, Welwick (East Riding of Yorkshire). Possibly commemorating William de la Mare (d. 1360) – Huggate's successor as provost of Beverley – the monument is a spectacular *tour de force* of the late Decorated style, incorporating a plethora of angels flying in and out of curvilinear tracery, very much in the visionary spirit of the Percy tomb.[47] No other sculpture has yet been attributed to him, although his influence is apparent in the 'fiery-haired' heads of the angels on the Harrington tomb at Cartmel (Cumbria).[48]

Assigning an extensive programme of sculpture to a team of carvers was a well-established medieval practice. Three of the sculptors, as already seen, were members of the workshop responsible for the sculpture of the nave and west front of York Minster. Here at Beverley, it is evident from the distribution of work outlined above that the most important zones of the Percy tomb were allocated to the Soul, Evangelist and Annunciation Masters, while the activities of the Clifford and Reredos Masters were restricted to the less prominent parts of the programme. It is significant, for instance, that the areas of cusping assigned to these two sculptors are both located on the outer face of the north arch, which is not visible from the high altar. Each master emerges as a distinctive artistic personality, although it is clear that in some areas the sculptors were following pre-established compositional guidelines, while correspondences between their work suggest that they had access to a common stock of model drawings.[49] There is even evidence to suggest that these were available to the sculptors engaged on the altar reredos. The similarities between the seated Christ on the south arch [50], for instance, and the Reredos Master's version of the same subject [51] suggest that both were based either on the same drawing, or else on two very similar drawings from the same source.

Bringing together a number of sculptors who were active individually in the North and Midlands, the Percy tomb was both a triumph of collaboration and a show-case for the richness and versatility of English sculpture on the eve of the Black Death. As an image of heaven, the canopy sculpture expressed the tomb owner's confidence that death – in their case – would be no more than a prelude to celestial bliss, culminating in their own resurrection at the end of earthly time. As part of the setting for the liturgy, the Percy tomb would have contributed greatly to the aura of sanctity surrounding the high altar, echoing the belief that heaven could be brought into mystical contact with the real world through the sacrament of the mass.

63 The tomb canopy in the south nave. The tomb, traditionally known as the Two Sisters' tomb, is a post-Reformation assemblage. William Collins' statue of King Athelstan can be seen through the arch.

THE TOMB OF THE TWO SISTERS OF BEVERLEY

Standing beneath one of the arches of the south nave arcade is an elegant fourteenth-century tomb canopy [**63**], incorporating a gabled roof supported on either side by a tall pointed arch embellished with large, foliage-filled cusps.[50] The latter were further enriched with open-work sub-cusps, which would have given the arches a delicate, traceried appearance. On either side of each gable is a bracket for statuary – an arrangement already seen in the Percy tomb and a standard feature of canopies of this type. Rising from each of the four corners of the canopy is a cluster of slender buttresses, whose bases have been crudely shaped to accommodate the bases of the adjacent nave piers - a clear indication that the canopy is not in its original location. The canopy was certainly designed to receive a tomb chest, since the shafts beneath its arches terminate well above ground level. At present, however, it is home to what appears to be the remains of a fifteenth-century tomb chest decorated with quatrelobes, sandwiched between two slabs of Purbeck marble.[51]

This hybrid arrangement is clearly post-medieval, and the tradition that it commemorates the two virgin daughters of Earl Puch – a Saxon nobleman whose wife was miraculously cured by St John of Beverley – is surely apocryphal. In the 18th century, the two virgin sisters were believed to have given the freemen of Beverley an area of pasture sufficient to graze three milk cows, but the land in question has not been positively identified.[52] However, the legend was already current in 1609, when Robert Clerk, one of the town governors, left his body to be buried at the Minster 'near the Maidens Tombe'.[53] The Purbeck slabs are over six feet long, and,

64 A mermaid on the inside face of the north arch of the tomb canopy illustrated in **63**.

in the absence of any evidence to the contrary, it is not unreasonable to assume that they were originally associated with tombs. The connection with St John of Beverley may also be significant. On grounds of size, K.A. MacMahon suggested that the upper slab may have come from the supporting structure beneath his shrine.[54] Alternatively, it could have formed part of the saint's tomb in the nave – about which very little is known. The most that can be said with certainty is that the Two Sisters' tomb was a product of the depredations sustained by the church's shrines and monuments at the Reformation, and reflects a propensity on the part of the Minster's new masters to preserve what remained by combining items that were not originally associated with each other.

Where the canopy was moved from, and whose tomb it originally belonged to, are questions which have been largely overlooked by recent scholars, whose attentions have tended to focus on the even more sumptuous Percy tomb. In order to make good this lacuna, one may begin by considering the internal evidence for the date of the canopy. Firstly, the presence of curvilinear tracery motifs in the head of the main gable, and again at the tops of the miniature buttresses, is sufficient to suggest a date in the middle third of the 14th century, given the development of flowing tracery in Yorkshire.[55] Secondly, the treatment of the arch cusping includes decorative ideas which - again given the Yorkshire context - are best explained in terms of a knowledge of the Percy tomb. In particular, one may note the way in which the main cusps are enriched front and back with carved ornament and terminate in small figures. But whereas the sculpture in the cusping of the Percy tomb is fully integrated into a complex iconographical programme, the corresponding zones of the Two Sisters' canopy mostly contain foliage decoration. Equally telling are the figures terminating the cusping. Those on the Percy tomb all depict angels, whose appearance of aeronautic activity is greatly enhanced by their location. In contrast, those on the Two Sisters' tomb are secular in nature - one depicts a bagpiper - and gain no particular advantage from their 'thrust-into-space' positioning. It is inherently more likely, therefore, that the Percy tomb provided the inspiration for the Two Sisters' canopy, than *vice versa*. On this evidence, the Two Sisters' canopy ought to have been erected at some time between 1340 and 1370.

There is one major monument dating from this period that is known to have been in the Minster when Leland visited Beverley, but which is as yet unaccounted for - the tomb of Idonea, wife of Henry Percy, second lord of Alnwick. Idonea died in 1365. At this period, moreover, tombs were not infrequently put in hand during a person's lifetime, and there would have been nothing remarkable about Idonea commissioning her memorial in the early 1360s. There is thus a strong possibility that the Two Sisters' canopy originally formed part of the monument commemorating Idonea Clifford, which – as noted above – initially occupied a position at the east end of the church.

The inside faces of two of the cusps of the canopy are carved with figures. One depicts a long-haired naked figure of indeterminate gender; the other is a mermaid [**64**]. Of ultimately classical origin, the mermaid reached the middle ages as the siren of the *Physiologus* - the forerunner of the later medieval Bestiary.[56] 'From the waist upward she is the most beautiful thing in the world, fashioned in the form of a woman', wrote Guillaume le Clerc in his early thirteenth-century rhyming Bestiary.[57] With a lower body in the shape of either a fish or a bird, sirens were renowned for their sweet voices, with which they lulled unsuspecting sailors to sleep before devouring them. Often shown holding a mirror and a comb, they were commonly associated with the sin of vanity and the power of women to lead men to perdition.[58] For Guillaume le Clerc, they symbolized the generality of moral perils facing all those journeying through the world, encompassing such deadly sins as lust, gluttony, sloth and avarice. On the other hand, allusions to mermaids in medieval literature are frequently more specific, equating their beguiling voices with the insincere and manipulative words of flattery. This is the meaning behind Chaucer's description of Chantecleer singing 'more merrily than a mermaid in the sea' in *The Nun's Priest's Tale*.[59] A cautionary reference to the dangers connected with flattery would not be out of place on the tomb of someone who had the reputation for being both 'circumspect and wise'.

Idonea, so Leland told us, was interred in a tomb of 'white alabaster'. This would seem to rule out the possibility, first raised by W. Longstaffe, that the Two Sisters' canopy may have originally been associated with the tomb chest beneath Huggate's effigy in the north transept. In fact, although Longstaffe went on to argue against the idea, he advanced a perfectly plausible solution to the 'white alabaster' problem. Leland, he suggested, was referring not to the tomb chest as a whole, but merely to the effigy.[60] Given the uncertainty surrounding the relationship between the tomb chest and the effigy of Provost Huggate, this allows one to frame the hypothesis that the chest originally bore an alabaster effigy of Idonea, and that both originally stood beneath the Two Sisters' canopy before it was moved into the nave. The contemporaneity of the two structures is well attested by their architectural detailing. The head of the gable over the southern arch of the canopy, for instance, contains diaper ornament similar to that on the north side of the tomb chest, while the tracery patterns decorating the miniature buttresses of the canopy find close comparisons in the blind tracery on the chest. Other considerations also need to be taken into account, however.

Longstaffe's conjecture that the tomb chest may have been connected with the canopy in the nave was based partly on size. The tomb chest is in fact slightly smaller than the available space beneath the canopy, but the discrepancy - approximately 15 cm in either direction - can be explained in various ways. The short sides of the tomb chest are made of plain blocks, designed not to be seen. These could have been trimmed to ensure that the width of the chest conformed to that of Huggate's effigy. The chest, in other words, could have been wider than it is today. The disparity in length is harder to account for, since it was normal for both chest and lid to abut the end walls of the canopy. However, it is quite possible – given the disturbed state of the stonework of the upper canopy – that the length of the canopy was slightly altered in order to accommodate it to its new location. How exactly the canopy was moved is not known, but those responsible were evidently concerned for its stability, since its upper stage is secured to the adjacent nave piers by means of iron struts. In order to provide additional support below, it is by no means impossible that the canopy was slightly stretched, thereby allowing the bases of its miniature buttresses to adjoin the bases of the nave piers. If - as thus seems possible - the canopy was originally slightly shorter, and the tomb chest slightly wider, there is no obvious reason why they should not have formed part of the same monument.

In its pre-Reformation state, it is not unreasonable to suppose, the Two Sisters' canopy formed part of an elegant memorial incorporating not only the lost alabaster effigy of Idonea, but also the sumptuous tomb chest in the north transept. Crowned with its company of gilded statuary and aglow with images of the saints, the monument would have presented an appearance of magnificence commensurate with the prestige of this distinguished northern lady.

THE EFFIGY OF A FOURTEENTH-CENTURY MERCHANT

Tucked away in the south-east corner of the east aisle of the north transept is the effigy of a secular male figure [**65**], traditionally believed to commemorate a Flemish merchant. The man is shown dressed in a long robe with pocket slits at the sides, through which his purse-belt can be seen. Around his shoulders, he wears a short cape, with the hood thrown back to reveal his long, flowing hair - trimmed to match the length of his short beard and drooping moustache. Two

65 Effigy of an unknown fourteenth-century merchant in the north transept.

angels hold the corners of the cushion beneath his head, while a watchful lion supports his feet. His hands joined in prayer, and his head framed by a cusped canopy, he presents a dignified image of lay piety - evidently a man of some substance and status. In the 18th century the effigy lay on a raised tomb in the north choir aisle, but where it lay before the Reformation is not known. According to Gough, it was 'dug up somewhere in the church'.[61]

The Beverley merchant was affiliated by Brian and Moira Gittos to a group of sandstone tombs – the 'Wolds Series' – whose geographical distribution stretches from Birdsall in the Yorkshire Wolds to Patrington in the south-east corner of Holderness. Beverley – approximately midway between the two, and the main town in this part of Yorkshire – may well have been the centre of production. In operation from the 1320s to around 1360, the workshop is best known for the de Mauley tomb at Bainton, whose canopy incorporates features inspired by the Percy tomb.[62] The Beverley merchant would suit a date of c. 1330–50.[63]

The tradition that the effigy commemorates a Flemish merchant draws attention to the importance of the town's commercial links with Flanders, stemming principally from the trade in wool and cloth. However, the tradition was not mentioned by Gent and appears to be of relatively recent origin. Indeed, Beverley had many rich merchants of its own, several of whom were sufficiently affluent to lend the king large sums of money to help finance the preparations for the Hundred Years War. There is nothing particularly Flemish about the effigy – certainly it was not made in Flanders – and in all probability it commemorates one of the wealthier burgesses of Beverley.

THE TOMB OF HENRY PERCY, FOURTH EARL OF NORTHUMBERLAND

During the hundred or so years that followed the erection of Idonea's tomb, a combination of factors conspired to prevent any further Percy burials at the Minster. The tombs of Eleanor Neville and George Percy marked a turning point, however, and in the later 15th and early 16th centuries four more members of the family chose Beverley as their final resting place. Despite Oliver's belief that George was a canon of Beverley, there is no evidence to support this, and his interment at the Minster, like that of his mother, is best explained in terms of the Percies' long-standing affection for their ancestral lands in Yorkshire.[64] Leconfield, where George was born, appears to have been the family's main residence in the later 15th century and, were it not for the fact that the first three Percy earls of Northumberland died on the battlefield, it is quite possible that the family mausoleum at Beverley would have been even more extensive than it eventually became.

The fourth earl - the 'mighty lion feared by sea and land' - fared no better than his predecessors, being slain at his manor at Topcliffe in 1489 during an uprising sparked off by his attempts to levy an unpopular tax.[65] In his will, made in 1485, he expressed the wish to be buried in Beverley Minster, should fortune dictate that he died in Yorkshire.[66] The result was the construction of the Percy Chapel on the north side of the Lady Chapel. The north window of the chapel was itself conceived as a memorial to the earl, and in the stained glass he was depicted together with his wife, Maud, and their children, kneeling on either side of a shield bearing his coat of arms. An accompanying inscription invited prayers for their souls.[67]

The jambs of the window are decorated with angels bearing shields carved with Percy armorials and badges, using the trappings of divinity to immortalize the earthly status of the earl in a manner reminiscent of fifteenth-century tombs, many of which substituted shield-bearing angels for the fashionably dressed weeper figures popular in the 14th century. Included among the heraldic insignia is Maud's family badge, a bascule – based on the counterpoise mechanism used to raise and lower drawbridges.[68] Maud, the daughter of William Herbert, earl of Pembroke, predeceased her husband and was already lying at Beverley when he made his will in 1485.[69]

The fourth earl's monument - an imposing table tomb, encased on all four sides with ogee-headed niches for statuettes - still dominates the Percy Chapel [**pl. 6**]. The miniature buttresses separating the niches are decorated with heraldic shields and badges, a compendium of the ancestral arms of the Percies and those Percy countesses who had contributed significantly to the greater estate of the family.[70] A drawing in *Dugdale's Yorkshire Arms* [**15**] shows that the niches were already empty in 1641, although their backs retain evidence of the attachments used to hold the statuettes in place. The lost figures may have depicted the earl's heirs and relatives, although apostles, saints and shield-bearing angels are also found on tomb chests of this period.

Until the 18th century, the tomb chest was surmounted by a battlemented canopy incorporating a flattened ogee arch resting on tall, freestanding supports [**15**]. The cornice bore the earl's motto, '*Esperance Ma Comfort*', while the spandrels of the arches were filled with heraldic beasts supporting garters containing his coat of arms and his favourite badge, the locket. Resplendent in its original colour and gilding, the sculpture and heraldry would have perpetuated the magnificence of the earl's funeral, an event requiring the manufacture of twelve banners, 100 silk pennons and sixty buckram shields – all bearing his arms or badge – and attended by 500 priests and over 13,000 poor people, each of whom received a sum of money for their trouble.[71] Associated with the tomb was an altar, at which five priests were bound to sing for the souls of the earl, his wife and their ancestors. In addition to stirring the saints into intercessory action, this regular round of prayers would have ensured that Henry and Maud were remembered by the living.

Leland began his account of the tombs at Beverley with a monument which he identified simply as that of 'Percy earl of Northumberland'. We know he was talking about the fourth earl's tomb because he went on to note the presence of a second tomb, belonging to 'his son, father to the last earl'. The 'last earl' in Leland's day was Henry Percy, sixth earl of Northumberland – 'Henry the Unthrifty' – who died childless in 1537 and was buried at Hackney. Thomas Percy, his brother and heir presumptive, was executed at Tyburn that same year for his role in the Pilgrimage of Grace, and Thomas's son – also called Thomas – did not succeed until 1557, on account of his father's attainder. The 'father to the last earl' was thus Henry Algernon Percy, fifth earl of Northumberland (1489–1527).[72]

The monument commemorating the fifth earl – Henry the Magnificent – has long since disappeared, but it was in this tomb that his wife, Catherine, was interred at her death in 1542 - the year after Leland's visit. In her will, dated 4 October 1542, she expressed the wish to be buried 'within the monastery of Beverley, and in the tomb there of my said late lord and husband'.[73] A drawing in *Sir Thomas Wriothesley's Book of Funeral Collections* shows the effigies of the earl and countess lying on a magnificent altar tomb, whose sides are decorated with large escutcheons separated by engaged baluster motifs.[74] Especially interesting from an art historical perspective is the complete renunciation of the decorative vocabulary of the Gothic style, marking the arrival of the Tudor Renaissance in Beverley.

On the eve of the Reformation, the array of Percy tombs at the east end of the Minster would have constituted a spectacular affirmation of the power and prestige of this remarkable family - an important link in a chain of memorials testifying to the antiquity of their lineage and the nobility of their blood line.

POSTSCRIPT

The ensuing period of religious upheaval had profound consequences both for the Percies and for the Minster's shrines and monuments. Insofar as the latter are concerned, the Protestants' rejection of the supernatural power of the saints removed the whole *raison d'être* for shrines and pilgrimages.[75] The fate of the glorious shrine of St John was sealed in 1541, when the Privy Council instructed the archbishop of York to ensure the destruction of all shrines throughout his province.[76] The idea of purgatory found no place in the reformed church and, under the Colleges and Chantries Act of 1547, chantry foundations were dissolved and their endowments confiscated to the Crown. As a further result of the act, the Minster lost its collegiate status, beginning a new life as a parish church in 1548 as discussed in chapter 4.[77]

Their former guardians replaced by a new administration with no financial incentive to take care of them, the Minster's monuments were left in an exposed position at the very moment when, under Edward VI, and again in the early years of Elizabeth's reign, attacks on religious images intensified. Stephen Gardiner, bishop of Winchester, voiced the fear that iconoclasm had a political dimension, which, if unchecked, could spread to images symbolizing the hereditary authority of the nobility, so undermining the established order of society. The extent to which these fears were justified is reflected in the proclamation, issued by Elizabeth in 1560, prohibiting the destruction or defacing of tombs and monuments 'set up in the churches or other public places for memory, and not for superstition'.[78]

It is against this background that one must view the depredations and losses that had overtaken the monuments by the time of Dugdale's visit in 1661.[79] The fourth earl's effigy had been removed, along with the statuettes that formerly surrounded his tomb chest. The monument of Henry and Catherine is nowhere in evidence. Eleanor's tomb had also disappeared, and the north-east transept chapel was being used as a vestry. The Percy tomb had been stripped of its brass and Idonea's canopy was standing under an arch of the south nave arcade, purporting to be the tomb of two Saxon virgins, while her tomb chest had been redeployed to support the effigy of Nicholas of Huggate in the north transept.

The only beneficiary of all this would appear to have been Maud Percy, claimed in *Dugdale's Yorkshire Arms* to be the occupant of the Percy tomb. Whether this was simply a mistake, as has been assumed, or a reinterment following the removal of her original tomb - which was not mentioned in Leland's account - is difficult to say. However, a tomb chest believed to be that of Maud and described by Dugdale as 'near unto' that of the fourth earl, was opened in 1678, revealing a stone coffin containing an embalmed body covered with cloth of gold. Also in the coffin were a wax lamp, a candle and a plate candlestick.[80] When the contents of the tomb chest associated with the Percy tomb were inspected in 1824, they found a wooden coffin containing the bones of a person estimated to have been no older than fourteen, encased in sheet lead.[81] This hardly corresponds to the description of the earlier finds and it is legitimate to ask what on earth had been going on at the Minster in the interim. Part of the answer may lie in the activities of a certain sexton, who, in the company of others, opened and ransacked both the Percy tomb and the earl of Northumberland's monument in 1793.[82] A good time was evidently had by all: games of skittles were played, skulls were bowled down the aisle, bones were stolen and one of the fourth earl's fingers finished up as a silver-tipped tobacco stopper!

The final chapter on the post-medieval history of the Percy mausoleum remains to be written, and will undoubtedly make interesting reading. In the meantime one can do no more than emphasize the historical importance of the remaining medieval monuments, whose fortunate survival helps bring us closer to some of the people whose lives shaped the town and Minster of Beverley. Indeed, the very existence of the Percy tomb - quite apart from the excellent state of preservation of its sculpture - is nothing short of a miracle!

NOTES

1   P. Binski, *Medieval Death: Ritual and Representation* (1996), p. 32.

2   Leach, *Memorials*, ii, pp. lxi–lxii, 122–5; R. McDermid, 'The Constitution and the Clergy of Beverley Minster in the Middle Ages' (unpublished MA thesis, University of Durham, 1980), pp. 365–97; idem, *Beverley Minster Fasti* (YASRS, 149, 1993), pp. 37 n. 5, 124 n. 7; R. Kemp, 'Tomb of an Unknown Priest at Beverley', *Aspects of Heraldry*, 8 (1994), 7–9.

3   R. Gough, *Sepulchral Monuments in Great Britain* (2 vols, 1786–96), ii, pt 3, p. 312.

4   B. & M. Gittos, 'The Goldsborough Effigies', *Journal of the Church Monuments Society*, 9 (1994), 3–32.

5   College of Arms, MS RR 14.C, 'Dugdale's Yorkshire Arms' (1667), f. 85v.

6   W. Longstaffe, 'The Old Heraldry of the Percies', *Archaeologia Aeliana*, new series, 4 (1860), 170 n. 15, 172. The effigy is 197 cm long, 33 cm shorter than the tomb chest.

7   Oxford, Bodleian Library, Gough Maps 227; Gough, *Sepulchral Monuments*, ii, pt 3, pl. CXIV.

8   Longstaffe, 'Old Heraldry', 172; N. Pevsner and D. Neave, *The Buildings of England: Yorkshire: York and the East Riding* (Harmondsworth, 1995), pp. 292–3.

9   For this, and the following account, see Leach, *Memorials*, ii, pp. lvi–lxii; McDermid, *Fasti*, pp. 8, 36–7.

10 McDermid, 'Constitution and Clergy', pp. 371–2.

11 I. Roper, *The Monumental Effigies of Gloucestershire and Bristol* (Gloucester, 1931), pp. 191–4. I am grateful to Philip Lankester for drawing my attention to these two figures.

12 M. Michael, 'The Little Land of England is Preferred before the Great Kingdom of France: the quartering of the royal arms by Edward III', in D. Buckton and T. Heslop, eds, *Studies in Art and Architecture presented to Peter Lasko* (1994), pp. 113–18.

13 For this group of monuments, see E. Panofsky, *Tomb Sculpture* (1964), pp. 59–61; L. Gee, 'Ciborium Tombs in England 1290–1330', *Journal of the British Archaeological Association*, 132 (1979), 29–41.

14 G. Oliver, *The History and Antiquities of the Town and Minster of Beverley* (Beverley, 1829), p. 337 n. 64.

15 P.J.P. Goldberg, 'The Percy Tomb in Beverley Minster', *YAJ*, 56 (1984), 65.

16 Oxford, Bodleian Library, Gough Maps 227; Gough, *Sepulchral Monuments*, ii, pt. 3, pl. CXI; P. Binski, 'The Stylistic Sequence of London Figure Brasses', in J. Coales, ed., *The Earliest Figure Brasses: Patronage, Style and Workshops* (1987), p. 128 and fig. 126; S. Badham, 'Monumental Brasses: the development of the York workshops in the fourteenth and fifteenth centuries', in C. Wilson, ed., *Medieval Art and Architecture in the East Riding of Yorkshire* (British Archaeological Association Conference Transactions, 9, 1989), p. 166. This dating is consistent with the view of Ms Badham - expressed in conversation with the writer - that the lost brass from the Percy tomb was a precursor of the group of London brasses known as Series A, the subject of a forthcoming article to appear in the *Antiquaries Journal*.

17 J. Russell, *A History of Heaven* (Princeton, 1997), pp. 66, 89, 91–6, 137–8.

18 Dante Alighieri, *The Divine Comedy, Vol. III: Paradise*, trans. M. Musa (Harmondsworth, 1986), p. 169.

19 II Timothy 4:8: 'Henceforth there is laid up for me a crown of righteousness, which the Lord, the righteous Judge, shall give me at that day; and not to me only, but unto all them also that love his appearing'.

20 Dante Alighieri, *The Divine Comedy, Vol. II: Purgatory*, trans. M. Musa (Harmondsworth, 1985), p. 112.

21 Jacobus de Voragine, *The Golden Legend of Jacobus de Voragine*, trans. G. Ryan and H. Ripperger (1948), pp. 708–16.

22 L. Toulmin Smith, ed., *The Itinerary of John Leland* (5 vols, 1906–10), i, p. 46.

23 M. Martin, ed., *The Percy Chartulary* (Surtees Society, 117, 1911), pp. 179–80.

24 BIHR, Prob. Reg. 4 f. 220v.

25 Oliver, *History and Antiquities*, p. 342.

26 D. O'Connor, 'The Medieval Stained Glass of Beverley Minster', in C. Wilson, ed., *Medieval Art and Architecture in the East Riding*, p. 72.

27 T. Gent, *The Antient and Modern History of the Loyal Town of Rippon* (York, 1733), p. 95.

28 *Cal. Close Rolls 1349–1354*, p. 422.

29 William Peeris, *Chronicle of the Family of Percy*, ed. J. Besly, (Reprints of Rare Tracts and Imprints of Ancient Manuscripts, etc., chiefly Illustrative of the Northern Counties, Newcastle, 1845), p. 29.

30 Poulson, *Beverlac*, ii, p. 696; Longstaffe, 'Old Heraldry', 172.

31 P. Binski and J. Blair, 'The Tomb of Edward I and early London Brass Production', *Transactions of the Monumental Brass Society*, 14, iii (1988), 234–6.

32 College of Arms, MS RR 14.C, f. 89v.

33 York Minster Library, MS LI (10), James Torre, 'Church Peculiars within the Diocess of York... Collected out of the peculiars & other registers A.D. 1691', p. 167; Gough, *Sepulchral Monuments*, ii, pt 3, p. 311; Goldberg, 'Percy Tomb', 68–9.

34 Goldberg, 'Percy Tomb', 68; Longstaffe, 'Old Heraldry', 170; G.E. Cockayne, ed., *The Complete Peerage* (13 vols, 1910–59), v, pp. 267–72.

35 C.H. Hartshorne, *Feudal and Military Antiquities of Northumberland and the Scottish Borders* (1858), p. 275 and Appendix I, p. vi; J. Raine, ed., *Testamenta Eboracensia*, i (Surtees Society, 4, 1836), p. 57.

36 C.H. Hunter Blair, 'Medieval effigies in Northumberland', *Archaeologia Aeliana*, 4th series, 7 (1930), 21 no. XIX, 26–7 no. XXXII and pls XIII (figs 1, 2), XVI (fig. 2); N. Dawton, 'The Percy Tomb at Beverley Minster', in F.H. Thompson, ed., *Studies in Medieval Sculpture*, Society of Antiquaries occasional papers, new series, 3 (1983), pp. 126–7 and pl. LI(a).

37 J. Britton, *The History and Antiquities of the See and Cathedral Church of Norwich* (1816), p. 60; F. Nichols, 'On the Age found in Inquisitions post mortem, and on the Parentage of Thomas Percy, Bishop of Norwich, 1355', *The Genealogist*, new series, 4 (1887), 14–16.

38 Dawton, 'Percy Tomb', pp. 126–7, 143 and pls. LI(a), LIII(b); E. Prior and A. Gardner, *An Account of Medieval Figure-Sculpture in England* (Cambridge, 1912), fig. 366; H.M. Colvin, ed., *The History of the King's Works: The Middle Ages* (2 vols, 1963), i, p. 484.

39 J. Alexander and P. Binski, eds, *Age of Chivalry: art in Plantagenet England 1200–1400* (Royal Academy of Arts, 1987), pp. 344–5 no. 340.

40 L. Stone, *Sculpture in Britain: The Middle Ages* (Harmondsworth, 1972), pp. 125–7.

41 N. Dawton, 'The Percy Tomb Workshop', in C. Wilson, ed., *Medieval Art and Architecture in the East Riding*, p. 126; P. Binski, *Westminster Abbey and the Plantagenets* (1995), p. 177.

42 D. Turner, 'The Development of Master Honoré', *British Museum Quarterly*, 33 (1968–9), pp. 53–65; R. Marks and N. Morgan, *The Golden Age of English Manuscript Painting 1200–1500* (1981), p. 17; Alexander and Binski, *Age of Chivalry*, pp. 340–1 no. 329.

43 P. Williamson, *Gothic Sculpture 1140–1300* (1995), pp. 217–18 and pl. 324.

44 Cf. Stone, *Sculpture in Britain*, pl. 107(A).

45 Binski, *Westminster Abbey*, pp. 182–4.

46 O. Pächt, 'A Giottesque Episode in English Medieval Art', *Journal of the Warburg and Courtauld Institutes*, 6 (1943), 57–70.

47 Dawton, 'Percy Tomb', p. 127 and pls LIIa, LIIb.

48 M. Marcus, '"An Attempt to Discriminate the Styles" - the sculptors of the Harrington Tomb, Cartmel', *Journal of the Church Monuments Society*, 11 (1996), fig. 14.

49 Dawton, 'Workshop', pp. 128–9.

50 Located between SP 6 and SP 7.

51 Pevsner and Neave, *York and the East Riding*, p. 293.

52 Gent, *History of Rippon*, p. 95.

53 Oliver, *History and Antiquities*, p. 320 and n. 28; Torre, 'Church Peculiars', f. 165.

54 K.A. MacMahon, *Beverley* (Clapham, 1973), p. 28.

55 See N. Coldstream, 'The Development of Flowing Tracery in Yorkshire, c. 1300–1380' (unpublished PhD thesis, University of London, 1973), pp. 55–94, 161–209.

56 F. McCulloch, *Medieval Latin and French Bestiaries* (Chapel Hill, 1962), pp. 166–9; N.C Flores. '"*Effigies amicitiae ... veritas inimicitiae*": antifeminism in the iconography of the woman-headed serpent in medieval and Renaissance art and literature, in idem, ed., *Animals in the Middle Ages* (1996), p. 173.

57 G. Druce, tr., *The Bestiary of Guillaume le Clerc, Originally written in 1210–11* (Ashford, 1936), pp. 36–7.

58 A. Weir and J. Jerman, *Images of lust: sexual carvings on medieval churches* (1986), pp. 48–53; C. Grössinger, *The World Upside-Down: English misericords* (1997), pp. 139–41.

59 G. Owst, *Literature and Pulpit in Medieval England* (Oxford, 1961), p. 201; L. Houwen, 'Flattery and the Mermaid in Chaucer's Nun's Priest's Tale', in idem, ed., *Animals and the Symbolic in Medieval Art and Literature* (Groningen, 1997), pp. 77–92.

60 Longstaffe, 'Old Heraldry', 172.

61 Oxford, Bodleian Library, MS Top. Gen. e. 25, f.311v.

62 B. & M. Gittos, 'A Survey of East Riding Sepulchral Monuments Before 1500', in C. Wilson, ed., *Medieval Art and Architecture in the East Riding* , pp. 96, 99, 107 n. 28.

63 I am grateful to Brian and Moira Gittos for this suggested dating, based on a variety of evidence.

64 Oliver, *History and Antiquities*, p. 323 n. 33; J. Raine, ed., *Testamenta Eboracensia*, iii (Surtees Society, 45, 1865), p. 210 n.

65 *Complete Peerage*, ix, p. 718.

66 *Test. Ebor.*, iii, p. 305.

67 O'Connor, 'Medieval Glass', p. 73 and pl. XVIA.

68 Longstaffe, 'Old Heraldry', 193, 198.

69 *Test. Ebor.*, iii, p. 310.

70 Longstaffe, 'Old Heraldry', 193–4.

71 *Ibid.*, 192 n. 46.

72 *Complete Peerage*, ix, pp. 717 sqq.

73 J.W. Clay, ed., *Testamenta Eboracensia*, vi (Surtees Society, 106, 1902), p. 166.

74 BL, Additional MS 45131, f. 89v.

75 J. Phillips, *The Reformation of Images: destruction of art in England, 1535–1660* (California, 1973), pp. 54–5.

76 *L. & P. Hen. VIII*, xvi, p. 553.

77 A.F. Leach, 'The Inmates of Beverley Minster', *TERAS*, 2 (1894), 100–2.

78 Phillips, *Reformation of Images*, pp. 82 sqq., 90–1, 117–8; N. Boulting, 'The Law's Delays: conservationist legislation in the British Isles', in J. Fawcett, ed., *The Future of the Past: attitudes to conservation 1174–1974* (1976), p. 11.

79 College of Arms, MS RR 14.C, ff. 87–90.

80 Longstaffe, 'Old Heraldry', 192.

81 *Ibid.*, 168 n. 9.

82 Oliver, *History and Antiquities*, p. 344.

10 · The Misericords

The Beverley stalls were executed around 1520, the date carved on the sacrist's misericord.[1] Those who gave towards the erection of ecclesiastical monuments were usually anxious that their piety should be publicly, if discreetly, recognized – for those who were armigerous, a heraldic emblem or rebus was the obvious solution. The sacrist's stall is inscribed on the left-hand supporter, *arma wilhelmi tait doctori[s]*, and on the right-hand, *thesaurarii huius ecclesie 1520*. Tait's coat of arms is the central carving of this misericord, supported by a hawk and dog, and on the canopy of his stall there is further a small corbel supporting the blank arcading which repeats the demi-sunburst motif and the inscription *tate*.

The precentor's stall is similarly identified by an inscription divided between the two supporters: on the left, above a pelican in her piety, we read *arma magistri thome* and on the right, *donyngto[n] p[re]centoris hui[u]s eccl[es]ie*. The central carving depicts a fanciful shield of arms, but the right-hand supporter depicts a collared and chained DOE sitting ON a TUN, i.e. a rebus, that popular late-medieval device, which yields the name Donington [77].

Another misericord inscribed with the name of one of the Minster's officers is that belonging to William Wight. Surrounding a shield of arms is a banderole inscribed *Will[el]mi Wyght tempore cancellarij huius ecclesie*. The chancellor's arms clearly provide an example of canting heraldry, with the weights depicted on his shield punning on his surname, and to drive the point home the two supporters also humorously feature men carrying weights. Somewhat puzzlingly, the same composition is repeated just three seats away. Did Wight perhaps contribute financially to the work to such an extent that it was felt fitting he should be commemorated in a second seat?

The last named member of the chapter is John Sparke, recorded on a banderole in the left-hand supporter in the form *Johannes Sperke*, while the inscription in the right-hand supporter gives his office as *clericus fabrici* or clerk of works. The supporters to Sparke's misericord are a dog gnawing a bone and a cockerel - both might conceivably have a symbolic significance or merely be genre scenes. Clearly Sparke had no coat of arms, for the main subject of his misericord is a hawking scene depicting a gentleman with a hawk on his wrist – Sparke himself? – and two hounds running off to his right, as a manservant with another dog on a leash runs in from the left.

A misericord on which we might expect to find some personal heraldic device is that of the stall of the archbishop of York, none other than Thomas Wolsey (consecrated 1514). Wolsey was not just the spiritual lord of the people of Beverley, but their temporal lord too and the townsfolk were well aware of their lord's power and went out of their way to keep him sweet. During 1522–3, for example, almost all of the town's expenditure on 'great men' went to his officials. He appointed his illegitimate son provost of Beverley at an unknown date, but certainly before March 1526. The birds carved on the supporters of Wolsey's stall have been described as a pelican and 'probably an eagle'. The chough was Wolsey's badge - is this what the Beverley carver has attempted?

Sadly, we know nothing about the carvers of the Beverley stalls and yet we are surely entitled to suspect some playful self-reference on at least one of the misericords they crafted. The stalls

66 The choir from the east, showing the stalls. Much of the woodwork at the upper levels is eighteenth- and nineteenth-century.

provide several incidental examples of significant gesture, but one misericord in particular may be said to consist entirely, main carving and supporters, of the representation of gestures. On the seat in question, two carvers are depicted, one raises a mallet, the other holds a chisel. If it is a quarrel then it can hardly be serious, for both men are smiling. The right-hand carver points at the man on the right-hand supporter who appears to be thumbing his nose at his colleague. The whole composition seems best interpreted as a piece of affectionate 'signing' of their work by the craftsmen of the Beverley *atelier* [**6**]. The two principal carvers are depicted with the tools of their trade threatening in a jocular manner two of their playfully insubordinate juniors or apprentices who, fittingly occupying subordinate and necessarily smaller positions in the supporters, direct gestural insults at their masters.

The importance of the Beverley misericords is as a representative body of late-medieval iconography. They were carved at a particularly interesting time. Chronologically, they are one of the latest English sets to be made, only shortly before the Reformation and the break with Rome, and stylistically they also provide important negative evidence for the penetration of the Italian Renaissance into English woodcarving, despite the availability of Italianate motifs, even in Yorkshire, at this time. From the Beverley stalls we sense that the middle ages are far from dead in 1520 and that the early modern era is still some way off. The year of their carving also saw the extraordinary Anglo-French spectacle of the Field of the Cloth of Gold, an occasion of lavish magnificence, but, despite the application of renaissance motifs to the royal pavilions, a spectacle still articulated in the chivalric idiom of the middle ages.

In terms of their style and iconography, the Beverley misericords may be usefully compared with those at Bristol, which must be very closely contemporary as they bear the arms of Abbot Robert Elyot (1515–26); the royal commissions associated with Edward IV at Windsor (c.1480) and Henry VII at Westminster (c.1512); but principally with the set at Manchester (c.1506).

Iconographically, the misericords at Bristol are perhaps the closest in feel to the Minster set. The four designs which the Bristol carver took from early printed Parisian *Horae* of the type printed by Pigouchet for Vostre compare with the three such used by the Beverley carver (see below). There is also a similar interest at Bristol in proverbial absurdity, and stylistically too, the Bristol seating shares with that at Beverley an absence of full-blooded renaissance motifs. A significant proportion of the misericords of the two royal chapels can be shown to derive their designs from German and Flemish prints – an important pointer to the availability of 'Germanic' prints to English stall-carvers in the decades around 1500 – and an influence also evident at Beverley (see below).

Tracy has stated that the carver of the Manchester stalls must have been acquainted with those at Windsor and 'what is more, the decorative carving has a distant stylistic affinity'.[2] Maybe it was directly from Windsor that the Manchester carver derived the conceit of the leaf 'tie' on the supporters, from where, presumably, the Beverley master derived his use of it, for we can be certain that the Beverley carver was familiar with the stalls at Manchester and probably those now at Durham castle as well. There can be no doubt, for example, that the entire Beverley misericord of the bagpiping sow including the supporters [**67**] is a reversed copy of that at Manchester. Similarly, there can be no doubt that the Beverley carver copied the Manchester design of the fox stealing a goose. Another striking correspondence is the Beverley ape-urinanalyst, clearly copied from that flanking the pedlar robbed by apes misericord at Manchester. Similarly, the opposite supporter to the Beverley carving, depicting an ape holding a swaddled baby, is copied from the opposite Manchester supporter.

We can be sure that there has been no change in the layout of the Beverley misericords since 1879, the year in which Tindall Wildridge published his book, *The Misereres of Beverley Minster*, but what of the intervening three-and-a-half centuries since their original placement? It is

67　A bagpiping sow, misericord 18 (for the location of the misericords see fig. 3). On the right, a harping sow.

undeniable that there are certain series of subjects portrayed on the misericords. An obvious example is the 'bear-hunt' quartet: if these represent four episodes in the capture of wild bears, then, as presently arranged, a sequence of three bear scenes is interrupted by that of a stag being disembowelled. Similarly, the preaching fox and its pendant, the geese hanging the fox, are now separated by two intervening seats, but must surely have been originally intended to be neighbours. The conclusion to be drawn from the evidence of these and other examples of interruptions in series at Beverley must be that the misericords were re-arranged at some point between the date of their carving and the late 19th century.

The Beverley misericords are quintessentially English in design: a central carved subject beneath the ledge of the upturned seat, flanked on either side by a smaller supporter. The relationship of supporters to central carving varies at Beverley as elsewhere. Sometimes there is reason to believe that the supporters offer some sort of comment on the central subject, sometimes they are merely 'emptily' decorative, occasionally all three scenes are to be read as a continuous narrative.

It is too readily assumed that all imagery to be found in a medieval context when not overtly religious in subject matter must be 'symbolic', so that, for example, any animal which is also to be found in the Bestiary must have been intended to be moralized. Some misericord carvings come close to being 'art for art's sake' – certainly, on the continent contracts contemporary with the Beverley stalls suggest that the carvers had a more or less free hand as to subject matter, subject matter which was, after all, to be hidden from view for most of the time. The misericords of the Amiens Cathedral stalls were to be decorated, according to the early sixteenth-century order 'de feuillaige ou mannequins et petis bestiaux et *autre chose a plaisance*' [with foliage or little people and animals and *anything else, as it pleases you*]. Similarly, the carver Gillis van Dickele was instructed to decorate the misericords of the new stalls of the abbey of St Clare in Gentbrugge with figures 'corresponderende eenighe bysprake *of dies ghelycke*' [corresponding to some proverb *or the like*]. Both orders make a token display of specificity but then abandon the pretence of a detailed instruction, plainly leaving the choice of subject matter, in practice, to the carver. From a study of the extant examples there is every reason to believe the situation was no different in England, where no contracts survive.

The Beverley stalls are no exception among the English misericord corpus in depicting only a tiny proportion of motifs which one could describe as overtly religious. One of the very few motifs of undoubted Christian reference is the Bestiary-derived pelican in her piety, one of the commonest of all Christian emblems, amply represented in the English misericord corpus. At Beverley it appears, significantly, as the central carving of the misericord on the stall reserved for the archbishop of York. A supporter carved with a smaller version of this subject also flanks the arms of Thomas Donington. The correlation between the subject matter of these two stalls and the status of the dignitaries to whom they were allotted, holders of the two highest-ranking offices represented in the Minster, can hardly be accidental. However free a hand the carvers had in the choice of decoration of the other stalls, the imagery of these two seats must have been closely specified.

The stall bearing the design of the spies returning from Canaan [Numbers xiii. 23] is the only truly scriptural subject and is copied from the block-book *Biblia Pauperum*. This popular religious work, printed in the Netherlands in the mid 15th century, is undoubtedly the ultimate source for this design, and responsible for its widespread popularity, though whether the Beverley carver had the book itself in front of him is another matter. The fact that this subject is found on only two other extant English misericords, at Ripon and Manchester, we are surely entitled to regard as more than mere coincidence.

If there are few overtly religious motifs in the Beverley misericords, and, as has been suggested, there is reason to doubt the moralizing symbolism of other subjects so readily inferred by many earlier commentators, can we nevertheless interpret some images as didactic in some way, or even satiric, rather than merely decorative?

A subject which must still have retained some of its original satiric bite is that of the preaching fox. The religious were not immune from satirical attack, and in particular the mendicant orders were always a comfortable target as far as the regular clergy were concerned. In his comprehensive survey of medieval fox iconography, Kenneth Varty showed how the motif of the preaching fox, or fox-friar preaching to a bird-congregation, was originally intended as a satirical hit at the rapacity of the various mendicant orders. The two misericords at Beverley which illustrate this theme are relatively late examples of a tradition which has its beginnings in thirteenth-century English art. The Beverley fox-friar is a fairly standard presentation of the subject. Holding a rosary (and therefore perhaps implying that he is a Dominican) Brother Reynard preaches from a pulpit to a congregation of seven proverbially silly geese [**21b**]. The scene of the revenge of the geese, who are depicted hanging Reynard, is frequently, as here at Beverley, paired with that of the fox's sermon. The best contemporary parallel in English woodwork for the pairing of these scenes is to be found at Bristol.

There is at least one subject (apart from the personal rebuses discussed above) that seems to embody a contemporary topical reference. Along with his sponsorship of various types of formal and informal drama, Henry Percy the 'Magnificent', fifth earl of Northumberland, sponsored a bearward named John Grene who travelled about the country with his performing bears. In the very year our stalls were carved, there is a municipal record of the payment of 6s 8d to this *ursarius* for exhibiting his dancing bears [*agitationis ursonum*] in the Beverley marketplace.[3] The supporters to one misericord show a bear squatting patiently on all fours while the bearward fastens the muzzle behind the animal's neck [**68**], and a smallish bear standing on its hind legs, its forepaws grasping the top of the bearward's left leg while he appears to pat it. Another supporter depicts a bear dancing to the sound of bagpipes played by an ape, perhaps one of the acts John Grene staged to amuse the Beverley public.

At Beverley it is the elephant's 'castle' that betrays its ultimate Bestiary derivation (compare the similar composition at Manchester), unlike the more naturalistic elephant depicted on an Exeter stall in the early 1240s. An even more splendid elephant and castle is carved in the round as one of the Beverley stall-end 'poppyheads' [**69**]. It must be stressed, however, that Bestiary derivation does not necessarily imply the associated Bestiary symbolism. One of the Beverley lions, with its paw on the head of a prostrate man, is probably to be derived from the Bestiary tradition, in which the lion's alleged unwillingness to get angry unless wounded and its sparing of the prostrate are both commended to the attention of every decent human being. It is

68 A man muzzling a bear; the left supporter of misericord 10.

69   The elephant and castle bench end.

possible that the other misericord which depicts the confrontation between a man and a lion, in which the man spears the lion, was originally paired with this, and that it is to be interpreted as illustrating the Bestiary assertion that despite its courageous nature, the lion would not look directly at a hunter's spear.

At least two subjects at Beverley, the misericords depicting the cat catching mice [**70**], and the hen with her chicks, might be considered as possible illustrations of *exempla*, short anecdotes or observations of everyday life which were inserted into sermons for the preacher to moralize. Historically, the tendency has been for scholars to assume such Bestiary-derived imagery brings with it its original Bestiary symbolism, more recently, however, such animal subjects have increasingly been seen as no more than observations of natural history. The carving of the mobbed owl is another such subject, the owl sometimes representing, as in the Bestiary, the Jews. Whatever the metaphorical possibilities of such a representation, however, I suspect that, here again, the motif of the owl attacked from all sides by smaller birds simply afforded the artist the opportunity of executing a satisfying, aesthetic composition – a composition particularly well suited to the circular roof boss, for example, as at Sherborne.

Some Bestiaries were enlarged by the inclusion of a humanoid bestiary, the so-called Monstrous Races, and the mysterious subject called by Anderson (who records seven examples),[4] 'Child rising from shell to fight dragon', is, I believe, based ultimately on a Monstrous Races prototype in which a pygmy (the 'child') emerges from its hole (the shell) adjacent to a hydra (the dragon).

A figure related, thematically at least, is that of the wild man or wodehouse / wodewose, covered in shaggy hair and usually carrying a club. Several misericords depict the wild man at Beverley at a date by which he had usually come to be thought of as a kind of late-medieval noble savage, but it is just possible that his presence here owes something to the *Life* of the Minster's patron, St John of Beverley. A Flemish *Life* printed c.1512, the *Historie ende Leven Vanden Heilyghen Heremijt Sint Jan Van Beverley* – for which we must posit a lost English original – tells how St John became a wildman when he retired into the wilderness after having murdered his sister, and it seems inconceivable that the carvers were unaware of this tradition regarding the town's patron saint.[5]

70 A cat catching mice,
    misericord 26. On the left,
    the cat and fiddle.

At Beverley carvings of fools abound, as might be expected historically in the town where the popular medieval Feast of Fools seems to have survived longest in England. Archbishop Arundel's ordinances of 1391 concerning the better government of the church at Beverley forbid celebration of the ancient custom of the *Rex Stultorum*,[6] though he is prepared to countenance the continuation of *les Fulles* as one of the Christmas games permitted to the laity. The Beverley fool carvings fall into two groups: three misericords which present the fool's head in classic eared hood, and a fourth misericord depicting three fools dancing.

One fool confronts us grinning, the forefinger of his right hand in the right-hand corner of his mouth, while the forefinger of his left hand rests above or pulls at his left eyebrow. As for the meaning of this fool's face, it might, of course, be purely whimsical, a piece of *grotesquerie* merely, yet both gestures considered separately can be assigned conventional meanings. The iconography of historical gesture is still in its infancy but, in an admittedly modern survey, the gesture termed 'the eyelid pull' signifies, 'I'm alert, I'm no fool'. Could this fool, paradoxically, be trying to tell us he is no fool? Both supporters depict geese. However unjustly, the goose is considered a proverbially foolish bird in English as in other European languages, compare the contemporary poet Skelton's 'as witless as a wild goose'. It is also the bird *par excellence* associated with the fool. A contemporary misericord at Christchurch in Dorset (1515) depicts a jester offering a plate of bread to a goose, and the privy purse expenses of Henry VII's queen, Elizabeth of York (1465-1503), record payment to 'John Goose, my lord of York's fool'. Peculiarly appropriate is a phrase in the homily *Against Contention*, intended for preaching throughout the churches of Henry VIII's realm in 1547: 'Shall I stand still, like a goose or a fool, with my finger in my mouth?' This quotation significantly combines three of the elements which go to make up this misericord carving – the fool, the goose, and the finger in the mouth – and constitutes valuable proof that the goose supporters are not merely whimsical, decorative additions.

The neighbouring misericord, which also features two goose supporters, presents a fool's head in an eared hood on top of which stand two birds which I believe are intended to be coots. It is Skelton again who first styles the bird 'the mad coot' in *Philip Sparrow* (c.1508). The third misericord in this group, situated nearby but possibly moved, shows a grinning fool's head in the usual ass-eared hood but with somewhat puzzling supporters: an elderly man smiling, full-face, on the left, and a face of indeterminate sex with apparently puckered lips in profile on the right. Is he perhaps whistling in derision at the fool he faces?

A feature which has not been noted before in studies of the Beverley stallwork is the number of small subjects carved in low relief in the spandrels afforded by the projection of the elbows which divide each seat from its neighbour. Three such spandrel carvings depict standard fools' heads; to at least one of these a commentary function may be attributed. The fool in question grimaces straight at the misericord supporter which depicts the feeble husband washing the

71 Putting the cart before the horse, misericord 58. On the right, milking a bull.

dishes (see below), while a grim-looking fool's head regards the two nude men fighting on the adjacent misericord with evident disapproval - it seems clear here that the carver has wished to point up the folly of such violence.

The misericord of the three dancing fools is of particular interest for English fool iconography, and I see it as simply depicting an exhibitionist dance of fools in the tradition of the Feast of Fools, a tradition which we know to have been still vigorous in the Beverley of the early 16th century. The right-hand fool holds a scimitar behind his head, but the contemporary figure for whom the wooden sword or dagger is a *sine qua non* at this date is the Vice. A most suggestive entry in the Revels accounts for 1551 records a payment to one Nycolas Germayne for 'one Vice's dagger & a ladle with a bauble pendant by him garnished & delivered to the Lord of Misrule's fool ... in December'.[7] The Beverley seat carved in 1520 is thus important evidence that the Fool might borrow the Vice's dagger at a time when the morality plays were still a living tradition. Of the fools carved on the supporters, the right-hand one plays a pipe and tabor, the instruments which traditionally accompany the morris dance, such as we see, for example, in both Van Meckenem's engravings of the subject,[8] but in such representations the musician is not usually shown in fool's garb. The left-hand supporter fool holds in his right hand a stick from which a decidedly phallic bladder dangles. With his right hand he points upwards with his index finger [18]. Certainly, fools do point out scenes of folly for us, but our fool's finger points up in the air. Given the form of the decidedly phalliform bladder he wields, together with the pelvic thrust which has the effect of emphasizing his codpiece, his erect finger may have been intended as a phallic suggestion.

As it happens, we are fortunate enough to have precisely contemporary evidence of this continuing tradition of the Feast of Fools locally in the Household Books of Henry Percy, fifth earl of Northumberland (1478-1527), one of whose seats was at nearby Leconfield. The earl's household regularly celebrated the Twelve Days of Christmas with all the traditional types of both learned and popular theatre at the very period during which the Beverley stalls were being carved. That the earl also observed the Feast of Fools we can deduce from the following entry in the First Household Book: 'My Lord useth and accustometh to give yearly when his Lordship is home and hath an Abbot of Misrule in Christmas in his Lordship's House upon New Year's Day in reward - xx s'.[9] Moreover, the fact that the Minster provided the earl with a Boy Bishop when he passed Christmas at Leconfield testifies to a close association between Northumberland's household and the Minster.

As well as fools, typically for the corpus, the Minster misericords include several proverbial follies. The 'Putting the Cart Before the Horse' is well known and justly celebrated, but the right-hand supporter is no ordinary milkmaid as catalogued, for close examination reveals no udder to her cow [71]. There can be no doubt that she is attempting to milk a bull, a traditional

72 The snail combat. (a) the left supporter of misericord 17. (b) the illustration of the scene from Vérard's *Shepherd's Calendar* (Paris, 1493), upon which the carving may be based.

impossibility: 'Who goeth a mile to suck a bull, Comes home a fool, and yet not full' (c.1548). Grössinger has drawn attention to this motif as the subject of one of the playing-card designs of Hans Schäuffelein (c.1535),[10] and indeed, it seems possible that the hair hanging down under the cap of the Beverley milkmaid may be a reminiscence of some lost earlier version of the pigtails of Schäuffelein's milking crone.

The right-hand supporter to the misericord carved with the preaching fox depicts a goose being shod. The bird's neck is secured within the shoeing-frame (of the type normally used for horses) while the blacksmith holds its left foot in the air and raises his hammer – a horseshoe of the normal pattern is clearly discernible on the goose's webbed foot [21b]. This proverbial folly enjoyed great popularity throughout northern Europe in the late middle ages, appearing, for example, on another misericord at Walcourt in Belgium, contemporary with our Beverley stalls. In England, the second oldest literary citation is a rare inscription accompanying a carving of the subject on a misericord at Whalley in Lancashire, datable to the abbacy of William Whalley (1418-38). Here a couplet points the moral: *Whoso melles hy[m] of th[at] al me[n] dos / let hy[m] cu[m] hier and sho the ghos* [Whoever meddles in everyone else's affairs, let him come here and shoe the goose].

Riding a pig might not be technically impossible, but it must surely be regarded as foolish. The right-hand supporter to another Beverley misericord depicts a boy riding a pig, albeit unsaddled, and holding its tail. The riderless saddled pig supporter to the porcine bagpiper seat – a mirror-image of that at Manchester – has been carefully provided with teats by the carvers and so we must more properly call it a sow with a saddle [67]. As so often in such short folk-idioms, the guiding principle of the (absurd) logic is alliteration, but, importantly, our saddled sow provides an antedating of the earliest literary attestation in Heywood's proverb collection of 1546 where the expression 'As meet as a sow To bear a saddle' is first recorded.

There are many carvings in the English misericord corpus, and the stalls at Beverley are no exception, which may broadly be described as satirical, at least in origin - though once again the question of how long a motif, originally intended satirically, retains that satiric intent in later copies, before becoming purely decorative, is problematic.

One motif, originally of quite specific satirical application, is that of the snail-combat in which an armed warrior, sometimes mounted, is depicted attacking or even fleeing from a snail. Lilian Randall has shown that the snail-combat was in origin a satirical attack aimed at the alleged cowardice of the Lombards, though it would seem most unlikely that it was still recognized as such by the artist who carved the misericord supporter in Beverley in 1520 [72a].[11] The snail-combat appears nowhere else in English woodwork, as far as I am aware, though it is found depicted on at least two Spanish misericords, one on a seat at Talavera de la Reina carved by Germanic craftsmen contemporary with our seat. The Beverley snail-fighter thrusts the tip of his spear down through the snail's head as it emerges from its shell – a mode of attack which suggests derivation from the woodcut in Vérard's original *Shepherd's Calendar* (Paris, 1493), rather than one of the English editions derived from it. A telling confirmation of this is the detail of the carved attacker's hood which, if compared with this putative woodcut source, can now be seen to represent the shape of the helmet worn by the French spearman, who is similarly presented in profile [**72b**].

Less than a generation after the Beverley stalls were carved, the attack of the cowardly soldier on the snail could be seen on the English stage. In the Tudor interlude *Thersites* of 1537 the eponymous hero is a *miles gloriosus* who, despite his outrageous boasting, dares not fight the snail single-handed, even though at his first entry one of his boasts is that 'when I am harnessed well, I shall make the dastards to run into a bag To hide them from me, as from the devil of hell'.[12] The supporter opposite the Beverley snail-spearer is a kneeling man with his head, shoulders, and one arm in a sack – a gesture which is surely now explained by this threat of Thersites to make his opponents run into a bag. The only other example of this motif known to me (in any medium) also appears on a misericord, carved in 1474 by the Fleming, Arnt Beeldesnider, at Kleve on the Lower Rhine in Germany, just over the Dutch border. This right-hand supporter thus depicts another cowardice motif, so that both supporter subjects constitute a deliberate contrast to the courage displayed by the main carving's dragon-fighter.

Anti-feminist satire – if that is not rather too dignified a name for medieval misogyny – is exemplified by at least four Beverley misericords, three of which clearly constitute a series. In an atmosphere in which every Tudor schoolboy (there were no schoolgirls, of course) learned to translate into Latin such sentences as 'It is the property of a woman to use scolding',[13] and viragoes were a commonplace of both the traditional and the new humanist drama, it is not surprising that such fearsome women should also figure in these carvings. The corollary to this anxious attack on the increasingly emancipated woman of the late-medieval and early modern era was, of course, a similar holding up to ridicule of the feeble husband. In their reflection of the relations between the sexes and anxieties about them, the Beverley misericords are absolutely typical for their date, and careful examination reveals a series of scenes symbolic of an inversion of the traditional marital gender roles.

73 An effeminate husband washing the dishes, left supporter of misericord 57.

The figure usually described as a man warming himself by the fire on one of the seats, for example, is rather, I believe, an old woman, and the now broken figure who wears an apron and chases a dog who has been at the cooking-pot is certainly a man who has signally failed in this household chore, while his crone of a wife takes her ease - it would not be difficult to find parallels to this scene in contemporary art. The left-hand supporter is another aproned man, kneeling down, and doing the washing-up in a large bowl [**73**]. The man who acted what was felt to be exclusively the housewife's role was known to the Tudors as a *cotquean*,[14] but it is to later literature that we must turn for useful citations, for example 'opprobrious words, of coward, *cotquean*, milksop, *dishwash*, and the like', and 'I cannot abide these *apron* husbands: such cotqueans ....'[15] A previously unnoticed detail concerning this *dishwash* supporter is the small spandrel fool's head which surely functions as a commentary here, pointing up the belief that for the man to undertake this traditionally female chore is folly. In the light of this reading, what of the other supporter depicting the man pulling his stocking off, his shoes lying on the ground beneath him? I suggest that he embodies an expression familiar in the medieval misogynist tradition since Chaucer, which implicitly compares marriage to an ill-fitting shoe, and survives in English as 'I know best where the shoe pinches', a commonplace of medieval anti-feminist literature.

On another seat, between two men (i.e. the same man shown twice) chopping firewood and blowing the fire, stands a now broken figure of a woman with the remains of her distaff at her side. The distaff as well as being the pre-eminent feminine attribute implying virtuous industry, is also the weapon of the virago. Watkin, a braggart soldier in a contemporary mystery play from the Digby MS 'dread[s] nothing more than a woman with a rock [distaff]'.[16] With this we may compare the several English (and continental) misericords which show a (sometimes armed) man threatened by a woman with her distaff; not least, the third of these virago scenes at Beverley, which depicts the woman clutching the man by his hair, and thrashing him with her (now broken) distaff for allowing the dog to get at the pot [74]. The supporters to this seat are an old woman grinding in a mortar and a man chopping a sausage (apparently). I suggest they symbolize this 'unnatural' *ménage* of the dominating virago and the emasculated husband. The action of pounding the pestle in the mortar is a commonplace of late-medieval European erotic diction, though, of course, symbolizing the sexual act from the male perspective. As for the opposite supporter, the man who chops into the sausage – or *pudding* as it would more usually have been called in the English of 1520 – it is another commonplace of European erotic diction that words meaning sausage may stand for penis, and precisely contemporary with our carving is a verse from a late-medieval carol, which constitutes quite unequivocal evidence of this phallic sense of pudding:

> Puddings at night and puddings at noon;
> Were not for puddings the world were clean done ...
> I will have a pudding that will stand by himself ...
> I will have a pudding that grows out of a man.[17]

Another repeated theme in the Beverley misericords is the animal musician, that is animals playing musical instruments such as we would expect to see only human musicians play. This was a commonplace of late-medieval *drôlerie*, though even here it is possible to make out some method in the apparently arbitrary madness. On the Beverley misericords we are concerned initially with a musical cat and two musical pigs.

The left-hand supporter of the cat catching mice seat features a cat and fiddle [70]. The very fact that we have this ready-made oral formulation in English should give us pause; we traditionally associate the cat with this particular instrument and no other. So do the French, and what is more, it is an association of venerable antiquity in both languages. An English document dated 1361 mentions a tenement (probably an inn) named *le Catfithele*, and in medieval Amiens there was a house called *le Chat qui vielle*. Closer to the date of our stalls, we hear of a London inn called *Le Catte cum le Fydell* in Bucklersbury in 1501. However recently attested the literary history of the nursery rhyme, the fiddling cat is undeniably attested in the *artistic* record

74 A woman holding a man by the hair while she beats him, misericord 65. The supporters develop the theme of masculine woman and emasculated man.

of late-medieval England, and a well-known example is carved on a bench-end at Fawsley, Northamptonshire, of similar date to the woodwork at Beverley.

We turn now to the misericord depicting a sow bagpiping to her four piglets (copied from Manchester) while on the right-hand supporter another *sow* – again the sex of the animal is significant – plays on the harp [**67**]. Numerous examples of the bagpiping pig on the continent and in England (including a precisely contemporary roof boss in St Mary's, Beverley) testify to the great popularity of the motif. The *harping* sow, however, is otherwise only found in English woodwork on a Windsor supporter (where there is an audience of three dancing piglets), a bench-end finial at Stowlangtoft in Suffolk and – once again – on a roof boss in St Mary's. We are fortunate, however, to have contemporary literary references to the harping sow in late fifteenth-century English nonsense verse. As a genre, Middle English nonsense verse has been little studied (in comparison with the French *fatras*, for example), but, like all literary nonsense, it has its own clichés. In a passage featuring nine animal musicians in a contemporary nonsense-poem, the cacophonous concert is introduced by the line, 'The sow sat on a high bench, and harped *Robin Hood*' [harped (a tune/ballad called) *Robin Hood*].[19] It is significant that each of the remaining eight animal musicians alliterates with its instrument – 'the turbot trumpeted ... the fox fiddled' – unlike the sow (and despite the availability of *hog*). The inescapable conclusion is that the harping sow was already a well-established collocation which the author could not lightly avoid or adapt.

There are also examples in medieval art of images in which the animal itself becomes the instrument. On one Beverley supporter an ape 'plays' a dog as if it were a bagpipe [**75**]. This motif is found twice elsewhere on English misericords: at Lavenham in Suffolk (late 15th century), where the animal-bagpipe is a pig, and at Boston in Lincolnshire (1390), a particularly attractive composition, depicting two fools in ass-eared hoods and with bells on their sleeves and shoes, biting the tails of two cats. Though the motif is also found in fourteenth-century French manuscript illumination, it is not necessary to look so far afield as Paris, or even Boston, to find the probable inspiration for this Beverley supporter for, on a corbel of the nearby Percy tomb in the Minster itself, dating from the 1330s, the sculptor has shown us a man playing a bagpipe whose bag is the body of a pig. Admittedly this is not quite the same situation as 'playing' the live animal, but it may perhaps have given the hint.

But who or what – if anyone or anything, indeed – is being satirized in these animal musician and animal-as-musical-instrument images? Wildridge, in tune with the cultural historians of his generation such as Wright, writes of the bagpiping and harping sows: 'These have evidently sarcastic reference to the decline of minstrelsy, and the degradation of the minstrels of the period, in which the harp ... was either neglected for the bagpipes or tabor, or borne by unworthy disciples of the lyric art....' He also suggests they may be a gibe directed at the guild of minstrels who are commemorated on a pillar in St Mary's carved in the early 1520s. I find myself in agreement with Schouwink, however, whose conclusion seems to me the common-sense one that, whether or not such humorous motifs began life as intentional satires, certainly by the time our stalls were carved they are devoid of any such serious moral purpose, but are merely representatives of a traditional repertoire of 'emptily' amusing images.[20]

The same is true of the ape-urinanalyst (another direct copy of the same scene at Manchester) on the right-hand supporter of the Beverley lion and dragon combat misericord. While this very common motif may originally have parodied the medieval physician's apparently sole diagnostic technique, one suspects that by the date of the Beverley stalls it had lost whatever satirical function it originally possessed.

The other supporter to the misericord featuring the lion and dragon combat depicts a seated ape holding a baby in swaddling clothes. Remnant believes that it is 'obviously

75   An ape 'playing' a dog, right supporter of misericord 16.

connected with the next misericord', that depicting the apes robbing the pedlar [**76**], in which case the ape is holding not a baby but a doll, yet I believe the situation is by no means quite so obvious. This particular supporter is admittedly a straight copy of one at Manchester, which does indeed flank the scene of the rifling of the pedlar's pack, but dolls are not to be found in other representations of this popular late-medieval subject,[21] or, indeed, in the other English misericord examples, at Windsor (c.1480) and Bristol (c.1520). Rather, I suggest that an independent motif of an ape with swaddled baby, first found in Flemish sources, has not unnaturally been drawn into the orbit of the scene of the robbing of the pedlar.

Increasingly, in this era of the final flowering of medieval English woodcarving, more and more examples of the use of particular printed sources are coming to be recognized. These design sources fall into two main groups, the metal-cut motifs to be found in the borders of Books of Hours (*Horae*) printed in Paris in the decades around 1500 (as at Bristol), and contemporary engraved and woodcut prints from Germany and Flanders (as at Windsor).

M.D. Anderson first pointed out that the carver of three misericords of the contemporary Bristol series took his designs from border-scenes in an early printed Parisian Book of Hours.[22] One of these designs, the ape riding an 'equine' pursued by a naked wild man holding the mount's tail and brandishing a club, is to be recognized at Beverley, though reversed, and with the whole ape – not just the head – turned to face the pursuing man. In Bristol Cathedral the dragon with a second head in its belly pursuing three naked boys is found in a very faithful copy, but the Beverley carver has reduced it to the distinctive gastrocephalic dragon and entirely omitted the *putti*.

Another Beverley design based on one of these small *Horae* cuts is the seat formerly catalogued as 'hare riding fox', and 'hare on the back of an animal whose species is uncertain'. This can now, with the identification of the metalcut source, be shown to be a snail riding on a dragon which it controls by means of the reins held in its 'paws', and is to be seen, for example, in a relatively early *Horae*, such as that of 1498 [*STC* 15889] now in the John Rylands Library, Manchester, printed by Pigouchet for Vostre – one of the foremost Parisian publishers, who established a shop in St Paul's churchyard in London – which contains all the designs discussed here.

76 Apes rifling the pedlar's pack, misericord 6.

77 The Donington rebus: a doe on a tun, right supporter of misericord 12.

What we may conveniently term 'Germanic' sources are also well represented. The return of the spies from Canaan, found only otherwise at Manchester and Ripon, serves once again to demonstrate the close iconographical link between these sets of stalls, and it is a moot point whether the Beverley carver took his design immediately from the block-book *Biblia Pauperum* or from the Manchester misericord. Another Germanic design shared with Ripon is the misericord depicting a man pushing a woman in a wheelbarrow which derives from a very popular print by an engraver known as the Master bxg, active in the Middle Rhine area c.1470–90; once again, though, the Beverley example seems more likely to derive from a copy of that at Ripon than from the print. The scene of the apes robbing the pedlar [**76**] discussed above (found also at Bristol and Manchester) is also most plausibly derived from a Germanic print (now known only from Italian copies).

One of the Beverley supporters features a bird with a distinctive long swept-back crest scratching its head, which certainly derives from the 8-of-Birds card engraved by the so-called Master of the Playing Cards, whose original card designs belong to the 1430s. Thus the Beverley stalls provide important evidence of the surprising longevity of these widely disseminated images. The playing card engravings of another anonymous German Master are also most probably to be identified behind the design of another Beverley misericord. A nude man (his right arm and most of the spear-shaft now missing) thrusts with a spear at his similarly nude adversary whose shield has the profile of a human face. It is principally this shield, but also the naked or semi-naked condition of the two hirsute combatants, which suggests their ultimate derivation from one of the Wild Men suit of playing cards. The naked wild man brandishing an upraised club in one hand and holding his face-shield in the other, occurs, for example, on the 5-, 6-, and 9-of-Wild-Men copy-cards.

The Minster misericords have much to tell us about early Tudor culture in general; not least, and contrary to the received wisdom, they show that Germanic influences loom considerably larger in the history of late-medieval and renaissance English art than Italian or even French influences. There is also the regional component. In 1955, in what was to become a standard text-book, *Sculpture in Britain: The Middle Ages*, Lawrence Stone could describe the 'woodcarvers north of the Trent' in the period c.1460–1540 as if they were living in some benighted cultural backwater, 'cut off by their geographical remoteness from the French and Flemish influences that were affecting artists farther south ....'[23] This seems to me to be adequately refuted by what we can now say about the sources of many of the Beverley carvings.

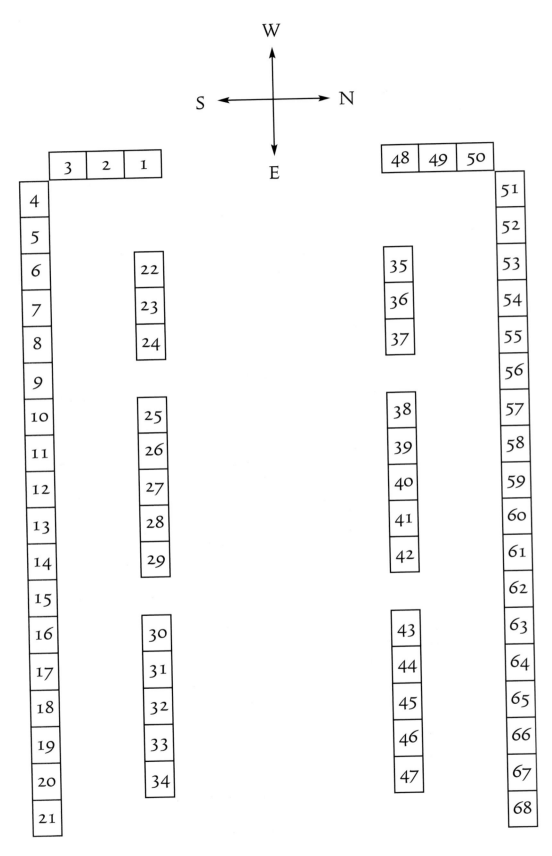

fig. 3 Misericords

APPENDIX: DESCRIPTIVE LIST OF THE BEVERLEY MISERICORDS

The list is keyed to fig. 3.* denotes a misericord discussed in the text; † a misericord illustrated in the text.

*1   Pelican feeding its young with the blood of its own breast ['pelican in her piety']. Left: a bird. Right: a bird pecking at a serpent [?] at its feet.

2   Ape on equine, followed by wild man armed with a club. Left: ape on a cat's back combing it. Right: boy riding a pig.

3   Winged demi-angel holding a heart; fruit and foliage on either side.

*4   Shield containing three weights [rebus of Wight]. Left: man carrying two weights. Right: man carrying scales and two weights.

*5   Fight between lion and dragon. Left: ape nursing a baby or doll. Right: ape with a urine flask.

*†6   Apes robbing a pedlar. Left: ape in foliage. Right: ape with staff chasing a cat among foliage.

*7   Shield with three weights [rebus of Wight]; on either side a man lifting weights.

8   Conventional foliage; foliage on either side.

9   Kneeling man blows fire with bellows, and standing woman [broken] watches a man split logs; fruit and leaves on either side.

*10   Three men pulling a wheelbarrow to which a bear is tied. †Left: man muzzling a bear. Right: man and bear wrestling or dancing together.

11   Man astride a sheep in the act of shearing it, another applying salve to sheep's hoof. Left: shepherd, crook in hand, patting his dog. Right: two rams butting each other.

*12   Shield [?fanciful] supported on either side by griffin. Left: pelican in her piety. †Right: Doe on tun [rebus of Donington].

13   Two men with a muzzled bear, and a third with a wheelbarrow. Left: huntsman with a dog. Right: bear licking its paw.

14   Two huntsmen dismembering a stag on its back watched by two dogs. Left: man holding a dog on a leash. Right: man blowing a horn while four dogs jump up and bark.

15   Huntsman attacking a bear assailed by dogs. Left: man training an ape. Right: bear dancing to bagpipes played by an ape.

*16   Man on horseback leads three muzzled bears by a chain. Left: muzzled bears. †Right: dog employed as bagpipes is made to howl by an ape biting its tail.

*17   Man [pygmy] rises from a hole to fight dragons flanking him. †Left: man spearing a snail. Right: man with his head in a sack.

*†18   Sow plays bagpipes while piglets dance, pig trough in foreground. Left: saddled sow. Right: sow playing a harp.

19   Fox run to earth by hounds and shot at by an archer. Left: fox ridden by an ape. Right: fox in bed attended by an ape.

20   Fox runs off with a goose pursued by a woman. Left: two foxes. Right: fox and captured bird.

21   ?Bramble-fruit and foliage; ?bramble-fruit and foliage on either side.

22   Devil pursuing a man or a soul [damaged]. Left: devil and miser with treasure-chest. Right: devil watching a glutton.

23   Fruit and foliage; fruit and foliage on either side.

24   Owl with a mouse; foliage on either side.

25   Two birds, perhaps cranes, eating corn in a sack; similar birds on either side.

*†26   Cat catching mice. Left: cat playing the fiddle to dancing mice or kittens. Right: cat tossing a mouse in its paws.

*27   Snail riding a dragon. Left: archer shooting. Right: three rabbits.

28 Lion [crown damaged] and antelope. Left: crowned lion couchant. Right: unicorn couchant.

*†29 Two half-length carvers in tightly-fitted jerkins. Left: man touches his nose. Right: man appears to thumb his nose.

30 Mermaid and fish [mirror and comb broken off]. Left: large fish seizing a smaller one. Right: three fishes interlaced.

31 Foliage; foliage on either side.

*32 Return of the Spies, Joshua & Caleb, with an outsize bunch of grapes. Left: vine leaf and tendril. Right: leaf and grapes.

33 Two lions couchant; conventional flowers on either side.

34 Elephant and castle, driven from behind by an ape. Left: a camel. Right: a lion.

35 Two lions couchant, one crowned. Left: a boar. Right: a bird.

*36 Combat between a naked figure with a spear and a man with a sword; foliage on either side.

37 Hawk. Left: falconer feeding a hawk. Right: hawk preying on a small bird.

38 Branch of rose-tree. [?Tudor] roses on either side.

39 Crested bird. Birds scratching their heads on either side.

*40 Lion with prostrate man. Left: a dragon. Right: a griffin.

*41 Two birds, perhaps coots, pecking at a fool's eared hood. Left: ?goose. Right: ?swan.

*42 Grimacing fool's head; geese on either side.

*43 Owl mobbed by small birds; birds [?hawks] on either side.

44 Dragons fighting; birds on branches on either side.

*45 Grinning fool in eared hood. Left: elderly male head. Right: head with puckered lips.

46 Foliage; foliage on either side.

47 Hen and chickens. Left: a cock. Right: hen with chickens under her and one on her back.

48 Stag-hunting scene. Left: a man on horseback. Right: a doe scratching.

*49 Man fighting lion. Left: lion passant regardant. Right: lion passant.

50 Unicorn; foliage on either side.

*†51 Fox wearing a friar's cowl and gown, with a rosary in his paws, preaching from a lectern to a congregation of seven geese, an ape standing behind him with a goose hanging from a stick over his shoulder; a fox runs off with a goose in his mouth at the extreme left. Left: an owl. Right: a man shoeing goose.

*52 Hawking scene. Left: dog gnawing a bone above a banderole inscribed *Johannes Sperke*. Right: cock above a banderole inscribed *clericus fabrici*.

53 Deer browsing. Left: a stag. Right: deer and young.

*54 Fox hanged by geese. Left: fox and sleeping geese. Right: ape takes the rope from the neck of a [?dead] fox.

55 Grotesque mask with foliage coming from its mouth [a 'Green man']. Left: man cutting wood. Right: conventional leaves.

56 Combat between a human-headed monster and griffin. Left: long-headed beast with pole. Right: a beast.

*57 Old woman warming her hands at a fire while an aproned man [broken] chases a dog which has stolen meat from a cooking-pot. †Left: aproned man washing dishes. Right: man pulling his stockings off.

*†58 Putting the cart before the horse [damaged]. Left: bull licking itself. Right: woman attempting to milk a bull.

*59 Shield supported by hawk and hound. Left: bird beneath a banderole inscribed *arma wilhelmi tait doctori[s]*. Right: a bird, perhaps a hawk, beneath a banderole inscribed *thesaurii huius ecclesie 1520*.

60 Hunter spears boar while a dog seizes another by the ear; conventional roses on either side.

61 Man with sword and shield fighting a dragon; fruit and foliage on either side.

*62 Male head in an eared hat pulling at the corners of its mouth; lion masks with protruding tongues on either side.

63 Cock crowing. Left: bird above a banderole inscribed *Chot*. Right: cocks on a barrel or tun.

*64 Man wheeling a woman in a barrow [damaged] while she pulls his hair. Left: man lifting a plank. Right: woman perhaps removing fleas from a dog.

*†65 Woman pulling a man's hair and striking him with an implement [broken off], while a dog steals food from a cooking-pot. Left: woman pounds a pestle in a mortar. Right: man chopping a sausage with an axe.

66 Dragon with a face in its chest; dragons on either side.

67 Demi-angel. Left: grapes with foliage. Right: rose with foliage.

*68 Three fools dancing. †Left: fool with a bladder-stick and finger pointing upwards. Right: fool with a pipe and tabor.

NOTES

1 For discussion of the technical aspects of the Beverley stallwork, see C. Tracy, *English Gothic Choir-stalls 1400-1540* (Woodbridge, 1990), chapter III. The only scholar in recent times to address the question of the iconography and design-sources of the Beverley misericords specifically is Christa Grössinger, in two articles published in 1989, especially 'The misericords in Beverley Minster: their relationship to other misericords and fifteenth-century prints,' in C. Wilson, ed., *Medieval Art and Architecture in the East Riding of Yorkshire*, British Archaeological Association Conference Transactions, 9 (1989), pp. 186-94. Most of what follows is treated more fully in my unpublished doctoral thesis, 'The Misericords of Beverley Minster: a Corpus of Folkloric Imagery and its Cultural Milieu, with special reference to the influence of Northern European Iconography on Late-medieval and Early Modern English Woodwork' (Polytechnic of the South West, 1991).

2 Tracy, *Choir-stalls*, p. 27.

3 I. Lancashire, 'Orders for Twelfth Day and Night circa 1515 in the Second Northumberland Household Book', *English Literary Renaissance*, 10 (1980), 7-45, esp. 11; see also, T. Percy, ed., *The First Northumberland Household Book* (1827), pp. 365, 377f.

4 In G.L. Remnant, *A catalogue of the misericords of Great Britain* (Oxford, 1969), p. 210.

5 G. J. Boekenoogen, ed. (Leiden, 1903).

6 Quoted in S. Billington, *A Social History of the Fool* (Brighton, 1984), p. 3.

7 A Feuillerat, ed., *Documents Relating to the Revels at Court in the Time of King Edward VI and Queen Mary* (Louvain, 1914), p. 73.

8 A. Winther, 'Zu einigen Ornamentblättern und den Darstellungen des Moriskentanzes im Werk des Israhel van Meckenem' in idem, ed., *Israhel van Meckenem und der deutsche Kupferstich des 15. Jahrhunderts* (Bocholt, 1972), esp. pp. 88-100.

9 Percy, *Household Book*, p. 344.

10 C. Grössinger, 'Humour and folly in English misericords of the first quarter of the sixteenth century' in D. Williams, ed., *Early Tudor England* (Woodbridge, 1989), p. 76.

11 L. Randall, 'The Snail in Gothic Marginal Warfare', *Speculum*, 37 (1962), 358-67; supplemented by R. Pinon, 'From Illumination to Folksong: the armed snail, a motif of topsy-turvy land' in V. Newall, ed., *Folklore Studies in the Twentieth Century: Proceedings of the Centenary Conference of the Folklore Society* (Woodbridge, 1980), pp. 76-113.

12   M. Axton, ed., *Three Tudor Classical Interludes* (Cambridge, 1982), lines 16ff.

13   Translating the Latin *Ingenium est mulierem conuicia exercere*: B. White, ed., *The Vulgaria of John Stanbridge and the Vulgaria of Robert Whittinton* (EETS, os 187, 1932), p. 22 line 30. Wynkyn de Worde had issued at least seven editions of Stanbridge's *Vulgaria* by the date the Beverley stalls were carved.

14   Thomas Nashe's use of this word in *An Almond for a Parrot* (1590) takes us straight back to the satirical world of the earlier misericords: 'groping his own hens like a cotquean' (OED, *s.v. grope*), for the *hennetaster* [hen-groper], a type of the effeminate man in Flemish art, and - so it would seem - in the Elizabethan mind too, is depicted c.1500 in stallwork at Emmerich, Kempen and Aarschot, and, more familiarly, in Bruegel's *Netherlandish Proverbs* painting of 1559.

15   J. Smyth, *Lives of the Berkeleys* [1640] (3 vols, Bristol, 1883), ii, p. 372; Middleton & Dekker, *The Roaring Girl* [1611], III.ii.30; A. Gomme, ed., *The Roaring Girl* (1976), p. 65.

16   *The Digby Plays*, ed., D.C. Baker, J.L. Murphy & L.B. Hall (EETS, os 283, 1982), lines 159f.

17   Cited in MED, *s.v. podyng*.

18   B. Lilywhite, *London Signs* (1972), p. 97.

19   T. Wright & J.O. Halliwell, eds, *Reliquiae Antiquae* (2 vols, 1841-3), i, pp. 85f., from the late fifteenth-century manuscript National Library of Wales, Porkington MS 10, f. 152.

20   T. Tindall Wildridge, *The misereres of Beverley Minster* (Hull, 1879), pp. 24-5; W. Schouwink, *Der wilde Eber in Gottes Weinberg: zur Darstellung des Schweins in Literatur und Kunst des Mittelalters* (Sigmaringen, 1985), p. 101.

21   For example the English illustrations in the Smithfield Decretals (BL Royal MS 10.E. IV, ff. 149v - 151), or the two late fifteenth-century Italian engravings reproduced in A.M. Hind, *Early Italian Engraving: A Critical Catalogue* (7 vols, 1938-48), A.I.76 and A.I.77.

22   T. Cox [= M.D. Anderson], 'Twelfth-Century Design Sources of the Worcester Cathedral Misericords', *Archaeologia*, 97 (1959), 165-6.

24   L. Stone, *loc. cit.*, p. 213.

11 · The Post-Reformation Monuments

FAMILY MONUMENTS – *David Neave*

Unlike some cathedrals and large urban parish churches the Minster is not overflowing with post-Reformation monuments. There are however some 250 memorials, largely confined to the transepts and the nave and choir aisles The majority are simple wall tablets, or floor slabs, with little more than an inscription. The earliest, in the north transept, is a brass plate with a rhyming inscription commemorating Richard Ferrant, a London draper, who died at Beverley whilst attending the fair in May 1560. Another brass plate, by the altar rail on the south side of the choir, has a long epitaph in Latin to Thomasina, the first wife of Sir William Gee of Bishop Burton, secretary of the Council of the North. Thomasina, who died in 1599 aged 29, was a daughter of Matthew Hutton, archbishop of York and president of the Council of the North. Her kneeling figure, with those of Sir William Gee and his second wife, appears on a monument in the south choir aisle of York Minster.

The Gee family, together with the Hothams of Scorborough and the Wartons of North Bar House and Beverley Parks, provided most of the MPs for Beverley in the 17th and early 18th centuries and it is fitting that all three families are commemorated in the Minster. Hidden away in the choir vestry is the mutilated monument to Sir Charles Hotham (died 1722) [**78**]. The obelisk, which has arrangements of armour to the left and right, was reduced to its present height in 1874, at the suggestion of Sir George Gilbert Scott. Memorials to the Warton family and their descendants, the Pennymans and Ellisons, pack the retrochoir. The earliest has the figure of Sir Michael Warton, who died in 1655 [**25, 79**]. A staunch Royalist, he was in his eighty-second year when he died and he is portrayed as a bearded old man wearing armour and kneeling at a desk. The monument has been attributed to the stonemason Thomas Stanton (1610-74) of London, as has the nearby wall-tablet commemorating Warton's six-year old grandson John (died 1656). Stanton's workshop was in Shoe Lane, Holborn where the Wartons owned property and he may have been their tenant.

Thomas Stanton's nephew and successor William Stanton (1639-1705) was responsible for the monuments to Michael (died 1688) [**80**] and Susanna Warton (died 1682) that once stood either side of the figure of Sir Michael Warton. They were removed to their present position at the entrance to the Lady Chapel in 1874-5, because they concealed the rich carving at the back of the altar screen. The monuments stand back-to-back and are identical in design. Each has a base decorated with garlands of leaves, a central panel with an inscription on well-cut draperies and the whole surmounted by a coat-of-arms surrounded by luscious foliage and topped by an urn. Accounts for setting up the monument to Michael Warton in September 1689 record that William Stanton was paid £50 for carving it and a further £4 was spent on transporting it from London to Beverley and erecting it in the Minster.[1]

For the last and finest monument in the series, that to Sir Michael Warton (died 1725), the family turned to Peter Scheemakers, one of the Continental-born sculptors who were ousting old-established English firms such as the Stantons. The monument, against the east wall, has a Roman sarcophagus and urn flanked by two seated female figures, one reading a book and the other with an upturned torch and a serpent forming a circle with its tail in its mouth to represent Eternity [29]. Scheemakers, who signed the monument on the base of the left-hand figure, received 100 guineas as part payment in July 1728.[2] The monument was erected by Warton's nephew and executor Sir Michael Newton who commissioned an identical work by Scheemakers for his own memorial, in Heydour church, Lincolnshire. The inscription records Warton's many benefactions including the four thousand pounds he left to establish 'a perpetual fund for the repairs' of the fabric of the Minster and the bequests to almshouses in Minster Moorgate. A contemporary benefactor, Anne Routh (died 1722), who bequeathed property to establish the almshouses in Keldgate that bear her name, is commemorated by a bold rococo cartouche on a pillar near the entrance to the south choir aisle. The rather old-fashioned monument with well-cut drapery, cherubs' heads, an urn and a skull was probably carved locally.

Two later monuments by London-based sculptors are worthy of note. An elegant wall-monument, in the north choir aisle, commemorating members of the Strickland family (died 1780-1793), with a sarcophagus and weeping female figure is signed by Peter Chenu and that to Major General Barnard Foord Bowes in the south transept is signed Coade and Sealy and dated 1813 [81]. The latter, made of Coade artificial stone, cost £150 plus £26 carriage from the firm's Lambeth manufactory.[3] General Bowes, who was killed in June 1812 at the assault on Salamanca, Spain during the Peninsula War, is also commemorated by a monument in St Paul's Cathedral by Sir Francis Chantry. The Beverley monument has the winged figure of Victory, standing before an urn-topped column, flanked by cannons and other military trophies.

Amongst the many Georgian wall tablets and floor slabs are a number recording links with America including the wall tablet in the north transept to Brigadier General Oliver de Lancey (died 1785) of New York 'who possessed one of the most extensive and truly valuable estates in North America'. A Loyalist during the American War of Independence de Lancey sought asylum in Britain and settled at Beverley, as did his fellow New Yorker Captain Henry Law (died 1787) who is commemorated by a ledger stone in the north choir aisle. In the lesser south transept is a ledger stone to General George Garth (died 1819), who had been Governor of Placentia, Newfoundland. The county town of Beverley with its polite society and active social and cultural life attracted many to retire there after service abroad in the army or commerce. In the north transept is a Gothic-style wall tablet signed by Thomas Knowles of Oxford to Ebenezer Robertson (died 1825) formerly of Jamaica, who lived at Keldgate Manor.

The majority of the wall tablets are likely to have been produced by monumental masons in Beverley, Hull or York, although few are signed. The Fishers, an accomplished and prolific firm of sculptors working in York, signed a monument in the north choir aisle to Henry Roxby (died 1801), a merchant of London Bridge. A long inscription, detailing his ancestry, is topped by an elegant urn. In the north transept another urn-topped inscription, to John Storm (died 1832), is signed by George Earle, a member of Hull's leading family of masons. Beverley is represented by Thomas Hayes, who had his workshop in Butcher Row. He signed three of the more elaborate tablets including that to the Revd Joseph Coltman (died 1837).

As this selective account of the Minster monuments clearly shows, burial inside the church was for the well-to-do. A board just inside the south porch, dated 1824, records that the costs of burial ranged from 14s 8d in the nave and aisles to £4 13s 10d in the sanctuary. Burial in the churchyard cost 3s 6d and it is here that most of the parishioners were buried but few have a gravestone. Nevertheless the Minster churchyard retains over 650 stones dating from the early 18th century to the mid 19th century.[4] Burials inside the Minster came to an end in 1858 and in the churchyard, except for existing plots, in 1861.

78 (right) The remains of the monument to Sir Charles Hotham (d. 1722), now in the choir vestry. The monument was truncated in 1874 at the suggestion of George Gilbert Scott and only the tip of the obelisk remains on the plinth.

79 (bottom left) The monument to Sir Michael Warton (d. 1655). See **25** for its location immediately behind the reredos.

80 (bottom right) The monument to Michael Warton (d. 1688) by William Stanton.

SACRED TO THE MEMORY OF
MAJOR GENERAL BARNARD FOORD BOWES.
A BELOV'D & LAMENTED HUSBAND, WHOSE VIRTUES ARE RECORDED
IN THE HEARTS OF HIS SORROWING RELATIVES, AND FRIENDS.
HIS DEEDS OF VALOUR IN ARMS, ARE PERPETUATED ON
A MONUMENT ERECTED IN THE CATHEDRAL CHURCH OF St PAULS
BY HIS GRATEFUL COUNTRY, AS A TRIBUTE OF RESPECT
DUE TO HIS MERITORIOUS ACTIONS, PLACING HIM AMONG THE
FOREMOST IN THE LIST OF THOSE GALLANT HEROES, WHO HAVE
BLED IN THE DEFENCE OF THEIR KING AND CONSTITUTION.
HE FELL ON THE 23 OF JUNE 1812 IN THE 43 YEAR OF HIS AGE
AFTER ALMOST A LIFE DEVOTED TO THE SERVICE
AND WHILE LEADING THE FORLORN HOPE TO THE ASSAULT
OF THE FORTRESS LA MERCIA SALAMANCA

SO SLEEP THE BRAVE, NOW SUNK TO REST
BY ALL THEIR COUNTRY'S WISHES BLEST.

81 The monument to Major
General Barnard Foord Bowes
in the south transept

THE MILITARY MONUMENTS – *Ian Sumner*

In the summer of 1782, shortly before the end of the American War of Independence, His Majesty's 15th Regiment of Foot arrived in Beverley, released from captivity by the French. The regiment had taken heavy losses in the West Indies, and needed some time to refit and train new recruits. Earlier that same year, the government had decided to name each infantry regiment after a different part of the country, hoping that this would aid recruitment at a critical time during the war. A circular was sent to the colonel of each regiment, asking them to choose an appropriate title. Sadly, the reply from the Colonel of the 15th, Lt General Sir William Fawcett KB, does not survive. Fawcett (c.1720-1804) was a Halifax man by birth, and had no immediate connection with the Riding; it would seem likely that he asked for the name 'East Riding of Yorkshire' simply to bring his battered regiment back up to strength in the shortest possible time by attracting local men to the colours.

So it was that the 15th, or East Yorkshire, Regiment of Foot was named. But no sooner had it been baptized than the regiment marched off, first to Leeds in June, then to Berwick, and by the end of 1783 to Glasgow. Seven months later, the regiment was in Ireland, and seven years after that, it re-embarked for the West Indies. Apart from sending some recruiting parties to the Riding in 1804-5, the regiment made no effort to develop links with the area; indeed, it did not return to Beverley for almost a century. In this the 15th was typical. The inclusion of a county title rarely succeeded in giving regiments a fixed geographical base, primarily because the government failed to build the network of permanent depots which would allow each regiment to recruit and train local men. Recruitment remained an *ad hoc* affair undertaken by small parties of men scouring any likely area; new recruits were then marched to wherever the regiment was stationed for training. So there was no real opportunity for the 15th Foot to put down roots within the Riding after which it had been named, and become an East Yorkshire regiment in every sense of the word.

It was not until the reforms of two successive Secretaries of State for War, Cardwell and Childers, in the 1870s and 1880s that the 15th Foot finally found a permanent home in Beverley. As part of those reforms, the regimental number was abolished, and the regiment became simply the East Yorkshire Regiment; a local depot was established, and placed in the newly-built Victoria Barracks on Queensgate. The colonel was once more instructed to foster links between the regiment and its recruiting area. As chance would have it, there was an almost immediate opportunity to do this.

The regiment had recently returned from Afghanistan, where it had been involved in the campaigns of the Second Afghan War, and on returning home, erected a bronze plaque in the south aisle of the nave as a memorial to those who had been killed. From then on, the Minster became a focus for the regiment's memorials. That for Afghanistan was followed on 4th March 1905 by a memorial to the dead of the Boer War, in the form of a number of bronze plaques by the south door, and a memorial window in the wall above. Alongside these have been added a number of memorials to named individuals, some erected privately and others by the regiment. These include not only men who were killed in action (like Lieutenants Philip and Frank Green, two of the four sons of the proprietor of the *Beverley Guardian*, killed within three months of each other during World War I), but also distinguished soldiers of the regiment who died in their beds (like Major General Coleridge Groves, the Colonel of the Regiment, who had unveiled the Boer War monument).

It is significant that all these memorials date from the period following the East Yorkshires' move to Beverley. Such was the peripatetic life of a regiment in the first eighty years of the 19th century, that memorials to the dead had previously been erected in the church nearest to the regiment's then current home. In the years between the end of the Napoleonic Wars and the establishment of a permanent depot, the men of the 15th Foot had served in the West Indies, Canada, and Ireland, as well as in Ceylon, Gibraltar, India and the Channel Islands, spending perhaps only nine years in total in England – and the regiment was by no means unique in this respect. Whilst this was happening, the regimental depot moved its location approximately every three years, from Carlisle to Guernsey, from Cork to Tynemouth. The profusion of monuments following the Cardwell reforms is testimony to changing attitudes to the army in this period. The government succeeded in creating a structure in which close ties could at last develop between regiment and county – ties whose force is still in evidence today.

Whilst the south aisle has many memorials to the men of the East Yorkshires, the dead from the First World War are commemorated in the larger cenotaph in the south transept. Here there are niches containing carefully illuminated scrolls bearing the names of those killed, alongside screens filled with the 7,500 names of East Riding men killed serving with other regiments and corps, such as the Green Howards, who recruited in the north of the East Riding. The north-east chapel contains the Henin Cross, made from wood found on the Arras battlefield of 1917. Next to these is a small chapel and cross for the dead of the Second World War, carved by Robert Thompson, the Mouse Man of Kilburn, and an altar rail to commemorate those killed in Malaya. On the south wall are two tablets to the men of the East Riding Yeomanry, raised in 1902, which also had its headquarters in Beverley. A cabinet in front contains a Book of Remembrance, whose pages are turned a day at a time, listing the names of all the East Riding men and women who did not return from the campaigns of the Second World War. The difference in attitudes towards the dead between the First and the Second World Wars is apparent. In the Book of Remembrance, the names are in alphabetical order, regardless of rank or service; but on the darkly glittering cenotaph, the men of 1914–18 are arranged by regiment, then by battalion, then by rank. Even in death there was a place for everyone, and everyone was in their place.

82 A colour party laying up the 'colours' of the East Yorkshires in 1911. The photograph was taken outside the west door of the Minster, looking north west.

Above the heads of visitors to the south transept hang a number of flags, the East Yorkshires' regimental 'colours'. Every battalion of the regiment was presented with two colours, one in the form of the Union Flag (the King's, now the Queen's, Colour), the other in the colour of the collars and cuffs of the regimental uniform (the Regimental Colour – yellow for the East Yorkshires until 1881, white thereafter). On the Regimental Colour were embroidered the names of the battles in which the regiment had distinguished itself, under Marlborough, Wolfe and Wellington; the two World Wars resulted in so many honours that these were restricted to only ten from each war, and were embroidered on the King's Colour. The colours were made from silk, and when they became too tattered and worn out, were hung in an appropriate church, a custom which dates from regulations of 1898 [82]. The oldest colour belonging to the East Yorkshires in the Minster hangs from the west wall of the south transept, and was presented to the regiment's Second Battalion in Malta in 1859, before being retired in 1897. Here can be found not only the colours of the two regular battalions, but also those of the Pals Battalions of 1914–18, simple Union flags, issued in 1921 in a hurry and without much thought, by a government anxious to avoid expense, long after the battalions had been disbanded.

There are a small number of military monuments elsewhere in the Minster. Next to the World War memorial in the south transept is the extravagant Coade stone memorial to Major General Barnard Foord Bowes [81], and by the north door is a brass plate to Lieutenant-General Sir Harry Jones, who fought during the Crimean War. In the north aisle are two memorial tablets to the ex-pupils of Beverley Grammar School killed during the World Wars, whilst in the north choir, near the Percy tomb, hang the colours of the Beverley Volunteers, a regiment raised to defend against a possible invasion by Napoleon.

The memorials and regimental colours in the Minster not only act as a tribute and memorial to those who gave their lives for the country, but as a reminder of the contribution of local people to the war effort, and to the place of the local regiment within the community.

NOTES

1 D. Neave and D. Woodward, 'Memorials to a Yorkshire family', *Country Life*, 11.10.1979, pp. 1230-5.

2 Lincolnshire Archives Office, Misc. Dep. 197/200.

3 I. & E. Hall, *Historic Beverley* (York, 1973), p. 33.

4 *Beverley Minster (St John and St Martin) Monumental Inscriptions*, East Yorkshire Family History Society (1997).

ALAN SPEDDING

12 · Music in the Minster

From the outset music was at the heart of the worship offered to God on the site where Beverley Minster now stands and it could be said that to this day it is music in worship that brings the building fully to life.

The earliest music would have been Gregorian plainchant which had been established from the early 8th century as the standard for liturgical singing. There is a tradition that John of Beverley was educated at Canterbury where music formed an important part of the curriculum along with mathematics, astronomy and medicine, in addition to theological studies. John had further experience of liturgical music as a pupil of Hilda of Whitby, and as bishop of York he inherited forms of worship based on Gregorian chant, actively introduced and encouraged by his predecessors, notably Wilfred and Paulinus. John's connection with the Venerable Bede, himself a trained singer, is well documented and Bede's monasteries at Wearmouth and Jarrow were ruled over by Abbot Benedict Biscop, who delighted in all things Roman, including liturgical music. At Beverley, too, John's foundation would have included provision for boys, whose treble voices would have been used in contrast to those of the men.

After John's death in 721 his community lived on until the mid 9th century when the site is traditionally said to have been abandoned as a result of an attack by the Danes. If there was a break in continuity at this point, religious life had resumed within the precinct by the early 10th century, and the community's possession of the relics of Bishop John (canonized in 1037) ensured the Minster's continuing importance.

It was no accident that when the Minster was rebuilt in the early 13th century, the first part of the building to be completed was the choir so that the eucharist could be celebrated with music and due solemnity. The daily offices continued to be sung until the Reformation but with a wide variety in standards of performance and competence and there were times when the choir was not capable of chanting antiphonally (the style of singing in which two equal groups of singers stand on opposite sides facing one another and sing alternate verses).

During the middle ages the town of Beverley also gained a great reputation for secular music through its guild of waits and minstrels which catered for musicians from far beyond the confines of the town – 'twixt Tweed and Trent' according to one later account [84, 85]. Information about the minstrels is scarce apart from some vague references in the town documents and a very late charter of 1555. It is known that the guild met in Beverley on Ascension Day for its annual election of officers. On this day the shrine of St John returned to the Minster after its Rogationtide tour of neighbouring chapels and the minstrels and other entertainers would have taken an important part in the celebrations. The minstrels contributed to the rebuilding of St Mary's church in 1520 where the famous Minstrels' Pillar still commemorates the fact. This pillar may have been modelled on a similar one in the south transept of the Minster, sadly much damaged, depicting some very fashionably dressed musicians holding sumptuously carved instruments.

In all there are over eighty carvings of medieval musicians in stone or wood in the Minster representing upwards of twenty instruments. The crowning glory of the collection is on the label stops on both sides of the nave where their elevated position has saved them from the

83 The choir screen and the 1916 organ case from the crossing.

depredations of iconoclasts and religious fanatics [**86**]. Many more are to be found, much restored, at ground level along the arcading of the north nave aisle (c.1340) and still more, dating from 1520, are carved under the misericord seats in the choir. The earliest of all are behind the sedilia in the sanctuary. The three figures at the south west end of the nave are helmeted and armed - a possible reference to the fact that the minstrels were also the town waits or guardians.

Up until the Dissolution the musical life of the Minster was maintained, under the precentor, by nine vicars, eight choristers, seven *berefellarii* (also called parsons of the choir, who were responsible for singing services in the choir by this date) and a number of chantry priests, employed to sing masses for departed souls. The boys, who were paid £1 per annum after 1391, were educated and housed in the song-school and were given an annual treat on Holy Innocents Day (28 December). The feast of St Nicholas (6 December) was also a special day in the pupils' calendar, when one of their number was chosen as Boy Bishop – a sort of Lord of Misrule – for a short time. This harmless custom continued until the Dissolution and in 1532 the sum of 16s was lavished on its maintenance. The boys were given an extra penny each when they sang at commemorative masses. Their uniform, a tawny-coloured woollen gown, would have made them conspicuous when out in the town.

By the late middle ages, and probably earlier, the musical staff of the Minster included an organist and a separate master of the choristers. In the fabric roll for 1531–2 a chantry priest, George Morsell, was named as master of choristers and received an additional £2 6s 8d per annum. Robert Flee, a dedicated servant of the Minster, received 13s 4d extra per annum as organist in addition to his other positions as receiver general, warden of the fabric and rector of Leven. An even more illustrious name appears on the same roll. Four shillings was given to John Merbecke 'in reward for songs by him given to the church'. Merbecke, who was then in his early twenties, was the son of Robert Merbecke who rented the Tabard Inn in the Fishmarket from the provostry. Merbecke became a singing man and one of two organists of St George's chapel, Windsor by the end of 1531. He became a protestant theologian of note and published a concordance of the English bible. His greatest claim to fame was his collaboration with Archbishop Cranmer in the production of the first Anglican prayer book in English and Merbecke's 'Book of Common Prayer Noted' (i.e. set to music) was published in 1550. Merbecke's brief was to set Cranmer's text to simple melodies, 'for every syllable a note'. He was arrested for heresy under the Marian Catholic backlash but was spared the stake because Bishop Gardiner dismissed him as 'only a musician' and thus not worth burning. In later life, as he became more identified with the Calvinist wing of Protestantism he affected to despise elaborate sacred music. He wrote regretfully in his preface to his concordance, 'I have consumed vainly the greatest part of my life in the study of music and playing the organs'. He continued to devote himself to theological speculation, however, and published a number of works including the splendidly titled *A ripping up of the Pope's Fardel* (1581).

At the Dissolution in 1548 Henry VIII's agents destroyed the college of secular canons and after a period of uncertainty the Minster was re-established as a parish church. The new parishioners inherited a marvellous building and the style of worship changed from professional to amateur. The musical situation was probably as confused as in any other church at the time.

Pre-Reformation congregations had been passive participants in worship. They had simply observed mass being celebrated by the clergy at the altar, in Latin. The new Book of Common Prayer now expected congregations to take a more active part but did not tackle immediately the problem of providing suitable music for the psalms and canticles. As a result simple hymns and metrical psalms were imported from the Lutheran and Calvinist traditions and became standard fare for Anglican congregations. We know nothing of the music or of a choir in the

84 (above) A bagpiper on the
   north aisle dado.

85 (above right) A fiddler
   from the east face of the altar
   reredos.

Minster at this time, however, although it is generally assumed that the organ continued to be used for a time. When Edward VI's commissioners listed the ornaments of the Minster in 1552 they included 'one pair of great organs' in the choir. (The term 'pair' signified an instrument of two divisions played from two keyboards.) It seems likely that this instrument was confiscated soon after and there are no recorded payments to organists until the 18th century.

In the absence of evidence or reliable records it is impossible to comment on music in the Minster from the mid-16th to the mid-18th century. The musical life was revived in spectacular fashion at the climax of the restoration of the Minster fabric in the 18th century. The most prominent organ builder of his day, Johann (John) Snetzler, was commissioned in 1767 to build an organ for the Minster. Snetzler had already provided organs for many prominent cathedrals and churches and his fame had extended even further afield. At least four organs had been commissioned and supplied to churches in America by him.

The Beverley organ was Snetzler's largest instrument. It had three manual keyboards, swell, choir and great and, according to Poulson's *Beverlac*, an octave and a half of pedals. These had no pipes of their own but were 'pull-downs' and could be coupled to the manuals. It was very unusual for English organs to be fitted with pedals at this time and it was another century before they would become standard in this country. The organ had twenty-six stops and was housed in a fine case on the new classical stone screen which replaced the medieval one at the west end of the chancel [87]. The organist sat at the console on the north side of the organ case facing inwards – a position that has been retained until the present day. The organ retains thirteen complete Snetzler stops and parts of two others and it is very moving to handle these rather undistinguished-looking pipes and see Snetzler's original markings scratched on them in his characteristic German script (including the German classification of notes, i.e. H for B and B for B flat). Snetzler's pipes may look rather insignificant but they still sing most musically.

Snetzler's organ was opened, in 1769, with a great festival of the music of Handel, the first such event to be held north of the Trent. A notice of the time announced:

> The oratorios for the opening of the elegant organ now erected in Beverley Minster will be on the 20th, 21st and 22nd of September. On Wednesday, 20th, the sacred oratorio of the *Messiah*, on Thursday, 21st, the oratorio of *Judas Maccabaeus*, and on Friday, 22nd, the oratorio of *Samson*, and that being the anniversary of the King's Coronation the performance will conclude with Mr Handel's grand *Coronation Anthem*. The first violin, Mr Giardini. The band will be numerous, and will consist of the best performers, vocal and instrumental, that can be procured. No money will be received at the doors. The North door will be opened at 10 o'clock, and the performances will begin at 11 o'clock. The great aisle will be filled with benches.
>
> N.B. - To add to the solemnity of these performances, the chorus will be dressed in surplices. Mr Giardini will oblige the company with a solo. An organ concerto each day, composed by Mr Matthias Hawdon.

86 An angel with a tambourine from the south nave arcade. The angelic orchestra at this level represents Paradise.

Hawdon was the first organist to be appointed to the Minster, and the first known to have written and published music. For the festivities Hawdon wrote a set of pieces which were later published under the title 'The Opening of an Organ – a Choice set of Voluntaries'. He had been organist of Holy Trinity, Hull and left Beverley in 1777 to return to his native Newcastle as organist of St Nicholas's church (now the cathedral) where, at his own request, he was eventually buried under the organ.

Hawdon was succeeded as organist by George Lambert (1777 – 1818) who was followed in turn by his son George Jackson Lambert (1818 – 1874). The contract for G. J. Lambert's appointment states that an act of parliament, passed in 1766, had made provision for rents from lands in Lincolnshire to be used by trustees to pay for the Minster organ (in 1769) and the fund was also to pay the organist's salary. The fund had been set up by the dean and chapter of York and the contract was delivered on 12 August 1818 over the seals of the archbishop, the dean and chapter of York, the mayor (John Arden) and the recorder of Beverley. Lambert was to be paid 'a yearly sum not exceeding Forty Pounds by four quarterly payments'.

The earliest record of a choir at the Minster since the Reformation is in 1809 when John Armstrong, the parish clerk, was granted £14 a year for instructing singers under the direction of the curate. Like several others, Armstrong combined the office of parish clerk with the mastership of the Blue Coat School in Highgate (now a clergy house on the north side of the Vicarage front lawn). The 'chantry boys' of the school formed the treble line of the Minster choir for many years and they could also be seen taking part in funeral processions directed by John Armstrong, singing psalms and hymns along the route. By 1811 the Vicar, the Revd John Jackson, was involved in training the choir and by 1814 three or four songmen were being paid at the rate of 15s a quarter. By 1830 there was a small surpliced choir of four boys and four men – an early date for a robed parish church choir.

The choir gave a lead to a sizeable congregation. In 1813, 300 carol sheets were bought and a further 200 followed in 1817 together with 150 Easter hymn sheets. In 1839 the Minster began to use a 'Collection of Psalms, Paraphrases and Hymns adapted to the Service of the Minster'. By 1852 the opening sentences of morning and evening prayer were being sung to Anglican chant and 'full cathedral services on Sundays' were being contemplated.

Snetzler's organ continued to give stalwart service. It was cleaned and overhauled by John Ward of York in 1821 in consultation with George Lambert and then in 1848 the Hull firm of Forster & Andrews made considerable changes and additions, the most important being the provision of two independent stops for the pedal section. A new pedal board was fitted but the rest of Snetzler's console was retained. A new blowing plant was installed but it was always notoriously heavy and required two men to work it.

The programme for the opening recital in 1848 after these 'improvements' is a sad reflection on the musical taste of the time. Out of thirteen items rendered by George Lambert, his son Henry and Dr John Camidge of York Minster, only Camidge's 'Introduction and Fugue' was an original organ composition. The rest, ranging from Mozart's overture for *Zauberflöte* to Handel's 'Hallelujah Chorus', were all transcriptions and arrangements. This seemed popular with the public, however, and upwards of 2,000 people came. *The Hull Advertiser* reported that Dr Camidge's performance of 'The Heavens are telling' 'wrought the audience to perfect enthusiasm' and found the imitation of muffled drums by the new pedal pipes in the 'Dead March', 'most sublime'.

In the meantime the choir seemed to function with very little help from George Jackson Lambert who was plagued by increasing deafness. He remained nominally in charge until 1875 during which time matters musical went from bad to worse. After an unfortunate period (1856–7) with one G. F. Flowers as acting-choirmaster, when the Minster music lists were filled with his odd experiments, Lambert's son Henry took on some of his duties. Henry had studied in Leipzig but soon tired of work at the Minster and handed the choir over to two senior song-men, Joseph and William Coverdale, and to a talented local musician and proficient violinist, J. A. Ridgway.

Mr Ridgway clearly enjoyed the confidence of the perpetual curate of the day, the Revd William Burton Crickmer, a popular and fiery preacher. Ridgway set one of Crickmer's ballads to music and it was published (c.1870) in a splendid edition with a print of the Minster on the front. 'Respectfully dedicated to the Ladies of Beverley', it was entitled 'The True British Matron' and began:

> Oh! hast thou marked how dews be-gem
> With diamonds the rose?
> Thus she her heart's pure diadem
> On him she loves bestows.
> If thou the pearly down could'st see
> Which prisms angels' wings;
> A bloom like that would seem to be
> Upon her holy things...

The Choir, Beverley Minster

87 The choir from the east before the demolition of Hawksmoor's screen in 1876, showing the Snetzler organ. See also **pl. 2** for a view of the screen and organ from the west.

As none of these men enjoyed the position and status of Minster organist they had difficulties in managing choir discipline and it is not surprising that critical comments appeared among letters to the *Beverley Guardian*. There are complaints about 'discordant sounds, which agonise one each recurring Sunday' and claims that 'the organ was played in a very eccentric manner' (1867). Another correspondent remarked that the music would have disgraced the poorest village church (1873), and this prompted 'A Grumbling Choirman' to break ranks and inform readers on 12 July 1873: 'There is only a deputy organist, who is not considered responsible for the performance of the services and has no control over the selection of the music.... The clergy being incompetent to superintend choral matters, the choir may be said to be without any responsible head'.

The care of the organ had also been neglected under Lambert, and Forster & Andrews reported in September 1873: 'We found it in a deplorable condition.... Many of the metal pipes through neglect of trifling repairs at the proper time are becoming seriously injured; one has fallen from the front next to the choir and several others are ready to fall. One large one ... is only held up by a piece of small string. The organ ... is beyond the organist's control'.

The Minster at this time was in the grip of a particularly virulent form of puritanism when any church music other than simple congregational hymns was regarded with suspicion. Even what appears to have been a harmless Diocesan Choirs Festival in the form of a simplified evensong was described as 'Romish' by one critic. In 1866 the psalms and canticles were sung to single Anglican chants, and the hymns before and after the sermon were, respectively, 'Now thank we all our God' and 'Abide with me' – not a whiff of incense there!

One annual event which the bigots did not condemn was the Harvest Festival – an extraordinary affair by all accounts, starting with a stampede for the best seats and lasting over two hours. Long processional hymns were favoured and the choir was augmented by young ladies from Miss Stephenson's Boarding School and members of the Choral Society (whose tin trunk may still be seen in the Minster vestry). A long sermon was often interrupted by the noise from the crowd waiting to get in after the service to view the harvest decorations and the final organ voluntary was often Henry Lambert's arrangement of the 'Hallelujah Chorus' for organ.

The organ continued to deteriorate under the strain in spite of an effort to clean the grime and dirt out of it in 1874 at a cost of £50. But improvements were on the way. In 1874 George Lambert was persuaded to retire on a pension and Langdon Colborne from St Michael's College, Tenbury was appointed, technically as 'assistant organist'. The thirty-nine year old Colborne was well-connected in church music circles and he organized fund-raising concerts by choirmen from St Paul's and other famous choirs and advertised for 'Middle Class Boys' to sing in the Minster choir. The great improvement in the musical standards of Minster services was noted in the *Beverley Guardian* on 5 September 1874.

Colborne's musical influence extended beyond the Minster and during his sixteen months as organist, he founded a Beverley Musical Society. One of the items at its inaugural concert was 'Overture in C' by Schubert which, rather surprisingly, included a part for harmonium, an instrument unknown to the composer. Colborne moved to Wigan parish church in 1875, finally moving to Hereford Cathedral in 1877.

Meanwhile Lambert had resigned formally and the post of organist was now vacant officially. Arthur Henry Mann, an even more eminent musician than Colborne, was appointed in December 1875, aged twenty-five. He was energetic in following Colborne's policies as Minster organist and conductor of the Musical Society and in 1876 he instituted the custom of singing hymns from the north-west tower on Easter morning which is still observed by the Minster choir. After only seven months, Mann was appointed to King's College, Cambridge where he was to make the choir the most famous in the Anglican world and to direct the first of the famous Christmas Eve broadcasts of Nine Lessons and Carols.

On 29 June 1876 seven candidates for Mann's post appeared before four judges: the vicar, the mayor (Alderman Alfred Crosskill) and two representatives of the Minster New Fund (which contributed to the organist's salary), Messrs R. Wylie and Joseph Hind. Mann set the tests and acted as umpire. A sizeable audience assembled to hear the candidates rehearse the choir in psalms or a short anthem and play an organ piece each. (An arrangement of Handel's *Zadok the Priest* was a favourite choice.)

Ignoring Mann's advice, the judges invited Messrs Camidge and Wright (both from York) and Goulding (Beverley) to play one Sunday each in the Minster. Mann's last service was on 9 July and on 15 July the New Fund Trustees appointed the twenty-three year old John Camidge, whose family had already provided three consecutive organists of York Minster (1756 – 1858). He took up his duties on 23 July and the anthem at his first service was 'O taste and see' by John Goss.

John Camidge lost no time in building on the foundations laid by his two immediate predecessors and along with his father (who helped him in training the boys) soon transformed the Minster's music. The regular Thursday choral evensong was started in October 1876 and when Canon Nolloth was appointed as vicar in 1880 Camidge's enthusiasm for excellence in standards of public worship was matched by an incumbent with a powerful vision for the Minster. Nolloth's desire was to make the musical standards of the Minster equal to the best Oxford and Cambridge college chapels. For a year in 1888-9 there was a sung evensong every weekday.

In 1877 John Green of Beverley published a book of the words of 'Anthems for use in Beverley Minster'. The seventy-three anthems were standard cathedral choir repertoire. The second edition appeared in 1881 expanded to 160 items and with John Camidge's name on the title page. Modern composers such as Brahms and Dvorak now featured and no fewer than twelve anthems by Camidge himself were listed (only Mendelssohn had more). The anthem books may well reflect Camidge's aspirations for his choir, however, rather than the realities of Minster music, and the list of evensong music in April 1889 features few ambitious items.

The first great problem to be faced by Camidge and Nolloth was the Minster organ. The annual church meeting in July 1876 was informed that the organ had been placed temporarily in the north aisle of the nave and the classical screen demolished. The effect on the already ailing organ can only be imagined. By 1885 Gilbert Scott's new organ screen had been completed by James Elwell, and Hill & Son commissioned to rebuild the organ [**88**]. Hill retained no fewer than twenty of Snetzler's original stops and added thirty-six of his own, including eight independent pedal stops. A new four-manual console was provided and the organ was blown by three hydraulic engines.

The opening ceremonies took place on Thursday 14 April 1885 and comprised a service at 3pm at which the archbishop dedicated the organ and preached, followed by a recital by Dr John Naylor, organist of York Minster. Evening prayer followed at 7pm when a hundred singers from the choirs of the Minster, Holy Trinity, Hull and St Mary's, Beverley combined to sing Mendelssohn's 'Lauda Sion', Hallelujah Choruses by Handel and Beethoven, Evening Canticles in F by Hopkins and offertory and processional hymns. John Camidge played the organ for both services and the choirs were conducted by Frederick Bentley, organist of Holy Trinity, Hull.

At the beginning of his sermon the archbishop pleaded for generous donations to the collection towards the cost of completing the organ. After digging deeply the congregation of about 1,500 gave a total of £21. The archbishop pronounced the blessing and Dr Naylor began his recital, much of which was inaudible owing to the uncouth behaviour of the departing congregation. Even more people (2,500) attended the 7pm service and £15 was donated but again the noise of the people was so intense that Mr Bentley had to appeal to the vicar for quiet and order so that his recital could be heard.

Writing in 1960, J. F. Shepherd, a former pupil of Camidge, recalled the day. As a boy of thirteen he had been thrilled by the opening of the new organ: 'It seemed as though the trumpets of Heaven had been borrowed!' His only criticism was reserved for the noisy hydraulic blowing engines: 'That was the problem at that time – to get wind into the organ with less noise'. Mr Shepherd also recalled the Snetzler organ standing 'behind the pulpit at the angle of the aisle and transept, over each drawstop was a paper label with the name of the stop printed on it'.

Thomas Hill, whose firm had rebuilt the organ, saving much of the original pipework from oblivion, was not without his critics who asked, in the newspaper columns, 'Where is the old mellow tone? What have they done to our beautiful Snetzler stops?' Others emerged as experts in organ voicing and wind pressure. Hill's short answer was that inches of dust had mellowed the tone and many of their precious Snetzler pipes had been closed and dumb for nearly a generation as a result of being often tuned by a smart blow from a hammer. Dr Arthur Hill (Thomas Hill's brother and subsequently head of the firm) stated unequivocally that 'all the original stops of Snetzler... are absolutely untouched as regards either voicing or wind pressure'.

Snetzler's organ had been housed in an elegant case but nothing comparable was provided in 1885. The pipes for the new organ could not all be accommodated on the screen and most of the large pedal pipes and other divisions were allowed to spill over into the south choir aisle. Gilbert Scott wanted to house the organ in two cases on either side of the chancel (the typical heard-but-not-seen attitude of an architect). The decision was made to site the organ on the

88 The choir from the north east, showing Scott's new screen and the Hill organ, dedicated in April 1885.

Beverley Minster, Choir West.

screen behind a rather clumsy arrangement of uncased, stencilled pipes, looking like a row of giant pencils. The situation was remedied in 1916 when the organ was further enlarged and rehoused in its present form in Dr Arthur Hill's inspired organ case [**83**], paid for by Canon Nolloth, a further act of generosity by the Minster's remarkable vicar.

The organ was re-dedicated on Thursday, 11 May 1916 by the archbishop of York at a service which also celebrated Beverley Grammar School Founder's Day. Great Britain was at war and the band of the East Yorkshire Regiment played before the service and led the singing of all three verses of the National Anthem at the end. The opening recital - an enterprising programme of works by Bach, Franck, Reubke, Guilmant and Harwood - was given by the eminent assistant organist of Westminster Abbey, Walter Alcock, who also included one of his own pieces and two improvisations.

During his long tenure of fifty-seven years, John Camidge appears to have stuck to a regular repertoire of choral music. He wrote a number of unpublished anthems, several of them for men's voices only and some chants and canticle settings in the prevalent Mendelssohnian style. His diary for 1922 records the title of each Sunday's anthem with a comment on its performance (mostly 'g' or 'vg') and most of the items are listed in his 1881 anthem words book. The diary (a tiny 'Letts Quikref' measuring only 7 x 5 cms) reveals that life was not all plain sailing. On 8 and 29 January there was not enough water in the town supply to power the massive hydraulic blowing plant for the organ and Camidge had to resort to a harmonium. The diary also reveals him as a thrifty man since he managed to cram week by week entries for 1923 and 1924 on the spare pages at the back.

On Thursday 15 July 1922 the diary entry proclaims 'I was appointed to this church in 1876'. On that evening in 1926 Camidge gave his Golden Jubilee Recital in the Minster. Reflecting the fashions of the time, only one of the four pieces was an original composition, the others all being orchestral transcriptions. The vicar's notes on his copy of the recital programme refer to 'Mr Camidge's record - never missed a Christmas, Easter, Whit or Harvest service in 50 years & never late'.

In 1933, aged eighty, John Camidge retired [**89**] and was succeeded by one of the century's most eminent church musicians, Herbert Kennedy Andrews. The thirty-two year old Andrews galvanized the music of the Minster. His choristers were recruited from the Minster Boys' School where the headmaster, Mr Whitehead, was also a churchwarden. Suitable boys were press-ganged (as Andrews humorously remarked) into the choir, one incentive being that they missed morning lessons for choir practice three times a week. A strict disciplinarian, Andrews instituted a system of fines and quarterly pay was distributed formally in the Minster. He also instituted the wearing of mortar boards (which he provided) to and from the Minster, thus rendering his choristers open to the sort of abuse their medieval counterparts in their tawny gowns must have suffered from their uncouth peers.

Dr Andrews gained the respect and affection of his choristers, however, and introduced them to a wealth of good music, according to the music lists. His uncompromising approach brought him into conflict with some of his songmen from whom he withdrew payments, as is evident from one or two indignant letters to the Parochial Church Council.

At one time Andrews suggested the setting up of choral scholarships to Beverley Grammar School, one of which he offered to fund himself. He would also pick up two or three songmen from York Minster by car after evensong (at 3pm) and bring them to sing at Beverley in the evening with sometimes a recital to follow, also at his own expense.

Early in his time at Beverley, Andrews was seriously ill and needed to convalesce for over six months during the winter of 1934-5. During his absence one of those events occurred which reflected the cultural range still to be observed in Minster congregations. Dr Rigg, writing in the parish magazine for November 1934, announces the visit of the eighty-eight year old Prebendary Carlisle, the greatly respected founder of the Church Army: 'There is to be an organ recital at 5.45pm. Mr F. Marshall will play two trumpet solos – "Holy City" and "Lost Chord." During the evening service there will be a solo, "There is a green hill" sung by Marjorie Jones, contralto (Gold Medallist) and community singing. I do not know whether Prebendary Carlisle will play on his trombone...'. An eye-witness reported that the great man did indeed play his trombone but he preached at such length that very few remained for the final blessing.

In April 1937 a further appeal for £800 was made to repair the Snetzler pipework in the organ which was still being maintained by the primitive and destructive method of cone-tuning, which involved fitting a brass cone into the top of a pipe and striking it with a hammer. With the advent of electricity the hydraulic blowers had been replaced in 1935 by an efficient electric motor which was to last for nearly sixty years. By August £260 had been raised and a further appeal was made.

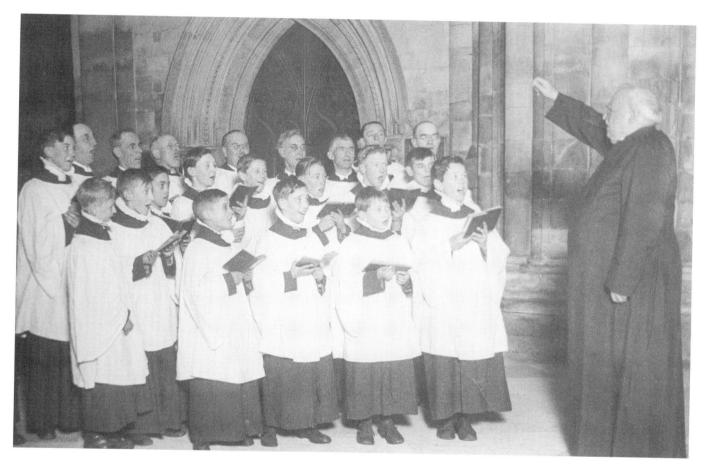

89 The Minster choir with John Camidge in 1933, the year of his retirement.

In 1938 Dr Andrews moved to Oxford as university lecturer, fellow and organist of New College. Even his most devoted admirers admit that H. K. Andrews was not a great organist. His successor John Herbert Long, aged thirty, was a fine player whose tasteful organ accompaniments in particular made an immediate impact on the choristers. Long came to Beverley in 1938 from Brighton parish church having previously held appointments at Lambeth Palace and Merton College, Oxford. He took over a flourishing choir and maintained a high standard of music until war service took him into the RAF.

During World War II the temporary organist was a Mr Murdoch. The then vicar, the Revd D. T. Dick, took it upon himself to undo much of the musical good work of the previous decade and when John Long returned after the war he found that even the Oxford Psalter (instituted by Andrews and favoured by the best Anglican choirs and choirmasters) had been discarded in favour of an ancient (and discredited) psalter and a battle ensued to restore it. It was possibly no coincidence that the anthem chosen for the vicar's final service at Easter 1947 was Henry Ley's 'The strife is o'er'.

In order to accommodate the younger men returning from the war, John Long instituted a choral evensong service on Monday, at which only the young men sang, with boys, in addition to the well-established Thursday service, sung by the full choir. The repertoire on Mondays was noticeably less elaborate. As the choir picked up again, Long was able to introduce an increasing amount of excellent church music, including anthems by Purcell, Boyce, Palestrina and Howells and canticle settings by Byrd, Gibbons, Ireland, Stanford, Murrill and Howells.

The Minster choir was called on to play an important part in the St John of Beverley Festival instituted in 1950, during Canon Collwyn Hargreaves' time. The festival took place for a week around the saint's day, 7 May. In 1953, for example, John Long conducted the choir and an orchestra in a concert of music by Victoria, Palestrina, Byrd, Batten, Blow, Purcell, Mozart, Bach and Barber, and other concerts were given by Nina Milkina (piano), Lady Susi Jeans (organ) and the Laurence Turner String Quartet. The festival opened with Festival Evensong sung by the choir attended by many civic heads of Yorkshire towns and cities, an event which still continues annually.

90 The Minster choir, July 1969. The author of this chapter is in the centre of the front row.

Canon Hargreaves' vision for the Minster included raising its profile in the town and beyond and it is interesting to note that readers at carol services in the 1950s included the mayor of Beverley, the stationmaster, the postmaster, the Chief Constable, the Grammar School headmaster, a doctor and a works foreman.

John Long resigned in 1956 and David Ingate, formally assistant organist of Chichester Cathedral, soon established himself as a brilliant organist, improviser and choir trainer. During his time broadcasts of organ recitals and choral evensong in the regular BBC series were undertaken for the first time. In his quest for excellence Ingate was discriminating in his choice of choristers and at one of his broadcasts fewer than ten choristers took part.

By 1960 the organ was once again in need of serious attention. Whereas in 1885 it was held together by pieces of string, in 1960 adhesive tape was employed. An appeal was launched for £9,000 for a complete overhaul by the firm of Hill, Norman & Beard, in consultation with David Ingate. The organ rebuild, although conservative in approach (a good thing in the 1960s when some fine English organs were ruined in deference to prevailing fashions in organ design), was something of a disappointment and critical articles appeared in the musical press. From the correspondence it appears that Peter Fletcher (who had replaced Ingate as organist in 1962) entered into the controversy with great enthusiasm and had to be restrained from making too many intemperate pronouncements for fear of legal repercussions.

Peter Fletcher inherited a lively musical tradition and soon put his own stamp on the repertoire, introducing music from his Cambridge days and discarding much standard repertoire. Needing additional employment to supplement the organist's salary which had hardly changed in thirty years, he was appointed music advisor to the East Riding Local Education Authority and very soon his considerable energies were devoted more to his educational work than to the Minster. He found a further outlet in the St John of Beverley Festival which became ever more ambitious under his musical directorship.

It was no surprise when Peter Fletcher moved, in January 1966, to the prestigious post of music advisor to the Inner London Authority. Alan Spedding, organist of the parish church, Kingston upon Thames was chosen by the Revd E. B. Bull from a field of fifty-six candidates, taking up his duties on 1 January 1967 after an interregnum of five months during which the assistant organist, Andrew Leach, had ably directed the music.

The first concern of the new organist was to recruit more choristers. He inherited eleven boys, three of whom were individually put to singing bass and alto parts, leaving eight effective choristers. By March 1967 there were twelve choristers, nine probationers, seven songmen and six junior songmen [**90**].

The pattern of Sunday services in the late 1960s was as follows:

1st Sunday	10.30am Family Service	6.30pm Evensong & Sermon
2nd Sunday	10.30am Mattins & Sermon	6.30pm Evensong & Sermon
3rd Sunday	10.30am Choral Eucharist	6.30pm Evensong & Sermon
4th/5th Sunday	10.30am Mattins & Sermon	6.30pm Evensong & Sermon

The best-attended service was the Family Service when the nave was fairly full. Congregations for the Choral Eucharist were small enough to be accommodated in the chancel but the evening congregation was sizeable. The choir sang anthems at most services but canticles were rarely sung to choral settings in the (largely mistaken) belief that the congregation would appreciate the opportunity of singing the canticles to simple Anglican chants. The choir sang its more ambitious repertoire at choral evensong every Thursday.

The liturgical upheavals of the 1970s and 80s, including the production of the Alternative

Service Book in 1980, were reflected in the Minster patterns of worship, as the vicar, Canon Peter Harrison, attempted to cater for the diverse tastes of his congregation. At one time ASB service forms (mattins, evensong and eucharist) alternated weekly with Book of Common Prayer services, creating confusion, especially among the protagonists of the old versus the new in the congregation. A music group was set up during this period to perform worship songs at some services and one Sunday evening a month was set aside specifically for informal worship. Adjustments continued to be made to Sunday worship until the arrival of the Revd Dr Peter Forster as vicar in 1991 when he established the general rule that morning services should conform to ASB forms and evening services to BCP.

The choral repertoire was extended during these turbulent years and the choir was heard not only in the Minster but further afield through a number of broadcasts on radio and television. Beverley Minster was even included in a BBC Radio Three series entitled 'Great Cathedrals and their music', in 1979, the only non-cathedral church to be included. The organ also gained wider recognition and the organist broadcast many recitals and made a number of recordings.

A number of annual events have been established since 1967 including the processional services at Advent, Epiphany, Palm Sunday and Good Friday. An Ash Wednesday evening eucharist was instituted in the 1990s at which, thanks to the breaking down of ancient prejudices, the service has been sung in Latin, for the first time since the Reformation. The choir and the clergy make an annual visit to Harpham, the reputed birthplace of St John of Beverley, for a procession to St John's Well, followed by choral evensong in the village church. The custom of climbing to the top of the north-west tower to sing on Easter morning, started in 1876, is still observed.

By the 1990s, the organ was again in need of urgent attention. The blower which had given excellent service since the installation of electricity in the 1930s finally failed and a new machine was installed in 1993. The improved wind supply soon found out many of the problems in the rest of the organ and under the energetic leadership of the vicar, Dr Peter Forster, an appeal was launched and £160,000 was raised in a matter of months for a thorough rebuild. The work was entrusted to Wood (Organ Builders) of Huddersfield whose dedicated craftsmanship and enthusiasm resulted in happy solutions to many problems which had persisted in the organ as far back as 1885. Not only was the organ passed on to the next generation in excellent condition but provision was made for an on-going fund to pay for future renovations.

The rebuilt organ was re-dedicated by the Rt Revd James Jones, bishop of Hull, at a great service on 10 September 1995. The opening part of the service was unaccompanied but as soon as the organ had been blessed by the bishop it played a full part in the hymns and anthems and in accompanying the choir in Stanford's Evening Canticles in G in which the bass soloist was Mr Arnold Bennett who had sung the treble solos in the same music some sixty years before as one of Dr Andrews' head choristers. The organist played one of Matthias Hawdon's compositions written for the 1769 opening and the final voluntary, 'Toccata - Carillon' specially written by Alan Spedding for the occasion, was listened to in unprecedented silence by the vast congregation.

In compiling this chapter, I have drawn extensively on material collected and generously given to me over a number of years by the late Philip Brown, Deputy Borough Librarian of Beverley and former secretary to the Parochial Church Council of the Minster. His pamphlet, *Victorian Themes, Music and Manners in Beverley Minster,* published for the St John of Beverley Festival, May 1966, was of particular help and I acknowledge my debt to one who was a good friend to me and to the music in the Minster.

My thanks are due to Arnold Bennett, a life-long member of the Minster choir since the days of H.K. Andrews, and to Andrew Leach, former assistant organist of the Minster, for taking the time to share their reminiscences at length and for allowing me to use their researches.

91 The procession entering the
great west door of the Minster
for the memorial service for
King Edward VII, 20 May
1910. The brick churchyard
wall seen in the background
of **36** was replaced with iron
railings in 1905.

SUSAN NEAVE

13 · The Precinct

> The prebendaries' houses stand round about St John's churchyard. Whereof the
> bishop of York has one moated, but all in ruin. The fairest part of the provost's house is
> the gate and the front.[1]

This description by Leland, of about 1540, suggests Beverley Minster was once surrounded by
collegiate and other associated buildings, though the precinct was apparently never enclosed in
the formal sense. Five major medieval streets converge on the Minster: Highgate, which was the
principal route from the church to the town, Eastgate, Flemingate, Keldgate and Minster
Moorgate. There are no documentary references to gateways into the precinct with the possible
exception of the 'Minster Bow'; this was probably located towards the south end of Highgate,
but may have been simply a bridge or vaulted sewer. Foundations that could relate to a gateway
have been found towards the east end of Minster Moorgate, on the south side of the street, but
an association with the Bedern complex, rather than an entrance into a formal close, seems
most likely. A gateway near the Minster in either street would have excluded several important
collegiate buildings from the precinct.

THE BEDERN AND PROVOST'S HOUSE

The communal residence of the Minster clergy was the Bedern, which originally provided
accommodation for the provost and vicars, the *berefellarii* or parsons, and also housed the canons
until they acquired their own prebendal residences. The provost's court and gaol were also part
of the complex. An illustration of the fourteenth-century residence of the vicars choral at
Southwell shows a half-timbered building which formed one side of a quadrangle, with a
central gateway which led into the inner courtyard. The arrangement of the communal buildings at Beverley is unknown, but may have been similar.

Documentary evidence suggests the Bedern and associated buildings occupied a substantial
block of land between Keldgate and Minster Moorgate, bounded by the modern St John Street
to the east. (A on fig. 4) An early fifteenth-century rental of the provostry lists under Keldgate
rent paid by the parsons for property within the Bedern close. A reference to the Bedern garden
occurs at the beginning of the Minster Moorgate section. In a seventeenth-century survey of
the holdings of the Warton family, land called 'Bardon [Bedern?] grounds' and property known
as 'Bardon stable' come between the sections headed Minster Moorgate and Keldgate. The early
eighteenth-century antiquary John Warburton presumed 'Barton Hall Garth' in Minster
Moorgate to be the site of the Bedern.[2]

An inventory of the provost's goods in the Bedern made in 1304 mentions the great and
small halls, great and small kitchens, larder, buttery, brewhouse, bakehouse and granary. Two
years later the Bedern cooks asked for absolution from excommunication for building a little
chamber in the Bedern kitchen without permission. In the late 13th century one of the vicars
had built a chamber with a chapel next to the dormitory. The fourteenth-century will of Alan
of Humbleton, one of the vicars, mentions the vicars' chamber where he had a chest and other

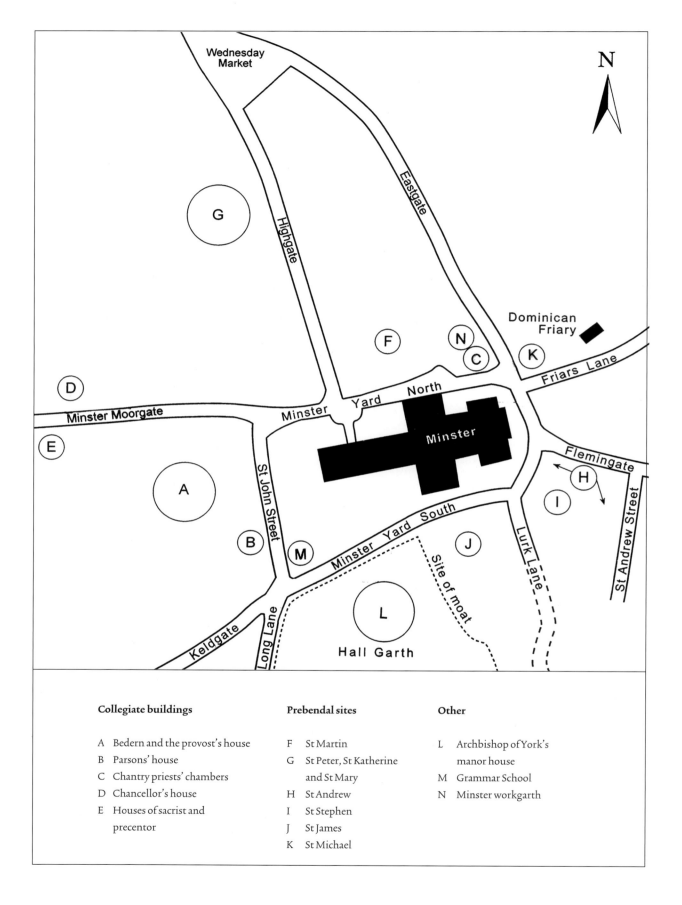

Collegiate buildings

A Bedern and the provost's house

B Parsons' house

C Chantry priests' chambers

D Chancellor's house

E Houses of sacrist and
precentor

Prebendal sites

F St Martin

G St Peter, St Katherine
and St Mary

H St Andrew

I St Stephen

J St James

K St Michael

Other

L Archbishop of York's
manor house

M Grammar School

N Minster workgarth

household items. Money was given towards the building or rebuilding of a dormitory in the mid 14th century.[3]

Robert Neville, who held the provostship from 1422–7, added a tower to the Bedern. Leland's notes suggest that in the later medieval period a new Bedern was built adjoining the old one, the latter becoming the provost's house. Repairs to the roof and stable at the provost's house, and to the kitchen and several chambers at the Bedern were mentioned in 1530, indicating separate buildings. According to Leland the 'fairest part' of the provost's house was the gate and the front. The gatehouse, which measured twenty feet by ten feet (6.1 x 3.1 metres), had a flat roof covered with lead. After the Dissolution the lead, valued at £60, was stripped off, melted down and sold. The building may have faced the west end of the Minster, with the new Bedern lying behind in Minster Moorgate. The provost's house, together with several prebendal sites and the houses of the chancellor, precentor, sacrist and 'seven rectors' or parsons were granted to Sir Michael Stanhope and his associate, John Bellow, in 1548. The following year they were granted the 'mansion of the nine vicars choral'.[4]

An inventory drawn up following the death of provost Thomas Dalby in 1526 provides information about his house at Beverley. Dalby was also prebendary of St James, but would have lived in the provost's house. A hall is mentioned, decorated with hangings of green cloth, and a great parlour, which had a large table and other furniture and blue and yellow hangings. The great chamber and bedchamber, both with four-poster beds, were hung with painted cloth of damask work. Hangings in the chapel depicted the story of St Katherine. Other rooms mentioned in the inventory are the steward's chamber, wardrobe, pantry and kitchen.[5]

THE PARSONS' HOUSE

Separate provision for the *berefellarii* or parsons, who originally lived in the Bedern, was made in 1399 when they were granted a piece of land in the Bedern close, on which they built their own mansion house. The grant gave them free access through the great and little gates of the Bedern. The land they were given was bounded on the east by the common way between the church and the Bedern. The width on the eastern boundary was sixty-two feet (18.9 metres), measured from the tenement in which John Tickhill lived, which has been identified as a property on the corner of Keldgate and St John Street. On the western boundary the width was ninety-six feet (29.3 metres), measured from the common sewer (which at this point ran parallel to Keldgate) northwards. The depth of the plot was 177 feet (54 metres). The northern boundary is not mentioned, but is assumed to have been the Bedern itself. In 1472 the mansion house of the *berefellarii* was described as lying 'beside the Bedern'.[6] The internal arrangements of the house are unknown, but it was probably a two-storeyed building with timber-framing to the first floor, with a hall and communal dormitory.

The site of the mansion of the seven parsons can be identified with nos 9–11 St John Street, where the base of a medieval wall survives within the post-medieval structure. (B on fig. 4) The street frontage of these properties measures sixty-two feet (18.9 metres), corresponding with the measurement given in the 1399 grant. A house on this site, possibly the five-hearthed house of William Smith listed in the 1672 hearth tax returns, and adjoining land, were sold to Joseph Lambert, master of Beverley Grammar School, in 1701. In his will Lambert describes how he had rebuilt the house, '*almost* all the old house being pulled down', suggesting he retained the foundations of an earlier building. Lambert's new house extended further north, incorporating the present no. 8 St John Street (the front wall of which is considerably narrower than at nos 9–11), and had a large rear wing. This building is described in more detail below.

fig. 4 *The Minster Precinct* Conjectural sites of collegiate and other buildings

THE CHANTRY PRIESTS' CHAMBERS

Some of the chantry priests also lived communally, in chambers in or near the Minster church-yard which belonged to the fabric fund. In 1532 six chambers and two 'low houses' were listed in the fabric accounts under the 'workgarth' and eight chambers are mentioned in a later document. At the Dissolution the priests who served the chantries of St Mary and St Peter were amongst those living in the chambers. In the early 18th century the curate's house at the corner of Minster Yard North and Eastgate (now known as the Old Vicarage) and other buildings were said to occupy the site of the chantry priests' chambers.[7] (C on fig. 4)

A *cubiculum* in the Minster churchyard was granted to William Wynlove and Edward Pease in 1549. It formerly belonged to St Anne's chantry, and was perhaps one of the 'low houses' mentioned earlier. Other priests may have lived in houses belonging to the chantries they served. The chantries of St Michael and St John of Beverley, for example, owned properties in Eastgate and Keldgate respectively.

The corporation records include payments in 1610-11 for the repair of 'Mr Pettye's chamber in the minster garth'. Petty was the master of the Grammar School. This was presumably the building in Minster Yard 'formerly in the occupation of Mr Pettie' which adjoined the curate's house, said in 1664 to be in a ruinous condition. It was pulled down soon after. The building probably pre-dated the Reformation and may have been part of the former chantry priests' chambers. There is also a reference in the corporation records, in 1703, to the reroofing of a 'low room' on the north side of the Minster which may have been another remnant of the medieval buildings.[8]

THE HOUSES OF THE CHANCELLOR, PRECENTOR AND SACRIST

The three principal officers of the collegiate church, the chancellor, precentor and sacrist, had houses in Minster Moorgate. The fifteenth-century provost's book describes the chancellor's house there as lying west of 'Ryngandlan' which can be identified with 'Ryngoldlane' (now lost), which ran north from Minster Moorgate to Fishmarketmoorgate (later Well Lane and now Champney Road). A deed of 1545 describes property on the north side of Minster Moorgate as bounded by the land of the chancellor of the collegiate church of St John on the east. Chalk footings of a substantial medieval building have been found on a site towards the eastern end of Minster Moorgate. Associated pottery indicates it went out of use around the time of the Dissolution, suggesting it was a collegiate building, and perhaps therefore the chancellor's house.[9] (D on fig. 4)

In 1273 the precentor was granted a court and house in 'Moregate' (Minster Moorgate). The precentor's mansion was mentioned in 1325, when dilapidations were assessed at 100s. The provost's book indicates that by the early 15th century the houses of both the precentor and sacrist were in Minster Moorgate, and more specifically in the part which lay within the parish of St Nicholas.[10] This suggests they were on the south side of the street. (E on fig. 4)

THE PREBENDAL HOUSES

In the early middle ages the canons or prebendaries would have lived communally in the Bedern, but later they acquired separate prebendal houses. Several of these houses occupied sites facing the Minster, as Leland's account implies.

St Martin. The prebendal house of St Martin was situated on the north side of the church, between Highgate and Eastgate. (F on fig. 4) It was rebuilt in the early 14th century, when the old house was said to be small and in a poor state of repair, apart from the stables and a room above the gate. The new house comprised a hall and double room with two fireplaces, a chapel, kitchen, brewhouse, bakery and a room which linked the hall and gate. Some timber from the old house was used in the rebuilding.[11]

In 1376 Richard of Ravenser, prebendary of St Martin, negotiated the exchange of a narrow plot of land measuring 147 feet (44.8 metres) by nineteen feet (5.8 metres), abutting on Highgate, for a rather more substantial plot, measuring 108 feet (33.0 metres) by forty-eight feet (14.6 metres), dedicated to the fabric of the church. The larger plot lay on the east side of his mansion, and enabled him to enlarge the prebendal garden. His justification was that houses or shops could be built on the smaller plot, providing income for the maintenance of the church fabric. Later documents show that shops were built on this piece of land. The Minster fabric accounts for 1445-6 include rent from eleven shops in Beverley 'by the mansion of the prebend of St Martin' which were part of the manor of Bentley.[12] The fabric lands passed to the Crown at the Dissolution, but were later granted back to the corporation to provide funds for the upkeep of the Minster. Compensation had to be made for some fabric land which had already passed out of Crown hands, in the form of a grant of the manor of Bentley to the duke of Northumberland. A deed dated 1626 refers to eleven shops in Highgate, described as 'parcel of the manor of Bentley'. Also conveyed at this date were 'a stable called Prebend Stable and Prebend Garth in High Street', evidently the site of St Martin's prebend, indicating that by the early 17th century the plot of land exchanged in 1376 and the rest of the prebendal site had been reunited.[13] The descent of these properties can be traced through to the early 18th century, when they were sold to Sir Charles Hotham. Prebend Garth was said to measure approximately one acre, and deeds show it occupied a block of land between Highgate and Eastgate, towards the southern end of these streets.

St Martin's prebend was granted to Sir Michael Stanhope and John Bellow in 1548. Stanhope, the brother-in-law of Protector Somerset, was executed in 1552 for plotting against the duke of Northumberland, and the prebendal site passed back to the Crown. By 1626 it had changed hands privately on at least two occasions.

St Peter, St Katherine and St Mary. Three blocks of prebendal land lay in Highgate, the street which runs north from the Minster to the town. In 1307 the prebendary of St Peter granted 'eight shops lately built on my prebend, in length from land of St Katherine's prebend to that of St Mary's, and in breadth between the high street called Fishmarketgate, and the wall situate on my prebend'.[14] At this date the northern part of Highgate was sometimes known as Fishmarketgate.

The grant suggests St Peter's prebend occupied a fairly narrow plot fronting Highgate, with the prebendal lands of St Katherine and St Mary lying on either side. If the prebendal house was on this plot, it was apparently set back, allowing commercial development to take place on the street frontage. In 1553 four workshops in Highgate formerly belonging to St Katherine's prebend are mentioned, suggesting a similar arrangement.[15]

In 1461 it was reported that the twelve governors of Beverley had assembled at the prebend of St Mary to eat four wildfowl sent to them by Lord Neville – the brother of Warwick 'the Kingmaker'– who was beginning to take over the former Percy interest in the East Riding. In 1549 St Mary's prebendal house, then in the occupation of Thomas Barton, was granted to Stanhope and Bellow. They had already been granted the prebendal houses of St Peter and St Katherine the previous year.

The precise location of these prebendal lands in Highgate is uncertain, but the most likely site is the block of land on the west side now fronted by nos 6–26, which lay between the Minster fabric lands to the south and a medieval house known as Englebert Hall to the north. (G on fig.

4) A jettied timber-framed building with decorative woodwork and original three-light window (nos 6-8 Highgate, demolished late 1958 or 1959) may have been one of the last surviving remnants of property formerly in prebendal ownership.

St Andrew. St Andrew's prebendal house was mentioned in 1318 and again in 1322 when assessments of dilapidations were made following the appointment of new prebendaries. Benedict of Paston, who was appointed in July 1322, carried out repairs to the house, although as a lawyer and diocesan administrator pursuing his career in the south, he was usually absent from Beverley. In 1323 Queen Isabel slept at the house when she visited the Minster, suggesting it was in good repair and comfortably furnished.[16]

The last prebendary, Thomas Thurland, surrendered to Sir Michael Stanhope in 1547. Following Stanhope's attainder St Andrew's reverted to the Crown, and was included in the grant of lands to the corporation in 1585 for the upkeep of St Mary's church. The grant refers to a 'messuage, tenement, burgage or mansion house, two little garden places, one dove cote and one close to the same adjoining'. The site, 'now or late in the occupation of Abraham Metcalf' was said to cover about an acre, and abutted Flemingate to the north.[17] (H on fig. 4) Burrow's plan of 1747 shows a large block of land between Flemingate and Minster Yard South in the ownership of Mr [Thomas] Clarke.[18]

The mid nineteenth-century Ordnance Survey plan has 'St Andrew's Garth' marked at the south end of Sigston Street (later renamed St Andrew Street) though whether the prebendal lands extended this far south of Flemingate is doubtful. The prebendal house probably lay close to the Minster, perhaps at the corner of Flemingate and Minster Yard South, where a timber-framed building stood until 1912. Illustrations of the house at Flemingate corner suggest a fifteenth- or early sixteenth-century date [**92**]. The house was demolished in 1912 and

92 The east end of the Minster from Flemingate c. 1850 (from a lithograph by Andrew Newman). The timber-framed house on the left-hand side, demolished in 1912, may have been the remains of the prebendal house of St Andrew.

replaced by the Constitutional Hall. An excavation of the site in 1985, following demolition of the hall, revealed the foundations of two medieval stone walls, running east-west, the larger 1.6 metres wide and 2.2 metres deep.

St Stephen. In 1319 Henry Carlton, prebendary of St Stephen, gave the vicars of St John a messuage in Lurk Lane which lay next to his prebend. Other documents indicate the prebendal site was on the east side of Lurk Lane, with the prebendal house facing the Minster, fronting the section of lane which is now part of Minster Yard South.[19] (I on fig. 4)

An inventory of the goods of William Duffield, prebendary of St Stephen, who died in March 1453, gives some indication of the size and contents of a prebendal house. Duffield, who was archdeacon of Cleveland and also held prebends at York and Southwell, would have spent a limited amount of time at Beverley. His house near the Minster had three principal rooms: a hall, chamber and chapel together with a kitchen, pantry and a brewhouse. The rooms were modestly furnished by comparison with his residence at York. Red was the dominant colour in the hall, the room used for entertaining, with curtains and other furnishings of this colour. The chamber contained a number of beds, including a four-poster, and various items of bedding, for example coverlets decorated with roses and fleur-de-lys. Other furnishings included a small wainscot chest and another chest painted green.[20] The house was mentioned in the grant of collegiate lands to Stanhope and Bellow in 1548, and its subsequent fate is not known. By 1747 the site, together with the prebendal sites of St Andrew and St James which lay on either side, was owned by the Clarke family.

St James. West of St Stephen's prebend, on the opposite side of Lurk Lane, lay the prebend of St James. The prebendal house, mentioned in 1305 and again in 1338, was included in the properties acquired by Stanhope and Bellow in 1548. The house was seemingly chosen as a local base from which to administer these acquisitions, for in September of that year Bellow ordered various building materials to be taken there and certain work carried out including the 'making of a study or checker'.[21] After Stanhope's attainder the house and adjacent buildings, orchards and gardens were granted in 1552 to Lord Clinton and Saye and Henry Herdson of London. By 1585, when the prebendal site was granted by the Crown to the corporation of Beverley, the house was no longer standing. In the grant the site is described as a 'close or orchard with the appurtenances in Beverley aforesaid containing by estimation one acre of land lying near the hall garth there commonly called St James prebend garth'.[22] This has been interpreted as a reference to a close or orchard which lay *near* a 'hall garth ... known as St James prebend garth', perhaps located in Eastgate. But there is no doubt it was the actual prebendal site which was granted to the corporation, described as a close or orchard, 'commonly called St James prebend garth', which lay in Beverley 'near the hall garth there', this being the site of the archbishop's manor house on the south side of the Minster. This places the prebend of St James on the west side of Lurk Lane, facing the Minster, and bounded on the west by Hall Garth. (J on fig. 4) This is supported by a reference in 1342 to a messuage in Lurk Lane which lay between the lane and the 'archbishop's great ditch' (the eastern boundary of Hall Garth). This property was bounded by Minster fabric land to the south, and 'land of the altar of St James' to the north.[23] These fabric lands were granted to the corporation after the Dissolution, and were later known as Lurk Lane Closes. Their location places the messuage granted in 1342 in the vicinity of Minster Boys' School (now demolished) with land of St James occupying the site between there and the Minster. Dr Clifton, who can be identified as William Clifton, last prebendary of St James, rented a close in Lurk Lane which belonged to the Minster fabric, presumably to augment his prebendal lands.

In 1979–82 the site bounded by Lurk Lane, Hall Garth and Minster Yard South was excavated prior to redevelopment, and evidence of a substantial fifteenth-century timber-framed building found [**93**]. This building, which replaced an earlier timber-framed hall, was set on heavy chalk foundations and may have had an undercroft. A stone building was located to the south. In the 16th century the timber-framed structure was rebuilt, and the ground sills replaced in brick. The original function of the building was not known but it was thought to have been associated with the collegiate church, perhaps a prebendal house or one of the communal buildings of the clergy. Medieval finds included parchment prickers, fittings thought to have come from book bindings, and the remnant of a wooden effigy taking the form of a pair of hands clasped in prayer. There was no indication of domestic occupation of the site after the 16th century.[24] The documentary evidence leaves little doubt that the principal building excavated was the prebendal mansion of St James, which was probably demolished in the mid 16th century. In 1747 the site is shown as an orchard, and is referred to in early eighteenth-century deeds as 'Prebend Orchard', further confirmation of its previous history. In the early 19th century it was used as a wood yard and later for allotments.

St Michael. A late thirteenth-century reference to land belonging to St Michael's prebend suggests the site lay between Friars Lane and Eastgate, close to the Minster. (K on fig. 4) The prebendal mansion of St Michael is mentioned in 1321. In 1547 William Giles, the last prebendary, relinquished his lands to Sir Michael Stanhope.[25] The prebendal site was apparently included in the lands granted to the corporation in 1585. An associated document of this date refers to a house or tenement 'once a prebend house' in the occupation of William Walker. The grant itself refers to 'one messuage tenement or mansion house one garden and one orchard to the same adjoining...in Eastgate...containing by estimation one acre of land now or late in the occupation of William Walker'.[26] Like many other properties mentioned in this grant, the prebendal site was sold by the corporation within a short space of time. By 1590 it was in the hands of Michael Warton, who died that year. At the time of his death his property included a capital messuage called Black Friars (the former Dominican friary, in Friars Lane), where he lived, and a house called St Michael's prebend with a garth, garden, orchard and gatehouse.[27] Warton, one of the twelve governors of the town, had no doubt acquired the prebendal site with a view to extending the grounds of his house. Black Friars was left to his wife Joan for her life, but she remarried soon after his death. Michael's eldest son and heir, Michael II, married in 1592 or 1593, and it was probably around this time that he demolished the prebendal buildings and rebuilt the friary, adding an extension to the west. The surviving range is now considered to be chiefly post-Reformation in date, incorporating earlier building materials, and has a number of late sixteenth-century features. Michael II remained there until his death in 1655.

Eastgate was once thought to form the boundary of the land occupied by the Dominicans, but the excavation of a section of wall, believed to be part of the precinct wall, c. 75 metres east of the street, indicates that this was not the case. Documentary evidence shows that Eastgate formed the boundary of the Warton holding, which extended at least 67 metres north of Friars Lane. This represents a space of considerably more than an acre for a prebendal site between Eastgate and the friary precinct wall, even allowing for a narrowing of the plot at its southern end. A suggestion that the land between the friary and the street was occupied by housing seems unlikely. Although foundations of tenements were found during excavations in Eastgate in the 1980s, the area excavated lay at the northern edge of the Warton holding and would not have been part of the prebendal site.

An excavation did take place in the area west of the friary building, close to Eastgate, in the 1960s, and substantial medieval wall footings and other features were discovered. It was not

93 The prebendal house of St James as it might have looked in c. 1300. (A reconstruction of the phase 7c building from the 1979-82 Lurk Lane excavation.)

clear what these represented, but it now seems certain they must relate to the prebendal house or its associated buildings. Some material from the site may have been used in rebuilding the friary and precinct wall (see below) in the late 16th century.

THE ARCHBISHOP OF YORK'S MANOR HOUSE

The archbishop's manor house stood on the moated site known as Hall Garth, south of the Minster. (L on fig. 4) A hall and kitchen were mentioned in 1388, and the great hall, where the archbishop's court was held, in 1444. Surviving earthworks indicate a large complex of buildings, which included a gaol. Work was carried out at the manor in the early 15th century, but it later fell out of use. Only six apartments, including the gaol, were mentioned in 1536 and Leland, who visited Beverley around 1540, reported that the manor house was 'all in ruin'.[28] The extensive deer park of the archbishops – a standing temptation to medieval townsmen, who were regularly excommunicated for poaching the archbishop's game - lay to the south, in the area now known as Beverley Parks.

The manor of Beverley was exchanged with the Crown in 1542. Six years later stone from Hall Garth was used in building a hunting lodge in Beverley Parks, and soon after the 'great kitchen' of the manor house was taken down and the lead, timber and stone sold. According to one account, the materials were worth £20, but the cost of building a new kitchen of a similar nature would have been £100.[29] This suggests the kitchen was a substantial building, detached from the manor house as, for example, at the bishop's palace in Lincoln. At the same time a derelict timber-framed building adjacent to the kitchen was demolished and some of the materials sold.

The archbishop's gaol later served the manor of Beverley Water Towns, the court of which was held at Hall Garth from the 17th to the late 19th century. A gaol and court house are mentioned in 1827, when part of these buildings was used as the Hall Garth Inn.[30] The inn, alternatively known as the Admiral Duncan, became a farm house in 1896 and was demolished in 1958. Illustrations of the building suggest an eighteenth-century date, but it may have had a much earlier core. The rest of Hall Garth remained empty, although wooden buildings used for theatrical performances were periodically erected there during the 19th century. The site was probably chosen because it lay just outside the jurisdiction of the borough.

THE GRAMMAR SCHOOL

The Grammar School attached to the medieval Minster was accommodated in a building in the churchyard. An early fourteenth-century document places the responsibility for keeping the schoolroom in repair on the schoolmaster, but if rebuilding was necessary this fell to the master of works. The school came under the control of the chancellor, who appointed the schoolmaster. A Precentor's or Song School was also mentioned in the mid 15th century; the gift of an oak to this school suggests it too may have had its own building, but no further reference to it is made.[31] The Grammar School continued after the Reformation, and there are detailed accounts of the rebuilding of the schoolhouse 1606-10. The new building, in the south-west corner of the churchyard, was a brick structure with stone detail to the windows and porch, and a flat-tiled roof [24]. (M on fig. 4) Some of the stone used came from a wall in Lurk Lane, perhaps from one of the prebendal sites.[32]

The school flourished in the late 17th century under the mastership of Joseph Lambert (1674-1717). Celia Fiennes, who visited Beverley in 1697, remarked that the school was said to be 'the best in England for learning and care', and in 1703 it was reported to have more than 120 pupils.[33] The schoolhouse was extended to the south in 1702–3, when part of the churchyard wall was taken down and the bricks used in the addition. In 1816 the building was demolished and the materials used to build a new school in Keldgate.

THE MINSTER WORKGARTH

The workgarth was in Eastgate, north of the Minster. (N on fig. 4) An inventory made in 1549 of 'all the wood, tiles, stone and other things' remaining in the 'late work garth' mentions the house within the gates, three houses adjoining, the long work house and the garth.[34] Materials stored there were used for work at the Minster and to maintain and rebuild property which belonged to the church. The workgarth was also the location of the chantry priests' chambers, which were owned by the fabric fund. In the 18th century the building now known as the Old Vicarage was said to stand on the site of these chambers, which suggests the workgarth was on the west side of Eastgate. A tenement and orchard there called the Workgarth measuring about one acre were included in the 1585 grant of lands to the corporation.[35]

THE MODERN PRECINCT

Although little survives from the medieval period, there are several buildings of historic interest. The following survey works clockwise round the Minster, starting in Minster Yard North. At the western end of the street, near the junction with Minster Moorgate and St John Street, stands a row of modest nineteenth-century houses formerly known as St John's Place. This terrace, which is shown on Wood's plan of 1828, has tie-plates dated 1825 on the east gable. Immediately opposite the north porch of the Minster is the entrance to Highgate, the principal route from the church to the town. The annual Cross fair, which attracted London merchants, was held in Highgate, giving rise to the alternative name Londoners' Street, in use from the mid 17th century. Externally most of the houses in Highgate date from the 18th century or later, but there are remnants of timber-framing, notably in the Monks Walk public house on the east side of street. On the west side stands the former Blue Coat School (no. 38), a mid eighteenth-century building which in recent years has been occupied by one of the Minster curates, and adjacent to it the modern vicarage.

Further east along Minster Yard North, where the gatehouse to St Martin's prebend probably stood, is the parish hall. It was built in 1885 as the Minster Girls' School, to the designs of F.

S. Brodrick of Hull. The building is of red brick with stone detail, in the Gothic style, with decorative tracery to the windows and a bellcote. It replaced the small building to the right, which adjoins the old Minster vicarage and was built in 1825 by the incumbent, the Revd Joseph Coltman. An inscription inside records that the eastern part of the schoolroom was built on the site of 'an old stable belonging to the Crown, with a chamber over it belonging to the curate' with the remaining part built on freehold land belonging to Coltman. From 1826 it was occupied by Graves's School, a charitable foundation which later became the Minster National School. After the new school was built in 1885 the old building became the parish room.

The former vicarage dates from 1704, and replaced an earlier building. In 1599 a valuation was made of some fittings of the curate's house in 'Minster Garth'. This house had a parlour, kitchen and buttery, with stairs leading to two chambers. A door from the foot of the stairs led into an orchard. It may have been part of a larger building; two years later, when the Grammar School was being repaired, the corporation agreed that the schoolmaster should be allowed to use 'a chamber room for teaching his scholars in some of Mr Crashaw [the incumbent] his chambers'. In 1655 a house abutting the Minster Yard on the south and west, where the curate lived, had 'about six rooms above stairs and six below' and a small garden. The town surveyors were ordered to fence in the garden belonging to the minister's house in 1680. In the first half of the 17th century the house was the meeting place for the court of the manor of Beverley Chapter.[36] It may have been a remnant of the collegiate buildings; the chantry priests' chambers, for example, were in this area. The building had probably fallen into a state of disrepair by the late 17th century, for in December 1703 it was agreed that 'the house in Minster yard late in the possession of Mr Clark deceased be rebuilt'.[37] The will and probate inventory of the late incumbent, Stephen Clark, indicate he had not in fact been living in the minister's house, but in a house which he owned.

The new minister's house was built for the corporation (acting as trustees for the Minster) by a local craftsman, Edward Robinson, in 1704. Glebe terriers mention a little hall, a part-panelled dining room, front and back kitchens, first-floor chambers (two of which were papered) and a garret which ran the full length of the building. In front there was a yard or garden plot. There were no outbuildings apart from the adjacent stable referred to earlier, which was converted to a schoolroom in 1825.[38] The house retains its early eighteenth-century panelling, and has a fine contemporary open-well staircase. It was refronted in grey brick in the early 19th century, probably around the time the conversion of the stable took place. The Gothic stone bay with heraldic glass dates from 1886. A Victorian extension at the east end of the house was demolished in the 1960s, when Eastgate was widened. The early nineteenth-century stable block which stands behind is not mentioned in the glebe terriers and was probably built on freehold land.

The eastern boundary wall of the vicarage plot, on Eastgate, contains pieces of medieval ashlar masonry. This section of wall, incorporating a brick gateway, was moved there from the opposite side of the road in 1964 [**94**]. The pedimented gateway originally led into the grounds of the Wartons' house, Black Friars, which almost certainly encompassed the site of St Michael's prebend by the end of the 16th century. The wall was probably built around this time, reusing some materials from the friary or prebendal buildings.

Cottages dating from the 18th century, formerly Minster property, face the east end of the Minster. Close by, where Flemingate commences, is the Sun Inn (now called the Tap and Spile), a partially half-timbered building which may have sixteenth-century origins. Further along the street are the remains of a substantial fifteenth-century timber-framed building with crown post roof, partly concealed behind the later facade of the Lord Nelson Inn. Although the

94 A brick gateway in Eastgate, 1862. It probably dates from the late 16th century and led to the grounds of Black Friars, the Wartons' house. The gateway survives, but was moved to the opposite side of the street in 1964.

building lies close to the Minster there is no record of any collegiate buildings on this site, and it may have been a merchant's house.

On the opposite side of Flemingate is the entrance to St Andrew Street (formerly Sigston Street), developed in the mid 19th century on land which had once belonged to St Andrew's prebend. The timber-framed house at the corner of Flemingate and Minster Yard South, perhaps part of the prebendal house, was pulled down in 1912 [**92**]. The Constitutional Hall which replaced it has also been demolished, and a featureless apartment block dated 1987 now stands on the site. More in sympathy with its setting is the low-level courtyard housing on Minster Yard South, a controversial development of the early 1980s. The scheme, which incorporated the rehabilitation of the Victorian houses in St Andrew Street, met with considerable opposition from a body of conservationists who fought to preserve the south view of the Minster. It should be remembered, however, that the medieval church was encircled by collegiate buildings, with the prebendal mansions of St Stephen and St James standing on this particular site. An impressive view of the Minster is still possible from Hall Garth, the scheduled moated site of the archbishop's manor house, west of the housing development [**pl. 1**].

95 8-11 St John Street, built as one house c. 1701. The range incorporates the foundations of the medieval parsons' house south of the Bedern.

Minster Yard South and North are linked by a narrow road at the west end of the Minster, known by the early 19th century as St John Street [**95**]. Nos 9–11 rest on a medieval stone base and were almost certainly built on the foundations of the house of the seven parsons, which stood next to the Bedern (see above). These houses, together with no. 8, date chiefly from c. 1701 when Joseph Lambert, master of the nearby Grammar School, purchased and rebuilt an old house on the site.[39] Internally many features of this date survive. Later in the 18th century Lambert's house was divided into two, and subsequently converted to three and later four houses. The two centre houses are now occupied as one.

The grounds of Lambert's house extended north as far as Minster Moorgate, and must have covered the site of other communal buildings of the clergy. As late as 1729 the plot is described as 'formerly a parcel of the possessions of the College of St John'.

An architectural survey carried out in 1996 suggests Lambert's house originally had a ten-bay facade with a central doorway, and a second entrance to the right. The windows (now sash) would have been casements with broad wooden mullions and transoms, an example of which can been seen at the rear of no. 10. At the north end of the 'old house' (nos 9–11), most of which he rebuilt, Lambert added a two-bay brick range of two storeys and attic with a rear wing (no. 8). Both the wing and northern end of the front elevation of the house have ashlar quoins, which may have come from an earlier building. A medieval carved head is incorporated at eaves level at the southern end of the front elevation.

South of the rear wing Lambert built a small three-storey staircase tower with a hipped roof. The position and relative simplicity of the staircase, and clues from elsewhere in the building, suggest there was a second staircase wing, later demolished, to the rear of no. 10. Pupils at the Grammar School, a number of whom came from gentry families outside the town, may have boarded in part of the house. In his will Lambert mentions his 'lodging chamber' where the family portraits hung, and his library.

Joseph Lambert died in 1717 and was survived by his three children, Sarah, Anne and Robert, who later became Master of St John's College, Cambridge. The house and gardens at the west end of the Minster were sold in 1729 to a tanner, John Croft. Croft already owned an adjacent plot of land to the west, stretching back to the newly-built workhouse on Minster Moorgate. Croft used some of the land as a tanyard.

In 1777 the house was purchased by Joseph Beaumont, a local fellmonger. By this date it had been divided into two, and there was also a brewhouse, bark mill, outbuilding, two gardens, orchard and tanyard. Two more houses (nos 6 and 7) were subsequently built on part of the gardens, and the old house was extended at the rear and further sub-divided. In the last quarter of the 19th century five more houses (nos 1-5) were built to the north, completing the development of St John Street, where members of the Beaumont family continued to live until the mid 20th century.

The Minster precinct has altered beyond all recognition since the middle ages. Documentary evidence suggests that some of the collegiate buildings were pulled down soon after the Reformation, and few probably survived beyond the 17th century. Excavations carried out at sites around the Minster have produced evidence of medieval buildings, but no remains survive above ground, other than the remnants in St John Street. Nor are there any known illustrations, other than of the timber-framed houses in Flemingate and Highgate which may have been prebendal properties. There is, however, sufficient documentary evidence, much of it from the post-medieval period, to locate the majority of the collegiate buildings. With the exception of Hall Garth, all the medieval sites are built on, preserving the sense of enclosure round the Minster. The problem of traffic passing by the south and east sides of the church needs to be addressed, but to the north and west the precinct still manages to retain something of its former tranquillity.

NOTES

1 L. Toulmin Smith, ed., *The Itinerary of John Leland in or about the Years 1535-1543* (5 vols, 1907-10), i, p. 46.

2 Leach, *Memorials*, i, p. 316; Hull Local Studies Library, transcription of 1684 Warton survey; Poulson, *Beverlac*, p. 575.

3 Leach, *Memorials*, i, pp. 28-9, 168-9; Bodleian Library, Oxford, University College MS 82, pp. 40, 44; M. J. Hebditch, ed., *Yorkshire Deeds*, ix (YASRS, 111, 1948), p. 13.

4 Leach, *Memorials*, ii, pp. lxxxv, 352; Poulson, *Beverlac*, p. 622; Toulmin Smith, *Itinerary of John Leland*, i, p. 46; W. Page, ed., *The Certificates of the Commissioners Appointed to Survey the Chantries, Guilds and Hospitals etc. in the County of York*, ii (Surtees Society, 92, 1895), p. 553; *Calendar of Patent Rolls, 1548-9*, pp. 37, 204.

5   L. & P. Hen. VIII, iv, pt 2, p. 876.

6   P. Armstrong et al., Excavations at Lurk Lane, Beverley, 1979-82, Sheffield Excavation Reports, 1 (1991), p. 242; Hebditch, Yorkshire Deeds, ix, p. 28.

7   Poulson, Beverlac, p. 635; Leach, Memorials, ii, pp. 364-5; Page, Chantries, ii, pp. 532-3; BIHR, Bp. C. & P. XVIII/7.

8   A. F. Leach, Early Yorkshire Schools, i (YASRS, 27, 1899), p. 128; ERAO, BC/II/7/5 ff. 30, 306.

9   Leach, Memorials, ii, p. 317; HUL, DDCV/15/7; Humber Archaeology Partnership, Sites and Monuments Record, 7463.

10 Leach, Memorials, ii, pp. 71, 295-6, 317, 331.

11 Leach, Memorials, i, p. 324.

12 Calendar of Patent Rolls, 1374-7, pp. 97, 239; A. F. Leach, ed., 'A Fifteenth-century Fabric Roll of Beverley Minster', TERAS, 6 (1898), 63.

13 Leach, Memorials, ii, pp. 353-7; HUL, DDCV/15/27.

14 Leach, Memorials, i, p. 206.

15 Calendar of Patent Rolls, 1553, p. 255.

16 Leach, Memorials, i, p. 353, ii, pp. 17-18, 37.

17 Poulson, Beverlac, App., p. 36.

18 ERAO, BC/IV/4.

19 Leach, Memorials, i, p. 369; Bodleian Library, Oxford, University College MS 82, passim.

20 J. Raine, ed., Testamenta Eboracensia, iii (Surtees Society, 45, 1865), pp. 137-8.

21 Leach, Memorials, i, p. 92, ii, p. 125; ERAO, DDCC/139/65.

22 Poulson, Beverlac, App., p. 36.

23 Armstrong, Excavations at Lurk Lane, p. 241.

24 Ibid., passim.

25 BL, Lansdowne MS 402, f. 60; Leach, Memorials, i, p. 389; Calendar of Patent Rolls, 1547-8, p. 170.

26 HUL, DDMC/9/15; Poulson, Beverlac, App., p. 36.

27 PRO, C 142/224, no. 31.

28 Calendar of Inquisitions Miscellaneous, iv, pp. 215-6; ERAO BC/II/7/1, f. 69; VCH Beverley, p. 14; L. & P. Hen. VIII, x, p. 30; Toulmin Smith, Itinerary of John Leland, i, p. 46.

29 PRO, E 101/458/24; ERAO, DDCC/139/65.

30 ERAO, Registry of Deeds, EC/136/148.

31 Leach, Memorials, i, pp. 222-3; Leach, 'Fifteenth-century Fabric Roll', 67.

32 Leach, Early Yorkshire Schools, i, pp. 121-6.

33 D. Woodward, ed., Descriptions of East Yorkshire: Leland to Defoe (EYLHS, 39, 1985), p. 49; N. Hardwick, ed. and transl., A relation of the journey of the gentlemen Blathwayt into the north of England in the year seventeen hundred and three by P. de Blainville (Bristol, 1977), p. 16.

34 ERAO, DDCC/139/65.

35 BIHR, Bp. C. & P. XVIII/7; Poulson, Beverlac, App., pp. 40-1.

36 ERAO, BC/II/7/4/1, f. 3; BC/II/7/5, f. 113; DDX/683/16; Leach, Early Yorkshire Schools, i, p.118.

37 ERAO, BC/II/7/5, f. 316.

38 ERAO, BC/II/6/102; BIHR, TER I (Beverley St John), 1764, 1809.

39 The following paragraphs are based on S. Neave, unpublished history and architectural survey of 8-11 St John Street, Beverley, 1996.

Suggestions for further reading

The place of publication is London unless otherwise stated.

PRINTED PRIMARY MATERIAL

Colgrave, B. and Mynors, R.A.B., eds, *Bede's Ecclesiastical History of the English People* (Oxford, 1969)

Dennett, J., ed., *Beverley Borough Records 1575–1821*, YASRS, 84 (1933)

Leach, A.F., ed., *Memorials of Beverley Minster: the chapter act book of the collegiate church of S. John of Beverley AD 1286–1347*, 2 vols, Surtees Society, 98 and 108 (1898–1903)

Leach, A.F., ed., 'A fifteenth-century fabric roll of Beverley Minster', *TERAS*, 6 (1898), 56–103, ibid., 7 (1899), 50–83

MacMahon, K.A., ed., *Beverley Corporation Minute Books 1707–1835*, YASRS, 122 (1958)

Raine, J., ed., *The Historians of the Church of York and its Archbishops*, 3 vols, Rolls Series (1879–94)

SECONDARY READING

Allison, K.J., ed., *The Victoria County History of York, East Riding. VI: The borough and liberties of Beverley* (Oxford, 1989)

Allsopp, B., 'A Note on the Arcading and Sculpture in the South Aisle of Beverley Minster', *Architectural History*, 2 (1959), 8–18

Armstrong, P., Tomlinson, D. and Evans, D.H., *Excavations at Lurk Lane, Beverley, 1979–1982*, Sheffield Excavation Reports, 1 (1991)

Aveling, H., *Post Reformation Catholicism in East Yorkshire 1558–1790*, EYLHS, 11 (1960)

Barnwell, P.S., '"The Church of Beverly is fully repaired." The roofs of Beverley Minster', *Transactions of the Ancient Monuments Society*, 44 (2000), 9–24

Bilson, J., 'Beverley Minster', *Architectural Review*, 3 (1898), 195–205, 250–9

Brown, G.P., *Minster Life: some historical themes of Beverley* (Beverley, 1979)

Brown, G.P., *Victorian Themes: Music and Manners in Beverley Minster 100 years ago* (Beverley, 1966)

Bull, E.B., *The statues of Beverley Minster* (Beverley, 1967)

Dawton, N., 'The Percy Tomb at Beverley Minster: the style of the sculpture', in F.H. Thompson, ed., *Studies in Medieval Sculpture*, Society of Antiquaries occasional papers, new series, 3 (1983), pp. 122–50

Dickens, A.G., *Lollards and Protestants in the Diocese of York, 1509–1558* (2nd ed., 1982)

English, B.A. and Neave, D., eds, *Tudor Beverley* (Beverley, 1973)

Evans, D.H., 'The Archaeology of Beverley', in S. Ellis and D.R. Crowther, eds, *Humber Perspectives: a region through the ages* (Hull, 1990), pp. 269–82

Goldberg, P.J.P., 'The Percy tomb in Beverley Minster', *YAJ*, 56 (1984), 65–74

Grössinger, C., *The World Upside-down: English Misericords* (1997)

Hall, I., 'The first Georgian restoration of Beverley Minster', *The Georgian Group Journal*, 3 (1993), 13–31

Hall, I. & E., *Historic Beverley* (York, 1973)

Harvey, A., 'A Priest's Tomb at Beverley Minster', *YAJ*, 38 (1955), 504–23

Hiatt, C., *Beverley Minster; an illustrated account of its history and fabric* (1898)

Hoey, L., 'Beverley Minster in its 13th-century context', *Journal of the Society of Architectural Historians*, 43 (1984), 209–24

Jones, R.J., *A History of the 15th (East Yorkshire) Regiment (Duke of York's Own) 1685–1914* (Beverley, The Regiment, 1958)

Lamburn, D., 'Politics and religion in early modern Beverley', in P. Collinson and J. Craig, eds, *The Reformation in English Towns, 1500–1640* (Basingstoke, 1998), pp. 63–78

MacMahon, K.A., *Beverley: a brief historical survey* (Beverley, 1965)

MacMahon, K.A., *Beverley* (Clapham, 1973)

McDermid, R.T.W., *Beverley Minster Fasti*, YASRS, 149 (1993 for 1990)

Miller, K., Robinson, J., English, B. and Hall, I., *Beverley: an archaeological and architectural study*, RCHME supplementary series, 4 (HMSO, 1982)

Montagu, G. & J., 'Beverley Minster reconsidered', *Early Music*, 6 (1978), 401–15

Oliver, G., *The History and Antiquities of the Town and Minster of Beverley* (Beverley, 1829)

Palliser, D.M., 'The "minster hypothesis": a case study', *Early Medieval Europe*, 5 (1996), 207–14

Pevsner, N. and Neave, D., *The Buildings of England: Yorkshire, York and the East Riding* (Harmondsworth, 2nd edition, 1995)

Poulson, G., *Beverlac; or the antiquities and history of the town of Beverley* (1829)

Tracy, C., *English Gothic Choir-stalls 1400–1540* (Woodbridge, 1990)

Wildridge, T. Tindall, *The Misereres of Beverley Minster* (Hull, 1879; reprinted Hutton Driffield, 1982)

Wilson, C., 'The early thirteenth-century architecture of Beverley Minster: cathedral splendours and Cistercian austerities', in P.R. Coss and S.D. Lloyd, eds, *Thirteenth Century England*, 3 (Woodbridge, 1991), pp. 181–95

Wilson, C., ed., *Medieval Art and Architecture in the East Riding of Yorkshire*, British Archaeological Association Conference Transactions, 9 (1989 for 1983)

Witty, J., *A History of Beverley Grammar School c. 706–1912*, revised by R.M. Scrowston (unpublished typescript in Beverley Library)

Index